The NEW ENCYCLOPEDIA *of* SOUTHERN CULTURE

VOLUME 7 : FOODWAYS

Volumes to appear in

The New Encyclopedia of Southern Culture

are:

Agriculture and Industry	*Law and Politics*
Art and Architecture	*Literature*
Education	*Media*
Environment	*Music*
Ethnicity	*Myth, Manners, and Memory*
Folk Art	*Race*
Folklife	*Recreation*
Foodways	*Religion*
Gender	*Science and Medicine*
Geography	*Social Class*
History	*Urbanization*
Language	*Violence*

The NEW

ENCYCLOPEDIA *of* SOUTHERN CULTURE

CHARLES REAGAN WILSON General Editor

JAMES G. THOMAS JR. Managing Editor

ANN J. ABADIE Associate Editor

VOLUME 7

Foodways

JOHN T. EDGE

Volume Editor

Sponsored by

THE CENTER FOR THE STUDY OF SOUTHERN CULTURE

at the University of Mississippi

THE UNIVERSITY OF NORTH CAROLINA PRESS

Chapel Hill

This book was published with the
assistance of the Anniversary Endowment Fund
of the University of North Carolina Press.
Designed by Richard Hendel
Set in Minion types by Tseng Information Systems, Inc.
Manufactured in the United States of America
The paper in this book meets the guidelines for permanence and
durability of the Committee on Production Guidelines for Book
Longevity of the Council on Library Resources.

Library of Congress Cataloging-in-Publication Data
The new encyclopedia of Southern culture / Charles Reagan
Wilson, general editor ; James G. Thomas Jr., managing editor ;
Ann J. Abadie, associate editor.

p. cm.

Rev. ed. of: Encyclopedia of Southern culture. 1991.
"Sponsored by The Center for the Study of Southern Culture
at the University of Mississippi."
Includes bibliographical references and index.
Contents: — v. 7. Foodways
ISBN 978-0-8078-3146-5 (cloth : v. 7 : alk. paper)
ISBN 978-0-8078-5840-0 (pbk. : v. 7 : alk. paper)
1. Southern States—Civilization—Encyclopedias. 2. Southern
States—Encyclopedias. I. Wilson, Charles Reagan. II. Thomas,
James G. III. Abadie, Ann J. IV. University of Mississippi.
Center for the Study of Southern Culture.
V. Encyclopedia of Southern culture.

F209.N47 2006

975.003—dc22

2005024807

The *Encyclopedia of Southern Culture*, sponsored by the Center for
the Study of Southern Culture at the University of Mississippi, was
published by the University of North Carolina Press in 1989.

cloth   11 10 09 08 07   5 4 3 2 1
paper   11 10 09 08 07   5 4 3 2 1

Tell about the South. What's it like there.

What do they do there. Why do they live there.

Why do they live at all.

WILLIAM FAULKNER

Absalom, Absalom!

CONTENTS

General Introduction *xiii*

Introduction *xix*

SOUTHERN FOODWAYS *1*

African American Foodways *15*

Appalachian Foodways *18*

Barbecue *22*

Beef *26*

Beverages *27*

Cajun Foodways *32*

Caribbean Foodways *37*

Civil War *39*

Cookbooks *41*

Cookbooks, Community *45*

Ethnicity and Food *47*

Farming *50*

Funeral Food and Cemetery
    Cleaning *53*

Game Cookery *55*

Gender and Food *58*

Gulf Coast Foodways *62*

Hispanic American Foodways *64*

Jewish Foodways *67*

Literature, Food in *70*

Lowcountry Foodways *73*

Lunch Counters (Civil Rights
    Era) *77*

Meals *79*

Music and Food *81*

New Orleans Foodways *83*

Pork *88*

Poultry *92*

Religion and Food *95*

Roadside Restaurants *100*

Social Class and Food *102*

Soul Food *104*

Aunt Jemima *109*

Barbecue, Carolinas *110*

Barbecue, Memphis and
    Tennessee *112*

Barbecue, Texas *115*

Beans *119*

Beaufort Stew/Frogmore Stew *121*

Benne *122*

Biscuits *122*

Black-eyed Peas *125*

Bourbon Whiskey *127*

Brennan, Ella *129*

Brown, Marion Lea *130*

Brunswick Stew *131*

Burgoo *132*

Cakes *134*

Catfish *136*

Chase, Leah Lange *138*

Chess Pie *140*

Chicken, Fried *141*

Chitterlings *143*

Claiborne, Craig *145*

Coca-Cola *146*

Coons and Possums *147*

Corn *151*

Cornbread *152*

Country Captain *154*

Country Ham *155*

Crawfish *158*

Deviled Eggs *160*

Dull, Henrietta Stanley *161*
Fast Food *162*
Fish, Rough *164*
Fish Camps *166*
Goo Goo Clusters *167*
Gravy *168*
Greens *170*
Greens, Collard *172*
Greens, Turnip *174*
Grits *175*
Gumbo *177*
Hash, South Carolina *179*
Hearn, Lafcadio *181*
Hill, Annabella Powell *182*
Hines, Duncan *182*
Hot Tamales *184*
Hushpuppies *185*
Jack Daniel Distillery *186*
Jambalaya *188*
Jefferson, Thomas *189*
King Cakes *190*
Krispy Kreme *190*
Lagasse, Emeril *193*
Lewis, Edna *193*
Maque Choux *195*
Mickler, Ernest Matthew *196*
Mint Julep *198*
MoonPies *199*
Moonshine and Moonshining *200*
Muddle *202*
Mullet *203*
Neal, Bill *204*
Okra *206*
Onions, Vidalia *207*
Oranges *208*
Oysters *210*
Oysters Rockefeller *212*
Panfish *213*
Peaches *214*

Peanuts *216*
Pecans *218*
Pepper Vinegar *219*
Peppers, Hot *219*
Persimmons *221*
Pickling *221*
Pies *222*
Pimento Cheese *226*
Po' Boy *227*
Poke Sallet *228*
Pots and Skillets *229*
Pralines *231*
Preserves and Jellies *231*
Prudhomme, Paul *234*
Puddings *235*
Quail *236*
Ramos Gin Fizz *238*
Ramps *239*
Randolph, Mary *240*
Rawlings, Marjorie Kinnan *241*
Red Beans and Rice *243*
Restaurants, Atlanta *244*
Restaurants, Charleston *245*
Restaurants, Nashville *247*
Restaurants, New Orleans *249*
Rice *251*
Rice, Red *253*
Roux *254*
Rum *255*
Sanders, Colonel Harland *257*
Sandwiches *259*
Saunders, Clarence *261*
Sazerac *262*
Sorghum *263*
Spoonbread *264*
Squash *265*
Stack Cake *266*
Sugar and Sugarcane *267*
Sweet Potatoes *269*

Tabasco *270*
Tasso *272*
Tea Rooms *273*
Tomatoes *274*
Uncle Ben's *277*
Waffle House *278*
Walter, Eugene Ferdinand *279*

Washington, George *281*
Watermelon *282*
Wilson, Justin *285*
Wine *287*

Index of Contributors *291*
Index *293*

In 1989 years of planning and hard work came to fruition when the University of North Carolina Press joined the Center for the Study of Southern Culture at the University of Mississippi to publish the *Encyclopedia of Southern Culture*. While all those involved in writing, reviewing, editing, and producing the volume believed it would be received as a vital contribution to our understanding of the American South, no one could have anticipated fully the widespread acclaim it would receive from reviewers and other commentators. But the *Encyclopedia* was indeed celebrated, not only by scholars but also by popular audiences with a deep, abiding interest in the region. At a time when some people talked of the "vanishing South," the book helped remind a national audience that the region was alive and well, and it has continued to shape national perceptions of the South through the work of its many users—journalists, scholars, teachers, students, and general readers.

As the introduction to the *Encyclopedia* noted, its conceptualization and organization reflected a cultural approach to the South. It highlighted such issues as the core zones and margins of southern culture, the boundaries where "the South" overlapped with other cultures, the role of history in contemporary culture, and the centrality of regional consciousness, symbolism, and mythology. By 1989 scholars had moved beyond the idea of cultures as real, tangible entities, viewing them instead as abstractions. The *Encyclopedia's* editors and contributors thus included a full range of social indicators, trait groupings, literary concepts, and historical evidence typically used in regional studies, carefully working to address the distinctive and characteristic traits that made the American South a particular place. The introduction to the *Encyclopedia* concluded that the fundamental uniqueness of southern culture was reflected in the volume's composite portrait of the South. We asked contributors to consider aspects that were unique to the region but also those that suggested its internal diversity. The volume was not a reference book of southern history, which explained something of the design of entries. There were fewer essays on colonial and antebellum history than on the postbellum and modern periods, befitting our conception of the volume as one trying not only to chart the cultural landscape of the South but also to illuminate the contemporary era.

When C. Vann Woodward reviewed the *Encyclopedia* in the *New York Review of Books*, he concluded his review by noting "the continued liveliness of interest in the South and its seeming inexhaustibility as a field of study." Research on the South, he wrote, furnishes "proof of the value of the *Encyclopedia* as a scholarly undertaking as well as suggesting future needs for revision or supplement to keep up with ongoing scholarship." The decade and a half since the publication of the *Encyclopedia of Southern Culture* have certainly suggested that Woodward was correct. The American South has undergone significant changes that make for a different context for the study of the region. The South has undergone social, economic, political, intellectual, and literary transformations, creating the need for a new edition of the *Encyclopedia* that will remain relevant to a changing region. Globalization has become a major issue, seen in the South through the appearance of Japanese automobile factories, Hispanic workers who have immigrated from Latin America or Cuba, and a new prominence for Asian and Middle Eastern religions that were hardly present in the 1980s South. The African American return migration to the South, which started in the 1970s, dramatically increased in the 1990s, as countless books simultaneously appeared asserting powerfully the claims of African Americans as formative influences on southern culture. Politically, southerners from both parties have played crucial leadership roles in national politics, and the Republican Party has dominated a near-solid South in national elections. Meanwhile, new forms of music, like hip-hop, have emerged with distinct southern expressions, and the term "dirty South" has taken on new musical meanings not thought of in 1989. New genres of writing by creative southerners, such as gay and lesbian literature and "white trash" writing, extend the southern literary tradition.

Meanwhile, as Woodward foresaw, scholars have continued their engagement with the history and culture of the South since the publication of the *Encyclopedia*, raising new scholarly issues and opening new areas of study. Historians have moved beyond their earlier preoccupation with social history to write new cultural history as well. They have used the categories of race, social class, and gender to illuminate the diversity of the South, rather than a unified "mind of the South." Previously underexplored areas within the field of southern historical studies, such as the colonial era, are now seen as formative periods of the region's character, with the South's positioning within a larger Atlantic world a productive new area of study. Cultural memory has become a major topic in the exploration of how the social construction of "the South" benefited some social groups and exploited others. Scholars in many disciplines have made the southern identity a major topic, and they have used a variety of methodologies to suggest what that identity has meant to different social groups. Literary critics have adapted cultural theories to the South and have raised the issue of postsouthern literature to a major category of concern as well as exploring the links between the literature of the American South and that of the Caribbean. Anthropologists have used different theoretical formulations from literary critics, providing models for their fieldwork in southern communities. In the past 30 years anthropologists have set increasing numbers of their ethnographic studies in the South, with many of them now exploring topics specifically linked to southern cultural issues. Scholars now place the Native American story, from prehistory to the contemporary era, as a central part of southern history. Comparative and interdisciplinary approaches to the South have encouraged scholars to look at such issues as the borders and boundaries of the South, specific places and spaces with distinct identities within the American South, and the global and transnational Souths, linking the American South with many formerly colonial societies around the world.

The first edition of the *Encyclopedia of Southern Culture* anticipated many of these approaches and indeed stimulated the growth of Southern Studies as a distinct interdisciplinary field. The Center for the Study of Southern Culture has worked for more than a quarter century to encourage research and teaching about the American South. Its academic programs have produced graduates who have gone on to write interdisciplinary studies of the South, while others have staffed the cultural institutions of the region and in turn encouraged those institutions to document and present the South's culture to broad public audiences. The center's conferences and publications have continued its long tradition of promoting understanding of the history, literature, and music of the South, with new initiatives focused on southern foodways, the future of the South, and the global Souths, expressing the center's mission to bring the best current scholarship to broad public audiences. Its documentary studies projects build oral and visual archives, and the New Directions in Southern Studies book series, published by the University of North Carolina Press, offers an important venue for innovative scholarship.

Since the *Encyclopedia of Southern Culture* appeared, the field of Southern Studies has dramatically developed, with an extensive network now of academic and research institutions whose projects focus specifically on the interdisciplinary study of the South. The Center for the Study of the American South at the University of North Carolina at Chapel Hill, led by Director Harry Watson and Associate Director and *Encyclopedia* coeditor William Ferris, publishes the lively journal *Southern Cultures* and is now at the organizational center of many other Southern Studies projects. The Institute for Southern Studies at the University of South Carolina, the Southern Intellectual History Circle, the Society for the Study of Southern Literature, the Southern Studies Forum of the European American Studies Association, Emory University's SouthernSpaces.org, and the South Atlantic Humanities Center (at the Virginia Foundation for the Humanities, the University of Virginia, and Virginia Polytechnic Institute and State University) express the recent expansion of interest in regional study.

Observers of the American South have had much to absorb, given the rapid pace of recent change. The institutional framework for studying the South is broader and deeper than ever, yet the relationship between the older verities of regional study and new realities remains unclear. Given the extent of changes in the American South and in Southern Studies since the publication of the *Encyclopedia of Southern Culture*, the need for a new edition of that work is clear. Therefore, the Center for the Study of Southern Culture has once again joined the University of North Carolina Press to produce *The New Encyclopedia of Southern Culture*. As readers of the original edition will quickly see, *The New Encyclopedia* follows many of the scholarly principles and editorial conventions established in the original, but with one key difference; rather than being published in a single hardback volume, *The New Encyclopedia* is presented in a series of shorter individual volumes that build on the 24 original subject categories used in the *Encyclopedia* and adapt them to new scholarly developments. Some earlier *Encyclopedia* categories have been reconceptualized in light of new academic interests. For example, the subject section originally titled "Women's Life" is reconceived as a new volume, *Gender*, and the original "Black Life" section is more broadly interpreted as a volume on race. These changes reflect new analytical concerns that place the study of women and blacks in broader cultural systems, reflecting the emergence of, among other topics, the study of male culture and of whiteness. Both volumes draw as well from the rich recent scholarship on women's life and black life. In addition, topics with some thematic coherence are combined in a volume, such as *Law and Politics* and *Agriculture and Industry*. One new topic, *Foodways*, is the basis of a separate volume, reflecting its new prominence in the interdisciplinary study of southern culture.

Numerous individual topical volumes together make up *The New Encyclopedia of Southern Culture* and extend the reach of the reference work to wider audiences. This approach should enhance the use of the *Encyclopedia* in academic courses and is intended to be convenient for readers with more focused interests within the larger context of southern culture. Readers will have handy access to one-volume, authoritative, and comprehensive scholarly treatments of the major areas of southern culture.

We have been fortunate that, in nearly all cases, subject consultants who offered crucial direction in shaping the topical sections for the original edition have agreed to join us in this new endeavor as volume editors. When new volume editors have been added, we have again looked for respected figures who can provide not only their own expertise but also strong networks of scholars to help develop relevant lists of topics and to serve as contributors in their areas. The reputations of all our volume editors as leading scholars in their areas encouraged the contributions of other scholars and added to *The New Encyclopedia*'s authority as a reference work.

The New Encyclopedia of Southern Culture builds on the strengths of articles in the original edition in several ways. For many existing articles, original authors agreed to update their contributions with new interpretations and theoretical perspectives, current statistics, new bibliographies, or simple factual developments that needed to be included. If the original contributor was unable to update an article, the editorial staff added new material or sent it to another scholar for assessment. In some cases, the general editor and volume editors selected a new contributor if an article seemed particularly dated and new work indicated the need for a fresh perspective. And importantly, where new developments have warranted treatment of topics not addressed in the original edition, volume editors have commissioned entirely new essays and articles that are published here for the first time.

The American South embodies a powerful historical and mythical presence, both a complex environmental and geographic landscape and a place of the imagination. Changes in the region's contemporary socioeconomic realities and new developments in scholarship have been incorporated in the conceptualization and approach of *The New Encyclopedia of Southern Culture*. Anthropologist Clifford Geertz has spoken of culture as context, and this encyclopedia looks at the American South as a complex place that has served as the context for cultural expression. This volume provides information and perspective on the diversity of cultures in a geographic and imaginative place with a long history and distinctive character.

The *Encyclopedia of Southern Culture* was produced through major grants from the Program for Research Tools and Reference Works of the National Endowment for the Humanities, the Ford Foundation, the Atlantic-Richfield Foundation, and the Mary Doyle Trust. We are grateful as well to the College of Liberal Arts at the University of Mississippi for support and to the individual donors to the Center for the Study of Southern Culture who have directly or indirectly supported work on *The New Encyclopedia of Southern Culture*. We thank the volume editors for their ideas in reimagining their subjects and the contributors of articles for their work in extending the usefulness of the book in new ways. We acknowledge the support and contributions of the faculty and staff at the Center for the Study of Southern Culture. Finally, we want especially to honor the work of William Ferris and Mary Hart on the *Encyclopedia of Southern Culture*. Bill, the founding director of the Center for the Study of Southern Culture, was coeditor, and his good work recruiting authors, editing text, selecting images, and publicizing the volume among a wide network of people was, of course, invaluable. Despite the many changes in the new encyclopedia, Bill's influence remains. Mary "Sue" Hart was also an invaluable member of the original encyclopedia team, bringing the careful and precise eye of the librarian, and an iconoclastic spirit, to our work.

INTRODUCTION

For much of the South's history, southerners have borne chips on their shoulders about all manner of our cultural creations. Food is no exception.

We have long accepted the epithets. Singer Bette Midler once told a Charleston, S.C., audience that grits tasted like "buttered kitty litter." We even joined the fray. "Southern cooking has been perverted by slatterns with a greasy skillet," wrote Atlantan Ralph McGill in a 1940s dispatch. "Its good name has been sullied by indigestible 'Southern fried chicken' . . . with piano-wire sinews and dubious gooey gravy which encourages the chicken to skid off the plate; by various 'fries'; by much bad Bar-B-Q and worse Brunswick stew; and by too much grease."

This volume is not a corrective. A bowl of instant grits, cooked carelessly and slicked with margarine, goes a long way toward proving Midler's point. And it is true that great traditional barbecue—pit cooked over hardwood by a cook of long tenure—is scarcer than ever. Instead, the entries that follow constitute an attempt to transcend the quips and stereotypes, to document and showcase southern foodstuffs and cookery, not to mention southern cooks and eaters, in all their diversity.

An appreciation of southern foodways has always depended upon more than an examination of the food on the table. With this volume as your guide, you will come to see food as a marker of class, gender, race, and ethnicity. You will come to understand how fund-raising cookbooks can be read as community histories. You will appreciate food events like barbecues and fish fries as sites for southern self-definition.

You will meet fabled cooks like Freetown, Va., native Edna Lewis, the woman who reintroduced the South to the idea of *terroir*, and Craig Claiborne of Sunflower, Miss., the man who reinvented the food pages of the *New York Times*. You will ponder the import of grocery store staples like Tabasco brand pepper sauce and the pride of Chattanooga, Tenn., the MoonPie. And you will comprehend the metaphorical power of southern provender, a phenomenon illustrated by A. J. Liebling in his biography of Louisiana politician Earl Long: "Southern political personalities, like sweet corn, travel badly. They lose flavor with every hundred yards away from the patch."

In the two decades since the original *Encyclopedia of Southern Culture* was published, America in general, and the South in particular, has awakened to the cultural import of regional foodways. Writers and researchers have applied rigor to the study of what we eat and why we eat it. Organizations such as the Southern Foodways Alliance—an institute of the Center for the Study of Southern Culture at the University of Mississippi—have begun documenting the lives of working-class fry cooks and pitmasters. Cooks have rediscovered the receipts of their forebears. And chefs have interpreted traditional recipes for white-tablecloth consumers and in, the process, become celebrities. Consider this volume the next step in that process, an attempt on the part of the contributors to knock those chips from our shoulders and deliver honest, unflinching portraits of southerners in the field, by the stove, and at table.

The NEW ENCYCLOPEDIA *of* SOUTHERN CULTURE

VOLUME 7 : FOODWAYS

SOUTHERN FOODWAYS

The first white men to come into the South ate what the American Indians ate. From the southern Indians the Europeans learned much about cultivated plants, wild fruits and nuts, the animals of the forest, and the fish in ocean, rivers, and lakes. They had to learn these lessons to survive and later push their way westward.

The Indian diet included a variety of game, and Indians near the coast ate large quantities of fish and shellfish. In their fields they grew corn, beans, squash, and other vegetables. They harvested wild plums, hickory nuts, chestnuts, blackberries, and other forest foods. Indians elsewhere on the continent domesticated the turkey and had developed the potato, tomatoes, eggplant, all kinds of peppers except black pepper, probably sweet potatoes, and possibly cowpeas. Both Indians and European settlers drew from other cultures, too. Originating in Brazil, the peanut was carried to Africa and later, bearing the African name "goober," was brought to Virginia aboard slave ships.

As settlers reached the frontier, they planted corn and other food plants, but until these could be harvested, they relied on game or fish (although fish played a large role only along the coasts of the Atlantic and the Gulf of Mexico). The pioneer in the interior was happy to have a catfish, especially a large one, but he trusted his rifle more than his rod, net, or fish trap.

Buffalo provided the best meat, but they were quickly exterminated east of the Mississippi River. The pioneer also relished the meat of the black bear; he even salted it and cured it like pork. If killed in the autumn, the bear provided fat for shortening or other uses. Some southerners ate bear more or less regularly throughout the 19th century, but in most areas the animal disappeared as settlers multiplied. That left as big game the white-tailed deer, and venison was a frequent dish on southern tables until—and in some areas long after—the Civil War. Wild turkeys were astonishingly abundant and unbelievably unwary in the pioneer South, and they played a large role in the pioneer diet. So did smaller game, especially rabbits, squirrels, raccoons, and opossums.

One should not think of the pioneer as baking a bear ham, roasting an opossum, or turning a haunch of venison on a spit. As often as not, the southern frontiersman had only one cooking pot, and whatever was available went into that pot to mix with the previous day's leftovers.

The Indians lived in a feast-or-famine condition much of the year, and when

Fixing plates at dinner on the grounds, part of an all-day community sing, 1940
(Russell Lee, photographer, Library of Congress [LC-USF33-012785-M2], Washington, D.C.)

food was abundant, they stuffed themselves. In the England that the earliest settlers called home, a host took as much pride in the quantity of the food he served his guests as in its quality. This background, combined with the abundance of food in the South as compared to the diets of German, English, Scotch, or Scotch-Irish peasants in the Old World, carried the concept of "big eating" over to the southern frontier and from the frontier forward to the Old South and eventually to the modern South.

As soon as he could, the pioneer farmer planted corn and established a herd of swine. Thus, the primary items in the diet of most southerners when the frontier had passed were cornbread and pork. Wild hogs were already in the forests, and those that the settlers brought with them were little tamer than their wild kin. High in the shoulder, low in the rear, thin, with a long head and snout, and very swift of foot, they were often killed in the woods. More often, however, the owner carried out a "roundup" each fall, castrated excess boars, marked the ears of pigs born since the last roundup, and took those destined for killing home to be fattened on corn. Gradually, better-quality boars were brought in, and the quality of southern swine improved.

Hog killing usually took place during the first spell of cold weather that seemed likely to last for several days. Chitterlings (small intestines), livers, knuckles (ankles), brains, and other edible parts that could not be preserved had to be eaten quickly, and an orgy of pork eating followed hog-killing day. During those hectic days, the fat was boiled in a large pot and rendered into lard. Cracklings, the crisp remnant of this process, were delicious baked into a pone of cornbread, called cracklin' bread. Scraps of leaner meat were pounded or ground into sausage.

Hams, shoulders, jowls, and sides of bacon could be cured to last indefinitely. After being trimmed, these pieces were buried in salt for four to six weeks. Then in the smokehouse they were smoked, preferably with smoke from hickory wood. Farmers differed as to whether to use sugar, spices, and the like to flavor hams and shoulders, but almost all rubbed red pepper into exposed areas to prevent contamination by skipper flies, whose larvae would burrow through the meat.

So long as they had pork, southerners ate it every day and at nearly every meal. Fried ham, shoulder, bacon, or sausage was almost an essential part of breakfast. The main meal, in the middle of the day, usually included pork and, unless it was Sunday or some special occasion, the pork was fried. Vegetables were frequently fried, but often they were boiled with a piece of fat cured pork. A dish of green beans, for example, was not good unless it had enough grease in it to "wink back" when one lifted the lid and looked at it. Vegetables were cooked this way in most southern households well into the 20th century.

Southerners did eat meat other than fish, game, and pork from time to time. Once the frontier stage had passed and predatory animals had begun to follow the Indians into oblivion, it was possible to raise poultry; and chicken, duck, goose, and turkey became fare for Sundays and holidays. Fried chicken became the delicacy that it has remained ever since, and hen eggs and, occasionally, duck eggs became table items. Southerners sometimes ate beef, but it appeared on the table far more often in Texas and on the prairies of Louisiana than elsewhere in the South. Technically, what southerners ate was not really beef but veal, or "baby beef." The meat of animals that had reached maturity was too tough to chew.

Milk cows, on the other hand, were prized possessions. Compared to the dairy cows of today, they were inferior creatures that produced little milk, an important food for the antebellum southern family as well as for families in later eras. In general, mutton was not a favorite southern meat, but Virginians seem to have been fond of it, and it was certainly not unknown in Tennessee, Kentucky, and Louisiana.

Cornbread was the primary bread of nearly all antebellum southerners. Most southern mills ground corn well but could not handle glutinous wheat, though there were flour mills in the Upper South. Moreover, rust reduced the yield of wheat in most of the South. The more prosperous families did eat yeast bread; beaten biscuits were a common item on plantation tables, but this was not true of the ordinary farmer's or townsperson's table.

Cornbread took many forms, from the elementary hoecake baked on a hoe blade or board in front of the fireplace to various sophisticated mixtures of cornmeal with milk, buttermilk, eggs, shortening, and even sometimes flour or sugar. Cracklin' bread has already been noted. Hushpuppies were balls of cornbread, with additives such as onion, that were fried in grease alongside, or just after, fish. Cornbread did not keep well, and this led to the expectation of hot bread with meals, a fact that delayed and infuriated many a Yankee or foreign traveler.

Corn itself was an important vegetable, and for breakfast or supper many a living southerner has eaten cornmeal mush, which in modern parlance is a cereal. Green corn, "roasting ears," could be roasted in the shuck, boiled as corn on the cob, or sliced off the ear and cooked in various ways. Ripe corn, treated with lye obtained from an ash hopper, became hominy; and hominy, dried and broken into small bits, became hominy grits. Hominy grits, next to cornbread, was the most nearly universal southern food. It was, and still is, delightfully good served with butter or gravy—or even solidified, sliced, and fried.

In one or another part of the South almost all vegetables eaten anywhere else were served. Southerners were especially fond of green beans, butter beans (a variety of lima bean), okra, eggplant, red beans, and white or navy beans. Carrots, parsnips, squash, cabbage, and even green peas (usually called English peas) were eaten, but with less enthusiasm. Southerners enjoyed Irish potatoes, but they could not be kept over the winter for seed, and the necessity for imported seed limited their popularity.

The great triumvirate of southern vegetables was turnips, cowpeas, and sweet potatoes, and it would be difficult to say that one of the three was more important than the others. Turnips were often planted in an open space near a pioneer's house site even before the house was built, because they could be planted in late summer and would produce turnips and greens before a freeze ruined them. The greens were more valued than the turnips themselves, and in the spring they met the residents' almost desperate need for a green vegetable.

Cowpeas were of many varieties. Today, black-eyed peas, crowder peas, and "blue hulled peas" are almost the only variations known, but many others flourished earlier, including whippoorwills, britches and jackets, cuckold's increase, and tiny lady peas. Better green but good dry, peas were boiled with a piece of fat salt pork. With cornbread they provided enough calories and enough protein to sustain a hard day's work, and that was what the southern farmer

Bobby Willis getting some canned goods off the shelves his father built in the family home near Yanceyville, N.C., May 1940 (Marion Post Wolcott, photographer, Library of Congress [LC-USF346-056228], Washington, D.C.)

needed. The liquid in which any vegetable had been cooked—the "pot liquor"— could be eaten with cornbread, but the pot liquor of cowpeas was especially delicious. Local custom and preference determined whether the cornbread was dunked or crumbled.

It would be difficult to exaggerate the role of the sweet potato. From the harvest in late summer until as long as they lasted into the winter, sweet potatoes were a major item in the antebellum southern diet. Like turnips, they could be preserved in a "hill" of earth and decaying vegetable matter, but some farmers had a "potato house," partly or wholly underground, in which the potatoes were stored for protection. Sweet potatoes could be boiled, baked, candied, fried, or made into pudding or pie. Most often they were baked in the coals of the fireplace, and a hot sweet potato with butter was an especially delectable dish.

On great plantations the food in the mansion's dining room was far more elaborate and abundant than it was in the house of the ordinary southerner. Travelers and Yankee tutors have left accounts of gargantuan meals: turtle, venison, ham, turkey, and chicken might grace the same table, with fruits and vegetables in equal abundance. These plantation meals were often accompanied by good wines, whereas in the farmhouse or the town home, milk, coffee, or whiskey was more likely to serve as the drink. Indeed, once the Scotch-Irish had learned to make whiskey from corn, tremendous quantities of that beverage were drunk on the frontier and in the antebellum South.

The food of the slaves, though generally sufficient, was as modest as the food of the great planter was abundant. In most of the South the basic slave ration was two to three pounds of cured pork and a peck of cornmeal a week per adult. In coastal areas fish might be substituted for pork much of the time, and in southwest Louisiana and Texas slaves often got beef, but these were exceptions. The basic ration was supplemented by vegetables in season, and especially by turnip greens, cowpeas, and sweet potatoes. On large plantations the slaves' meals might be prepared in a common kitchen, but in most instances they were cooked in the cabin. This meant primarily in a pot in the fireplace, and southern blacks became accustomed to boiled foods; until recently, and probably to this day, black people of the South tend to eat more boiled foods than do southern whites.

The Civil War left the South impoverished, and the lowest economic classes of society bore the hardest burden. The vast majority of former slaves became sharecroppers, and they were soon joined by millions of southern whites. Sharecroppers got their food and other necessities from a plantation commissary or from a general store. It was still cornmeal and pork, but the cornmeal now came from the Corn Belt, and in the milling much of the nutrition had been removed. The pork was no longer grown and killed on the plantation; it too came from the Midwest, but rather than being bacon, it was fatback, the layer of meat between the skin and the ribs, containing little protein. The basic diet of cornbread and fatback was supplemented by fruits and vegetables far less often than it had been in antebellum days. Diseases associated with malnutrition, especially pellagra, which had seldom been observed before the Civil War, began to take a heavy annual toll. Nor was malnutrition confined to sharecroppers: cotton mill workers and poor townsfolk, including the slum dwellers of developing southern cities, also suffered.

Some of the poorer yeoman farmers who managed to hold on to their land were malnourished as well. In general, however, they ate pork that they had raised and killed themselves, and they took their own corn to the mill. They may have had to buy fatback from the general store part of the year, but most had milk from a scrub cow or two. Also, they planted a vegetable garden, and the old triad of turnips, cowpeas, and sweet potatoes helped them survive. Yeoman farmers were much more likely than tenants to have a fruit orchard.

Two very significant changes, one in food itself and the other in food pro-

Making cookies on a Sunday morning in the McLelland kitchen, Escambia Farms, Fla., 1942
(John Collier, photographer, Library of Congress [LC-USF34-082645-C], Washington, D.C.)

cessing, took place during the later 19th century. As a result of increased wheat production and new milling methods, the great flour mills of the Midwest brought the price of flour down so low that even relatively poor southerners could afford it. Even comparatively prosperous farmers or townspeople had seldom eaten wheat bread before the Civil War, but by 1900 wheat flour biscuits had become as common as cornbread. People ate huge quantities of biscuits. Many farmers bought one or more barrels of flour before the onset of winter weather isolated them from the store. It could be purchased in lesser amounts, but the smallest amount available in most stores was 24 pounds in a cloth sack.

Food patterns formed on the southern frontier persisted well into the 20th century, and indeed until after World War II in many small towns and rural areas. Canned goods, commercial bread, and the refrigerator joined the cookstove and cheap flour in making a difference, albeit a relatively small one. Eventually, however, urbanization, the dislocation brought on by two world wars, the ease of travel in the age of automobiles and interstate highways, and the homogenizing effect of radio and television effected major changes in southern eating habits.

Probably the most basic change was the growth in "eating out," a trend spurred by the availability of reasonably good restaurants in the cities (superb ones in some cities) and, especially, by the advent of so-called fast foods. The hamburger emporium, the fried catfish stand, and the fried chicken establishment provide meals for a tremendous number of southerners every day. It is noteworthy that two of these foods, chicken and catfish, have been a part of the southern diet for 200 years. Furthermore, they are still fried!

American food culture is heavily regionalized. Southern foods accompanied southerners who migrated out of the South, and barbecue and fried chicken became more Americanized than ever in the 20th century. Movements of new populations into the South similarly transform regional foodways today. Sushi restaurants are found throughout the South and certainly in small towns that are home to a Nissan or Toyota factory. Indian curry and other dishes can be found at convenience stores as well as in restaurants. Mexican grocery stores have ceased being exotic, and Mexican restaurants are pervasive. Many of the South's new populations, in turn, enjoy the various regional styles of barbecue, which may be as authentic a surviving icon as we have from the earlier South. Cookbooks for the southern kitchen proliferate, and national food magazines tell readers about frying Cajun turkeys or making fried pies. The meat-and-three plate lunch may be an endangered species, but good ones are still prized.

Since the publication of the *Encyclopedia of Southern Culture* in 1989, the study of foodways has intensified and matured. Commentary relating to southern foodways is, of course, of long note. Lafcadio Hearn's *La Cuisine Creole* (1885) comprised recipes, food vendor street cries, and Creole proverbs from New Orleans, and the collection is an excellent example of the anecdotal nature of much early foodways work. In *The Old Virginia Gentleman and Other Sketches* (1910), George Bagby observed that the Old Dominion archetype "gets religion at a camp-meeting, and loses it at a barbecue or fish-fry."

Jay Anderson's article "The Study of Contemporary Foodways in American Folklife Research," published in the *Keystone Folklore Quarterly* in 1971, is among the pioneering contemporary works in the field. Anderson argued that the study of foodways should include a historical and regional emphasis, but should also embrace "the whole interrelated system of food conceptualization and evaluation, procurement, preservation, preparation, consumption, and nutrition shared by all the members of a particular society." Modern scholarship defines foodways as the study of what we eat, as well as how and why and under what circumstances we eat. In a 1978 dissertation, "America Eats: Toward a Social Definition of American Foodways," Charles Camp proposed that researchers emphasize food events as well as foodstuffs themselves.

Much academic work, from Karen Hess's *The Carolina Rice Kitchen: The African Connection* (1992) to Marcie Cohen Ferris's *Matzoh Ball Gumbo: Culinary Tales of the Jewish South* (2005), follows Camp's proverbial lead, taking into account how members of a society define themselves at table.

Foodways scholars have come to recognize cultural representations as integral to an understanding of the field. And the effects of poverty as well as the brand of geography have been brought into relief. Scholars have also emphasized the importance of African American contributions.

Cultural Representations. Musical expression is much informed by foodways, as in songs like Uncle Dave Macon's "Eleven Cent Cotton, Forty Cent Meat," Dan Penn's "Memphis Women and Fried Chicken," and Memphis Minnie's "I'm Selling My Porkchops (But I'm Giving My Gravy Away)." The traditional song "Chitlin Cookin' Time in Cheatham County" gives voice to how and why chitterlings matter:

> When it's chitlin cookin' time in Cheatham county,
> I'll be courtin' in them Cheatham county hills.
> And I'll pick a Cheatham county chitlin cooker.
> I've a longin' that the chitlins will fill.

Food figures large in southern literature, too. In a passage from *Intruder in the Dust* William Faulkner posits that food provides universal passage into the community of man, that one may read the history of food as the history of man: "Man didn't necessarily eat his way through the world but by the act of eating and maybe only by that did he actually enter the world . . . by the physical act of chewing and swallowing the substance of its warp and woof."

In *Invisible Man* Ralph Ellison uses sweet potatoes (known colloquially as yams) to evoke the emotional tether of food to place for expatriate southerners of African heritage: "I saw an old man warming his hands against the sides of an odd-looking wagon, from which a stove pipe reeled off a spiral of smoke that drifted the odor of baking yams slowly to me. . . . We'd loved them candied, or baked in a cobbler, deep-fat fried in a pocket of dough, or roasted with pork and glazed with the well-browned fat; had chewed them raw—yams and years ago."

To Richard Wright, food is fodder for representations of both symbolic and sustentative want. In his autobiographical work *Black Boy* Wright observes, "I lived on what I did not eat. Perhaps the sunshine, the fresh air, and the pot

FREE BARBEQUE

ALL QUALIFIED VOTERS OF BUTLER COUNTY ARE
CORDIALLY INVITED

To Beeland Park
Tuesday, April 3rd.
AT 5:30 P. M.

TO HEAR
Hon. George C. Wallace
Candidate for Governor
ADDRESS CITIZENS OF BUTLER COUNTY
ALL COUNTY CANDIDATES AND A NUMBER OF STATE CAN-
DIDATES, INCLUDING CONGRESSMAN GEORGE GRANT, WILL
BE THERE. DON'T FORGET THE HOUR—
★ 5:30 P. M. — TUESDAY, APRIL 3rd ★
PLEASE CALL, COME BY OUR OFFICE OR DROP US A CARD IF YOU PLAN TO ATTEND!
WALLACE COMMITTEE FOR GOVERNOR
PHONE DU 2-4903   605 EAST COMMERCE STREET
GREENVILLE, ALABAMA

FREE BARBEQUE

Political rally barbecue poster, Butler County,
Ala. (Edward H. Hobbs personal collection)

liquor from greens kept me going." Zora Neale Hurston employs food as a descriptive trope. In *Their Eyes Were Watching God*, Janie, the protagonist, said of her husband, "Ah hates the way his head is so long one way and so flat on de sides and dat pone uh fat back uh his neck."

Traditional Geographic Regions. Owing to a diversity of topographies and climates, the South may be best understood in terms of pluralities. Although a diet of meat, (corn) meal, and molasses was common throughout much of the region, there were exceptions. Corn was not the dominant grain in the Atlantic South, where, on the marshlands, rice cultivation was accomplished by means of African labor and expertise. There, in addition to composed rice dishes like pilaus, rice waffles and other rice-based breads were enjoyed. Of course, seafood was available in abundance, and the prevalence of oyster stews and deviled crab dishes reflected the bounty of the waters.

Along the crescent of the Gulf South, life has long revolved around the catching and cooking of crustaceans and fish. Oysters from Galveston Bay in Texas, shrimp from the waters beyond Biloxi, Miss., and Mobile, Ala., and pompano from Pensacola Bay, Fla., are the stuff of sustenance and ceremony. While barbecues may have been the community-building and fund-raising feeds elsewhere, along the Gulf of Mexico, fish fries and oyster roasts were the important events. Gumbos and other one-pot stews made with shrimp and crab and such and thickened by roux, filé, or okra, or a combination of the three, have long been considered totemic dishes of the region, eaten by people of all classes.

In the southern interior, peanuts and pecans thrived. Pecan trees, though native to the region, did not become a major crop until after the Civil War, when planters began working cultivated orchards. Both Union and Confederate soldiers prized peanuts—actually legumes like beans, rather than true nuts—during the Civil War. They were not planted often, however, until the early years of the 20th century, when the boll weevil ravaged much of the cotton crop and farmers sought an alternative.

The region's northernmost states, where cold weather came earlier and lasted longer, were favored for the curing of hams and other pork products. To prevent spoilage, hog killings took place after the first frost, when cold weather set in. The hills and hollers of the mountains were also inhabited by distillers, who employed techniques of their Scotch and Irish forefathers to make whiskey from corn, out of sight of federal revenue agents.

Effects of Poverty. Though much of the region boasts a long growing season for vegetables, and a wealth of game and fish, the South has not been immune to economic downturn. The ravages of the Civil War took their toll, as reflected in the *Confederate Receipt Book*, originally published in 1863, which offers instructions for preserving meat without salt and making ersatz coffee from acorn shells.

In the wake of the war, privation was, for many, a constant. To supplement meat and flour purchased from the city grocer or country store, many southerners turned to kitchen gardens. When pellagra, a nutritional deficiency, was rampant during the early years of the 20th century, homegrown green vegetables like collard greens proved to be the underclass's cure-all, its tonic.

The Great Depression was also devastating, though in 1931 it did engender a lighthearted debate between the editors of the *Atlanta Constitution* and Huey Long, U.S. senator-elect from Louisiana, over the proper consumption of two frugal foods: potlikker and cornbread. Long was a dunker of cornbread. The *Constitution* advocated crumbling, and the debate raged for more than three and a half weeks in February and March of that year.

African American Influence. Many of the dishes that southerners think of as distinctive, from hog's head cheese to collard greens to desserts like chess pie, owe their origins to European recipes and techniques. But the introduction of enslaved Africans transformed the South's diet in fundamental ways. African

Americans reinterpreted European cookery and American Indian ingredients, applying African-inspired techniques and constructions. In the kitchen, African American cooks slipped in a pepper pod here, an okra pod there. Indeed, some of the foodstuffs we now recognize as elemental to the southern diet owe their presence to the slave trade: okra came from Africa, as did benne, also known as sesame, and watermelon.

Southerners of African descent cooked in deep oil, as they had done in Africa. They mastered use of the sweet potato, the available tuber closest in appearance to the fibrous yams of Africa. Historian Eugene D. Genovese characterized this general tendency as an example of "the culinary despotism of the quarters over the big house." In the modern as well as the historical South, there is ample evidence supporting Genovese's theory.

Modern Foodways. Modernity, in the guise of improved transportation and a more homogenous food supply, has knitted together the various regions of the South. In the 20th century, companies such as Coca-Cola of Atlanta and Viking Range of Greenwood, Miss., came to prominence, selling their goods in the international marketplace. Concurrently, the movement of southerners from farms to cities and suburbs spurred an increased reliance upon prepackaged foods and a spike in the number and quality of restaurants.

Roadside food of the sort peddled by Harland Sanders's Kentucky Fried Chicken and thousands of independent purveyors came to be a constant. Foods like fried chicken and barbecue, once proudly provincial, found their markets. And as local-option prohibition laws were repealed, white-tablecloth restaurants began to proliferate in cities beyond the fine-dining mainstays of Charleston and New Orleans.

In the late 1960s "soul food," the urbanized food of rural southern blacks, came into vogue at the same time as soul music and other celebrations of black southern life. By the early 1970s soul food was moving upscale as restaurants like Atlanta's Soul on Top o' Peachtree opened downtown, on the 30th floor of the Bank of Georgia building. In 1976 a farmer named Jimmy Carter from the southern Georgia town of Plains became president, and the nation was soon smitten with the foods of his home state, most famously peanuts and grits.

During the later years of the 20th century a growing national fascination with regional foods found a foothold in the South, as cookbooks were published touting southern cooking. In 1986 Nathalie Dupree, born in New Jersey but raised in the South, published *New Southern Cooking*, a work that would help define the genre. Preceding Dupree were Edna Lewis, a native of Freetown, Va., author in 1976 of *The Taste of Country Cooking*, and Bill Neal, chef of Crook's Corner in Chapel Hill, N.C., author in 1982 of *Bill Neal's Southern Cooking*. Contemporary with Dupree's work was John Egerton's *Southern Food: At Home, on the Road, in History*, the book that comes closest to claiming definitive status.

At the cusp of the millennium, the region was rife with restaurants serving updated takes on traditional recipes (fried green tomatoes topped with crab, pecan-crusted catfish). Chefs like Frank Stitt of Birmingham's Highlands Bar and Grill rose to prominence cooking updated dishes like grits soufflés and butter bean crostini. Their work inspired younger southerners to embrace the foods and foodways of their forebears. Farmers, responding to this trend, began planting older varieties of vegetables and fruits that might have been recognizable to a southerner of 100 years ago.

During the late years of the 20th century scholars of the South began to embrace the study of foodways. Among their works was a 1995 dissertation by Doris Whitt, "What Ever Happened to Aunt Jemima?: Black Women and Food in American Culture." In the mid-1990s two organizations dedicated to studying southern food culture, the Society for the Preservation and Revitalization of Southern Food and the American Southern Food Institute, started and stopped operations. In 1999 the Southern Foodways Alliance, a member-supported institute of the Center for the Study of Southern Culture at the University of Mississippi, assumed the member rolls of the previous organizations and launched a campaign to document and celebrate southern foodways by staging symposia and sponsoring oral histories and documentary films.

JOE GRAY TAYLOR
McNeese State University

JOHN T. EDGE
University of Mississippi

John T. Edge, *A Gracious Plenty: Recipes and Recollections from the American South* (1999); John Egerton, *Southern Food: At Home, on the Road, in History* (1987); Damon Lee Fowler, *Classical Southern Cooking: A Celebration of the Cuisine of the Old South* (1995), *Damon Lee Fowler's New Southern Kitchen: Traditional Flavors for Contemporary Cooks* (2002); Jessica B. Harris, *The Welcome Table: African American Heritage Cooking* (1995); Sam Bowers Hilliard, *Hog Meat and Hoecake: Food Supply in the Old South, 1840–1860* (1972); "Our Food, Our Common Ground," *Southern Exposure* (November–December 1983); Barbara G. Shortridge and James R. Shortridge, *The Taste of American*

Place: A Reader on Regional and Ethnic Foods (1998); Stephen A. Smith, in *American Material Culture*, ed. Edith Mayo (1985); Joe Gray Taylor, *Eating, Drinking, and Visiting in the South: An Informal History* (1982); Gertrude I. Thomas, *Foods of Our Forefathers* (1941); Rupert B. Vance, *Human Geography of the South: A Study of Regional Resources and Human Adequacy* (1935); Eugene Walter, *American Cooking, Southern Style* (1971).

African American Foodways

The food of the African Diaspora has had a larger influence on the cooking of the American South than previously acknowledged. The majority of Africans who were enslaved and brought to this country, and their descendants, spent their time working in agriculture-related pursuits and in domestic service of one sort or another. They were, ironically, by their condition of enslavement well placed to subtly influence their masters. This pervasive influence extended not only to the dishes they ate and served, but also to foodstuffs grown, methods of agriculture, culinary techniques, and, arguably, ideas of hospitality.

It all begins on the African continent. The continentwide culinary paradigm of a soupy stew eaten over a starch was certainly in effect prior to European contact, with the starch and the stew varying from region to region: the north boasted millet and hard wheat; the west, true yams and rice; the Horn of Africa, its own grains like teff and elusine. In other areas, the corn that was brought by the Columbian Exchange and other New World and European foodstuffs had largely supplanted them. Culinary techniques, in most areas, were limited to those that could be accomplished on variations of the simple three-rock stove: boiling in water, toasting near the fire, roasting in the fire, steaming in leaves, baking in ashes, and frying in deep oil. These techniques would form the matrix for the cooking that African Americans would excel at and add to the foodways of the South.

With the beginning of the Atlantic slave trade to northern colonies in 1619, the transformation of the foods of Africa began. Many of the foods that were given to the enslaved on the Middle Passage, such as black-eyed peas, corn cakes, and cornmeal or rice mush, would become their last culinary contacts with Africa and serve as an indicator of the sagaciousness of the traders. Traders took note of African culinary preferences and made sure to provision their ships with victuals that were appropriate to the Africans they were carrying. Once on the African coast, ships would go to a particular port (timed to coincide with harvest) to obtain additional provisions appropriate for the region from which it was to obtain slaves. Bulk quantities of rice would be bought on the Upper Guinea Coast, corn (probably maize) on the Gold and Slave Coasts (usually at Anomabu), and yams at Bonny and Old Calabar.

Plantation owners would later call on that same wisdom as they imported African foodstuffs in their ever-ranging quest to find cheap fodder for the enslaved. In such manner, okra, black-eyed peas, and more were added to the South's cooking pots, where they remain emblematic of the cooking of African Americans.

The growth of slavery in colonial America was slow at first, but by the end of the 17th century enough Africans were enslaved in the American South for the beginnings of of an African American communal life to take some form. The experience of slaves, however, was not monolithic and ranged from subsistence farming on small spreads to labor on large plantations that produced everything from tobacco to indigo to rice and later cotton.

What slaves ate often depended on where they lived. In South Carolina, cracked rice was predominant in the diet, and on the Sea Islands slaves were able to maintain the African tradition of seasoning food with dried shrimp. In much of the rest of the South, for the enslaved, as well as for the yeoman farmer, corn and pig meat prevailed. For slaves, the corn was usually consumed as hominy, which was eaten with molasses and, when available, fatback. The hominy was transformed into ashcakes, porridges, or mashes that harked back to the foodways of the African continent.

Each household also maintained its own system for the distribution of food. In some, the enslaved ate communally; in others, they were given their own rations to prepare; and in still others, they were required to produce the foodstuffs that would sustain the plantation and its labor force. A few slaves were given their own small plots and allowed to farm them in their few off hours.

The culinary responsibilities of the enslaved, though, went beyond the preparation and often cultivation of their own food. They were also tasked with the feeding of the master's household. Some, like Thomas Jefferson's James Hemings, even benefited from training in Europe. Here, the line of culinary transmission becomes blurred. For, in the big house kitchen, while the mistress and occasionally the master gave orders and recipes to the cook (or cooks), in the cook's hands the recipes were transformed in ways that are hard to define and harder still to trace specifically. Historian Eugene D. Genovese uses the term *culinary despotism* to describe this phenomenon. The result of this Africanizing of the taste of the South is a predilection for okra, both fried and cooked in a variety of soupy stews often called gumbo; the tradition of eating black-eyed peas and rice on New Year's Day for luck; a taste for spicier food than is favored in most other regions of the country; and a consumption of leafy greens, be they mustards, collards, turnips, or gumbo z'herbes. These preferences transcend race and often class and were evident in the early culinary literature of the region: Mary Randolph's *The Virginia House-wife* (1824) includes two okra dishes, one for a plain buttered okra and the other for "gumbs, a West India dish," which is an okra gumbo. *The Carolina Housewife* (1847) includes another recipe for okra soup, as well as recipes for a peanut soup, a sesame soup, and a New Orleans gumbo.

Away from the plantations, in coastal urban areas, the lives of the enslaved were more closely intertwined with those of their masters. Culinary know-how was still a mark of the African population, and many urban slaves were noted street vendors. African traditions of huckstering prevailed, and slaves enlivened the markets and walked the streets of the towns hawking everything from fresh fish and vegetables to dainties such as cakes, candies, and, in New Orleans, a West African rice fritter known as a cala.

The Emancipation Proclamation of 1863 freed the enslaved but left most of them without education and the ability to translate their numerous skills into cash-making endeavors. The Civil War had reduced many members of the planter class to eating what formerly was considered slave fodder, even more inextricably binding together the foodways of the black and white people of the South.

The years following the Emancipation Proclamation saw an increasing number of African Americans find work with food. In 1881 Abby Fisher published *What Mrs. Fisher Knows about Old Southern Cooking.* Fisher, a former slave from Mobile, Ala., had taken the westward trek along with so many others, settling in San Francisco like another southerner, Mammy Pleasant, who would also make her reputation in the world of food and hospitality.

Others of the formerly enslaved would find their way westward as cowboys. Fully one-third of cowboys in the late nineteenth century were African Americans, a large number of whom served as cooks, transporting across the West spicing styles, culinary techniques, and tastes from the South. Many former slaves hoped to find their way to prosperity via work on the new Pullman and dining cars that were instituted on American railroads at the time slavery ended. By 1921, 51 of 63 railway lines surveyed reported that they employed African Americans as cooks.

The Great Migration of the first part of the 20th century moved many African Americans from the South to homes elsewhere around the country. They brought with them the tastes of Africa that they had made southern. In both the South and the North, African American women found work as housekeepers and cooks, spreading the tastes of African American food still more widely in our national culture. The civil rights movement of the 1950s and 1960s brought many African Americans back to the South. Lunch counters and restaurants served as battlegrounds as African Americans who had traditionally cooked the region's food demanded the right to eat it where they had always cooked it. African American restaurants often served as meeting headquarters and planning places for the movement.

Today, while African American chefs have still not attained the acclaim and financial rewards of their white counterparts, they can increasingly be seen at the helm of their own restaurants in the major cities of the South. Leah Chase and Edna Lewis are legendary eminences. South Carolinian Sylvia Woods has created a culinary empire that encompasses restaurants in New York and Atlanta and a line of canned goods and spices available nationwide. Products ranging from pralines to chowchow are bringing the tastes of the African American South to the country's supermarkets. In increasing numbers, cookbooks are being written about all aspects of African American cuisine, and finally the descendants of generations of enslaved cooks are taking their bows as the creators of a cuisine that has marked the South with the taste of Africa and of African Americans.

JESSICA B. HARRIS
Queens College

John Blassingame, *The Slave Community* (1979); George Francis Dow, *Slave Ships and Slaving* (1970); John Egerton, *Southern Food: At Home, on the Road, in History* (1987); Abby Fisher, *What Mrs. Fisher Knows about Old Southern Cooking* (1881, 1995); Eugene D. Genovese, *Roll, Jordan, Roll: The World the Slaves Made* (1976); Jessica B. Harris, *The Welcome Table: African American Heritage Cooking* (1995), *The Africa Cookbook: Tastes of a Continent* (1998); Karen Hess, *The Carolina Rice Kitchen: The African Connection* (1992); Howard Paige, *Aspects of Afro-American Cookery* (1987); James D. Porterfield, *Dining by Rail* (1993); Robert Roberts, *Roberts' Guide for Butlers and Other Household Staff* (1993); Lorenzo Dow Turner, *Africanisms in the Gullah Dialect* (1949).

Appalachian Foodways

With the nation's most ancient mountain range at its core, the Appalachian region stretches from southern New York to northern Mississippi, encompassing all of West Virginia and portions of 12 other states.

Since colonization, the region's foodways have been shaped by immigrants primarily from Scotland, Ireland, England, Germany, and Africa. The most pervasive and lasting influences on the cooking of Appalachia, however, come from the practices of Native American populations.

The region's reliance upon corn, beans, and squash, for example, is a legacy of white settlers' first encounters with tribes such as the Cherokee and Iroquois. One of Appalachia's most common meals, beans and cornbread, represents the coming together of white and Native American traditions. Seasoning the iconic pot of beans is lard, the rendered fat of the pig. Beans were cultivated by Native

Americans long before white settlement, as was corn, used to make the corn-bread that has become a standard accompaniment to a bowl of soup beans and a symbol of the South.

True Appalachian cooking remains, today, unadorned and loyal to its origins in the earth. It is a cooking style that grew out of hard times. A popular gravy in the mountains is called redeye, made from the simplest of ingredients—browned particles from a fried cut of ham or bacon, the grease from the meat, water, and, oftentimes, leftover coffee. Writer John Egerton has described it as a "divine elixir," and, despite health concerns, the region is experiencing a redeye gravy renaissance of sorts. The gravy is featured for breakfast at white-tablecloth establishments such as the Martha Washington Inn, in Abingdon, Va. Meanwhile, it remains on the menus of classic mountain eateries. At the Southern Kitchen in Charleston, W.Va., slabs of ham swim in the two-toned, briny broth, bordered by fresh-baked biscuits.

Although Appalachian mountain people are prolific gardeners, they use herbs and spices sparingly. Salt, pepper, and sugar are frequently the only seasonings in an entire meal.

The simplicity of the Appalachian table bespeaks the cuisine's working-class, even hardscrabble, origins—food that fed farmhands, coal miners, and mill-workers. It is not uncommon for mountain cooks, particularly those raised during the Great Depression, to spread the table with the treasures of the farm and then humbly apologize for the "scarcity" of the repast.

Offerings on Appalachian tables are governed, in large part, by the cycles of the seasons. As a first sign of spring, Cherokees herald the appearance of ramps, a pungent wild mountain leek, the first green plant to pop through the leaves on the forest floor, valued for its reputed ability to cleanse the blood after a winter of relative inactivity.

Strawberries, spring's earliest fruit, have been found in archaeological contexts in the Southeast dating to around 500 B.C., and the first bowl of sugared strawberries in early May is still cause for celebration. For Cherokees, strawberries symbolize happiness and home. In the Cherokee story of creation, the first woman, Selu, the Corn Mother, leaves her husband, the first man, in a fit of anger. He calls upon the Great One for help in bringing her back. As she flees, the Great One places before Selu a tree full of ripened Juneberries, a bush of juicy huckleberries, and a patch of blackberries. None of these, not even the scratchy blackberry vines, stop her flight. And then the Great One creates a field of strawberries. The fragrance causes Selu to bend down on her knees and taste. Her anger disappears. "Some say that strawberry preserves were born that day. Maybe they were. What we can say for sure is that every well-meaning Chero-

Appalachian homemaker with some of her canned goods in the cellar, Barbourville, Knox County, Ky., 1940 (Marion Post Wolcott, photographer, Library of Congress [LC-USF34-056421-D], Washington, D.C.)

kee housewife keeps strawberries in the house year-round, whether frozen, or canned, or preserved, or fresh," write Paul Hamel and Mary Chiltoskey.

Spring's first lettuce and green onions are picked from the garden and "killed" with a mixture of hot bacon grease and vinegar. When oak leaves are the size of squirrels' ears, mountaineers comb poplar thickets for the precious morel mushroom, to be taken home, battered, and fried as "dry land fish."

Along the region's streams, in the coolness of spring, mountain folk gather cresses, transformed into "creasies" in many highland dialects. They are eaten rinsed and raw, in salads, as last-minute additions to pots of other greens, and on tea room–style sandwiches.

Appalachians' veneration of vegetables is so deep that, in midsummer, tables are oftentimes devoid of meat. A typical meal might include boiled sweet corn, seasoned only with a pat of butter and a shake of salt, pork-flavored green beans cooked until no trace of a crunch can be found, new potatoes just grabbled out of the ground, sliced tomatoes on a stark white plate, and garden-fresh cucumbers bathed in ice water. The best mountain cooks see no reason to embellish nature's creations.

Then, as the summer garden wanes, end-of-season green tomatoes and peppers are gathered to make a type of relish called chowchow, used as a topping for the ever-present bowl of soup beans.

Perhaps Appalachia's greatest contributions to the world's cuisine are the ingenious ways mountain cooks have devised to preserve the bounty of the farm. Fall, usually around Thanksgiving, is the traditional time for hog killing. Biting winters and steamy summers provide the perfect conditions for the salt-curing of hams, aged for as long as two years. Mountain people savor side meat, or bacon, called, by some, with an Elizabethan-inflected second syllable, "streaked."

The bean harvest is preserved well into the winter by canning and freezing, in addition to the time-tested method of drying. "Leather britches" are string beans dried in wind and sun and threaded, to be reconstituted months later in a pot of boiling water.

Likewise in the fall, church groups and families unite around brass kettles for the making of fruit butters, boiled down, thickened, and spiced. Apple butter, spiked with cinnamon, is a common offering at roadside stands and flea markets. In addition to being used as a filling for pies, the meat of the cushaw, a green-and-white-striped squash prized by Native Americans, is cooked into a golden yellow butter served as a biscuit accompaniment.

When not eaten straight out of the field, summer's corn is blanched and frozen, ground into cornmeal for cornbread, or converted into corn liquor, popularly known as "moonshine."

Home-dried apples provide the filling for the dessert most closely associated with the Appalachian highlands. Rarely found in restaurants, seven-layered dried apple stack cake resembles a Central European torte. The time-consuming confection must cure, allowing the apple flavor to permeate the cake, a source of stern discipline for mountain children without the patience to wait the required three days.

Carrying on the influence of the German settlers who wagoned down the Blue Ridge to North Carolina and across the Appalachian spine into Tennessee, home canners make sauerkraut, adhering strictly to the signs of the Zodiac and the phases of the moon.

Along with honey, one of the region's oldest sweeteners is sorghum syrup, produced when sorghum cane is squeezed and the liquid boiled down into an amber thickness. Typically, sorghum syrup is used as a "sop" for biscuits at breakfast time, either alone or mixed with butter. Sorghum "stir-offs" were communal events in the days when the liquid was extracted from the cane by the circular tramping of a horse or mule. An all-natural product, sorghum syrup is experiencing a resurgence in Appalachia today, and Kentucky and Tennessee are making more of it than any other states.

As tobacco farming has declined, sustainable agriculture and aquaculture have reemerged. Operations like Davidson's Country Store and Farm in Hawkins County, Tenn., which once grew tobacco and raised beef cattle, have converted to the production of heirloom vegetables—greasy beans, Turkey Craw beans, and supersweet corn varieties. At Johnson County High School in Mountain City, Tenn., an area hit hard by the loss of tobacco profits, students learn the science of farming tilapia. Near the western North Carolina town of Canton, Sunburst Trout Farm has been in the business of sustainable aquaculture since 1948 and now sells trout caviar, a product that was once discarded.

As they have done for ages, those who live in the Appalachians, even in the modern age of convenience food and rootless mobility, continue to grow green beans, bake cornbread, can apple butter, harvest black walnuts, and cure hams. While the encroachment of chain food establishments threatens mountain cookery just as it does traditional southern cuisine in general, Appalachian fare has always been centered in the home and in the garden and guided by the seasonal variety of the land and the larder. Those in the region who attend church dinners on the grounds and family reunion feasts may see more commercially prepared fried chicken and store-bought cakes on the tables nowadays, but those dishes, cooked by unknown hands in corporate kitchens, have yet to supplant home-canned half-runner beans, home-baked fruit pies firmly in the English tradition, sun-warmed tomatoes, and primeval sweet corn, foods as persistent as the mountain people who have rejoiced in their life-sustaining simplicity for nearly four centuries.

FRED W. SAUCEMAN
East Tennessee State University

Joseph E. Dabney, *Smokehouse Ham, Spoon Bread, and Scuppernong Wine: The Folklore and Art of Southern Appalachian Cooking* (1998); John Egerton, *Southern Food: At Home, on the Road, in History* (1987); Paul Hamel and Mary Chiltoskey, *Cherokee Plants and Their Uses: A 400-Year History* (1975); Ronni Lundy, ed., *Cornbread Nation 3: Foods of the Mountain South* (2005).

Barbecue

Of all the signature foods of the South, none unites and divides the region like barbecue. When it comes to barbecue, southerners cannot agree on meat, sauce, technique, side dishes, or even how to spell the word. What they can agree on is that barbecue in all its variety is one of the fond traditions that makes the South the South. It drifts across class and racial distinctions like the sweet vapors of pork hissing over hickory embers.

Southern barbecue has its roots in the Caribbean, where Spanish explorers of the early 1500s found islanders roasting fish and game on a framework of sticks they called (in translation) a barbacoa. The Anglicized word *barbecue* first appeared in the *Oxford English Dictionary* in 1661 to mean any such framework, whether used for cooking or some other purpose, like supporting a mattress. A century later, the word had narrowed to mean the food and the social event where it was served. "Went up to Alexandria for a barbicue," George Washington wrote in his diary in 1769, pioneering another spelling.

The first barbecuers were usually African slaves who combined their native methods of roasting meat with know-how picked up from their passage in the West Indies. The most important point, then and now, was the knowledge that barbecue takes hours to absorb its smoky flavor and must be cooked very slowly over indirect heat, usually over hardwood coals, and not over the fire itself. Authentic barbecue is still cooked the old-fashioned way, and a disproportionate number of the cooks are still African American.

Early barbecues were occasions for family and community to gather, for southerners to show off their growing reputation for hospitality. Margaret Mitchell captured the scene in her novel *Gone with the Wind* when she describes Scarlett O'Hara's arrival at a plantation barbecue near Atlanta: "Even before Twelve Oaks came into view Scarlett saw a haze of smoke hanging lazily in the tops of the tall trees and smelled the mingled savory odors of burning hickory logs and roasting pork and mutton."

From the beginning, politicians were drawn to those savory odors like swarms of gnats. Elected officials from the Talmadges of Georgia to President Lyndon B. Johnson of Texas have used barbecues to raise funds and rally the faithful. At one of the largest such assemblies, in 1923, Oklahoma governor Jack Walton celebrated his inauguration with a mass feeding that consumed 289 cattle, 70 hogs, 36 sheep, 2,540 rabbits, 134 possums, 15 deer, 1,427 chickens, and an antelope.

Around the beginning of the 20th century, barbecue went commercial as meat markets and restaurants began to sell to the public. Some of the nation's earliest drive-ins, like the Pig & Whistle chain out of San Antonio, Tex., were barbecue places. But barbecue is slow food, requiring great patience, and quicker dishes like hamburgers and fried chicken proved more suitable to the fast-food businesses that transformed the American landscape. Few enterprises

Foster's Bar-B-Q, Reagan, Tenn. (*Courtesy Amy Evans, photographer*)

have managed to successfully franchise barbecue. Most barbecue pits in the South remain independently operated, their peculiarities an essential part of their appeal.

Barbecue joints come in all shapes and sizes, from storefront rib shacks in the inner city to cinder-block roadhouses with sawdust-covered floors in the country. The classic of the genre is a decidedly downscale affair with red checkered tablecloths, knotty pine paneling darkened by smoke and grease, and a sign out front showing a smiling pig that seems to be inexplicably happy about its contribution to the menu. Pickup trucks and expensive cars sit cheek by jowl in the parking lot, evidence of the food's ability to cut across cultural barriers. Barbecue lovers will drive many miles to make the pilgrimage to beloved places like Wilson's in Goldsboro, N.C., or Fresh Air in Jackson, Ga., or Dreamland in Tuscaloosa, Ala., or McClard's in Hot Springs, Ark., or the Salt Lick in Driftwood, Tex. The repast lives on in endless good-natured debates about who's the best and who's slipped a notch.

The South's devotion to barbecue began to spread across America after World War II. Southerners moving to other regions took their meat-smoking ways with them; when black Mississippians left the Delta in droves, for instance, they turned the south side of Chicago into a smoldering porkopolis of rib shacks. A more amateur strain of barbecue enthusiasm swept through the suburbs as outdoor grilling became part of the good life. The popularity of charcoal and gas grills has blurred some distinctions, however; to the chagrin of purists, back-yard chefs tend to refer to anything they char as barbecue.

Most southerners know (or should know) that an incinerated chicken or a hot dog with burn stripes is not barbecue. But that does not mean they necessarily see eye to eye on what constitutes the real thing. Take the most basic variable, meat. In most of the South, barbecue means pork—hams, shoulders, ribs, the whole hog (particularly in the Carolinas, where pig-pickin's are an institution). Pork barbecue is so widespread that University of North Carolina sociologist John Shelton Reed once suggested the South ditch the controversial Confederate battle flag and adopt a curly-tailed porker as an official symbol everyone could feel good about. But that gesture might draw fire in western Kentucky, where mutton is the preferred meat, or in much of Texas, where the cattle culture rules in the form of sliced beef brisket. Texans also enjoy barbecued sausage and goat, nods to the state's German and Mexican stock.

Sauce is another disputed matter. Academic papers and books have been written about the balkanized sauce styles of the South, a map of which can resemble a map of the wine regions of France. The Carolinas are a patchwork quilt of their own, with mustard sauces in central South Carolina, tomatoless vinegar sauces in eastern North Carolina, and ketchup-based sauces to the west. As in the rest of the country, most barbecue sauces in the South are red. But there are exceptions: white mayonnaise sauces in Alabama and black mutton-dipping sauces in Kentucky, while in whole stretches of Texas people believe that sauce is irrelevant if the meat was smoked properly. Memphis deserves special mention, riven as it is by two sects; the wets slather ribs with sweet tomato sauce, and the drys powder their pork with seasonings but nothing liquid.

Naturally, there is little consensus about appropriate side dishes. From Virginia to Georgia, barbecue usually comes with Brunswick stew—although South Carolina stands apart with pork hash served over rice. Kentucky has its own stew called burgoo. Coleslaw accompanies barbecue across the region, although here too there are quirks. In North Carolina, the slaw tends to be fine and vinegary and served on the side with hushpuppies. In Memphis, the slaw is creamier and often comes smeared on a bun in a barbecue sandwich.

Several towns claim to be the world capital of barbecue, among them Owensboro, Ky., the epicenter of mutton barbecue; Kansas City, Mo., where southern barbecue customs meet Midwestern feed lots; and Lexington, N.C., which must have the highest barbecue joint-to-population ratio anywhere. Memphis hosts the Memphis in May World Championship Barbecue Cooking Contest, a Mardi Gras of wigged-out piggery that draws competitive teams from all over the country and beyond. Memphis certainly takes the ribbon for unusual side dishes; its restaurants invented barbecue spaghetti and barbecue pizza, the latter a favorite of America's most notorious omnivore, Elvis Presley.

JIM AUCHMUTEY
Atlanta Journal-Constitution

Jim Auchmutey and Susan Puckett, *The Ultimate Barbecue Sauce Cookbook* (1995); Rick Browne and Jack Bettridge, *Barbecue America: A Pilgrimage in Search of America's Best Barbecue* (1999); John Egerton, *Southern Food: At Home, on the Road, in History* (1987); Lolis Eric Elie, *Smokestack Lightning: Adventures in the Heart of Barbecue Country* (1996), ed., *Cornbread Nation 2: The United States of Barbecue* (2004); Bob Garner, *North Carolina Barbecue: Flavored by Time* (1996); John Thorne and Matt Lewis Thorne, *Serious Pig: An American Cook in Search of His Roots* (1996); Robb Walsh, *Legends of Texas Barbecue Cookbook: Recipes and Recollections from the Pit Bosses* (2002).

Beef

As early as 1550, the first cattle arrived in Florida, brought by Spanish settlers. Weighing 600 to 800 pounds, these Florida Crackers or Florida Scrubs, as they were known, flourished and are still around today. Virginia welcomed its first cows in the early years of the 17th century; soon after, Governor Thomas Dale proclaimed that "no man shall dare kill any bull, cow, calf . . . whether his own or appertaining to another man." Within four decades, there were an estimated 30,000 cows in the colony.

Though five of the top ten beef-producing states today are in the South—Texas, Oklahoma, Florida, Tennessee, and Kentucky—perhaps Dale's proclamation against killing cattle should be read as a foreshadowing of southern dietary preferences for centuries to come. Cattle were raised throughout the region, but most often for the milk, butter, and leather they provided. With large amounts of land in the South still unclaimed and unsettled through the 18th century, cattlemen were able to let their cows roam and graze freely, a lifestyle that, while almost certainly preferable to the cow itself, hardly resulted in tender cuts of beef come slaughter time. So, despite its early arrival in what would eventually become the southern United States, the cow never caught on as an eating animal the way that the pig did, even after the means of raising a tenderer animal had been introduced.

A preference for pork made good, practical sense in the days before refrigeration, when meat had to be eaten fresh or preserved. In sparsely populated rural areas, the much larger cow would have provided too much beef to go around before spoiling, making fresh beef an impractical commodity. And preserved beef—whether dried, cured, or potted—couldn't compete with pork for a southerner's palate. Even after refrigeration made transporting and storing fresh beef possible, and the rest of the country had developed a preference for beef over pork—around 1900—the South stuck to the tastes it had already developed.

That is not to say that beef has been absent from the southern plate. Far from it. As Sarah Belk writes, "Beef cured in a solution of sugar, salt, and spices has probably been popular in the South since the first bovine was slaughtered and eaten." In east Texas barbecue, beef brisket replaces pork shoulder. Gravy-smothered country fried steak—in which a cheap cut of beef is pounded thin, dredged in flour, and pan-fried—is common throughout the South. And north Mississippians still celebrate the slugburger, a legacy of the Depression developed to stretch its main ingredient—ground beef—and a cook's budget by mixing in cornmeal, breadcrumbs, or, more commonly today, soybean meal. The fried slugburger, whose unappetizing name is likely derived from the slang for a nickel rather than from the slimy critter, gets a festival in its honor each July in Corinth, Miss.

Even today, when cuts of high-quality beef are available at supermarkets and on restaurant menus throughout the South, it is, according to John Egerton, the cheaper cuts of beef that recipes in southern cookbooks call for. "As far back as the early 1800s, the North had a reputation for good beef and bad pork, but in the South it was the other way around," writes Egerton. The spirit of that sentiment certainly remains today.

MATT MCMILLEN
Washington, D.C.

Charles E. Ball, *Building the Beef Industry: A Century of Commitment* (1998); Sarah Belk, *Around the Southern Table: Innovative Recipes Celebrating 300 Years of Eating and Drinking* (1991); John Egerton, *Southern Food: At Home, on the Road, in History* (1987); Waverly Root and Richard Rochemont, *Eating in America: A History* (1976); Andrew Smith, ed., *The Oxford Encyclopedia of Food and Drink in America* (2004); Robb Walsh, *Houston Press* (1 May 2003).

Beverages

The first mechanical refrigeration plant for the manufacture of ice was built in New Orleans in 1865, but long before that inventive southerners found ways to slake the thirst of long, hot summers in the region. In springhouses, cellars, and underground icehouses, 19th-century housekeepers cooled sweet milk, buttermilk, cider, and other liquids. Using winter ice insulated with straw, they made special-occasion pitchers of lemonade and iced tea. In winter they drank hot coffee, tea, and cocoa, imported beverages consumed widely in the South before the Civil War. Mineral water from the hot springs of Arkansas was first bottled in 1871. Orange juice and other juices from Florida-grown citrus fruits became universally popular.

Southerners have used lemonade for refreshment since colonial times. Too strong to be eaten straight from the tree like other citrus fruits, lemons required dilution with water and sweetening with sugar to be pleasing to the palate. Thus the recipe for lemonade incorporates these very modifications of lemon juice to produce a pleasant, cooling beverage suitable for the hot southern climate. All three of the 19th-century southern "Housewife" cookbooks—from Kentucky, Virginia, and South Carolina—contained recipes for lemonade.

In her cookbook *The Taste of Country Cooking* (1976), Edna Lewis reminisces about drinking lemonade to keep cool on scorching summer afternoons at home in rural Virginia "when a stone crock of tangy lemonade was brought out with a big, free-form piece of ice and thin slices of lemon floating on it. It would be ladled out in tall glasses and the cool drink always fitted the occasion." Zora Neale Hurston incorporates a similar scene into her novel *Their Eyes Were Watching God*. During their courtship, Janie and Tea Cake enjoy summer evenings on Janie's porch, talking and eating: "Near eleven o'clock she remembered a piece of pound cake she had put away. Tea Cake went out to the lemon tree at the corner of the kitchen and picked some lemons and squeezed them for her. So they had lemonade, too." Using mint and lime to enhance the flavor, southerners continue to make lemonade today to combat the heat of the summer.

Iced tea also survives as a popular southern beverage from earlier times. Loose-leaf orange pekoe provided the tea base for generations, although now southern grocers offer seemingly infinite choices, from decaffeinated teas to herbal teas to teas in flow-through bags. Most commonly, iced tea is referred to simply as "tea" and comes in both sweet and unsweetened varieties, often with lemon for flavor. Iced tea emerges in the tradition of southern cooking as a creative revision of the ancient practices of tea making and drinking, adapted for refreshment to the hot southern climate. Iced tea appears on menus at a diverse array of restaurants in the South across the seasons.

Historically, southerners also drank homemade beer, wine, and whiskey. In the late 1700s Kentucky became a mecca for whiskey makers, and the sour-mash bourbon that originated there is now world renowned; in fact, almost all whiskey made from corn and limestone water comes from Kentucky and Tennessee.

Drinking sodas at a picnic at Irwin Farms, Ga., on May Day, 1939 (Marion Post Wolcott, photographer, Library of Congress [LC-USF 33-03071-M4], Washington, D.C.)

Besides the generic liquids just mentioned, a number of brand-name beverages originated in the South and now enjoy wide popularity, including Maxwell House coffee, roasted and blended by Joel O. Cheek in Nashville, Tenn., beginning in 1892; Dixie beer, first brewed in 1907 by Valentine Merz in New Orleans, La.; and Gatorade, developed by Dr. Robert Cade, a University of Florida kidney specialist, in Gainesville, Fla., in 1965. But southern inventors have most famously contributed the largest number of brand-name beverages to the world of soft drinks.

Everyone has heard the story of Coca-Cola, concocted in 1886 by Atlanta druggist Dr. John Pemberton as an over-the-counter tonic, containing extracts of coca leaves and caffeine-rich kola nuts. Asa Candler perfected the mass manufacture of the beverage, and in the 1920s his successor, Robert Woodruff, took Coke to a global market, making himself and Candler two of the South's richest men in the process. This history is enshrined in the World of Coca-Cola Museum, a museum and tourist attraction not far from company headquarters in the heart of Atlanta.

Pepsi began in much the same way, thanks to pharmacist Caleb Bradham in the coastal North Carolina city of New Bern. He mixed a concoction of pepsin and kola nut extract in 1898, patented it in 1903, and began franchising the bottling rights in 1905 to plants in the cotton mill towns of Charlotte and Durham. Pepsi remained based in the South until 1935, when its headquarters moved to New York State.

Today America's fourth-most-popular soft drink—after Coke, Pepsi, and Diet Coke—is Mountain Dew. Its complicated all-southern genealogy goes back to 1948, when Knoxville, Tenn., bottlers Barney and Ally Hartman created the trademark—depicting hillbilly moonshiners Barney & Ally—for a lemon-lime beverage. Then along came Sun-Drop, a highly caffeinated orange juice–tinged soft drink credited to a Missouri inventor but first bottled in Gastonia, N.C., in 1953. Sun-Drop, billed as "Golden Cola—Refreshing as a Cup of Coffee," gave a caffeine rush that proved just the thing for factory workers in the Carolinas and Tennessee. To compete against Sun-Drop, a Mountain Dew franchisee in Fayetteville, N.C., reformulated his drink in 1962, creating the now-familiar flavor. Customers loved it, and in 1964 Pepsi bought out the company and took Mountain Dew national.

Coke and Pepsi reign as the corporate powers in pop, but nipping at their heels is Dallas-based Dr Pepper/7-Up. Dr Pepper, created in 1885 by a Virginia druggist who had moved to Waco, Tex., flourished for many years in southern markets before finding a national audience in the 1970s. 7-Up, born in St. Louis in the 1920s, joined the Dr Pepper product line in 1986, and nine years later British candy and ginger ale giant Cadbury-Schwepps bought the whole operation. RC Cola and Nehi came under the Dr Pepper corporate umbrella in 2000. Their story starts back in 1905 when Columbus, Ga., pharmacist Claud A. Hatcher began bottling Chero-cola. The company added Nehi fruit flavors in 1924 and reformulated its cola in 1934 under the name Royal Crown. By 1940 Royal Crown and Nehi were available throughout the United States—but southerners claimed a special affinity and eventually their nickname—"RC"—became the brand's official moniker.

Coke and Pepsi have squashed nearly all of the hundreds of local brands that once flavored southern regions. In the early decades of the 20th century, bottlers in every city had their own specialties. Dixie Grape, "The Hospitality Drink" from Charlotte, N.C., included the hoop-skirted silhouette of Southern Belle on the bottle along with musical notes from "It's True What They Say about Dixie." Tom's, whose slogan "It's better" modestly eschewed any claim to be "best," was distributed by Tom's snack food route salesmen in South Carolina. White Light-nin, developed in Highlands, N.C., but found as far afield as Arkansas, was a Sun-Drop/Mountain Dew competitor. The James E. Crass Bottling Company of Richmond, Va., made the fearlessly named Crass available in several fruit flavors as well as ginger ale.

A handful of regional holdouts still exist, however. Blenheim's Ginger Ale, brewed in three degrees of hotness, is now owned by the promoters of South Carolina's famous South of the Border tourist complex on I-95, but continues to be made with water from the Blenheim Artesian Mineral Springs in the tiny village of Blenheim, S.C., where the drink originated in the 1890s. Cheerwine, a highly caffeinated (but nonalcoholic) cherry beverage first sold in 1913, is still bottled in its native Salisbury, N.C. Ale-8-1 hails from Winchester, Ky., steadfast since 1926, distributed only in Kentucky and parts of adjacent states. Double-Cola dates back to a 1933 decision by a Chattanooga entrepreneur to debut a 12-ounce bottle, countering the industry standard of 6 ounces. Sun-Drop still finds its staunchest customers in the Carolinas and Tennessee—though that may change as it gains attention as a NASCAR sponsor. Barq's root beer, first bottled and sold in Biloxi, Miss., in 1898 by Edward Charles Edmond Barq, is now among the top-selling soft drinks in the world; the Mississippi legislature has designated Barq's the official state soft drink.

Why the South? Long, hot summers offer one obvious explanation. Before air-conditioning, southerners took summers slowly, seeking a breeze on the porch with a cold drink in hand. Industrialization also spurred soda pop sales. In Virginia, the Carolinas, and Georgia, the rise of textile, tobacco, and furniture manufacturing put thousands of men, women, and children inside hot buildings year-round. Cotton mills, in particular, were notorious for their heat and humidity, necessary to keep threads from breaking. Workers drank lots of soda pop, which they nicknamed "dope," likely in honor of the stimulant effect of caffeine. The "dope wagon," a cart selling snacks and soft drinks, rolled through most mills at least once each shift.

To be sure, soft drinks are deeply intertwined with southern culture. Coca-Cola cake, a moist chocolate confection that substitutes Coke for some of the expected sugar, has been a southern tradition at least since the sugar-rationing days of World War II. "Give Me an RC Cola and a MoonPie (and Play Me Some of that 'Maple on the Hill')" became a hillbilly hit for singers Lonzo and Oscar in 1951. And in May 2005 the town of Bell Buckle, Tenn., proudly held its 10th annual RC Cola and MoonPie Festival.

Today, the South, once the most isolated region of the country, has become a magnet for immigrants from around the world—all of whom are bringing their own soft drinks. A single corner in Charlotte, N.C., illustrates the diversity. There, the Dominican restaurant offers Country Club fruit drinks in glass bottles. The Middle Eastern deli has Fayrouz lemonade from Egypt and the English fruit drink Vimto, a favorite in former outposts of the British Empire. The Salvadorean diner sells LaCascada pineapple pop. The cooler at the Indian grocery includes Thums-Up cola and beerlike Malta India. Two Asian shops display stunning arrays of exotics, from Pink Guava flavor, to Pearl Pineapple (with black basil seeds throughout the liquid), to jelly drinks that recall the recent fad for "bubble tea." Mexicans comprise the South's biggest immigrant group, and they've brought their thirst for fruit beverages. At the corner *tienda* (grocery), crowded shelves offer thick, sweet Jumex nectars of mango or strawberry, the wonderfully named Boing! orange drink, and Senorial nonalcoholic sangria, as well as Jarritos and rival brand Barrilitos in half a dozen flavors from *tamarindo* (tamarind) to *toronja* (grapefruit).

JOHN EGERTON
Nashville, Tennessee

TOM HANCHETT
Levine Museum of the New South

FRANCES ABBOTT
University of Mississippi

Frederick Allen, *Secret Formula: How Brilliant Marketing and Relentless Salesmanship Made Coca-Cola the Best-Known Product in the World* (1994); *Beverage World: 100 Year History, 1882–1982* (1982); John Egerton, *Southern Food: At Home, on the Road, in History* (1987); Harry E. Ellis, *Dr Pepper: King of Beverages* (1979); Constance L. Hayes, *The Real Thing: Truth and Power at the Coca-Cola Company* (2004); Sam Bowers Hilliard, *Hog Meat and Hoecake: Food Supply in the Old South, 1840–1860* (1972); E. J. Kahn Jr., *The Big Drink: The Story of Coca-Cola* (1950); Kathryn W. Kemp, *God's Capitalist: Asa Candler of Coca-Cola* (2002); Edna Lewis, *The Taste of Country Cooking* (1976); Martha McCulloch-Williams, *Dishes and Beverages of the Old South* (1913, 1988); John J. Riley, *A History of the American Soft Drink Industry: Bottled Carbonated Beverages, 1807–1957* (1958); Bob Stoddard, *The Encyclopedia of Pepsi-Cola Collectibles* (2002), *Pepsi: 100 Years* (1997); Jasper Guy Woodruff and G. Frank Phillips, *Beverages: Carbonated and Noncarbonated* (1981).

Cajun Foodways

A pervasive but mistaken belief in French Louisiana is that Acadian refugees introduced Cajun cuisine to the area two and a half centuries ago. Cajun cuisine is, instead, a product of the 20th century and the result of extensive cross-cultural borrowing by the diverse ethnic and racial groups that have coexisted in the bayou country since the late 18th century. Anyone who has had the opportunity to sample both Cajun cuisine and "traditional" Acadian fare in the Canadian Maritime Provinces needs no further persuasion.

The evolutionary tract followed by Acadian cuisine in North America was shaped by the variety of available foodstuffs, the accessibility of gradually improving cooking technology, and the population's pragmatism and willingness to experiment with new modes of food preparation. The last characteristic is the legacy of the Acadians' historical experiences.

The Acadians' ancestors sprang almost exclusively from the French peasantry, whose 16th- and 17th-century diet consisted primarily of soups and whole-grain breads. Once transplanted to Acadia on the shores of the Bay of Fundy in the early 17th century, however, the French colonists changed their diet radically as readily available fresh game, fish, and shellfish found their way to the table. The Acadians, however, maintained a great affinity for pork, particularly salted pork, which they reportedly ate twice daily.

Despite the infusion of meat into the Acadian diet, the settlers' culinary tradition changed very little. Because their cooking technology remained unaltered, their foods were prepared and consumed as they had been in France. Like their French ancestors, the Acadians used two basic types of pots to prepare their meals. The first was the cauldron, suspended by hooks in the hearth. Cauldrons were used to slow-cook foods, particularly soups. The second major cooking vessel was a deep skillet. Without a lid, this cast-iron pot was used for frying foods, particularly fish or eggs. Covered by a lid, the pot was transformed into a Dutch oven capable of baking whole-wheat breads that remained a staple of the Acadian diet until 1755. Acadian cuisine in the 17th and 18th centuries thus bore little outward resemblance to its modern Louisiana descendant. Neither would the taste remind anyone of any dish in the present Cajun culinary repertoire.

Acadian cuisine began to acquire some of its present characteristics following the settlement of approximately 3,000 Acadian exiles in Louisiana's bayou country between 1765 and 1785. Wheat and barley, cereal grains widely cultivated in Acadia, would not grow in south Louisiana. The refugees were consequently compelled to produce maize, a crop largely unknown in their pre-dispersal homeland. Corn served as the staple of the Acadian diet in Louisiana until the early 20th century. Rice, which supplemented corn in the 1920s in many Cajun communities, was a marginal crop in most south Louisiana parishes until the late 19th century, when midwestern immigrants introduced steam-powered irrigation into the Pelican State's prairie region. Corn and rice production was supplemented by the cultivation of large vegetable gardens and fruit orchards. Acadian refugees reestablished the broad lines of these agricultural endeavors in late 18th-century Louisiana.

As in their Canadian homeland, Louisiana Acadians supplemented the output of their gardens and orchards with wild game and fish taken from local woods and streams. Louisiana's Acadian population has continued to incorporate wild game and fish into its diet, but the importance of those food items waned as the community's economic condition improved. The void was filled by salted pork, fresh beef, and old, unproductive hens.

The types of meat consumed by Louisiana Acadians—dubbed Cajuns by their Anglo neighbors in the 19th century—dictated the perpetuation of traditional cooking techniques, despite the introduction of new cooking technologies in the 19th and 20th centuries. The stringy beef generated by local longhorn cattle, salt pork, and old hens (killed and eaten only when they became too old to produce eggs) all required lengthy cooking at low temperatures. In most Cajun homes, cooks relied upon the familiar cauldron to slow-cook, and thereby tenderize, meat. Throughout the 19th and early 20th centuries, slow-cooked meat was served with cornbread and seasonal vegetables. Extant documentation suggests that there were few desserts, and those that existed, like *gateaux de sirop* (syrup cakes), were quite simple, combining seasonal fruits and homemade syrup.

Between 1765 and 1900, travelers through Louisiana's Cajun parishes found local cuisine in no way unusual, with one notable exception—gumbo. Gumbo first appears in the historical record at the dawn of the 19th century. The two initial references point to the use of gumbo at a gubernatorial reception in New Orleans in 1803 and at an Acadian house dance along the Mississippi River in 1804. The dish's origins remain cloudy, but it is clear that gumbo had supplanted *soupe de la toussaint* (All Saints' Day soup, a meatless cabbage and turnip soup) as the Acadian community's favorite dish before Louisiana achieved statehood in 1812. Cajun gumbo, distinguished from its New Orleans Creole counterpart in the early 19th century by its use of both a roux base and okra, was so popular within Louisiana's Acadian community that State Supreme Court Chief Justice Joseph A. Breaux identified it as the group's "national dish." Throughout the 19th and early 20th centuries Cajun hosts routinely served gumbo at special gatherings, particularly at weekly house dances. By the Civil War era, innovative Cajun cooks had developed numerous gumbo varieties. Seafood was both expensive and accessible only to those Cajun settlements in close proximity to the Gulf of Mexico, so seafood gumbo, if it was consumed at all, was quite rare in the Cajun parishes before the introduction of refrigeration in the 20th century.

The introduction of refrigeration, the improvement of Louisiana's highway system in the 1920s and 1930s, and the increasing affluence of the Cajun population after World War II provided the underpinnings of a culinary and dietary revolution. In the post–World War II era the newly constructed ranch-style houses of Cajuns usually featured two-car garages and a storage area for fishing boats. Cajun offshore oil workers made frequent use of these boats during their "free time," and by the 1970s many Cajun homes featured a second deep freezer filled to capacity with frozen bream, *sac-à-lait*, catfish, and bass.

Crawfish, a shellfish now intimately connected with Cajun cuisine, played only a minor role in the local diet until the mid-twentieth century. Before then, Cajuns customarily harvested small amounts of crawfish that they boiled and consumed during the meatless days of the Catholic vernal Lenten season. As with lobster consumption during the early 20th century, crawfish consumption bore a social stigma because the crustaceans were popularly viewed as "the poor man's food" (which indeed it was). Cajun consumption of crawfish increased significantly only with the establishment of the Breaux Bridge Crawfish Festival (1959), which launched a public relations campaign to improve the food's image. The resulting increase in demand gave impetus to the development of a cottage industry producing ever-increasing quantities of peeled crawfish. The ready availability of peeled crawfish at affordable prices made it convenient for south Louisiana cooks to incorporate the crustacean into mainstream Cajun cuisine, and by the early 1970s crawfish étouffée had become a fixture on restaurant menus, at social gatherings, and on dinner plates.

Like crawfish, seafood became a fixture in Cajun cuisine only in the second half of the 20th century, after improvements in south Louisiana's economic, educational, and transportation infrastructures had laid the groundwork for a remarkable culinary revolution. In the 1920s and 1930s regional newspapers sought to capitalize upon the rapidly expanding local pool of potential readers by publishing cookbooks featuring New Orleans Creole recipes. Cajun cooks, previously unable to use much seafood, became increasingly willing to experiment with these recipes as new highways, the establishment of municipal electrical systems, and the introduction of iceboxes made seafood both readily available and affordable—but only in urban settings.

The Cajun appetite for seafood increased significantly after World War II, when the unprecedented expansion of the Gulf Coast oil industry provided previously impoverished Cajuns with both the means and the incentive to experiment with finfish and shellfish that had formerly been extravagant luxuries. In the 1950s thousands of young Cajuns found employment in the offshore oil drilling industry. Most of these workers—particularly those from the southwestern Louisiana prairie region—had their first taste of seafood in the famed offshore oil rig galleys, and most soon developed an appreciation for red snapper and other saltwater fish, oysters, and shrimp.

Oil workers carried their acquired tastes home, and their families' growing affluence gave their wives, now liberated from the cotton, sugarcane, and rice fields, time to make seafood dishes in the modern kitchens of their new houses. By the late 1970s and early 1980s, virtually every Cajun housewife had an impressive repertoire of seafood recipes.

During the golden years of the oil boom, much of the seafood consumed by Cajuns in restaurants was fried. Home-cooked meals, on the other hand, generally continued to feature étouffées, fricassées, and brown gravies. In the post–World War II era, Cajun cuisine in the prairie region became synonymous with beef, rice, and gravy dishes, which, in most households, were consumed twice a day. This culinary duality has created considerable confusion among outsiders about what actually constitutes the hallmarks of Cajun cooking, and the problem was compounded by the national discovery of Cajun cuisine in the 1980s.

Widespread interest in Cajun cuisine spawned a host of imitators hoping to cash in on the national craze. National restaurant chains began to market "Cajun" products, such as McDonald's Cajun chicken sandwich and Pizza Hut's Traditional New Orleans-Style Cajun Pizza. Usually the only link between corporate America's products and actual Cajun dishes was cayenne pepper, which the imitators used to great excess.

The national Cajun culinary sensation, which peaked in the 1990s, coincided with dramatic changes in the typical Cajun household, changes that threaten to permit the cooptation of the culinary tradition's continued development by "outsiders." With the rise of the two-income household in the late 20th century, fewer Cajun women had the time or energy to cook, much less to engage in creative culinary experiments. The torch of creative culinary leadership has thus been passed by default to chefs in the Cajun parishes' leading restaurants. Many—perhaps most—of these chefs are not Cajun, and they freely meld their own cooking traditions with those developed organically within the Cajun community. Many young Cajuns committed to preventing fast food from dominating the area's culinary landscape have enthusiastically joined in the experiment. The resulting fusion, increasingly called nouveau Cajun or simply Louisiana cuisine, is represented by such dishes as crawfish fettuccini, Cajun enchiladas, crawfish cabbage rolls, and Cajun sausage spaghetti.

CARL A. BRASSEAUX
RYAN A. BRASSEAUX
Lafayette, Louisiana

Barry Jean Ancelet, Jay D. Edwards, and Glen Pitri, *Cajun Country* (1991); Carl A. Brasseaux, *Acadian to Cajun: Transformation of a People, 1803–1877* (1992); Carl A. Brasseaux, Keith P. Fontenot, and Claude F. Oubre, *Creoles of Color in the Bayou Country* (1994); Rima and Richard Collin, *New Orleans Cookbook* (1987); John

Egerton, *Southern Food: At Home, on the Road, in History* (1987); Peter S. Feibleman, *American Cooking: Creole and Acadian* (1971); Roy F. Guste Jr., *Antoine's Restaurant Cookbook* (1978); Howard Mitcham, *Creole Gumbo and All That Jazz: A New Orleans Seafood Cookbook* (1978); Paul Prudhomme, *Chef Paul Prudhomme's Louisiana Kitchen* (1984).

Caribbean Foodways

The links between the food of the Caribbean and the food of the American South go back to the days when the English-speaking areas of the South were referred to by those of the Caribbean as the northern colonies. Then, the coastal areas of the South were transit points for goods from the Caribbean including molasses and sugar products, slaves, and foodstuffs.

From first contact, the Caribbean region fascinated Europeans with the diversity of its foodstuffs and the culinary creativity of its people. The Arawaks cultivated sweet potatoes, yautia, maize, peanuts, and cassava and are known to have enjoyed guavas, pineapples, cashew fruit, and more. They baked, stewed, smoked, and roasted their meats, frequently seasoning them with casareep, a condiment prepared from cassava juice, salt, and chilis. The Caribs, who occupied the northwest part of Trinidad, the Lesser Antilles, and the eastern part of Puerto Rico, ate a diet that was more dependent on animal protein, but were best known for their love of hot sauces.

European arrival and the subsequent fight for dominion resulted in the unleashing of foodstuffs on the Old and New Worlds that came to be known as the Columbian Exchange. Tomatoes, potatoes, corn, and chilis made their way to Europe, while pigs and sugarcane made their way in the 15th century to the Caribbean, where they would become integrally intertwined with the diet. The 16th and 17th centuries saw other additions to the Caribbean larder, including bananas and plantains, rice, and breadfruit. The wars for supremacy that followed Columbus's arrival were aided by privateers and freebooters. Some of the brothers of the coast were known for a preference for smoked meats that they prepared in the native manner. They were also known for a love of the beverage called Kill Devil that would become the region's most emblematic culinary contribution: rum.

Pacification led to settlement, and by the mid-17th century the Caribbean was poised to become the center of the sugar revolution, which began in Barbados and soon spread to other islands, turning the region from one of multiple small farmers to one in which the monoculture of sugar dominated the landscape, changing Caribbean history forever. For more than 200 years sugar would rule, and King Sugar's wealth gave rise to a plantocracy that was known for its culinary excesses. Breakfasts consisted of multiple courses of bacon, ham, hung beef, fowl, roasted cassava or plantain, bread, butter, cheese, and more and was washed down by copious beakers of strong beer and sweet wines. The afternoon meal was even more lavish and, according to John Steadman, an 18th-century observer, "Nothing is wanting that the world can afford in a western climate of meat, fowl, venison, fish, vegetables, fruits, etc. and the most exquisite wines are often squandered in profusion." Evenings finished up with still more alcohol.

The excess of the planters was paid for by the misery of the enslaved Africans who labored in the cane fields. Feeding them was the other side of the culinary coin. The Caribbean climate was similar to that of their native Africa, and so planters transported and transplanted many African ingredients. Okra, true yams, and ackee arrived. Breadfruit was brought from the South Seas by Captain Bligh, of HMS *Bounty* fame, in 1793. In the slave yards of the towns and villages of the Caribbean, African culinary know-how was maintained and coupled with the techniques and ingredients of varying European powers to produce dishes like callaloo and funghi, coocoo, kenkeym, and dokono, which retained the tastes and, in some cases, the names of their African antecedents.

The post-Emancipation period brought new waves of immigrants from India and China to serve in the cane fields as indentured servants. They were joined by Syrians and Lebanese who followed from the Levant to become shopkeepers. All would maintain the culinary traditions of their homelands and add their own ingredients to the regional mix. Items such as pak choi and star anise, turmeric and mangoes, became local ingredients alongside those of the planter/slave society. Spices abounded. Grenada, with its nutmeg plantations, became known as the spice island of the region, and Jamaica exported ginger and allspice. Dishes such as Martinique's Colombo de porc, a pork curry, and Trinidad's dhalpurieroti, a split-filled crepe, bear witness to the Indian immigrants. Cuba's comidas chinas y criollas speak of the Chinese presence, while Trinidad's channa and tabaduile hint at the Levantine connection.

The 20th century further transformed the region, as tourism became its main industry, bringing with it everything from Kentucky Fried Chicken and McDonald's franchises to culinary competitions designed to preserve the integrity of traditional dishes. One of the lessons to be learned by tourists is the historical and culinary links between the region and creolized port cities of the American South.

JESSICA B. HARRIS
Queens College

Alfred W. Crosby Jr., *The Columbian Exchange: Biological and Cultural Consequences of 1492* (1972); David and Brinsley Samaroo Dabydeen, eds., *India in the Caribbean* (1987); Jessica B. Harris, *Sky Juice and Flying Fish: Traditional Caribbean Cooking* (1991); Jean-Baptiste Labat, *Nouveau Voyages aux Isles de l'Amerique* (1979); Walton Look Lai, *The Chinese in the West Indies 1806–1995: A Documentary History* (1998); Rosemary Parkinson, *Culinaria: The Caribbean, A Culinary Discovery* (1999).

Civil War

From President Lincoln's Proclamation of Blockade on Southern Ports on 19 April 1861 until well after Robert E. Lee surrendered at Appomattox, the Civil War made food shortages a way of life for the southern cook. In addition to the strain placed on supplies by blockades and severed transportation lines, pantries and larders were often emptied by homebound women who felt it to be their patriotic duty to give soldiers comestible comfort, providing milk, coffee, soup, cornbread, and, whenever possible, cakes and pies to augment the provisions of troops quartered nearby. The food shortage was further exacerbated in 1863 when the Union army targeted the salt mines in southwestern Virginia and Louisiana. Without salt, southern cooks could not preserve meats, pickle vegetables, or season their food.

Ingenuity, economy, and an ability to adapt were the most important skills to have as the cost of staples like bacon, butter, coffee, and flour doubled or tripled in the first year of the war and then rose at a rate of 10 percent a month by 1863. In 1863, West & Johnson, a publisher in Richmond, produced the *Confederate Receipt Book: A Compilation of Over One Hundred Receipts Adapted to the Times*, which included recipes for preserving meat and bacon without salt, baking breads and cakes without yeast or *saleratus* (a common leavening agent that had been imported from the North), and preparing coffee from acorns roasted in bacon fat.

Despite inflation and shortages, rural southerners remained able to subsist— much as they had done before—on what they could grow and store themselves. A staple diet of pork and corn ("hog and hominy" was often served for breakfast, lunch, and dinner) was complemented by chicken, wild game, sweet potatoes, greens, and field peas. As food prices rose, agricultural production fell, and provisions could no longer be transported, even plantation owners, previously used to the fancier fare of balls and dinner parties, were reduced to this basic southern diet, which had previously been reserved for the slaves in their households. These affluent southerners, as well as their urban counterparts, often complained bitterly over having to eat hominy instead of rice and settle for lesser cuts of pork in place of fresh seafood, farm-raised beef, or poultry.

Whenever possible, they tried to re-create the flavors and sensations of ante-bellum meals using the means at hand, preparing "artificial oysters" with green corn, beaten egg, and flour and sweetening desserts with sorghum, watermelon syrup, or persimmons in place of sugar.

Food was an everyday worry for Confederate soldiers, as military allotments were sparse after the first months of the war. Insufficient food supplies, spoiled meat, unripe fruit, and polluted water caused nutritional deficiencies that promoted diseases such as dysentery and typhoid. Standard military food included cornmeal, beef, hardtack (crackers), and, at times, rice, field peas, or potatoes. Soldiers became used to coffee substitutes, and their consumption of alcohol was notable. Soldiers supplemented their rations by bartering with local farmers, sometimes stealing, and often hunting available game. Soldiers who came from families of means could sometimes enjoy a higher standard of food fare, but as the war went on access to better supplies became rarer.

In the last years of the war, southern cities were the site of both the greatest luxury and the harshest famine. While regular citizens and refugees struggled to buy staples like flour and cornmeal, wealthy inhabitants spent small fortunes to dine in style on food and fine wines procured by blockade-runners. Varina Davis, the first lady of the Confederacy, continued, as late as 1865, to throw elegant parties in Richmond, featuring champagne and several courses of beef, seafood, and game served on her Sèvres china. After Lee's surrender, however, even those who had previously regaled themselves with the bounty of blockade-runners often had to join the lines of people accepting Federal handouts of cornmeal and dried cod, the only provisions the Union could at first afford to distribute.

MARY MARGARET CHAPPELL
Brooklyn, New York

Matthew Page Andrews, *Women of the South in War Times* (1920); Jan Carlton, *Richmond Receipts Past and Present* (1987); *Confederate Receipt Book: A Compilation of Over One Hundred Receipts Adapted to the Times* (1863); Mary Vereen Huguenin and Anne Montague Stoney, eds., *Charleston Receipts* (1950); Kristie Lynn and Robert W. Pelton, *The Early American Cookbook* (2000); Lila May and John Spaulding, *Civil War Recipes: Receipts from the Pages of Godey's Lady's Book* (1999); Helen McCully, ed., *The American Heritage Cookbook* (1964); Martha L. Meade, *Recipes from the Old South* (1961); Michael J. Varhola, *Everyday Life during the Civil War* (1999); Bell I. Wiley, *The Life of Johnny Reb* (1971); C. Vann Woodward, ed., *Mary Chesnut's Civil War* (1981).

Cookbooks

The first cookbooks in the South were brought from England by early colonists. Until near the end of the 18th century cookbooks in the United States were simply manuscript collections or printed editions of English recipes. The first cookbook published in the colonies appears to have been *The Compleat House-wife; or, Accomplish'd Gentlewoman's Companion* by E. (Eliza) Smith, printed in Williamsburg in 1742. Hannah Glasse's *The Art of Cookery, Made Plain and Easy* (1747) was the most popular volume in Virginia, but others, such as *The English Huswife* (1623), by Gervase Markham, also were found throughout the South.

The Virginia House-wife (1824), by Mary Randolph, has been called by Karen Hess "the most influential American cookbook of the nineteenth century." Randolph was a member of a prominent family, and her cookbook reflected a knowledge of regional produce, cooking practices, and overall social context. In addition to showing the dominant English influence, Randolph's cookbook reflected Indian contributions to southern food, through recipes that included Native American foods such as maize, sweet potatoes, squash, beans, fruits, and nuts. An African influence came through recipes learned from servants who prepared food using such ingredients as field peas, eggplant, yams, and tomatoes (which possibly were of African background). Randolph's recipes used 40 vegetables and 17 herbs, but did not specify the extended cooking for meats and vegetables that later became a trademark of southern cooking.

The ritual of setting a good table has been a veritable religion in the South since Mary Randolph's time. Cookbooks have been guides to southern ways of eating and have reinforced the southerner's belief that the food eaten and the manner of eating it have social significance. In antebellum times the great distance between homes (especially plantations) meant that any social gathering was a real occasion. The food was the entertainment. The Civil War had a profound effect on the way southerners were able to carry out this ritual of eating. Polly Alice Masten Körner (Mrs. Jule Gilmer Körner) wrote in her memoirs, as recorded in the *Körner's Folly Cookbook*, of the "troublous times toward the end of the War and for some time thereafter" when her father buried things of value, including her mother's "brown flowered china and tea set to protect them from the Yankee soldiers." Emma S. Layton in *I Remember When* recalled that "during the Civil War the Yankees came through taking everything they could get." Her grandmother "hid a peck of meal in the cradle with the baby" and had one of her boys "hide a ham in a big oak tree.... Grandmother hid her silver in a barrel of hog-feed."

Setting a good table began with the table covering. The standard "snow-white cover, damask or home-made" reflected the character of the housewife as well as her table, according to *Mrs. Elliot's Housewife* by Sarah A. Elliot (1870). Elliot admonished her housewife to keep "her castors bright and well-filled."

The food available in the South prior to the modern supermarket was primarily grown "on the place." Spring or young chickens were available only in the spring; new potatoes were the first potatoes to mature; and green peas (called English peas) were fresh from the vines for only a few days each year.

Before World War II most recipes, called receipts, were not written down. They were instead carried around in the cook's head. Some of these cooks, possessed of great intuitive skill, still exist and will explain in detail the art of preparing pinto beans or stewed potatoes. What they cannot explain is the special knack they bring to any cooking enterprise, which makes such a difference in the finished product.

Often, when a recipe was recorded, it was preserved simply as a list of ingredients on a piece of paper. There were no accompanying directions. It was assumed that once the cook knew the ingredients and their amounts, she could figure out the rest for herself. The following recipe by Mrs. Jed Giddings of Maryland was contributed to S. R. Rhodes's *The Economy Administration Cook Book* (1913):

Two Pound Cake by Measure

The whites of twenty-four eggs, seven teacups of flour, four and one-half teacups of granulated sugar, two teacups of butter, one of sweet milk, a heaping teaspoon of cream of tartar. Have the pan warm and bake as quickly as possible.

When bound cookbooks started to appear in great numbers, they were put out by people like Henrietta Stanley Dull. She edited the weekly food page in the *Atlanta Journal*, which appeared under the slogan "It covers Dixie like the dew." Dull's name was a household word when her book *Southern Cooking* was published in 1928. Another popular compilation of recipes in booklet form was by Sara Spano, a food editor in Columbus, Ga. Her recipe for deep chocolate cake called for eight plain 5-cent chocolate bars and two 10-cent cans of chocolate—an indication of staple grocery prices in the 1920s and 1930s.

An early example of the many popular cookbooks put out by food companies is *The Rumford Complete Cookbook* by Lily Haxworth Wallace, published in 1934. Cookbooks published by churches, clubs, schools, and Junior Leagues also began to appear, bearing a wealth of excellent recipes. One of the most successful of these was *River Road Recipes*, published by the Junior League of

Baton Rouge, La. Its first printing was in 1959. By the 70th printing in 2007, at least 1.3 million copies were in circulation.

Abby Fisher's *What Mrs. Fisher Knows about Old Southern Cooking* (1881) is credited as the oldest cookbook by an African American. African American cooking styles and recipes are indeed rooted in the South, and they are preserved in Sue Bailey Thurman, *Historical Cookbook of the American Negro* (1958), Jim Harwood and Ed Callahan, *Soul Food Cookbook* (1969), Vertamae Smart-Grosvenor, *Vibration Cooking; or The Travel Notes of a Geechee Girl* (1970), and Bob Jeffries, *Soul Food Cookbook* (1970). Norma Jean and Carole Darden assembled the recipes in *Spoonbread and Strawberry Wine* (1978) by visiting relatives in Alabama, North Carolina, Virginia, and Ohio. Included are recipes for sweet potato biscuits, Cousin Johnnie K's macaroni and shrimp salad, Aunt Marjorie Palmer's every-kind-of-cookie-dough, and syllabub (a drink made from cream, sugar, nutmeg, and rum or brandy). Jessica Harris's *The Welcome Table: African American Heritage Cooking* (1995) has quickly become a classic, and Joe Randall and Toni Tipton-Martin's *A Taste of Heritage: New African American Cuisine* (1998) updates a traditional form of southern cooking.

Chef Paul Prudhomme's Louisiana Kitchen (1984) helped usher in a national fad for Cajun cooking. Another volume, Marjorie Kinnan Rawlings's *Cross Creek Cookery* (1942), assembled recipes from rural north central Florida. John Martin Taylor's *Hoppin' John's Lowcountry Cooking: Recipes and Ruminations from Charleston and the Carolina Coastal Plain* (1992) preserves and expands traditional cooking from that distinctive culinary locale. Eudora Welty wrote the introduction to the Jackson Symphony League's *Jackson Cookbook* (1971), which includes a recipe for Squash Eudora. The recipes of other southern writers appear in Dean Faulkner Wells's *Great American Writers' Cookbook*, published by Mississippi's Yoknapatawpha Press in 1981. It includes Harry Crews's snake steak, Roy Blount Jr.'s garlic grits (and an "ode to grits"), and Willie Morris's John Birch Society beans (which cause a violent internal reaction).

Of course, southern cookbooks have their idiosyncrasies. In 1969, when Albert Brewer was governor of Alabama, his wife, Martha Farmer Brewer, helped produce the *Alabama First Lady's Cookbook* as part of the celebration of the 150th birthday of the state. The book offered 41 recipes for preparing chicken, but not one for preparing fried chicken. The assumption was that everyone already knew how to fry chicken.

Among many things, the 1960s brought popular cooking programs on television, hundreds of new cookbooks, and a magazine named *Southern Living* based in Birmingham, Ala. A 23 November 1981 *Wall Street Journal* article described the magazine's formula for success as simply giving the readers what they wanted to read. The article mentioned a recipe for a nutmeg feather cake, which had appeared in an issue of the magazine, and predicted that "it would be safe to wager that nutmeg feather cakes will shortly appear on tables from Biloxi to Kannapolis." In 1970 a cookbook named *Our Best Recipes* was published by *Southern Living*—the beginning of a series of cookbooks that is still tremendously popular. Their annual cookbook sells in excess of 1.5 million copies. Oxmoor House, *Southern Living*'s book division, began publishing an Antique American Cookbooks series in the 1980s, including historic southern volumes.

Several writers deserve special recognition for influential recent southern cookbooks. *Nathalie Dupree's New Southern Cooking* (1986) and *Nathalie Dupree's New Southern Memories: Recipes and Reminiscences* (1993) provided influential models for contemporary cookbook writers who combine anecdotes and stories, as well as memories. Edna Lewis was important as a model for African American cooks, writing *The Taste of Country Cooking* (1976) and, along with Mary Goodbody, *In Pursuit of Flavor* (1988). *The Gift of Southern Cooking: Recipes and Revelations from Two Great American Cooks* (2003), which Lewis authored along with Scott Peacock, embodied food's role in biracial southern society. That was also a theme in John Egerton's *Southern Food: At Home, on the Road, and in History* (1987), perhaps the single most influential book in the recent resurgence in the study, appreciation, and eating of specifically southern regional food. John T. Edge, *A Gracious Plenty: Recipes and Recollections from the American South* (1999), compiles the best community and church cookbook recipes from the region. Bill Neal influenced countless restaurant chefs, as well as home cooks, through *Bill Neal's Southern Cooking* (1985).

The library at the University of North Carolina in Greensboro has an extensive collection of southern cookbooks, as do the libraries at the University of Alabama, Tulane University, and North Texas State University. Southern cookbooks reinforce a regional appreciation for tradition and encourage southerners to continue to enjoy the old favorites. People may not live by squash casseroles alone, but a southern cookbook without a recipe for at least one is rare.

BETH TARTAN
Kernersville, North Carolina

Alabama First Lady's Cook Book (1969); John Egerton, *Southern Food: At Home, on the Road, in History* (1987); Sarah A. Elliott, *Mrs. Elliott's Housewife* (1870); Margaret Husted, *Virginia Cavalcade* (Autumn 1980); Mary Randolph, *The Virginia House-wife*

(1984, facsimile of 1824); Blanche S. Rhett, *Two Hundred Years of Charleston Cooking* (1984); Sarah Rutledge, *The Carolina Housewife* (1984, facsimile of 1847); Lena E. Sturges, *Southern Living: Our Best Recipes* (1970); Beth Tartan, *Körner's Folly Cookbook* (1977); Hazel Valentine, ed., *I Remember When* (1978); Lily Haxworth Wallace, *The Rumford Complete Cook Book* (1908); Eugene Walter, *American Cooking, Southern Style* (1971).

Cookbooks, Community

Community cookbooks (also known as charity, regional, and fund-raising cookbooks) are recipe collections published to support a charitable cause. The community cookbook, like jazz and musical comedy, originated in America, evolving during the Civil War, in conjunction with northern and southern women's efforts to raise money for medical corps. Cookbooks to benefit veterans, widows, and orphans of war followed, and the form was quickly adopted by religious and other philanthropic groups. Within two decades women in almost 30 states had authored such books.

By the early 20th century, southern women had published recipe collections to support churches and synagogues, libraries, schools, village improvement societies, and the Daughters of the American Revolution; divisions of the United Daughters of the Confederacy from Georgia to Florida published books to support war victims and veterans. Some community cookbooks achieved considerable fame, such as Kentucky's first charitable cookbook, *Housekeeping in the Bluegrass* (Ladies of the Presbyterian Church, Paris, Ky., 1875), with at least nine reprints, and *The Laurel Cook Book* (Women of St. John's Guild, Laurel, Miss.) published in 1900 and reprinted in 1910 and 1914. The 1879 *Dixie Cook-Book and Practical Housekeeper* achieved great popularity, being republished and revised numerous times. It was actually a close adaptation of one of the best-selling early community cookbooks, the *Centennial Buckeye Cook Book*, compiled originally by Estelle Woods Wilcox, with the women of the Marysville First Congregational Church in Ohio, in 1876.

Community cookbooks published before the mid-20th century reveal their authors' mainstream, class-conscious values in the prefatory pages, selection and arrangement of recipes and advertisements, and illustrations. Nonwhite contributors are absent or obscured; emphasis is on women as home managers, moral agents, and gracious hostesses. Contributing and collecting recipes, soliciting advertisements that would appear in a book (to cover the cost of publication), seeing the book through to publication, and then marketing it provided leadership and business training for many women. In the

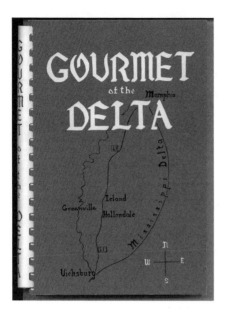

Front cover of Gourmet of the Delta,
recipes collected by St. John's Woman's
Auxiliary of Leland, Miss., and St. Paul's
Woman's Auxiliary of Hollandale, Miss.,
first published in October 1958 (James G.
Thomas Jr. personal collection)

early 20th century, women's business associations, Junior Leagues, and widely varied activist groups produced books with explicit regional flavors, frequently memorializing an area's or group's history. Gradually, after 1950, with the rise of the women's movement and the civil rights movement, community cookbooks (still mainly produced by women) become more inclusive and varied, reflecting new social values, ethnic pride, and cooking technologies, but usually retaining an emphasis on regional history and culture. Southern community cookbooks sometimes offer specialized local recipes (for dove and other game, for example, in Louisiana and Texas cookbooks), draw on ethnic traditions (Cajun and Mexican among others), or emphasize southernness itself (whether from a white or African American perspective, or both).

Since the 1980s, scholars in history, literature, women's studies, folklore, and other disciplines have studied community cookbooks as cultural artifacts that tell a great deal about changing culinary habits and technologies, along with women's history, their values and beliefs, their ways of building and maintaining community. The Tabasco Company (Avery Island, La.) celebrates community cookbooks via its annual Community Cookbook Awards and Walter S. McIlhenny Hall of Fame Awards for community cookbooks selling over 100,000 copies.

ANNE L. BOWER
Ohio State University

Anne Bower, ed., *Recipes for Reading: Community Cookbooks, Stories, Histories* (1997); Margaret Cook, *America's Charitable Cooks: A Bibliography of Fund-raising Cook Books Published in the United States, 1861–1915* (1971); Alan Grubb, in *In Joy and Sorrow: Women, Family, and Marriage in the Victorian South, 1830–1900*, ed. Carol Bleser (1991); Andrew F. Smith, introduction to *Centennial Buckeye Cookbook* (1876, 2000); Virginia M. Westbrook, introduction to *Buckeye Cookery and Practical Housekeeping* (1880, 1988).

Ethnicity and Food

A popular myth about the South is that the region is devoid of ethnicity. According to this myth, the region is populated solely by the descendants of white European colonists and enslaved African Americans. But if this were true, how could we explain the popularity of Greek-dressed blackened red snapper, Sephardic burekas, Creole étouffée, Caribbean gumbo, Choctaw hoecakes, German tortes, Indian curries, Vietnamese fish stews, Lebanese kibbe, crawfish wontons, tamales, sweet potato kugels, and Italian pastas at the dinner tables of card-carrying southerners? Generations of southerners have served these ethnic dishes to their families.

Throughout the nation food strongly defines ethnic and regional identity. But in the South, a region torn apart by war, slavery, and the aftermath of reconstruction and segregation, food assumes greater importance. It is true that fewer immigrants moved to the South than to other regions of the country because of the region's history of free labor, the dominance of agriculture over industry, and a general lack of tolerance for outsiders. These factors did not, however, preclude ethnic groups from making the region their home. Historian George Tindall traces the South's ethnic diversity to its earliest history. Prior to the 1700s the majority of southerners were Native Americans from a rich mosaic of cultural groups, each with its own chiefs and traditions. With the arrival of Europeans and African Americans, the region became the most polyglot of the English colonies, and foods served at southern tables confirmed this diversity. Tindall argues that the diverse population of the colonial South merged into black and white "ethnic" groups that had much in common, although few were willing to acknowledge this kinship.

Sociologist John Shelton Reed describes a persistent "southernness" and labels southerners a "quasi-ethnic" regional group. Reed argues that in the South a sense of place, family, and collective experience created a people who resemble an oversized ethnic community. Southern loyalty to regional foodways reflects this identity. By eating as they do, southerners affirm their solidarity and endurance as an ethnic group. Within this southern "ethnic family,"

Jews, African Americans, Italians, French, Chinese, and other immigrants were marginalized and used foodways to reinforce their own ethnic and racial boundaries.

This process was clearly present in the colonial experience of southerners in Savannah, Ga., and Charleston, S.C. Drawn by the economic opportunities these ports offered as trading centers, Jewish mercantile families settled in the Lowcountry, established businesses, and founded synagogues, philanthropic organizations, and cemeteries. Lowcountry Jews were closely tied to Jews throughout the Atlantic region by religion, commerce, kinship, memories of Europe, and shared foodways. A fundamental link within this extended Jewish community was a shared commitment to Jewish dietary rules, which created a healthy coastal trade in kosher meat. Food nourished the Jews of Savannah and Charleston and shaped their personal Judaism.

Colonial Jewish families with names like Sheftall, Minis, Harby, Moise, Moses, and Cohen encountered a rich mix of ethnic food traditions in Savannah and Charleston. There were Jewish immigrants from the West Indies, England, Alsace and the Rhineland, Poland, Prussia, and the Netherlands, as well as traders from northern cities like New York, Philadelphia, and Newport, all of whom brought foods of their homelands with them. These people mixed daily with enslaved African Americans, free black artisans and tradespeople, Gentile Anglo-American merchants and craftsmen, Scotch-Irish farmers, and British-descended white plantation owners, all of whom had their distinctive food traditions.

In the mid-19th century, immigrants traveled into the southern interior, where they became peddlers, grocers, dry goods merchants, tailors, artisans, and restaurateurs. Settling in the villages and crossroad communities of the rural South, ethnic southerners recreated the foodways of their homelands as best they could, depending upon the availability of supplies, their ingenuity with local ingredients, and the degree of assimilation they experienced. There was often only one ethnic family in a rural community, or perhaps a Jewish merchant, a Chinese launderer, and a Lebanese grocer. In these isolated circumstances, food was a powerful badge of both ethnicity and assimilation.

Although the foodways of ethnic newcomers differed from those of black and white southerners, immigrants in the South found much that appealed to their own tastes. They appreciated the southern table where "big eating" was the rule, as described by food historian Joe Gray Taylor. Ethnic southerners quickly embraced this southern food tradition that connected festivity, bounty, and hospitality.

The daily lives of ethnic southerners intertwined with African Americans in the workplace, at home, and in churches and synagogues. Food traditions passed back and forth between these communities as black cooks baked sweet potato pies and biscuits for their immigrant employers and went home with leftover chopped liver and stuffed grape leaves. Lifelong relationships developed over time, as African Americans and ethnic southerners formed an unlikely alliance because of their shared outsider status.

Ethnic patterns of settlement continually evolve, a fact clearly reflected in the contemporary South. Hispanics—a diverse community of Cubans, Mexicans, Puerto Ricans, and other Latin Americans—are one of the most significant ethnic groups in the South, and the largest ethnic minority in the United States. North Carolina's Hispanic population is growing faster than that of all but one other state, reflected in new tiendas, taquerias, and butcher shops frequented by all southerners, no matter their race or ethnicity.

Anthropologists, folklorists, and food historians argue that food is invested with symbolic meaning and that any food-related activity—from a simple meal at home to the most elaborate public celebration—is an important act that helps us understand the power of food and ethnicity in the South. Ethnicity is forever changing, as is its expression at the southern table. Folklorists John Allen Stern and Stephen Cicala argue that ethnicity "is constantly negotiated" as each generation struggles to redefine its ethnic and regional identity, and food is one of the strongest ways that people express this identity.

C. Paige Gutierrez explores the process of "creative ethnicity" in her study of Cajun foodways in southwestern Louisiana. The symbolic power of Cajun food is associated with ethnic identity, kinship, and strong ties to the region from which the Cajun people draw their livelihood. Gutierrez explains that crawfish became a regional symbol of Cajun perseverance and spirit, an identity that has now been adopted by non-Cajun Louisianans who achieve insider status because of their ability to peel and eat the crustaceans. Less observant Jews in the region ignore the nonkosher status of crawfish and proudly serve them at their tables as a symbol of their regional identity.

For generations southern ethnic groups have struggled to make sense of their experience through memory-making, and much of that struggle takes place at the dinner table. Memory and history are key to understanding the power of food for ethnic southerners, who connect to family and regional history at every meal. Today, in a rapidly changing South, Asian and Hispanic newcomers join an older world of black and white southerners to shape a new era of foodways, and indeed, to create memory rooted in the present rather than the antebellum past. Bill Smith, chef at Crook's Corner, a culinary institution in Chapel Hill, N.C., captures this new South in the dedication of his cookbook, *Seasoned in the South*: "To all my cooks. Love and kisses from 'the land of blood, meat, and fire.' A todos mis cocineros. Amor y besos desde 'la tierra de sangre, carne, y fuego.'"

MARCIE COHEN FERRIS
University of North Carolina at Chapel Hill

Frederik Barth, *Ethnic Groups and Boundaries: The Social Organization of Culture Difference* (1998); John Egerton, *Southern Food: At Home, on the Road, in History* (1987); Marcie Cohen Ferris, *Matzoh Ball Gumbo: Culinary Tales from the Jewish South* (2005); Donna R. Gabaccia, *We Are What We Eat: Ethnic Food and the Making of Americans* (1998); C. Paige Gutierrez, *Cajun Foodways* (1992); Susan Kalcik, in *Ethnic and Regional Foodways in the United States: The Performance of Group Identity*, ed. Linda Keller Brown and Kay Mussell (1984); John Shelton Reed, *One South: An Ethnic Approach to Regional Culture* (1982); Bill Smith, *Seasoned in the South: Recipes from Crook's Corner and from Home* (2005); Stephen Stern and John Allan Cicala, eds., *Creative Ethnicity: Symbols and Strategies of Contemporary Ethnic Life* (1991); Joe Gray Taylor, *Eating, Drinking, and Visiting in the South: An Informal History* (1982); George Brown Tindall, *Natives and Newcomers: Ethnic Southerners and Southern Ethnics* (1995).

Farming

The truism that agriculture underlies a region's foodways can and should be extended in the case of the American South. Farming activities there not only supported the traditional economy but also formed the backdrop for much cultural distinctiveness. Agriculture in the South has always been different from that in northern states, and in many ways more successful. The region is subtropical, with a combination of a long growing season, abundant and reliable rainfall, and gentle terrain that encourages the production of hundreds of different crops as well as many types of livestock. Although insect pests and fungal diseases also find these growing conditions to their liking, the overall situation is the envy of nearly all competitors.

Southern farming has featured both a commercial and a subsistence side since the earliest years of European settlement. The commercial aspects are well known, especially the tobacco, rice, indigo, and Sea Island cotton plantations that developed along the Atlantic Coast during the colonial years as a response to demand from England. Although the production of indigo and Sea Island cotton proved to be fairly short lived, plantations nevertheless increased in numbers and spread across most of the region's better soils. Sugarcane became the crop of commercial choice in the rich soils near the Mississippi River in

Louisiana. Elsewhere, across a wide, crescent-shaped band from the Virginia Piedmont, through Alabama's famous Black Belt, and into eastern Texas, the choice was short-staple or upland cotton. This expansion of acreage was aided by the invention of the cotton gin in 1793 and predicated on the availability of cheap labor for cultivation and harvest. By 1850 the South grew 80 percent of the world's export cotton.

Plantations, because of the money they generated, their occupancy of the best soils, and their visibility on the landscape, are often thought to have been more common than they were. If the presence of 20 or more slaves is accepted as a definition, the number of plantations in 1850 was only about 46,000. If 30 slaves form the threshold, then the plantation total for that year falls to 2,500. Even after the Civil War, the plantation economy continued to function much as before down until the 1930s. The African American laborers remained a dependent population, but now worked on shares and lived in dispersed (rather than centralized) housing.

Away from the plantation world in the antebellum years, many backwoodsmen made their living with herds of cattle and hogs. A host of small farmers also supported themselves in semisubsistence fashion. Their most important crop was corn, a plant native to tropical America that had scores of uses. Cornmeal made a good substitute for wheat flour, a mash from it worked well in distilleries, and the grain itself was basic fare in the diets of family members and favored livestock alike. This central food was supplemented by the harvesting of greens, game, and fish from the surrounding backcountry; by flocks of chickens and a few hogs kept near the houses; and by big gardens filled with beans, sweet potatoes, tomatoes, and other vegetables. In postbellum times, as cheap land disappeared and capital became scarce, many small farmers were forced to plant cash crops in order to obtain credit. This system increased the production of cotton but also initiated a cycle of erosion, poorer diets, and general poverty that began to end only in the 1930s with New Deal programs that provided money for restricting production.

Farming in the South changed nearly completely during the two decades following World War II. An exodus of black laborers led to a decline in the farm population of almost 60 percent between 1940 and 1960. Average farm size increased greatly, many shacks vanished, tractors and other machinery became common, and cotton growing retreated to the superior soils of the alluvial Mississippi Valley. The most abused uplands throughout the region (approximately half of the total land acreage) reverted to pine forest, and trees now blanket as much as 90 percent of many counties. Cattle graze most of this land and much of it is harvested regularly as pulpwood in a system that many people would regard as a type of farming. Another 40 percent or so of the rural landscape has been planted to grass. This decision, too, benefited long-abused soils and has gone hand in hand with a resurgence in cattle production. To be successful, European breeds had to be crossed with South Asian (Zebu) stock and new grasses introduced, but beef sales in the region have exceeded those of cotton for many decades. Much of this production is by part-time farmers.

The small portion of the rural South that is neither grassed nor forested is dominated by specialty crops. One of these, tobacco in central Kentucky and eastern North Carolina, is a continuation of an old pattern. The location of two others, sugarcane in southern Louisiana and southern Florida and citrus fruit in central and southern Florida, is dictated by a need for frost-free weather, but most of the others came about as local entrepreneurs sought ways to compete in the new global economy. Soybeans, a source for vegetable oil, proved profitable in the alluvial Mississippi Valley on land made available by government restrictions on cotton acreage. Rice, introduced into southwestern Louisiana in the 1890s, has become popular since the 1970s as the country's taste has moved away from potatoes. This crop now rivals cotton and soybeans for space in the vast delta landscape of Arkansas and Mississippi. Other specialty crop production includes truck farming on the Atlantic coastal plain, pecan harvesting in Georgia and Texas, and peanut farming in Georgia, Alabama, and Virginia. Poultry and hogs are similarly concentrated. These animals are often raised in confinement on a contract basis in areas that, in most cases, are marginal for other farming. (The negative environmental impact of such confinement farming is slowly coming to the fore.) Clusters of counties in northwestern Arkansas, northern Alabama, northern Georgia, central and eastern North Carolina, and a few other locations now produce some three-quarters of the nation's broilers. Wendell Murphy of Rose Hill, N.C., who initiated hog raising in this manner in 1974, has been largely responsible for his state's expansion of pork production, in which it now ranks second in the nation after Iowa.

BARBARA G. SHORTRIDGE
University of Kansas

Charles S. Aiken, *The Cotton Plantation South since the Civil War* (1998); Pete Daniel, *Breaking the Land: The Transformation of Cotton, Tobacco, and Rice Cultures since 1880* (1985); Gilbert C. Fite, *Cotton Fields No More: Southern Agriculture, 1865–1980* (1984); Lewis C. Gray, *History of Agriculture in the Southern States to 1860*, 2 vols. (1933); John F. Hart, *The Rural Landscape* (1998); John F. Hart and Chris Mayda, *Southeastern Geographer* (May 1998); Sam Bowers Hilliard, *Atlas of Antebellum Southern Agriculture* (1984); Terry G. Jordan, *Trails to Texas: Southern Roots of West-*

ern Cattle Ranching (1981); United States Department of Agriculture, *Agricultural Atlas of the United States* (1999).

Funeral Food and Cemetery Cleaning

Today's cemeteries are vistas of modern landscaping and efficient land use, vast fields of flattened markers and tasteful greenery. How ironic, then, that they seem less full of life than old-fashioned graveyards and burial plots, with their crooked stones, cracked cherubs, and snarled trees.

Burial today means perpetual care, regular swipes from wide-riding mowers, and the occasional dose of fertilizer. Burial 50 or 100 years ago meant yearly visits from one's family, armed with clippers, hoes, fresh flowers, and, yes, picnic baskets. In the South, even grave maintenance became an excuse to share a meal.

North Carolina fiction writer Clyde Edgerton did not have to reach far to find the connecting thread that ran through his 1988 novel *The Floatplane Notebooks*. The annual Copeland family visit to the burial plot weaves through the novel like wisteria through the woods. The plot device, though, came not from the author's imagination, but from experience. "My family cleans the graveyard every year," he says. On the Saturday before Mother's Day in early May, Edgerton's relatives return to the original family land, now in the middle of Umstead State Park in Wake County, N.C. The family's history in the area dates to about 1790, but the graveyard, once located behind the family home, was started about 1900.

The story, matching the one in the novel, stems from a field hand who died. No one knew the man's family, so he was buried in a field behind the house. As the years went on and infant mortality took its toll, several babies joined the field hand in their own plots, followed by elderly family members. By the 1950s it was a full-fledged burial ground with about 22 graves.

The house disappeared and people left the land, but throughout Edgerton's life, returning to the graveyard each year has kept the family together. Arriving with rakes, clippers, and eventually Weed Eaters and lawn mowers, they converge to put nature right, to catch up, and to share family stories of the people who came before, covering four or five generations. The food they eat is simple picnic fare, maybe ham and biscuits brought by the older people. "I'm embarrassed to say, somebody will go buy Bojangles'. Anybody who's been to a homecoming in a Baptist church would be ashamed." But elaborateness is not the point. The important thing is sharing together, in the presence of family history.

Despite his rich memories of the cemetery cleanings, Edgerton does not remember how the family settled on the date, the Sunday before Mother's Day. He thinks it was because people were likely to return for family visits then, but the date may have more significance than even the author realizes.

In the South, cemetery cleanings as a social ritual began soon after the Civil War. A war fought not on distant battlefields but across the eastern United States, the carnage stretched across yards and farm fields. Bodies were buried near where they fell, sprinkling the South especially with makeshift burial grounds.

Editor Robert Haven Schauffler recounted in 1911 the beginning of the tradition in *Memorial Day (Decoration Day)*, part of the series Our American Holidays. Right after the war, women in the South began placing flowers over graves, making no distinction between Confederate and Union dead. News of the ritual spread, and women in other parts of the country began doing the same, capturing a sentiment of healing desperately needed in the rejoined republic. In 1868 Adjutant General N. P. Chipman suggested to National Commander John Logan of the Grand Army of the Republic that the organization should support an official custom of spreading flowers on war graves. Logan issued an order naming 30 May 1868 as the date for Decoration Day. Supporting legislation was quickly passed in all state legislatures except those of Arkansas, Missouri, Montana, New Mexico, Texas, and West Virginia. The date varied slightly, from 30 May in the North and West to 26 April in Alabama, Florida, Georgia, and Mississippi and 3 June in Louisiana.

The name Decoration Day was thought to be too superficial to convey the idea of remembrance of America's fallen soldiers, so it was changed to Memorial Day. In the South, however, the name Decoration Day clung to the holiday well into the 20th century, immortalized in poetry and in songs such as John Lee Hooker's blues classic "Decoration Day."

In Schauffler's book, written only five decades after the Civil War, Decoration Day still had strong emotions associated with a conflict that had ripped a nation in two. In his preface, Schauffler noted, "No discrimination has been shown in this collection between the literature of the South and North. For our secular All Soul's Day knows neither North nor South, Blue nor Gray." The poems and speeches gathered in his book reflect the sad passion that still clung to Decoration Day as the new century began, as in poems such as "Decoration Day" by Henry Wadsworth Longfellow: "Your silent tents of green, we deck with flowers; yours has the suffering been, the memory shall be ours."

Schauffler also hit on a rich notion in dubbing Decoration Day "our secular All Soul's Day." Throughout the world, many cultures celebrate forms of sharing meals with the dead at their final resting place, from China's festival of Ching Ming, when families take their favorite foods to graveyard cleanings in April, to Mexico's Dias de Los Muertos on 1 and 2 November, when entire communities converge on the graveyard to celebrate through the night, sharing food with one another and presumably with visiting ancestors. Even the ancient Romans took food to tombs, long before the Roman Catholic church existed to declare All Souls and All Saints Days.

Caring for a graveyard, sharing food with one another in the presence of those who came before, is a powerful link. Edgerton, who now lives in Wilmington, far from the family plot, treasures the chance to return to it each spring. At the end of his own life, he hopes to end up back where his family started, "one way or another, ashes or whatever." Decades of visits with relatives have permanently forged his tie to that one remaining little piece of land. "When I think about war for land, I think about this little plot," this contemporary southern novelist says. "If somebody was to take it away, it would be difficult. I would fight for it."

Southerners like the Edgertons know that bringing food to grieving families is a token of caring. The casserole is emblematic. Dishes such as squash casserole, spinach pie, cheese grits, corn pudding, hoppin' John, and limpin' Susan are one-pot, covered dish meals that draw on traditional ingredients and are comfort foods at a time of loss. Fried chicken is also common for families that sit up with the dead in southern wakes. The South's women were the culinary caregivers with funeral and cemetery cleaning day foods, baking cakes and pies, setting up card tables or other serving places, and generally overseeing the food rituals of a southern way of death.

KATHLEEN PURVIS
Charlotte Observer

John T. Edge, *A Gracious Plenty: Recipes and Recollections from the American South* (1999); Rabbi Aaron Levine, *To Comfort the Bereaved* (1996); Robert Haven Schauffler, ed., *Memorial Day (Decoration Day)* (1911).

Game Cookery

Southerners have long prized game of all kinds as table fare. While folks in other regions of the country may have equated the consumption of wildlife with unsuccessful farmers and shiftless backwoods folks, southerners have generally exalted the hunting, cooking, and eating of game. From times when Native American and European colonists hunted for food and used game as a medium of exchange, the arrival of wild meat in the kitchen has been a cause for joy. In

1846 South Carolinian William Elliott rhapsodized about the "ample chest" and the "brave array of branches" from the wild turkey and the four white-tailed deer he and his companion had killed. Elliott even suggested that wild meat was so coveted that it might best serve as a gift.

Whether southern cooks received game from friends or killed it themselves, they had to adapt their cooking methods to its often uncertain condition—that is, young or old, tender or tough—and to their own cultural predilections. Wild animals and birds are usually most tender when cooked at the two extremes of rare or falling from the bone, and as rare meat has only recently been accepted in the South, many traditional game recipes involve substantial cooking time. Most animals are very lean, with little or no palatable fat. The fat of white-tailed deer, for example, lies inside the body cavity or on the outside of the muscles and is often a waxy tallow, useful in years past for candles but generally inedible. Native Americans and later colonists might add the fat of buffalo or black bear to their game dishes or even harvest the oil from hickory nuts for the same purpose. In the early South, in fact, the rendered oil from the black bear was easily as important as the meat itself. Perhaps because of the lack of natural fat in game, roasting never became as popular among rural southern folk as boiling, baking, frying, and combinations thereof. William Elliott praised the saddle of a whitetail doe, no doubt roasted, but his sophisticated Lowcountry kitchen almost certainly contained a set of larding needles. Although roasting is as old as hunting itself, in the South it has until recently either been a practice of the elite or a makeshift method when away from the kitchen. Mississippi planter James Gordon, on a hunt sometime after the Civil War, described a camp dish called "a filibuster" that overcame the problem of lean game. One of his companions took slices of the liver and muscle from a bear and interspersed them with thin slices of pork bacon and splinters of "Spicewood," possibly *Lindera benzoin*, or wild allspice, as he rolled the entire thing in a layer of bear fat before skewering and roasting over a fire.

Traditionally, boiling has been a much more common cooking technique. According to anthropologist Charles Hudson, Native Americans in the South were particularly fond of stewing their meat with various vegetables. He writes that they preferred their meat thoroughly cooked, and others have argued that they probably created the forerunner of Brunswick stew and burgoo, which employ game as a major component. Creating meals that incorporate various game meats, such as deer, duck, rabbit, squirrel, and raccoon (and maybe even possum), is still an important ritual in hunting camps and communal dinners. In parts of the South influenced by the Cajuns, complex gumbos and sauce picquantes using one or more types of game are common to both hunting camps and home kitchens. Ducks, geese, and deer lend themselves to both the spicy Cajun dishes and the milder stews of the Upper South. Some cooks use the entire duck or goose while others reserve the breasts for the grill. And almost all cooks keep the backstraps or loins of their whitetails (usually the tenderest part) out of the stewpot.

Southerners often begin the preparation of small- to medium-sized mammals like raccoons, opossums, muskrats, nutrias, or beavers by parboiling to eliminate any residual musk or unpleasant-tasting fat. The classic treatment of raccoons and possums followed parboiling with a thorough browning and baking in a slow oven for two to three hours with or without sweet potatoes. Cooks also sometimes barbecue small game after parboiling. Probably no animal is more associated with boiling and stewing than the squirrel. The large red and black fox squirrels and the smaller gray squirrels were the traditional bases for game stews. Lean, with a mild flavor, mature squirrels reach their perfection when, boiled for tenderness, they are simmered slowly with flour or cornmeal dumplings.

For many southerners, however, frying was and is the standard cooking method for game. Since hog lard supplanted bear oil, southern cooks have fried everything from small birds to deer. Quail, young rabbits, and young squirrels are often fried, and even old squirrels get that treatment after the customary boil. Cooks frequently cut the lean breast of a wild turkey into chunks for frying and reserve the carcass for stews. And for many southerners their first taste of venison was a thin slice, pounded with a tenderizing mallet or the mouth of a pop bottle, salted, peppered, floured, and fried. Browned, flour-based gravy and biscuits are the standard companions to the deer meat, and it is a preparation still familiar in the South with the contemporary substitution of vegetable oil for lard.

Today southerners probably eat more deer than any other game, if for no other reason than the volume of meat taken from the tens of thousands of whitetails brought in every year. Venison adapts well to the modern fascination with grilling. Cooks still have to overcome the leanness of venison, and cookbooks that feature game may seem to be simply lists of marinades that contain varying amounts of vegetable oils. Grilled game has also gained acceptance as southerners grow more accustomed to rare meat. Ducks and turkey breasts may be found on southern grills now along with venison, and may even come off rare.

WILEY C. PREWITT JR.
Lodi, Mississippi

Byron W. Dalrymple, *Hunting for the Pot, Fishing for the Pan* (1981); William Elliott, *Carolina Sports by Land and Water including Incidents of Devil-Fishing, Wild-Cat, Deer and Bear Hunting, Etc.* (1846); James Gordon, *Scribners Monthly* (October 1881); C. Paige Gutierrez, *Cajun Foodways* (1992); Charles Hudson, *The Southeastern Indians* (1976); Ichauway Documentary Project, Center for the Study of Southern Culture, University of Mississippi (interviews with Sol Brown, James Mott, Terry Hudson, and Elvonia Brown); Jens Lund, *Flatheads and Spooneys: Fishing for a Living in the Ohio River Valley* (1995); Lee Allen Peterson, *A Field Guide to Edible Wild Plants of Eastern and Central North America* (1977); Daniel H. Usner Jr., *Indians, Settlers, and Slaves in a Frontier Exchange Economy: The Lower Mississippi Valley before 1783* (1992).

Gender and Food

From the dismantling of the peculiar institution of slavery to the arrival of air-conditioning, southern history has been characterized by dramatic change. Throughout the region's history no two areas have remained more conservative than the food southerners eat and the gender of those who cook it.

When English settlers first tried to create a colony off the coast of present-day North Carolina on Roanoke Island in the 1600s, they encountered Native American people whose foodways differed greatly from their own. Memoirs of early white settlers reveal both their surprise and their disdain upon seeing Native American women doing the hard physical labor of planting, harvesting, and preserving food crops, while their menfolk pursued the more leisurely tasks of hunting and fishing. Although English colonists of the 1600s and 1700s, and later white frontiersmen of the 1800s, adopted many food traditions from the southern Indians that they encountered, few were willing to abandon Old World patterns that shaped their everyday meals. These patterns included a system in which men and women shared in the management of their domestic economy. Once land was cleared and home life became more stable, husbands assumed responsibility for chores outside the home, while wives oversaw food production such as garden plots, dairies, and poultry.

During the opening of the southern frontier white male settlers found themselves alone for months. Gender roles were often abandoned as they explored the western boundaries of southern settlement and were forced to prepare their own meals of deer stew and venison jerky. At times frontiersmen found a tavern or inn that provided food and lodging. Such establishments were usually operated by white women, often widows, whose financial and marital status required that they work outside the home. Eighteenth-century taverns, such as

Ann Vobe's and Christiana Campbell's in Williamsburg, Va., were well known as centers of both hospitality and politics.

By the 1830s the gendered responsibilities of men and women defined how daily meals were served in the plantation South. The role of the white "southern lady" stressed a woman's constant devotion to her family. Meals served to both family and guests reflected this devotion and were a means for the white plantation master to demonstrate his social status and financial success. Historian Bertram Wyatt-Brown argues that southern hospitality, and all that made it possible—the southern lady, slaves, well-equipped kitchens, stocked larders, fine china, silver, and an impressive home—became a central expression of the southern white male's honor. Black male and female slaves not assigned to the big house worked in the fields, where they planted, cultivated, and harvested food crops. White plantation masters determined which food crops to plant. Gendered divisions of labor and ritual were present at the table as well as in the kitchen and the fields. During an afternoon dinner at Shirley Plantation in Virginia in the 1830s a visitor described how Mrs. Carter, the plantation mistress, ladled soup at one end of the table, while her husband carved mutton at the other end. Young male slaves served additional meats and side dishes to the guests. Mr. Carter set out bottles of wine, filling his own glass and passing the bottles on to his guests. The black female cook and her female assistants worked in the kitchen outbuilding, and young slave boys served as runners to carry hot food from there to the house.

Although Reconstruction era tales of the Old South depicted plantations in which white women were gracious hostesses who spent their days in leisure and black mammies were good-natured cooks and loyal family retainers, in reality all southern women worked hard to produce meals for white and black families in the plantation South. White mistresses supervised slaves, oversaw the purchase of food supplies, directed seasonal preservation of food, planned menus, and directed dairy and poultry operations. Black cooks and house servants planted and harvested gardens, cooked three meals a day for the plantation community, cleaned the house, did the laundry, and waited upon guests who frequently visited for extended stays. Slaves were also charged with textile production, sewing, and mending.

Historians Catherine Clinton, Drew Gilpin Faust, and Lee Ann Whites stress the crisis in gender relations brought on by the Civil War, and food was a key part of this crisis. As food supplies were depleted, white women on plantations in the slaveholding South realized that the social contract they held with their husbands was failing. These elite white women no longer believed that, in return for devotion and subservience to their husbands, they and their families would receive adequate food, clothing, and protection. Women expressed their protests through food riots across the South, as well as in letters asking Confederate officers to release their husbands and sons so that they might return home and support their families.

After the war, newly freed black families established a gendered division of labor that had been denied by slavery. Black women left the fields to focus on their own homes and families, and former house servants finally cooked proper meals for their families rather than serve them leftovers from the big house.

The complexity of gender and food in this era is described in Charles Frazier's *Cold Mountain*, a novel that focuses on war-wearied southerners in the Appalachian Mountains. Ada, a white woman of means, is left to care for her family's derelict mountain farm after her father's death. She soon realizes that her training in fine needlework, classical piano, and poetry is of little use in helping her feed herself. Ada turns to Ruby, a poor mountain woman, who helps manage the farm. A pesky rooster has terrorized Ada for weeks, and she asks Ruby, "How will we run it off?" While Ada's words still hang in the air, Ruby captures and beheads the unruly beast and soon has it in a stewpot surrounded by gobs of biscuit dough. This scene illustrates how southerners redefined traditional roles connected to food production and preparation during the Civil War.

From the 1890s through the 1920s southerners created a New South that was evident in new lines of commercial food products that appeared in the general store and grocery. Although men's and women's roles in food preparation changed little from the end of the Civil War to World War II, access to canned goods, cooking stoves, and electric refrigerators and appliances significantly changed women's roles in the kitchen. Since few could afford to hire black domestic workers, white women found themselves solely responsible for food preparation and all their household chores.

Sharecroppers and farmworkers who were forced to move from rural areas to southern towns and cities during the agricultural depression after 1900 were deprived of garden patches, home-canned produce, and meat from hunting and fishing. Among those who remained on farms, men negotiated the sale of livestock for meat, while women supplemented family income with egg and butter money made from selling surplus dairy products and baked goods at weekly curb markets or by selling door-to-door to in-town customers.

After World War II, white middle- and upper-class women throughout the South hired black women as cooks and housekeepers, often for as little as three dollars a week. While black women managed their households, white women volunteered for community and religious organizations, and they raised funds for these groups through food-related events such as church suppers and the sale of community cookbooks. Completely removed from food preparation, white working husbands provided the weekly grocery money and presided over the family's evening meal. In the 1960s Southern Progress Corporation in Birmingham celebrated the white southern family in *Southern Living*, a monthly magazine that continues to portray wives as cooks and hostesses and husbands as tenders of the grill and the hunting camp.

The South has always been known for food events that range from political fund-raisers to dinner on the grounds at rural churches. Originating in the work frolics and religious revivals of the antebellum South, these events are marked by a gendered division of labor. House-raisings, corn shuckings, log rollings, and church picnics all required significant quantities of food to accommodate large crowds. Both white and black men cooked outdoor meals that featured Brunswick stew, catfish, and barbecue. Ingredients and side dishes that accompanied the meat and fish were prepared by female slave cooks and, after Emancipation, by both white and black women. These gendered patterns are still present at boucheries and crawfish boils in the Cajun country of southwestern Louisiana, at oyster roasts along the Chesapeake Bay, at ham suppers in Virginia, and at numerous other outdoor food events. Throughout the South, women remain the primary domestic cooks, while men are public performers who cook for and entertain hungry audiences at special occasions in their community.

Television has dramatically changed the gendered role of southerners in relation to food since the 1970s. Today both men and women reign as the region's finest chefs, caterers, food writers, restaurateurs, and culinary instructors. From rural cafés famous for their meat-and-three plates to the finest restaurants in New Orleans, men and women share the management and daily operation of southern eateries. Women have entered the professional ranks of southern food-related companies such as Viking Range Corporation, *Southern Living*, and White Lily Flour. They have also launched numerous southern Internet mail-order businesses that market pound cakes, salted pecans, and catfish paté. Southern specialties once limited to home tables are now delivered overnight across the country by Federal Express.

Southern literature, music, film, art, and folkways define mythic characters such as the pampered white southern belle, the nurturing black mammy, the poor white backwoods moonshiner, and the paternalistic white plantation master. Each of these stereotypes reinforces a popular understanding of southern food and the role of women within the kitchen. But reality is infinitely more complex than these stereotypes suggest when we consider foodways and gender in the South. While men and women are increasingly trading places in culinary worlds throughout the South, traditional gender divisions of southern foodways are far from extinct. Future generations of southerners will likely recognize the familiar sight of male hunters in camouflage, church ladies at their bake sales, men preparing barbecue outdoors, and women preparing the evening meal in their home.

MARCIE COHEN FERRIS
University of North Carolina at Chapel Hill

Catherine Clinton and Nina Silber, eds., *Divided Houses: Gender and the Civil War* (1992); Pete Daniel, *Standing at the Crossroads: Southern Life in the Twentieth Century* (1986); John Egerton, *Southern Food: At Home, on the Road, in History* (1987); Charles Frazier, *Cold Mountain* (1997); Sherrie A. Inness, *Dinner Roles: American Women and Culinary Culture* (2001), ed., *Cooking Lessons: The Politics of Gender and Food* (2001); Anne Firor Scott, *The Southern Lady: From Pedestal to Politics, 1830–1930* (1970); Joe Gray Taylor, *Eating, Drinking, and Visiting in the South: An Informal History* (1982); Bertram Wyatt-Brown, *Honor and Violence in the Old South* (1986).

Gulf Coast Foodways

Gulf Coast foodways evolved in an environment that is, for the most part, abundantly fertile and easily accessible. Brackish bayous, swamps, and river deltas gradually become sea, with fertile marshes and shallow waters yielding fish, shellfish, waterfowl, and other standard ingredients of the Gulf Coast cook's larder.

Much of the Gulf Coast is etched with inlets, bays, estuaries, and shallows that are easily accessible by wading, by piers, or by small craft. Traditional food procurement techniques in such settings involve a minimum investment in technology. For example, the hand gathering, or "cooning," of oysters is a Native American practice continued today from Texas to Florida where oyster beds are in wading reach in shallow waters. When cooning, people open and eat some of the oysters on the spot, open others to carry home, and replenish the reef by throwing back the empty shells. "Soft-shelling" refers to the nighttime catching of recently molted crabs by waders carrying lanterns in ankle- to calf-deep water over sandbars at low tide, sometimes gigging flounders in the process as well. Seines handled by two people on a beach can catch shrimp, crabs, and occasional flounders. Fishermen use piers or boats or wade deeper with cast nets for mullet or with rod and reel for speckled trout and other fish. Shrimp are caught from piers with brill nets. Adults and children catch crabs with nets dropped from piers. In the past, people scavenged turtle eggs on beaches, while fresh and saltwater turtles were more common foods. Men, women, and children of every background fish for a great variety of finfish from piers, boats, and banks. In Louisiana, crawfish join the list of foods caught locally in traps or with hand nets. The weather is rarely very cold, and something is always in season.

These traditional activities were once subsistence activities; today they are usually supplemental to store-bought food. Industrialized fishing, aquaculture, and foreign imports supply commercial outlets. Yet getting the ingredients for dinner directly from nature remains a form of recreation, as does preparation and cooking. Shrimp boils, crab boils, oyster-opening parties, and crawfish boils are social events that celebrate local foodways. Festivals and restaurants throughout the Gulf Coast region market local dishes to residents and tourists alike.

Cultural influences vary along the Gulf Coast, but they are usually notably distinct from those of nearby inland areas. The northern shore, from Pensacola, Fla., to Port Arthur, Tex., includes rural Cajun country and cosmopolitan New Orleans and shares a predominantly French, though multiethnic Catholic influence, a region "South of the South," that proudly distinguishes itself from the Anglo-Protestant interior. Creole and Cajun cuisines were born in this part of the New World, a fusion of European, African, and Native American influences in an especially productive natural setting. Creole or Cajun dishes such as gumbo (of many types), jambalaya, and boiled crawfish are now popular from Texas to Florida. In panhandle Florida, smoked mullet is a specialty. There are ethnic enclaves throughout the Gulf States: Greeks in Tarpon Springs, Fla., Cubans in Tampa, Croatians in southeastern Louisiana and coastal Mississippi, Mexicans in Texas and elsewhere. Vietnamese have entered the seafood business, especially shrimping, throughout the Gulf States.

Restaurant cooking focuses on local foods for both tourists and residents. Restaurants near or over the water on pilings serve fried or boiled seafood and fried seafood poor boy sandwiches. In New Orleans, venerable old restaurants specializing in Creole cooking are city landmarks. The national interest in Cajun food began with Paul Prudhomme's popularizing of his family's traditional cooking in the 1980s through his restaurants, cookbooks, and personal appearances. Other chefs, including adopted native and television personality Emeril Lagasse, continue in this mode. Elsewhere on the Gulf, trained chefs have created new cuisines such as Caribbean-inspired Floribbean and Mexican-influenced Texas Creole. New ideas in turn influence local home cooks. Countless cookbooks compiled in local communities help document and preserve traditional cooking.

Gulf Coast foodways unfortunately are threatened by pollution, loss of habitat, and overfishing. Unless these problems are reversed, Gulf foodways will depend on globally marketed imports for their local dishes, and the procurement aspect of Gulf Coast foodways will be but a memory.

C. PAIGE GUTIERREZ
Biloxi, Mississippi

Virginia Elverson, *Gulf Coast Cooking* (1991); Peter S. Fiebleman, *American Cooking: Creole and Acadian* (1971); C. Paige Gutierrez, *Cajun Foodways* (1992).

Hispanic American Foodways

Hispanic foods arrived in the American South at the margins, entering Texas from Mexico and Florida from the Caribbean. By the end of the 20th century, however, these foods had spread throughout the region and, indeed, the entire country. Latinos now comprise the largest minority group in the United States, but the category is as misleading gastronomically as it is politically because of the diverse histories of Native American peoples and of Hispanic colonialism.

Although Cubans, Mexicans, Puerto Ricans, and other Latin Americans define their Hispanic identity in opposition to Spain, the colonial power provides the basis for a common Latino culture. As part of the broader Mediterranean civilization, Spain holds the trinity of wheat bread, olive oil, and wine as the foundation of its cuisine. From a nutritional perspective, Spain bequeathed its greatest gift to the Americas in the form of livestock, particularly cattle, sheep, pigs, and chickens. Catholicism has also become an important part of Latin American culture, and Spanish foods are commonly eaten at Christmas and Lent, when meals feature dried cod and shrimp, lentils and chickpeas, dried fruits, nuts, and the invariable dessert, *capirotada* (bread pudding). The Moorish occupation of the Iberian Peninsula, from 711 to 1492, left a Muslim influence of citrus fruits, rice, and eggplants, brought by Arab traders from Asia, as well as a distinctive style of preparing spicy stews. Many widely eaten Hispanic dishes depend on non-European ingredients; for example, *moros y cristianos* (Moors and Christians) is named for its combination of black beans from the Americas and white rice from Asia.

This common Hispanic heritage blended with Native American and African civilizations to produce distinct Latin American cultures. In the Caribbean, Taino and Carib inhabitants employed a variety of hunting, gathering, and horticultural practices to make optimal use of local resources. The leading cultivar, manioc, was prepared by grating the root, squeezing out its toxic juice, pressing the meat into a flat cassava "bread," and baking it on an earthenware griddle.

The islanders also consumed a variety of native fruits, vegetables, rodents, fish, and mollusks. The arrival of Columbus in 1492 led to the decimation of the local inhabitants as a result of conquest and disease. The Spanish and later other European nations therefore imported millions of African slaves to work the lucrative sugar plantations established on the islands. West African skills at rice cultivation formed the basis for the regional staple, rice and beans, although Cubans favored black beans while Puerto Ricans and Jamaicans preferred red. Other patterns established by the slave diet, including the use of more dried than fresh fish and meat, remain common even today for working-class people throughout the Caribbean. In Florida, however, Spain left only a marginal cultural imprint, establishing a precarious line of missions and presidios to deny the strategic coastline to European rivals.

In Mexico, Spanish conquistadors found complex and diverse cuisines among the Maya, Nahua, Totonacs, and Zapotecs. The combination of corn and beans provided a complementary source of protein that ensured a healthy although largely vegetarian diet. Simmering the corn with lye to make hominy and then grinding and cooking it as tortillas offset the threat of pellagra. The addition of squash, avocados, and greens, as well as turkeys, small dogs, fish, and rodents, also helped round out the nutritional balance. Finally, chile peppers provided the basis for elaborate festive stews called *mollis* and made even the everyday tortillas and beans tasty. These indigenous foods mixed with those of Spanish newcomers to form the basis for Mexico's mestizo national cuisine; for example, mole poblano incorporated Old World spices into the Native American turkey and chile pepper stews. Wheat tortillas represented another hybrid food, especially common in the north, where Spanish settlers had few mills and ovens to bake bread. Texas, like Florida, remained peripheral to the Spanish empire and was colonized in the early 18th century for strategic reasons, to protect the silver mines of Zacatecas and San Luis Potosí from French incursion. Although most *norteños* were of mixed race, their foods tended toward Spanish rather than Indian styles, with more meat and fewer vegetables. Texas chili con carne thus began as a simple mole made of deer or goat meat as often as beef and spiced with red chiles, cumin, and oregano, which are still the distinctive flavors of the Tex-Mex kitchen.

When Texas gained independence from Mexico in 1836 and was annexed by the United States a decade later, Anglo newcomers viewed the Mexican people and their foods with both attraction and repulsion, a contradictory impulse that emerges in the history of chili. Arnoldo de Leon has documented the racism against Mexicans, who were called "greasers" and "chilis," and subject to widespread discrimination and frequent lynching. At the same time, Mexican women were referred to as "hot tamales" and became an object of desire, particularly in the case of the so-called Chili Queens. By the 1880s, Hispanic women had begun setting up tables in San Antonio plazas to sell their spicy stews, while carefully chaperoned by male relatives: chili became a prominent tourist attraction, but city officials nevertheless began an ongoing campaign to restrict the stands where it was sold by first ordering them off Alamo Plaza in 1890. In March 1936, just days before the centennial celebrations of the Alamo, chili vendors on Market Plaza were confined to screened enclosures, and after a brief revival in 1939, the stands were closed for good in 1943.

Chili had meanwhile spread far beyond south Texas, being appropriated and transformed by nonethnic entrepreneurs and consumers as a result. The dish first received national exposure at the 1893 World's Columbian Exposition in Chicago, where a San Antonio chili booth did a roaring business at a time when vendors could no longer sell chili at the Alamo itself. A few years later, in 1896, chili powder was industrialized by German immigrant William Gebhardt, whose company later began selling packaged dinners including canned chili and tamales by mail throughout the country. Already tamed-down for Anglo palates, chili underwent further alterations, with the side order of beans dumped into the mixture, and it was added to hot dogs and, in Cincinnati, even to spaghetti. Tamales, meanwhile, took root as a folk food in the Mississippi Delta region.

Although many think of the Cuban American community as a product of the Communist Revolution, the island's connections with the United States reach deep into the 19th century, when southern planters hoped to annex Cuba as a slave state. Fanny Calderón de la Barca, who visited the island in the late 1830s, described the foods of the elite as heavily Spanish. Common dishes included grilled meats, chorizo, fish *en escabeche* (pickled fish), *ropa vieja* (literally "old clothes," shredded beef), and very strong coffee. By the 1880s a substantial Cuban population had gathered in Tampa, and in the 1920s Miami became a haven for refugees from the island's unstable politics. The trickle of exiles turned into a flood in 1960, when the United States broke relations with Fidel Castro's government, and the Cuban middle class emigrated en masse to the United States, causing a massive growth in the existing Cuban markets and restaurants around Miami's Calle Ocho (Eighth Street). Subsequent waves of Central American and Haitian refugees added further to the complexity of ethnic foods in Miami as well as in New South cities such as Atlanta and Charlotte. One beneficiary of this growing population was Goya Foods, founded in New Jersey in the 1930s by a Spanish family that still manages the company, marketing primarily to Hispanics on the East Coast, from New York to Miami.

For most of the South, and indeed the United States, Hispanic food has meant Tex-Mex. One of the first pioneers of Mexican food outside the Southwest was the El Chico chain, founded in Texas in the 1930s, which opened franchises throughout the South in the postwar era. Many Mexican restaurants offered little more than ethnic and culinary stereotypes, one example being South of the Border, S.C., established in the 1950s as a tourist trap on Interstate 95. Recent scholarship suggests that we might consider Tex-Mex as more than a bastardized version of Mexican food, as a true regional cuisine, a melding of Mexican, Native American, and American tastes and traditions, in much the same way that southern cooking reflects European, African, and Native American traditions.

In recent years Hispanic cuisines have begun to emerge from the Tex-Mex shadow. In the early 1990s Miami-based chefs introduced Nuevo Latino as a new fusion cuisine, drawing on recipes from throughout Latin America; it remains to be seen whether taro root chips, tropical fruit salsas, and rum *mojitos* will mount a successful challenge to the margarita bar scene. Meanwhile, the recruiting of Mexican migrant workers to Alabama road construction and North Carolina slaughterhouses has brought authentic *taquerías* to countless southern communities. Given the traditional southern affinity for hominy, beans, pork, and hot sauce, Hispanic foods have a bright future in the region.

JEFFREY M. PILCHER
The Citadel

Fanny Calderón de la Barca, *Life in Mexico* (1966); Donna R. Gabaccia, *We Are What We Eat: Ethnic Food and the Making of Americans* (1998); Arnoldo de Leon, *The Tejano Community, 1836–1900* (1982), *They Called Them Greasers: Anglo Attitudes toward Mexicans in Texas, 1821–1900* (1983); Mario Montaflo, in *Useable Pasts: Traditions and Group Expressions in North America*, ed. Tad Tuleja (1997); Jeffrey M. Pilcher, *¡Que vivan los tamales! Food and the Making of Mexican Identity* (1998); George Pozzetta and Gary Mormino, *The Immigrant World of Ybor City Italians and Their Latin Neighbors in Tampa, 1885–1985* (1987); Earl Shorris, *Latinos: A Biography of the People* (1992); Robb Walsh, *The Tex-Mex Cookbook: A History in Recipes and Photos* (2004).

Jewish Foodways

Eating a meal in the Jewish South reflects how Jews balance their Jewishness in a world dominated by white and black Christian southerners. The story is repeated in each century and in each generation—from a meal of mutton enjoyed by an 18th-century Jewish merchant and self-trained shohet (kosher butcher) in colonial Georgia to a snack of hard-boiled eggs and crackers eaten by a 19th-century Jewish peddler on a rural Alabama road, collard greens sold by a Jewish storeowner to his black customers in Charleston, S.C., in the 20th century, and a shrimp boil fund-raiser organized by brotherhood members at a Reform congregation in New Orleans, La., today.

Jewish responses to kashrut in the South range from complete avoidance to strict adherence, a pattern that dates back to the first Jewish settlers and continues to the present. Today, many Orthodox and Conservative Jews in the South keep kosher, an especially difficult task in rural areas where kosher food must be ordered by mail, telephone, or the Internet. In Memphis, a kosher barbecue contest sponsored by an Orthodox synagogue features barbecued beef brisket. Corky's, a well-known local barbecue restaurant, is owned by Don and Barry Pelts, who are prominent members of the Reform Jewish community. In addition to their pork barbecue, the Pelts now sell kosher barbecue sauce and kosher barbecued turkeys.

Jewish immigrants brought food traditions to the South from their countries of origin—Ashkenazim from Central and Eastern Europe, and Sephardim from countries bordering the Mediterranean. From Germany came kuchens, strudels, breads, roasted goose, matzoh balls, and gefilte fish; from the Mediterranean, feta, olive oil, fish, rice dishes, and filo dough pastries; from Eastern Europe, chopped liver, kishke, stuffed cabbage, roasted chicken, kreplach, tzimmes, and herring; from Alsace and Lorraine, tortes, pastries, breads, onions and garlic, cheeses, baked and stewed fish dishes.

As southern Jewish identity evolved from the 18th century through the 20th, some women kept southern and Jewish dishes separate, while others mixed the cuisines by adding pecans, fresh tomatoes, okra, butter beans, rice, and sweet potatoes to holiday menus. They also substituted regional specialties such as fried chicken, gumbo, and beef ribs for the traditional roasted chicken at Friday evening Sabbath suppers. Today Jewish women prepare southern and Jewish foods in ways that celebrate the distinctive foodways of both their region and their religious heritage. Traditional Jewish dishes frequently prepared in the region include gefilte fish, chopped liver, matzoh ball soup, potato latkes, noodle kugel, kreplach, stuffed cabbage, borscht, brisket, strudel, and tzimmes. These traditional foods are prepared with regional ingredients and cooking methods as an important part of Jewish life in the South.

Southern cooks braise, stew, and fry meats, and most meals include vegetables slow-cooked over a low simmer. These techniques are also familiar to Jewish cooks, particularly stewing and braising. Few Jews had a tradition of vegetable gardening because of their urban backgrounds and restrictions against owning land in the Old World. Mildred Covert, a descendant of Eastern European Jews who moved to New Orleans in the early 1900s, recalls, "If my grandmother had a tomato bush, it was by accident." Jewish women did, however, bring traditions of pickling and preserving from Central and Eastern Europe that blended easily with the summer canning traditions of their Gentile neighbors.

Since many traditional southern dishes require lard for frying and butter as shortening, observant Jews faced a special predicament. How can one not serve fried chicken, pies, and cakes and still be considered a loyal southerner? The introduction of Crisco in 1912, a certified kosher vegetable shortening, solved a long-standing problem for Jewish women and for African Americans who cooked for observant Jewish families in the South. Crisco was considered parve, a neutral food by kashrut standards, and it was eaten with both dairy and meat dishes. When the product was first introduced, Procter and Gamble announced, "The Hebrew Race has been waiting 4,000 years for Crisco." And for observant southern Jews who lived within a culinary culture of cast-iron frying pans in which foods were fried in lard, it *felt* like 4,000 years.

Following World War II, the southern economy shifted from agriculture to industry, and as thousands of rural southerners moved to southern cities their eating patterns changed. Factory workers carried sack lunches from home, or bought sardines, pickles, crackers, and cheese from corner grocery stores, many of which were owned by Eastern European and Sephardic Jewish merchants.

Southerners consider food as sacred as religion, and eating is like a religion. "There is nothing we do here without food," says Rabbi Arnold Mark Belzer of Savannah's historic Congregation Mickve Israel, which was founded in 1733. Every week of the year the Saturday morning service is followed by a hot lunch prepared by the temple's catering staff. Until her recent retirement, Alberta Everett, an African American cook at Mickve Israel, was known for her delicious kugels and challahs.

Food events among Jewish southerners include both social gatherings where a meal is shared by congregants in a home or at a local restaurant and religious gatherings such as a Passover Seder. In the 19th- and early 20th-century South, Jewish food celebrations included "Purim entertainments," temple fund-raising fairs and bazaars, "Ballyhoo" luncheons, "Break-the-fast" dances, congregational picnics, "Simchat Torah Balls," nonkosher oyster roasts, strawberry festivals, wedding receptions, and candy pulls. Today food events include home-cooked meals for visiting rabbis, potluck suppers at the temple, community Passover Seders at the synagogue, Sabbath fried chicken at Jewish summer camp, sisterhood-sponsored food bazaars, Jewish golf tournaments, and synagogue-sponsored "barbecue" competitions.

Food traditions—both kosher and nonkosher, both deeply southern and deeply Jewish—endure and are reinterpreted by each generation of Jewish cooks who mix regional flavors and methods with Old World ingredients and techniques. Jewish grandmothers and mothers rarely change their recipes, as they try to preserve flavors that remind them of family, ancestral places, and historic memories. The newer generation creates healthier versions of Jewish favorites by reducing fat and adding fresh fruits and vegetables. Hispanic and Asian flavors now present in the South also find their way into Jewish dishes. At their dining tables, Jewish southerners—young and old, rural and urban—create a distinctive religious expression that reflects the evolution of southern Jewish life.

MARCIE COHEN FERRIS
University of North Carolina at Chapel Hill

Mark Bauman and Bobbie Malone, eds., *American Jewish History, Special Issue: Directions in Southern Jewish History* (September and December 1997); Arlene Belzer, Becky Civjan, Elaine Erlich, Diane Kuhr, Joan Levy, Margie Levy, and Sue Ruby, eds., *Shalom Y'all Cookbook* (1995); Anita Bernstein, Florence Kurtz, Bella Wallace, and Pearl Wolfson, eds., *Historically Cooking: 200 Years of Good Eating* (1985); Marcie Cohen Ferris, *Matzoh Ball Gumbo: Culinary Tales of the Jewish South* (2005); Joan Nathan, *Jewish Cooking in America* (1994); Dale and Theodore Rosengarten, eds., *A Portion of the People: Three Hundred Years of Southern Jewish Life* (2002).

Literature, Food in

In the section of *Killers of the Dream* called "The Women," Lillian Smith tells the story of a group of white middle-class Georgia women who come together in the 1930s as the Association of Southern Women for the Prevention of Lynching. These women believe that it is meaningless for them to take communion—the central ritual of the Christian church, a foretaste of the heavenly banquet that all believers are promised—unless "they break bread with fellow men of color." They gather in small groups to eat with African American women, deliberately breaking one of the strongest taboos of southern culture. It is a well-meaning attempt that does not go smoothly. After these early attempts at sharing a table, both black and white women become physically ill. What the women attribute to "food poisoning," Smith describes as a symptom of "how this eating taboo in childhood is woven into the mesh of things that are 'wrong,' how it becomes tangled with God and sex, pulling anxieties from stronger prohibitions and attaching them to itself."

Food and cooking have been, since the earliest days of southern literature, one of the primary ways by which southern culture has been defined and celebrated. In this telling episode, Smith sums up many of the food-related themes that run through the literature of the South: images of plenty, feasting, the banquet, hospitality, all of them qualified by questions of which races, gender, and classes are entitled to places at the table. The South's religious and political conservatism, racial segregation, and class consciousness have given southern writers the myth of a stable society with conventions that they can make use of or rebel against. In *The Generall Historie of Virginia* (1624), Captain John Smith pauses in his recounting of his capture by Powhatan and deliverance by Pocahontas to mention the hospitality of the king's brother Opitchapam, who invited him into his house and presented him with "many platters of bread, foule, and wild beasts" and gave him the leftovers to take home to the settlers. William Byrd II, writing in about 1738 in a journal that was published in 1844 as *The History of the Dividing Line*, described the ease of life in North Carolina, where "the easiness of raising provisions" led to a great "Disposition to Laziness" on the part of the men.

For Thomas Jefferson, accused in his own time of "abjuring his native victuals," good food and good eating were an integral part of his vision of a nation of independent yeoman farmers. Even though his commitment to the rational ideas he espoused has been called into question, for some, by his relation to the enslaved African Americans at Monticello, it was Jefferson in the gardens and kitchens of Monticello and the White House who fused native plenty to European traditions of fine dining that he found in France and Italy. Damon Lee Fowler eloquently sums up Jefferson's contribution to American food history: "He embraced the relationship between garden and table; he sought out quality ingredients both from home and abroad; he understood both the simplicity of classic dishes as well as the adventure of new foods; he preserved his own food roots and reached out to the cuisines of other cultures; he encouraged the connection between food and sociability and cherished lingering conversation over fine wine. . . . In this brilliant and complex man is a timeless articulation of the role and value of food in our lives."

John Pendleton Kennedy's novel *Swallow Barn* was the model for a whole genre of novels glorifying the myth of plantation life in the South. Central to the idealized life of Virginia planters is a vision of hospitality and shared plenty: "They frequently meet in the interchanges of a large and thriftless hospitality. . . . Their halls are large, and the boards ample; and surrounding the great family hearth, with its immense burthen of blazing wood casting a broad and merry glare over the congregated household and the numerous retainers, a social winter party in Virginia affords a tolerable picture of feudal munificence."

This benevolent feudal munificence is, however, often undercut by the narratives of the enslaved people who raised and cooked the food that made plantation hospitality possible. Frederick Douglass in *My Bondage and My Freedom* (1855) sees the heavy, elaborate dinners consumed by the Lloyd family as physically and spiritually poisonous: "Lurking beneath all their dishes, are invisible spirits of evil, ready to feed the self-deluded gormandizers with aches, pains, fierce temper, uncontrolled passions." Harriet Jacobs's *Incidents in the Life of a Slave Girl* (1861) shows the travesty of the generosity of the plantation system in her recounting of her mistress's habit of spitting in the pots after Sunday dinner was dished up in order to prevent the slaves from eating the leftover food. "The Lord's Supper," Jacobs muses, "did not seem to put [her mistress] in a Christian frame of mind."

The problems posed by questions of race in defining the food traditions of the South are further complicated by questions of gender. Many white southern women have enjoyed the reputation of being great cooks when the actual cooking was done for them and their families by African American servants. The stereotypical image of the mammy has played a large part in southern fiction, most notably Mammy in Margaret Mitchell's *Gone with the Wind* (1936), Disley in William Faulkner's *The Sound and the Fury* (1929), Berenice in Carson McCullers's *The Member of the Wedding* (1946), and Calpurnia in Harper Lee's *To Kill a Mockingbird* (1960). Trudier Harris has perceptively explored the Mammy stereotype in the works of African American writers such as Kristin Hunter, Toni Morrison, Richard Wright, and others.

The elaborate meals of *Swallow Barn* and of the Lloyd family are a way of asserting class as well as racial superiority. "Eating together," Mary Titus has pointed out, "signifies community and social equality." Descriptions of meals have given generations of southern writers a shorthand for describing the social class to which characters belong and for talking about class conflict in the changing South. In *I'll Take My Stand*, the manifesto of the Vanderbilt Agrarians (1930), Andrew Lytle and other writers see the midday dinner as symbolic of the family values that characterize life in the upper- and middle-class South, a world in which "everybody has had something to do with the long and intricate procession from the ground to the table." The meals in Kate Chopin's *The Awakening* (1899) show the dissatisfaction of Edna Pontellier with the strictures of the Creole society in which she lives. In Harper Lee's *To Kill a Mockingbird*, the class difference of the visiting Walter Cunningham is immediately apparent to the Finch family when he pours syrup on his dinner.

Eudora Welty is the master at using food as a shorthand for class differences and to show class conflict. The five family meals around which *Delta Wedding* (1946) is structured allow Welty to show the family conflict created by two disapproved-of marriages and its final resolution and acceptance. In *Losing Battles* (1970), the dinner assembled for the family reunion on the occasion of Granny Vaughn's 90th birthday provides a rich background for this comic portrait of family life and conversation.

Restaurants are also important in southern literature, and it is no accident that a significant part of the civil rights movement was fought over lunch counters. Only equals share a table and eat together, and while those who would restrict access to the table to those like themselves have not entirely disappeared from the South, most southerners now realize that any banquet is richer if shared.

THOMAS HEAD
Washington, D.C.

Damon Lee Fowler, ed., *Dining at Monticello* (2005); Peggy Prenshaw, ed., *Southern Quarterly* (Winter-Spring 1992); Mary Titus, in *Companion to Southern Literature*, ed. Joseph M. Flora and Lucinda H. MacKethan (2002).

Lowcountry Foodways

The low, flat coastal plain that hugs the shores of South Carolina and Georgia is limned by barrier islands. Stretching inland some 80 miles to the fall line, where sand dunes once hugged the oceanfront, the Lowcountry is a humid subtropical land of swamps and rivers spilling into the estuaries that twist and turn through the marshland. More than a fourth of the saltwater marshes on the eastern seaboard are found on the 300-mile coastline of the Lowcountry, and the often enormous tides (averaging nearly eight feet) bring into those brackish waters the crab, shrimp, oysters, and finfish that have helped define the regional cuisine for centuries.

After earlier attempts by the Spanish and French to settle the fecund land, the English established a permanent colony in 1670, when Charles II granted all of the land in the New World south of Virginia to eight gentlemen planters who had restored him to the throne. This expansive grant—the Heath Charter—was considerably larger than the rest of the British Empire, and the colony quickly became one of England's richest. Its settlers came first from overcrowded Barbados, where the king's supporters—now Lords Proprietors—had amassed great fortunes on their sugar plantations. With these already Creolized Barbadians came the model for the plantocracy that would distinguish Carolina from the start.

By the end of the 17th century, rice cultivation had become the principal source of wealth in the Lowcountry; the South Carolina plantation was one of the most successful financial ventures in North America. Charleston, the capital of the Lowcountry, was already a sophisticated city of great beauty, according to contemporary accounts. Built at the expense of human dignity, the city arose on the backs of the slaves who were imported directly from the rice-growing regions of West Africa. From more than two dozen ethnic groups speaking 40 different languages, the enslaved were imported by the thousands. By 1710 the colony had a black majority. The trend continued: by midcentury, blacks outnumbered whites two to one. From 1720 to 1775, 40 percent of the Africans imported into North America came through Charleston. By 1740 most of the enslaved were African born.

Savannah was settled on a high bluff of the river of the same name about 100 miles south of Charleston in 1733. Often called the best-planned city in America, it has continued to spread out from its original grid of small lots around 20 small parks. Nowhere in America was a colony more closely tied to Georgian England; prevailing English tastes prevailed in Savannah and the surrounding Lowcountry long after the Revolution.

Throughout the region, it was West Africans, expert planters of wetland rice, who cleared the land and constructed the complicated dikes and sluices that defined the rice plantation. They maintained the crop and prepared it for the table. Although they were shipped naked and in chains, the enslaved survived the Middle Passage with their extensive knowledge intact. With the slave trade came many African plants, words, religious beliefs, crafts, arts, idioms, and proverbs that have remained a part of the Lowcountry for over 300 years. Okra, sorghum, collards, black-eyed peas, circular cast nets, basket weaving, call-and-response field songs, and words such as *gumbo, benne* (sesame seeds), and *yam* entered the vernacular, along with New World plants such as peanuts, tomatoes, and peppers, which the Portuguese had taken to Africa earlier and with which the slaves were long familiar. Their rice cookery skills, which neither the English nor the French had, would influence not only the Lowcountry kitchen, but the cooking of the entire South. One-pot dishes such as gumbo, pilau, and hoppin' John became common in the Creole kitchen of the region.

The Restoration was witness to a revolution in the sciences and humanities. The Lords Proprietors had hired the forward-thinking philosopher John Locke to write a constitution for their colony, and, while his original was never fully adopted, his ideas greatly influenced how the colony's government operated and how its populace lived. Most distinctive and effective was the guarantee of religious freedom. The religious fugitives of Europe flocked to Carolina, and by 1750 fully half of the white settlers were French Huguenots. Throughout the 18th century, Charleston also had the largest Jewish population in America. Mostly Sephardic, the Jews brought with them their Mediterranean culinary traditions, which are still evident in the cooking of the area today. In 1730 Lutherans from the Palatinate settled in Orangeburg, about 70 miles inland, where they grew wheat and cabbage and raised cattle for the Lowcountry gentry. To this day, Orangeburg is the center of the dairy industry in South Carolina.

What quickly emerged was a Creole culture, perhaps most evident in the kitchen. From Carolina's inception, the Lords Proprietors had offered passage, land, and slaves to new settlers. Even in the modest plantation houses of the Huguenots, meals were prepared by Africans. With the advanced hunting, fishing, and cooking skills of the Africans, the superior meat-curing techniques of the Germans, the worldly pretensions of the aristocratic English, and the country French traditions of the Huguenot craftsmen who settled in Carolina, the Lowcountry kitchen evolved an exotic cuisine, with unprecedented combinations not unlike the fusion cooking of the late 20th century. Fiery peppers were added to bland Scottish soups. Tropical fruits from the Caribbean arrived in the Lowcountry's busy ports, a mere four days after being picked. American coconut cookery saw its beginning in the city, and melons were pickled with West Indian spices, in imitation of East Indian mangoes. Recipes for condiments such as *ats jaar* pickles were recorded in 18th-century ladies' journals. The recipe for *ats jaar*, originally from Malaysia, would have traveled on the spice and slave routes from Java, to India, to Madagascar, to South Africa (where the Dutch had Malaysian slaves), up the coast to West Africa, and on to the Lowcountry. As settlers moved further inland, the entire South began to embrace the sweet and sour tastes of the East—tastes evident in the still prevalent chowchow, piccalilli, chutney, spiced peaches, and other condiments that are one of the hallmarks of the southern table.

With its subtropical climate, and rich, loamy soil, the Lowcountry is a gardener's paradise. Many of the most accomplished botanists of the 17th, 18th, and 19th centuries spent years in the area. By the middle of the 18th century Charleston boasted not only the country's first formal gardens, theater, and opera house, but also its largest bookstore, replete with the latest cookery, gardening, and music books from England, France, and Germany. Gardeners regularly advertised seeds, plants, and herbs for sale in any of several newspapers.

Africans with cooking skills were considered part of the Lowcountry family. They worked side by side with the plantation mistress, who often was in charge of planning the meals and clothing not only for her own family, but for those of the enslaved as well.

With its task system, the Lowcountry plantation was different from plantations in other colonies. When a slave's task was done, he or she was free to hunt, fish, or garden a plot of land. Vegetables previously known in Africa, such as collards, peanuts, tomatoes, and guinea squash, were served at the table of master and slave alike. Recent archaeological digs have shown that duck, geese, and turkeys (both wild and domesticated), pigeons (brought from Europe by the settlers), guinea fowl (from Africa), and songbirds—particularly rice birds (bobolinks)—were daily fare. Pigs were allowed to roam free, then hunted and cured for the festive hams and the smoked parts that flavor many typical Lowcountry dishes. Native American oysters and corn became staples, with ground corn—grits—appearing on the table when rice did not. Because the land was more valuable when planted in rice than when used for animal husbandry, beef was rarely eaten. Most households, however, kept a cow for milk, and the calves were slaughtered for veal. More plentiful, therefore, than meat, oysters were used as fillers in sausages and casseroles.

The cooking of antebellum Charleston, Savannah, and the surrounding Lowcountry was often elaborate and grand in the European tradition, long after the Revolution. The cuisine almost died, however, after the Civil War, when much of the land was lost and rice cultivation moved to other areas where the soil could support the new machines that were too heavy for the marshy Lowcountry. After 50 years of struggling, with hand labor, to compete, the rice industry, crippled by storms and freshets and the silting caused by upriver cotton farming, was dealt a final blow by a devastating hurricane early in the 20th century. With the fall of the plantation, many of the traditional dishes of the Lowcountry were lost until the culinary renaissance of the 1990s.

By the year 2000 Charleston had become an international tourist destination, attracting over 5 million visitors each year. Savannah's historic district covers over 2.5 miles of easy walking and boasts over 20 tour companies. Hundreds of restaurants operate in the historical centers of the two cities; a few offer updated versions of some of the classic Creole dishes of the area, such as shrimp and grits, Frogmore stew (boiled spicy smoked sausage, corn on the cob, and shrimp), and Awendaw (a local version of spoonbread made with cornmeal and grits). Truck farmers continue to grow tomatoes, peppers, peanuts, greens, eggplants, sweet potatoes, and corn. *Charleston Receipts*, a cookbook of traditional recipes published by the city's Junior League in 1950, has sold nearly a million copies, and it remains in print. Both Savannah and Charleston have reinstated successful weekly farmers markets throughout their metropolitan areas. Savannah has seen a huge increase in tourism since the publication of the John Berendt's international best-seller *Midnight in the Garden of Good and Evil* in 1994 and the airing of several television programs that feature local cooks.

JOHN MARTIN TAYLOR
Charleston, South Carolina

Karen Hess, *The Carolina Rice Kitchen: The African Connection* (1992); Richard J. Hooker, ed., *A Colonial Plantation Cookbook: The Receipt Book of Harriet Pinckney Horry, 1770* (1984); Mary V. Huguenin and Anne M. Stoney, eds., *Charleston Receipts* (1950); Charles Joyner, *Down by the Riverside: A South Carolina Slave Community* (1984); Sallie Ann Robinson, *Gullah Home Cooking the Daufuskie Way* (2003); Sarah Rutledge, *The Carolina Housewife* (1847); John Martin Taylor, *Hoppin' John's Lowcountry Cooking* (1992).

Lunch Counters (Civil Rights Era)

The struggle over who sat down with whom at the tables and lunch counters of the South proved to be one of the signal issues of the civil rights movement. The modern sit-in movement began on 1 February 1960, when four freshmen at North Carolina Agricultural and Technical College—Joseph McNeil, Franklin McCain, David Richmond, and Ezell Blair Jr.—walked into an F. W. Woolworth Company store in Greensboro, N.C., and requested service at the lunch counter. They were refused. A larger group of students returned the next day. Within two weeks, students in 11 cities staged sit-ins, primarily at lunch counters in downtown department stores. Their efforts were well planned and nonviolent. Students in Nashville developed an etiquette guide for protesters: "Do show yourself friendly on the counter at all times. Do sit straight and always face the counter. Don't strike back, or curse back if attacked. Don't laugh out. Don't hold conversations. Don't block entrances."

By March, sit-ins spread to 30 cities in seven southern states. In Charlotte, N.C., a merchant unscrewed the seats from his lunch counter. Other stores cordoned off seats so that every customer had to stand. Writing in the *Carolina Israelite*, Harry Golden of Charlotte noted that "It is only when the Negro 'sets' that the fur begins to fly." As a tongue-in-cheek solution, he proposed the "Golden Vertical Negro Plan," stipulating that all sit-down lunch counters be refashioned for stand-up meals. Problem solved.

On the surface, the sit-ins were a struggle for equal access to public accom-

Ronald Martin, Robert Patterson, and Mark Martin stage a sit-in after being refused service at an F.W. Woolworth lunch counter, Greensboro, N.C., 1960 (Library of Congress [LC-DIG-ppmsca-08095], Washington, D.C.)

modations. But the symbolism of the table was also important. Sharing a meal signaled both physical intimacy and social equality, argues Diane McWhorter. McWhorter writes that Clark Foreman, a Georgian, often told the story of a white girl from his home state who would visit her mulatto child at the orphanage but declined the administrator's suggestions that she lunch with him. "Well I couldn't do it," said the child's mother. "Eat with niggers?"

As the sit-in movement caught fire across the South, the locus extended from lunch counters to all restaurants. Some white restaurateurs subscribed to the principles of massive resistance. Among the most well known were Maurice Bessinger, of Maurice's Piggy Park in Columbia, S.C.; Ollie McClung, of Ollie's Barbecue in Birmingham, Ala.; and Lester Maddox, of the Pickrick Cafeteria in Atlanta, Ga.

When, on 2 July, President Lyndon B. Johnson signed the Civil Rights Act of 1964, declaring segregation in places of public accommodation to be unlawful, many restaurateurs acquiesced. Others, like Bessinger, McClung, and Maddox, fought integration through the courts.

Others refashioned their restaurants into "key clubs." Most were clubs in name only, relying upon something akin to the "paper bag test" to screen admittance: if your skin was lighter in color than a paper bag, they let you sit down. Otherwise, it was backdoor service or take-out. By the late 1960s the key club system was on the wane; by the late 1970s most lunch counters and restaurants were fully integrated.

JOHN T. EDGE
University of Mississippi

William H. Chafe, *Civilities and Civil Rights: Greensboro, North Carolina, and the Black Struggle for Freedom* (1981); Bob Short, *Everything Is Pickrick: The Life of Lester Maddox* (1999); Juan Williams, *Eyes on the Prize: America's Civil Rights Years, 1954–1965* (1988); Miles Wolff, *Lunch at the Five and Ten: The Greensboro Sit-ins: A Contemporary History* (1970).

Meals

At mealtime, communication among diners gathered around the table is just as important as the food served. For rich or poor, black or white, shared eating opportunities provide valuable time and open lines to assess the day ahead or the day that is ending.

Traditionally, a southern meal relies upon an appreciation for the harvest, for farm food—fresh, local, and in season. The farming lifestyle set the tone for traditional southern meals. Southern economics were long driven by the tempo of agrarian life. Simply prepared, with layers of flavors, food served at wealthy as well as humble tables used the same basic recipes. The cooks who worked in the kitchens of the wealthy were preparing the same dishes served in their own homes, all based on the agricultural harvest. Necessity, availability, and innovation on the part of the cook wrote the recipes of the South. Such motivations and inspirations crossed ethnic and racial lines.

The region is famous for its huge breakfast plates that include farm eggs, cured or fresh pork such as bacon, sausage, or ham, and biscuits with gravy made from the fat of the pork. While the generous use of fat in cooking has been shunned in recent years, fat was long a precious commodity for frugal cooks intent upon imparting both flavor and caloric heft to dishes.

Fresh fruit in season and local honey, molasses, or sorghum mixed with fresh butter (for sopping biscuits), as well as strong coffee, play supporting roles in a traditional country breakfast. Although not everyone living south of the Mason-Dixon line is a farmer, the idea that starting out a work day with a farmer's breakfast to keep one's energy flowing is not lost on modern southerners.

Dinner is the name traditionally given to the midday meal in the South, which was long considered the principal meal of the day. Hearty meals served in the middle of the day brought the farmer in from the fields to refuel. They also brought the businessman home to eat with his family or to a boarding-house restaurant that served home-style meals. Preparing the main meal in the early morning allowed the cook to use the cool of the day to fire up the stove and ovens rather than add to the heat in the house later in the afternoon. On a summer day, dinner might consist of vegetables alone. Beans would serve as the main protein, and fresh summer vegetables such as corn, tomatoes, okra, squash, and cucumbers would be served with a slice of cornbread. For special occasions and on Sundays, two or three meats like beef, pork, or chicken would be added to that roster. Dinner was served family style, meaning that all food was placed in big bowls or on serving platters and passed around.

In today's South, the modern take on the tradition of dinner plays out in family-style or meat-and-three restaurants. Instinctually, southerners migrate to a hearty meal in the middle of the day—a square meal, shared with friends or family. Country cooking or soul food restaurants are popular in small towns as well as big cities.

Another midday meal that should be mentioned is lunch, food that is taken away from home to eat on the road or at work. Containers for carrying a meal might be a sack, box, or bucket. Factory, rail, and field workers, as well as schoolchildren, used metal lunch boxes often but relied on a more humble container that would be called a lunch bucket. Food packed for lunch away from home could include a piece of chicken or meat, maybe a biscuit left over from breakfast or cornbread, and perhaps a fresh tomato, cucumber, or piece of fruit that could be cut up with a pocket knife. Sandwiches wrapped in wax paper and a thermos full of coffee helped bolster a worker on the midnight shift.

In the days before the Civil Rights Act was passed in 1964, blacks traveling through the South had to take food with them. Whether by train, bus, or car, moving through town or country, African Americans were forced to carry their own meals because most restaurants would not allow them to dine. A shoe box lunch might contain fried chicken, biscuits, and cake wrapped in paper. While their home-cooked meal was probably better than what they would find in a restaurant on the road, for most blacks the food took on a bitter quality because of the lack of freedom to choose.

Supper, or the evening meal, was normally simple, reheated food from dinner, although it was still served at the table, family style. Again, the mealtime allowed for communication within the family and, very important to each meal, provided a moment to bow heads before digging in to say "grace" or a "blessing" over the food. Supper was served early in the evening and the meal took care of any leftovers from the day. Nothing was wasted. Leftover cornbread was crumbled into a glass and eaten with milk or buttermilk poured over it. Many claim that milk and cornbread are a natural sleep aid.

Mealtime in the modern South continues to change with the influence of national chain fast-food restaurants. Meals eaten on the go threaten to replace family communication around the table. It is encouraging, however, to note the rebirth and emergence of small, family farms that are finding success in sales to the public through green markets and produce stands as well as to restaurants and chefs who care about locally grown food. This blossoming interest in food grown locally and enjoyed in season may encourage southern diners to regularly gather round a communal table to enjoy their meals.

ANGIE MOSIER
Atlanta, Georgia

Joseph E. Dabney, *Smokehouse Ham, Spoon Bread, and Scuppernong Wine: The Folklore and Art of Southern Appalachian Cooking* (1998); John Egerton, *Southern Food: At Home, on the Road, and in History* (1993); Martha McCulloch-Williams, *Dishes and Beverages of the Old South* (1913, 1988); Kathy Starr, *The Soul of Southern Cooking* (1989).

Music and Food

The subject of southern food has been invoked in various types of music, particularly within the blues genre. Food-inspired songs were, and are still, written for novelty purposes. Some use lyrical analogies to represent love and sex. Others portray food as a reminiscence, be it about a place or a person, or use it as a device to further the storytelling element of their music.

Food images can be found in early American folk music and spirituals such as "Turkey in the Straw" and "Bringing in the Sheaves." It later made its way into the minstrel shows of the late 19th and early 20th centuries, in which food entered songs as a Tin Pan Alley tool to invoke the mammy figure in lyrical reminiscences of the South. "They Made It Twice as Nice as Paradise and They Called It Dixieland" is an example of this technique. The singer remembers being a small child in the company of his or her mammy, who told mythic stories about the creation of the South as a place of immense beauty and gentility. The chorus claimed that the woman was an angel who was brought to earth where "They put some fine spring chickens on the land / And taught my Mammy how to use a frying pan."

Early blues singers incorporated food terminology into their music as metaphors reflecting the new sexual freedoms of a post–Civil War society. Both male and female performers integrated food into their lyrics as a way of making the racy subject matter of their music more socially acceptable. These songs substituted for parts of the human anatomy terms such as *banana, pig meat, jellyroll, jelly bean,* and *pie. Biscuit* implied an attractive young woman, and *biscuit roller* conjured the image of an attractive young woman with desirable sexual skills. Coffee grinding was an action used in blues lyrics to connote sexual intercourse ("Coffee Grinding Blues" by Lucille Bogan), as was going to the mill to grind corn ("What's the Matter with the Mill?" by Memphis Minnie and Kansas Joe). According to lyrical analyses, the mill signifies female sexual organs, with the man serving as the miller. Grinding a woman is engaging in intercourse, and the result is meal, or a child.

Women, in particular, sang about food as commodity. Lucille Bogan sang in "Coffee Grinding Blues" and "Barbecue Bess" that she grinds her coffee "at two or three dollars a pound" and sells her barbecue "cheap 'cause [she's] got good stuff." Bogan took her sexual commodity to a literal level in "Groceries on the Shelf" when she sang, "My name is Piggly Wiggly and I swear you can help yourself / And you've got to have your greenback, and it don't take nothin' else." Artists have continuously incorporated the blues format into food songs. According to Roy Blount Jr., there are over 55 known food songs that use *blues* in their title, including "Texas Hambone Blues" by Milton Brown and His Musical Brownies, "Milk 'Em in the Evening Blues" by the McGee Brothers, "Your Greens Give Me the Blues" by Reverend Billy C. Wirtz, "Oreo Cookie Blues" by Lonnie Mack, "Jelly Whipping Blues" by Tampa Red, "Grunt Meat Blues" by the Memphis Seven, and "Ration Blues" by Louis Jordan and His Tympani Five.

Country music also embraced the use of food terminology but in a manner less sexual and more suited to storytelling. George Jones described his father's moonshine business, as well as efforts to stop it, in "White Lightning." In "Church" Lyle Lovett sang about being at a religious service in which the minister would not finish his sermon, resulting in the congregation's become ravenous; a dove flies into the sanctuary and lights upon the pulpit, whereupon the minister promptly consumes it. Robert Earl Keen touted the virtues of barbecue, singing,

> Barbeque makes old ones feel young
> Barbeque makes everybody someone
> If you're feelin' puny and you don't know what to do
> Treat yourself to some meat—eat some barbeque.

Probably the most famous country song involving foodstuffs is "Jambalaya" by Hank Williams Sr., which was released in 1952 and has been recorded by over 20 other artists.

At present, two of the most prominent purveyors of southern foodways in music are the band Southern Culture on the Skids and singer-songwriter Jimmy Buffett. Based in Chapel Hill, N.C., and started in the mid 1980s, Southern Culture on the Skids incorporates food into their stage shows, throwing fried chicken into the audience as well as singing about it in "Eight Piece Box" and "Fried Chicken and Gasoline." Their lyrics act to document and preserve aspects of southern culture, as exemplified in the song "Carve That 'Possum," which states, "The best darn eatin' in the whole southern land / well that possum meat is just all right by me / always so red and always so sweet." Jimmy Buffett, a native of Mississippi, has incorporated food into much of his music in the same storytelling manner employed by many country musicians. "Life Is Just a Tire Swing" invokes food from his childhood in the South in the lines "'Jambalaya' was the only song I could sing / Blackberry pickin', eatin' fried chicken." The song "I Will Play for Gumbo" pays homage to the southern dish, about which Buffett sings,

> Maybe it's the sausage or those pretty pink shrimp
> Or that popcorn rice that makes me blow up like a blimp.
> Maybe it's that voodoo from Marie Leveaux,
> But I will play for gumbo.

RENNA TUTEN
University of Mississippi

Roy Blount Jr., in *Cornbread Nation 1: The Best of Southern Food Writing*, ed. John Egerton (2002); Paul Oliver, *Screening the Blues: Aspects of the Blues Tradition* (1968); Stephen J. Whitfield, *Southern Cultures* (Summer 2002).

New Orleans Foodways

When the French nobleman Jean-Baptiste Le Moyne, Sieur de Bienville, founded New Orleans in 1718, he did not likely have cooking on his mind. But the city's French beginnings seem to have augured well for its future as a gastronomic capital. When Bienville stepped onto the soggy bank of the Mississippi River and named the spot for the Duc d'Orléans, classical French cuisine was still in the making; it would not come to full flower until the early 1800s, with the rise of such innovators as Antonin Carême.

France had a major role in shaping New Orleans gastronomy, before and after Louisiana attained statehood in 1803. But, as history would have it, so did the Africans and Caribbeans who also sailed up the river's mouth during the colonial period. Lesser influences came from the region's Native Americans and the small number of Spanish colonists present in the city during Spain's control of Louisiana from 1762 to 1803.

The predominant word used to describe traditional New Orleans cooking is *Creole*, which implies a mix of divergent cultures, especially those of Africa, Europe, and the New World. Up to the present day the staples of a Creole cook's pantry would likely include cayenne pepper, named for the southern Caribbean island of its supposed origin; the okra, sweet potatoes, squashes, and beans first transported from Africa, either directly or via the West Indies; and such contributions of the native Indian tribes as corn and sassafras, the leaves of which were ground down to become filé for thickening gumbo (a hybrid of soup and stew, often served with rice). There also would be an array of spices and herbs to enrich the flavor of the fish, shrimp, crabs, turtles, and oysters that were drawn from the vast and plentiful marshes and fishing grounds south of the city toward the Gulf of Mexico. As for meats, the Creole cook had a bounty of them at his or her disposal—not just chicken, beef, and pork, but venison, ducks, and other game brought into town by hunters and trappers from the outlying marshes and backwoods.

During most of the 1790s a slave rebellion, led by Toussaint L'Ouverture, raged on the Caribbean island of Saint Domingue (now Haiti). The widespread violence inflicted by L'Ouverture and his compatriots prompted a large number of French-descended colonists, as well as many slaves, to seek refuge in New Orleans. Many brought their island foodways with them. In the early 1800s a group of the exiles opened some of the city's first eating and drinking establishments, among them the Café des Réfugiés near the old French Market. The café kitchen's repertoire is unknown, although one contemporary reference mentions *sagamité*, a sort of cornmeal mush borrowed from the local Indian cultures.

Meanwhile, African-descended New Orleanians were contributing such iron-pot dishes as jambalayas (paella-like concoctions of shellfish, meat, rice, and tomatoes that might have had a Spanish ancestry as well); greens cooked down with salted pork; the Caribbean-style *congri* of cowpeas and rice; gumbos blending different combinations of pork sausage, chicken giblets, and seafood, and a host of stews thickened with roux (flour browned in fat or oil), all joining to form a cooking style using modest ingredients to create rich flavors.

Throughout the colonial period and afterward, the well-heeled French Creoles of New Orleans maintained close ties to the mother country. The classic cuisine that began developing in France during the 1800s quickly spread to the former colony. By the mid-19th century, moneyed New Orleanians were drink-

Red beans and rice, a New Orleans signature dish (Courtesy NewOrleansOnline.com)

ing burgundies and clarets from the vineyards of France. Kitchens in the finer homes and hotel banquet halls were turning out galantines, croustades, and potages, along with such classically French sauces as marchand de vin, béarnaise, ravigôte, rémoulade, and hollandaise. Most of these have become permanent mainstays of the city's gastronomy, especially in such "old-line" creole restaurants as Arnaud's, Brennan's, Broussard's, and—the oldest of them all—Antoine's.

Angelo (alias Antoine) Alciatore arrived in New Orleans around 1838. Born in Alassio, Italy, he had traveled from Marseilles, where, according to family lore, he had been a successful chef. In 1840 he opened a boardinghouse in the French Quarter on St. Louis Street that quickly gained a reputation for its food, prompting him to establish a restaurant. By 1874 Alciatore's restaurant business had prospered sufficiently for him to open a complex of handsome and spacious dining rooms at what is now 713 St. Louis Street, offering lavish, elegant French dishes—*escargots à la bourgignonne, pommes de terre soufflées, pompano en papillote,* and, the most famous of all Antoine's dishes, *huitres en coquilles* (oysters on the half shell) *à la Rockefeller.* More than 160 years later, Alciatore's descendants were still operating the restaurant he founded.

By the mid-19th century, New Orleans's location near the mouth of the Mississippi River had made it second only to New York as a shipping center. It also was a natural port of entry for European immigrants. Joining the steady flow of new arrivals from France were others from Germany, Italy, and Ireland. Many of their culinary traditions found their way into the local Creole mix.

Among the newcomers in 1853 was a young German, Elizabeth Kettenring, who had left her native Bavaria to join her brother, a worker in the old French Market on the riverfront. Kettenring eventually married Louis Dutrey, a French Market butcher. Ten years later the couple opened a restaurant across from the market at the corner of Decatur and Madison Streets. Local and out-of-town businessmen, market vendors, and their customers crammed into the Dutreys' restaurant for Madame Dutrey's cuisine, especially in the prenoon hours when she served hefty breakfasts. After the death of Louis Dutrey, Elizabeth married the restaurant's bartender, Hippolyte Begue. The restaurant, renamed Madame Begue's, became known for such dishes as sautéed calf's liver, roasted duck, creamed chicken in puff pastry, turtle soup, codfish à la bordelaise, and *daube à l'italienne*, along with Creole-style bisques, oyster omelets, jambalayas, and soups. By 1906, the year of Elizabeth Begue's death, she had acquired a national reputation as a chef, and many of her fellow German Americans had established themselves as some of New Orleans's leading hoteliers and restaurateurs. Large, lavish restaurants bearing such names as Kolb's, Fabacher's, Vonderbank's, and Gluck's prospered up to World War I and beyond. Most offered cross-cultural menus containing not only German, but also Creole and even Italian dishes.

In 1905 Jean Galatoire, who had recently arrived from the town of Pau in the French Pyrenees, joined two of his nephews in purchasing Victor's restaurant, a Creole-style bistro on Bourbon Street. A decade or so later, just a few blocks away from the renamed Galatoire's, came Arnaud's, founded by a French-born wine salesman and self-proclaimed count, and Broussard's, operated by two brothers from the Cajun town of Opelousas. All three restaurants traded in many of the warhorses of the French-Creole repertoire—delicately spiced gumbos and sautéed seafood and meats swathed in French sauces, rich with cream or butter.

By the 1920s the city's large Sicilian population began opening restaurants, the first being Turci's Italian Garden at 827 Decatur Street, where the celebrated tenor Enrico Caruso and his entourage dined during his appearances at the New Orleans Athanaeum. In addition to the 23 pastas on Turci's menu were truffled *paté de foie gras*, oyster omelets, caviar on toast, and shrimp *à la Créole* with rice.

Two sandwiches that have endured as New Orleans classics emerged during the early 20th century as well. Sicilian delicatessens in the French Quarter began selling the now-familiar muffuletta, a sandwich of cold cuts, cheeses, and olive salad on a large, mushroom-shaped Italian loaf. Also making its appearance was the poor boy sandwich, made by filling New Orleans's distinctive French-style bread with fried seafoods, roast beef with gravy, or any of a multitude of other hot and cold ingredients.

With the post–World War II era came a gradual move toward more variety in the repertoires of New Orleans's restaurant kitchens. In 1956 members of the Brennan family established their still-thriving restaurant dynasty with the opening of Brennan's Restaurant at 417 Royal Street. "Breakfast at Brennan's" was the draw in the posh and fashionable dining rooms. Beginning at 8 o'clock every morning save Christmas, the menu brimmed with lavishly sauced and garnished egg dishes, often paired with "eye-opener" cocktails such as brandy milk punch or absinthe frappé. Lunches and dinners were equally festive, frequently capped with the finale of bananas Foster, the restaurant's famous dessert of ice cream covered in bananas sautéed with brown sugar, butter, and banana liqueur.

The trendsetter of the 1960s was Leruth's, across the river from New Orleans in Gretna, where founder-chef Warren Leruth put his native Louisiana spin on an essentially French menu, with creations such as oyster-and-artichoke soup and sautéed soft-shell crabs topped with lump crabmeat.

In 1971 the founders of Brennan's Restaurant bought Commander's Palace, an old, traditional-style Creole restaurant in New Orleans's Garden District. Soon afterward the Brennan family members partitioned their restaurant properties, which had risen to five in the 15 years since the founding of Brennan's in the French Quarter. Siblings Ella and Dick Brennan became proprietors of Commander's, where, during the 1970s, they oversaw the creation of what they called "haute Creole" cooking—originally under chef Paul Prudhomme, who was born and raised in Louisiana's Cajun country. Prudhomme brought a more regional identity to the Commander's menu, going beyond the more polished Creole techniques and ingredients to the lustier traditions of southwest Louisiana's Cajuns.

Prudhomme left Commander's in 1980 to open his own K-Paul's Louisiana Kitchen, where he first created blackened redfish, a typical example of the peppery, assertively seasoned cuisine he called Cajun. Prudhomme became a virtual proselytizer for his earthy but complex cooking and sparked a virtual national craze for the Cajun style as he had defined it. He was succeeded at Commander's Palace by Emeril Lagasse, a Rhode Islander with French Canadian and Portuguese roots who brought his own innovative ideas to the Brennan establishment's culinary tradition of deep, full flavors wrought from ingredients that Creole cooks had used for generations. Prudhomme and Lagasse, and a succession of their disciples, brought a new open-mindedness to New Orleans restaurant cooking, forging the multifaceted, contemporary approach that now coexists with the city's much older Creole way of doing things.

The devastation caused to New Orleans by Hurricane Katrina, in August 2005, affected restaurants, as well as other aspects of the city's life. Some restaurants opened in Baton Rouge until they could return to the city, and numerous eating places faced a shortage of qualified employees, many of whom had fled the city. In general, restaurants in the French Quarter and Uptown were restored to operation, even if it was limited, within six months. The Southern Foodways Alliance organized efforts to reopen, in the spring of 2007, Willie Mae's Scotch House, a corner café in the Treme neighborhood. Dooky Chase's, in the same neighborhood, reopened soon after, a symbol of the city's Creole food tradition and its resiliency.

GENE BOURG
New Orleans, Louisiana

Mme. Bégué's Recipes of Old New Orleans Creole Cookery (1900); Pip Brennan, Jimmy Brennan, and Ted Brennan, *Breakfast at Brennan's and Dinner, Too* (1994); Rima and Richard Collin, *New Orleans Cookbook* (1987); Walter Cowan, Charles L. Dufour, and O. K. LeBlanc, *New Orleans: Yesterday, Today, and Tomorrow* (2001); John Egerton, *Southern Food: At Home, on the Road, in History* (1987); Peter S. Feibleman, *American Cooking: Creole and Acadian* (1971); Leon Galatoire, *Leon Galatoire's Cookbook* (1995); Lafcadio Hearn, *Lafcadio Hearn's Creole Cook Book* (1990); *The Picayune's Creole Cook Book* (1922).

Pork

When Hernando de Soto was roaming across the southeastern part of North America in the 1530s, he would not have used the term *South*, but his introduction of 13 pigs to Florida became the founding of an enduring hog kingdom that would define the region's cuisine and help to nourish southerners for centuries. By the time English settlers came to Virginia in 1607 with their own domesticated pigs, wild hogs were roaming the countryside. Pork, along with corn, soon dominated the foodways of colonial southerners, establishing the familiar "hog and hominy" diet that would last into the 20th century. The hog and its meat had a bad reputation with upper-class colonial southerners, though. The squeamish Virginian William Byrd II complained that frontier settlers he met ate so much pork, to the exclusion of other foods, that it caused scurvy and facial disfiguration. Another upper-class Virginian, Robert Beverley, wrote in 1705 that "Hogs swarm like Vermine upon the earth."

Southerners are said to eat every part of the hog "but the squeal"
(Photographer unknown, United States Department of Agriculture)

Beverley was complaining about a fundamental basis of hog raising from the colonial era through the 19th century—the open range where swine roamed, eating acorns and other grazing food in thickly forested woods of the Southeast and providing a headache for nearby farmers raising their tobacco or cotton. Yeoman farmers could easily keep hogs free, capturing them at the end of the year, fattening some up for slaughter, and driving others to market. Along with growing vegetables, this open-range grazing enabled them to maintain an independent way of life that included a diet rich in meat. Hogs thus moved across the Upper South with pioneer farmers and thrived in piney woods, the hill country, and scrub lands that often were not the best cotton-growing land but which were the source of an independent lifestyle for hog raisers. While the hog had special meaning for small farmers, pork was a pervasive food in the South. A magazine writer in 1860 noted that in the South "it is fat bacon and pork, fat and pork only, and that continually morning, noon, and night, for all classes, sexes, ages, and conditions." That same writer insisted that "hogs' lard is the very oil that moves the machinery of life," and that southerners would just as soon give up their coffee and tobacco as forgo "the essence of hog."

Southerners have indeed eaten many forms of pork, including cooking in lard. Hog killing was a familiar end-of-the-year ritual for farm families, yielding chitterlings (small intestines), livers, and brains that were consumed quickly. Other parts of the hog could be preserved to last longer. Country ham, for example, is made from the hindquarters of a year-old hog, cured with salt and (at times) sugar, smoked, and aged for a year or longer. The process was well known in such Upper South states as Virginia, Maryland, and North Carolina as far back as the colonial era, and it spread with westward settlement to Tennessee and Kentucky. These states remain what John and Dale Reed call the "ham heartland." The relative ease with which pork could be preserved was a prime reason for its pervasiveness in the South. Bacon, sausage, or fried ham was standard southern breakfast fare, but pork, usually fried, was also a centerpiece of the midday meal. Vegetables were likely boiled with a piece of pork to give desired flavor.

Production of pork spiraled downward after the Civil War, as southern yeomen found themselves increasingly caught up in a commodity-crop economy in which the diminishing open range often made it difficult for them to maintain their mixed economy that had included hogs. Their consumption of pork did not decline, but now their pork came from hogs raised in places like Iowa, as they increasingly purchased their pork from midwestern packing houses. The Midwest became the meatpacking region of the United States, with pigs first commercially slaughtered in Cincinnati, which soon became known as Porkopolis. Side meat has been a main course for poorer southerners and a seasoning agent for many more. It might be called fatback, salt pork, sow belly, middlings, white meat, streak-of-lean, bacon, white bacon, seasoning meat, or just meat. Bacon grease, or "drippings," remains a popular seasoning in southern cookbook recipes, and pots of beans and greens still call out for a bit of hog jowl or side meat.

Early in the 20th century southern state legislatures passed laws requiring fenced lands for livestock, bringing a final end to free-range grazing of hogs by small proprietors. U.S. Department of Agriculture demonstration agents taught southern farmers to raise hogs in pens, a midwestern-style confinement system. Confinement was successful, and southern farmers raised healthy hogs. In the 1920s eastern North Carolina and southeastern Virginia hog farmers adopted a system of indoor confinement of hogs in sheds and barns, a system pioneered by the southern poultry industry. Small, independent operators virtually disappeared, as economies of scale produced larger operators.

Wendell Murphy, a vocational agriculture teacher in North Carolina, developed the system to its fullest with his Murphy Family Farms. In the 1960s he had been one of those small-scale hog operators, but an outbreak of hog cholera and the threatened quarantine of his herd led him to disperse his swine to other farmers beyond the quarantine area. They raised the hogs for him, with Murphy soon requiring them to adopt the confinement system. This system made Murphy a celebrity—"Boss Hogg" who became an influential North Carolina legislator. The system made Murphy's farmers raising the hogs into dependents with less and less independence. The once free-ranging hogs, the symbols of southern farmers' independence, were now imprisoned in minuscule spaces, waiting to drop through adjacent ramps directly to the slaughterhouse. The system created a nightmare of pollution, with massive amounts of urine and feces waste stagnant in large "lagoons." The farms, lagoons, and slaughterhouses sit near rivers and creeks that spread pollution to wetlands, resulting in dire ecological harm to nearby flora and fauna.

North Carolina now is the second-largest pork-producing state. In 2001 there were 640 operations with 5,000 or more hogs in the state, with Iowa's 500 the next largest. The movement is toward consolidation. Between 1993 and 2002, there was an 80 percent decline in hog farms in North Carolina, and every other southern state, from Virginia to Texas, experienced a decline of between 60 and 100 percent. In 2004 the nation's hog herd was 60 million, with about 20 percent of that located in the South. Smithfield Farms recently bought Murphy Family Farms, securing its position as one of the great American meat-packing companies.

Today, southerners eat less pork than in the past, but barbecue remains an iconic food, whatever the tomato, mustard, vinegar, or other sauce that accompanies it across the region. Native Americans pioneered many aspects of the later cuisine of the South, including smoking meat before Europeans and Africans arrived. On the southern frontier, barbecues became social events, bringing a scattered community together over smoked hog. Plantations were sites of summer barbecue cooking, with slave men doing much of the long and hot work of cooking. Many of the surviving barbecue pit masters in the South are African American. Stephen A. Smith argues that "barbecue is taken as seriously as religion" in the South, with a reverence for traditional ways, evocation of the region's ancient camp meeting social life, an occasion for communal participation, egalitarian fellowship, and a shared interracial dimension. Meanwhile, the image of the hog can be seen on signs towering above contemporary barbecue shacks and restaurants, symbolizing its abiding place in southern culture.

CHARLES REAGAN WILSON
University of Mississippi

Rodney Barker, *And the Waters Turned to Blood* (1997); Joseph E. Dabney, *Smokehouse Ham, Spoon Bread, and Scuppernong Wine: The Folklore and Art of Southern*

Appalachian Cooking (1998); John Egerton, *Southern Food: At Home, on the Road, in History* (1987); Sam Bowers Hilliard, *Hog Meat and Hoecake: Food Supply in the Old South, 1840–1860* (1972); http://www.ers.usda.gov/Briefing/Hogs/Background.htm.

Poultry

Poultry is a common item in the food consumption patterns of southerners today, and the regional taste for fried chicken is one that has persisted for many years. Poultry, especially chicken, has served as a regular but supplementary meat to pork, which dominated southern diets during the 1800s and 1900s.

Chicken was most common in the diets of well-to-do farmers and was regarded among the less affluent population as a semiluxury item. It was a popular Sunday dish and was often served to visitors, including the local preacher. Humorous tales about the preacher's love for chicken abound in both black and white folklore. In addition to fried chicken, among the most popular chicken dishes in the South have been stewed chicken, with the bird slow-cooked until falling apart; chicken pilau or perloo, made with rice and seasoning vegetables (a dish having Mediterranean origins and likely entering the South through Charleston); chicken and dumplings, with the chicken again cooked to pieces and either cornmeal or flour dumplings added at the end; and country captain, a rather exotic dish, with currants, almonds, crisp bacon pieces, rice, and chutney all part of a recipe that is attributed to Savannah for its origins in the South and which has been more common along the Atlantic coast than in the interior.

A glance at cookbooks suggests that southerners have roasted, baked, fried, sautéed, grilled, and barbecued chickens for centuries. Chicken has been a key ingredient in such regional dishes as gumbo, jambalaya, and Brunswick stew. People prize different parts of the chicken, and its neck, liver, heart, feet, and gizzard are all consumed. Cookbooks since the 19th century have also included recipes for wild duck, turkey, and goose, as well as such fowl as blackbird, lark, quail, grouse, guinea fowl, peafowl, pigeon, and other game.

Chickens were kept on practically every farm and often ran loose in the barnyard area. As a result farmers virtually lived with their chicken flock. Chickens could be kept on a minimum of feed and were much more convenient to slaughter and prepare for eating than either pigs or cattle. Predators such as the fox and the hawk were a constant problem for the farmer's barnyard flock, thus requiring the farmer to keep both his dog and shotgun handy.

Since 1900 the per capita rate of consumption of chicken has increased markedly, outstripping the growth in demand for other meats such as beef and pork. During this period, and especially in recent decades, very important changes have occurred in the production of chickens, and these had an effect on both the economy and culture of the South. A few decades ago the rural population of the South was largely self-sufficient in terms of supplying its chicken and egg needs. Farmers maintained small flocks of chickens for their own use. Often city dwellers' demand for chickens and eggs was met by farmers who sold excess production to town merchants. This trade furnished butter-and-egg money for farm housewives. Women worked with county extension agents to improve and modernize their production and marketing of eggs and chickens, often setting up roadside stands or selling at special farmers' markets. Historians credit the profitability of women's egg and chicken sales with seeing many families through the Depression's hard times. Today it is rare indeed to find farm families that produce chickens and eggs. In place of this production system have come large-scale, highly specialized mass-production techniques involving the utilization of the latest technological advancements.

This modern era of poultry production dates from the 1930s; its methods had almost totally replaced the previous production techniques by the 1950s. The modern poultry farmer has one or more chicken houses, growing 10,000 to 20,000 birds per house. Ordinarily each batch is grown under contract with large agribusiness firms during a period of 7 to 10 weeks. Market-ready chickens are taken to processing plants for slaughtering, dressing, and packing, and are later transported by refrigerated truck to widely dispersed markets. The poultry industry is characterized by a vertical integration in which an agribusiness firm, either through direct ownership or contract, controls the entire production process. Such firms own processing plants, feed mills, and hatcheries, and contract with farmers to raise the chickens. Because of these arrangements the farmer has little voice in the industry. Some observers label this type of poultry farming a modern version of sharecropping. However, one advantage of this production system to the farmer is that it reduces the capital needed to start poultry farming.

Today a large proportion of southern poultry is produced by farmers who derive only a part of their total income from this source. The chief wage earner may have a full-time industrial or commercial job while the family raises chickens as a supplementary source of income, or chicken farming may be ancillary to other agricultural pursuits. Labor needs of poultry farming are minimal because of the automation of the process. The management of two chicken houses of 10,000 to 20,000 chickens each can usually be accomplished during the evenings and on weekends by family members.

Several of the nation's main poultry-growing areas are located in the South. Northeast Georgia was one of the first areas to begin large-scale commercial chicken production, with Gainesville serving as a processing plant center and the location for feed mills and hatcheries. Both northeast Georgia and north-west Arkansas began to develop as poultry centers in the late 1930s and early 1940s. They were followed in the 1940s by centers in south central Mississippi and central North Carolina, and in the 1950s by northern Alabama, around Cullman County. Today a trip through these areas provides visible indications of the industry's impact on the landscape, with the long, narrow chicken houses on farms and the specialized feed trucks and poultry-transport vehicles that operate between feed mills, farms, and processing plants.

The emergence of chicken production in these areas largely reflects chang-ing conditions of traditional subsistence farming. Many of these regions were from the beginning of settlement poor farm areas. They were populated by low-income farm families who had lost a previous source of farm revenue—cot-ton in northeast Georgia, northern Alabama, and south central Mississippi; tobacco in North Carolina; and fruit in northwest Arkansas. A new source of farm income such as chicken raising was welcomed enthusiastically by these farmers. Local entrepreneurs and agricultural officials were largely instrumental in establishing this industry. J. D. Jewell, for instance, played an important role in establishing production in northeast Georgia. He owned a small feed store in Gainesville in the 1930s and encouraged neighboring farmers to grow chick-ens, affording him a market outlet for feed and other supplies. Because cash with which to buy baby chicks and feed was seriously limited among farmers, Jewell supplied his customers with credit until their chickens were marketed. However, when the chickens reached the proper age and size for marketing, the farmer had no way to get them to market. Jewell provided transportation to haul the live chickens to urban markets. Later his company became one of the major vertical integrators in northeast Georgia, and he became nationally recognized as an industry leader.

Today southern poultry raisers dominate national chicken production, which all together produced over half of the 8.5 million chickens raised in the nation in 2002. The five leading states are Arkansas, Georgia, Alabama, North Carolina, and Mississippi. Four of the five most profitable chicken compa-nies began in the South: Tyson Foods in Springdale, Ark.; Gold Kist, a farm-cooperative business in Atlanta; Holly Farms in Wilkesboro, N.C.; and Perdue Farms Inc., in Salisbury, Md. Tyson Foods acquired Holly Farms in 1989, ac-quired diversified food production companies in the 1990s, and solidified its position as the world's largest poultry producer by merging with Hudson Foods in 1998. Critics have pointed to issues of pollution and inhumane treatment of poultry in this leading agribusiness. Chicken has become the fastest-growing part of the fast-food business, profiting such southern companies as Kentucky Fried Chicken, Church's Fried Chicken, Popeyes, and Bojangles.

J. DENNIS LORD
University of North Carolina at Charlotte

Karen Davis, *Prisoned Chickens, Poisoned Eggs: An Inside Look at the Modern Poultry Industry* (1996); J. Fraser Hart, *Annals of the Association of American Geographers* (December 1980); Sam Bowers Hilliard, *Hog Meat and Hoecake: Food Supply in the Old South, 1840–1860* (1972); Lu Ann Jones, *Mama Learned Us to Work: Farm Women in the New South* (2002); Edward Karpoff, *Agricultural Situation* (March 1959); N. R. Kleinfield, *New York Times* (9 December 1984); J. Dennis Lord, "Regional Marketing Patterns and Locational Advantages in the United States Broiler Industry" (Ph.D. dissertation, University of Georgia, 1970), *Southeastern Geographer* (April 1971); Irene A. Moke, *Journal of Geography* (October 1967); National Agricultural Center, National Poultry Museum, www.poultryscience.org/psapub/pmuseum.html; Malden C. Nesheim, *Poultry Production* (1979).

Religion and Food

The connection between food and religion runs deep in the southern Bible Belt. Eating has been an incentive for and aspect of going to church for many a southerner. Religious foodways have had a big hand in preserving and signaling change in southern cuisine. In the fellowship of church meals, many southerners feel strong connections to elements that sustain a southern as well as evangelical Christian worldview: the sacredness of family, the providence of God, and the holiness of place. Religious ways of understanding and using food also extend outside religious institutions to express the sacredness of southern culture.

Perhaps the first thing that comes to mind when thinking of southern food and religion is the practice of "dinner on the grounds" after worship. Sharing a potluck meal spread under the trees of the churchyard may have had practical origins in the evangelical camp meetings of the late 18th and early 19th centuries. Distances traveled to camp meetings might be almost as long as the sermons; worshippers were encouraged to bring provisions to share. When evangelicals (Methodist, Baptists, and others) established churches, eating "camp meeting style" persisted. After the Civil War, it proliferated and is still observed by many churches today. It is often called by the old name, although the "ground" is now more likely to be the church basement fellowship hall. The popularization of another name, "covered dish supper," parallels other changes: the evening main meal and the ubiquity of casseroles made with convenience products.

The blessing at a dinner on the grounds, 1940 (Russell Lee, photographer, Library of Congress [LC-USF33-012784-M1], Washington, D.C.)

Practical adaptations keep the church dinner feasible, but the feeling the food evokes ensures its endurance. The church dinner is a type of ritual, a practice that follows the sacred model of a community's myths or sacred stories. Rituals help to connect the truths of myths to human experience on a basic level through meanings attached to symbols. Food is highly symbolic, and food rituals exist in most religions. They tend to have similar functions, although a tradition might emphasize some functions over others. The dominant evangelical Protestantism of the South is no exception.

Dinner on the grounds, for example, is a type of feast that celebrates the idea of divine blessing on a particular land and people, especially when the foods reflect the bounty of the land. Feasts usually involve sacrifice, the ritual slaughter of an animal that invokes the divine. Overtones of sacrifice remain in church suppers, where game and barbecue are the main dishes.

Ritual meals reaffirm the boundaries of community, as often by the absence of forbidden foods as the presence of special dishes. The teaming of evangelical Protestantism with alcohol prohibitions is such a boundary marker. (It has not gone uncontested in southern Protestantism, however. For example, bourbon whiskey is often attributed to Kentucky Baptist preacher Elijah Craig.) While other traditions might employ alcoholic beverages to connote the sacred (wine in the Catholic Mass), southern Protestantism's prodigious use of sugar in church meals, from gallons of sweet tea to desserts by the dozens, reflects the special status of these meals as well as the sweet tooth of southern cuisine.

For evangelical Protestants, however, the primary religious functions of church meals follow their theological understanding of Christ's Last Supper. This is reflected in the parallel meanings of a term they use for the ritual meal in worship, *communion*, and the term they use to describe what a church meal is, *fellowship*. Both emphasize the community of believers. Partaking in activities such as church dinners reinforces the bond of community and belonging to the church family. The covered dish supper laid out for everyone to help themselves to food taken from the same pots and eaten at communal tables symbolically relates to the supper at which Christ and his disciples shared common dishes. This points to another function of church meals: commemoration. Christ told his disciples to continue to eat together, "in remembrance of me." Southern Protestants do this ritually in Communion and in their fellowship meals.

Remembrance and community are reinforced and extended on multiple levels through a variety of foodways that connect church to the rest of life. Church eating can symbolize the bond of community that goes back to early Christians and continues in the local congregation at present. It can remind churchgoers of community here and beyond. Particularly at homecoming celebrations, which center around a dinner on the ground, the idea of ancestral community is reinforced. People who no longer live in the community might return home for the occasion; it might take place in sight of not only the church building but also the church graveyard. A sense of the community's ancestry is evoked by foods associated with tradition. Cultural myths and food traditions overlap with church rituals—church food *is* southern food. Churches are among the remaining places where some traditional dishes appear with any regularity. The connections reinforce the holiness associated with both the church and culture of a special people and place.

The two-way flow between church and family is often expressed in food. A big Sunday dinner around grandma's table is sacred for many southerners, even if experienced more often in nostalgia than in reality. Churches express their family character in foodways that extend into homes. Especially during family transitions or crises, churches nourish bodies and souls alike. Church members take dishes to the homes of grieving families during mourning. After the funeral, a meal might be prepared by church members in the home or fellowship hall. The earliest evangelicals often substituted church family for kin, but the holiness of family for evangelicals today serves as a model for church community. Church meals are now frequently referred to as "family night suppers," reflecting as much an orientation to families and children as the idea of church as family.

The traditional role of nurturer of home and church assigned to women is foundational for this connection and central to foodways in southern churches. While churchmen may preside over cookouts, church eating has been largely the domain of women. Foodways both reinforce the gender hierarchy and subvert it. While the responsibility for church meals means more labor for women, it also provides opportunities for creative expression. Early church dinners might have been "make do" affairs and still might be depending on supply, money, and time. But even in tough times, church dinners have provided opportunities to celebrate as best one could through special fare. They gave cooks so inclined (or socially pressured) the chance to show off with dishes they might not make for home meals, providing a means for status and recognition. Church foodways also gave leadership and ministerial opportunities to women who were (and often still are) otherwise denied them. Through food events, women have raised money for church causes; enticed men into church participation; fed the hungry, sick, celebrating, and grieving; and acted as "ritual specialists" when they could not preside at the Communion table or preach "the bread of life" from the pulpit.

Churchwomen's cookbooks have been important sources of fund-raising for their communities. They also preserve a "herstory" of southern Protestantism and a means by which traditions are passed down. While the introduction to the cookbook of the Second Presbyterian Church of Spartanburg, S.C., gives a history of male leadership, the rest of the book documents women's activity in recipes and anecdotes. Cookbooks can be personal expressions of devotion as well as community legacies. Mrs. Rose Marie Horne, a south Georgia church cook, dedicated her recipe manuscript to "Jesus Christ, my Strength and Sustainer." When Mrs. Horne became gravely ill, women in her church financed the publication of her book as a testimony to her and to preserve the recipes that had become a part of the church's life.

Church cookbooks are important sources for charting preservation, innovation, and devolution in southern foodways as well as women's history. *The New Kentucky Home Cookbook*, published by Methodist churchwomen in 1884, is a valuable resource on southern white women who did their own cooking. But there is no better way to taste change and continuity in southern eating than to observe (or better, take part in) church meals themselves. A recent project in the Carolinas reveals that church foodways are still meaningful forms of fellowship, with things both lost and gained over time. One mill village church has only 60 members today; but over 300 "came home" to its recent homecoming celebration. The minister, usurping the women's duty, to some consternation, planned the menu of traditional foods as well as preached. The church maintains itself in part these days by providing space for an after-school meal program. A Holiness church recently employed a dietician to create lighter versions of traditional foods because of health concerns in the African American community. While covered dish suppers have waned in recent years at a suburban Methodist church, a small group eats every Sunday dinner at a southern-themed chain restaurant near the church. And a Baptist church that has grown to megachurch status employs a professional chef who oversees a number of food events and has introduced a popular feature to its Wednesday evening "family meals": a chocolate fountain in the center of the dining hall.

The dominant evangelicals are not the first or last groups for which the South has provided hospitable ground for the combination of religion and food. Native Americans had a rich ritual life involving foodways. Early Anglicans and Catholics often ate together in homes after services. Foods of religious sects like the Moravians have become part of southern cuisine. Jews in the pork-loving South have managed to maintain foodways that preserve their identity and also reach out to the broader community. Spartanburgers think of a certain typical American coffee cake as "Jewish" because it is a popular item at the local temple's bake sale. During the annual Greek Festival, Baptists come after "preaching" to eat at St. Nicholas Orthodox Church. The first introduction for many native southerners to the faiths of the growing number of Hindus and Buddhists in the South is through the foods offered at their festivals. And new groups adopt and adapt the covered dish.

Connections between religion and food are not exclusive to the South, but they are particularly prominent in southern culture. Friday night fish fries are accompanied by gospel music in some restaurants. Other eateries offer reduced prices to those who bring their church bulletins to the Sunday dinner buffet. Even when religion is not overtly expressed, the sense of holiness about food carries over in cultural symbols. Southern hospitality parallels fellowship. Fried chicken has symbolic power in part because of its association with Sunday dinners and church suppers. Convenience "bucket" versions play on southern heritage through commercial myths such as Colonel Sanders and PoFolks. Sweet tea and cornbread are "sacraments" for southerners: they commemorate and mark identity with the South. Maybe the best example of a foodway that expresses the connection between religious behavior and southern culture is barbecue. The ritual cooking and eating of a hog commemorates a mythic place and time, communal bond, and identity still sacred in the South.

CORRIE E. NORMAN
Greenville, South Carolina

John Egerton, *Southern Food: At Home, on the Road, in History* (1993); Marcie Cohen Ferris, in *Southern Jewish History* 2 (1998); Jean M. Heriot, *Blessed Assurance: Beliefs, Actions, and the Experience of Salvation in a Carolina Baptist Church* (1994); Corrie Norman, in *Phi Kappa Phi Forum* (2002); Wade Clark Roof, in *God in the Details: American Religion in Popular Culture*, ed. Eric M. Mazur and Kate McCarthy (2001); Daniel Sack, *Whitebread Protestants: Food and Religion in American Culture* (2000); Janet Theophano, *Eat My Words: Reading Women's Lives through the Cookbooks They Wrote* (2002).

Roadside Restaurants

The American roadside restaurant revolution began with the construction of larger factory districts throughout the industrial Northeast. Higher employment concentrations and longer journeys to work brought larger concentrations of potential patrons. Street peddlers purveying ready-to-consume food became more common in urban areas and were joined by horse carts in the 1870s and finally by fixed-location restaurants, most notably diners, along major arterial roads in the 1880s. The diner set the stage for the development of America's stereotypical roadside restaurant. Few of the thousands of diners scattered across the United States were ever erected in the South, but the only manufacturing company currently producing them is located in Atlanta.

Diners were joined by a new class of "white box" restaurants in the 1920s, most notably the Midwest-based White Castle and White Tower chains. The advantage of the "white box" restaurants was their lower overhead, created by smaller square footage, lower labor demands, and simpler menus. Initially almost always located along streetcar routes within urban areas, these factory-produced units were easily erected and easily moved as traffic patterns changed. White Castle and White Tower located virtually all of their stores in the Industrial Northeast and Midwest, with only a handful in the South. The Krystal chain, however, was created by Rody Davenport of Chattanooga, Tenn., as a conscious copy of White Castle in 1932, and it became a southern icon.

Numerically there were few true roadside restaurants in the South prior to the early 1950s, primarily because of the absence of concentrations of factory jobs and large-scale commuting, a lack of disposable income, and a general antipathy for eating away from home. Drive-ins began appearing in larger southern towns and cities soon after World War II, but in comparison to those in other regions their numbers were small. They were, however, a spawning ground for later regional chains, prominent among them Alex Shoenbaum's Charleston, W.Va., Parkette Drive-In, begun in 1947, which became Shoney's in 1953. Other important regional chains from this period include the Krystal clones, Huddle House (Decatur, Ga.) and Waffle House (Avondale Estates, Ga.), as well as the Kettle Restaurants (Houston, Tex.) and Jerry's (Kentucky).

The numbers, diversity, and locations of roadside restaurants exploded during the 1950s and 1960s. As more Americans found themselves away from home at mealtimes, restaurant dining became commonplace among a larger and larger spectrum of the population. The mobility of the automobile, coupled with the need for a place to park while dining, made suburban locations increasingly attractive, even in small towns. The demand, and then the reality, of the modern roadside restaurant, was born. Fast-food chains are the first of these that come to mind, but actually all kinds of restaurants began appearing at the edges of communities along main roads. Barbecues, cafeterias, chicken shacks, and other locally operated stores saw the opportunity to capture the automobile market outside of the establishment-dominated town center, especially in small and medium-sized cities. While many of the initial stores were franchisee or company outlets of national fast-food chains, tens of thousands were not. Soon it was the old café in downtown that was struggling for survival as the edge-of-town roadside venues began to dominate the restaurant scene.

A "hamburger alley" urban environment was created along the major suburban arterials of virtually every large town in the nation. One might assume that this was the beginning of the end of southern restaurant cuisine. Certainly larger markets have higher percentages of national chain store outlets than smaller ones. All, however, continue to serve a liberal dash of traditional southern fare, though often modified to meet more "national" tastes. A typical such strip might begin with an Applebee's (national, though founded in Atlanta), then a couple of national sandwich and pizza shops, then a Huddle House and a Sonic (Oklahoma), then a couple of independents, one Chinese and the other serving bagels, followed by two competing chicken fast-food outlets with a barbecue restaurant nestled between them, and so on. The decline of traditional southern fare in the larger roadside restaurant environments has created some backlash, and several chains, most notably Folks (née PoFolks; the two brands now operate separate chains) and Cracker Barrel, have been created to capitalize on this market. An inspection of their customer base reveals that they do not by any means cater exclusively to decrepit southerners. In many ways southern regional culture is being supported today more by incomers than by natives, who often do not comprehend what is being lost. Southern food is one of the most visible areas of this process. Not only are "old timey" ways being supported and reincarnated through fairs and festivals (often organized and supported by the newer residents), but everyday foods are being placed center stage with the patronization of older or creation of newer restaurants featuring traditional southern favorites, though often prepared in ways that your grandmother might have had trouble recognizing as authentic.

RICHARD PILLSBURY
Folly Beach, South Carolina

John A. Jakle and Keith A. Sculle, *Fast Food: Roadside Restaurants in the Automobile Age* (2002); Richard Pillsbury, *From Boarding House to Bistro: The American Restaurant Then and Now* (1990).

Social Class and Food

During the early 20th century the South ranked dead last among regions nationally in every conceivable economic category, and when the Great Depression gripped the country in 1929, many southerners grimly joked that they did not notice any difference in their circumstances. In the 1930s President Franklin D. Roosevelt described southern poverty as the most serious economic problem facing America.

At the dawning of the New Deal economic recovery program, the majority of the South's African American population and about half of its whites subsisted on a hunger diet. "It seems indisputable that the condition of the poor, whether sharecroppers in the black belt, millworkers in the Piedmont, or scratch farmers in Appalachia, began to reach its nadir about 1925," writes Joe Gray Taylor.

As it had been during much of the South's past, from the early colonization of Virginia, pork continued to be a mainstay on the region's tables well into the 20th century, and at the same time a symbol of the inequitable distribution of food products. The phrase "eating high on the hog," used to describe periods of prosperity, had its converse in the scraps of fatback and gristly ham hocks allocated to slaves for 200 years on the plantations and dispensed to white and black patrons alike at general stores and company commissaries. Pigs have played a central role in southern survival largely because they are one of the most efficient sources of food, as their weight can increase 150-fold in the first eight months of life, and most of the animal is edible.

One of the great paradoxes of the southern table is the fact that African

Americans, the southerners subjected to the worst forms of class as well as race discrimination, have made some of the greatest contributions to the region's cookery. African slaves enriched the diet of the South by introducing products from their homeland such as okra, black-eyed peas, and benne, or sesame, seeds. The kitchen was one of the few places where displaced and enslaved Africans could exercise their creativity, raising common, often even discarded, foods to grandeur. "It is difficult to reconcile the glory of the feast with the ignominy of slavery," writes John Egerton. Ironies continued after the end of slavery. In the Jim Crow South, from the end of the Civil War into the 1960s, blacks who cooked in restaurant kitchens were not usually allowed to step out front and eat in the dining room. Poverty caused many blacks to be confronted with class deprivation as well as racial oppression. Writer Richard Wright recalls sheer hunger from lack of family resources for food as a child, as well as racial limitations.

The image of the frilly-frocked southern belle, presiding over a table set with silver and porcelain, is a marked contrast to the hard-working lives of so many plantation matrons and especially to the hardscrabble existence of countless southern farm women, who sold eggs to supplement the family income and turned used cotton chicken feed sacks into curtains and clothing. Until recently, the cooking of the aristocratic, planter class was preserved in southern cookbooks, to the exclusion of the marginalized. Most southerners never owned slaves.

Half the poor families in the United States, one-seventh of the white poor and two-thirds of the nonwhite, lived below the Mason-Dixon line as late as 1966. Throughout the first half of the 20th century, the meat in the diet of poor southerners in the Appalachian region consisted largely of fatback—very little bacon or ham—and cornbread or flour biscuits, all low in protein and vitamins, resulting in the proliferation of diseases such as pellagra brought on by nutritional deficiencies. By the end of World War II, milling companies had begun to fortify their flour and cornmeal with vitamins, which brought a significant improvement in the health of southerners.

Amid troubles and triumphs, economically disadvantaged southerners of all races have resourcefully combined the lowliest of foodstuffs—the simple fare of field and farm—to create some of America's most memorable dishes: lard-seasoned soup beans and cornbread flecked with pork cracklings; redeye gravy, a simple combination of grease, water, and perhaps some leftover coffee; and pain perdu, "lost bread" or "French toast," an ingenious way of using leftover bread as dessert, perked up with precious sugar and spices. Hard times resulted in clever ways to preserve meat, vegetables, and fruit. Country hams, cured with salt and smoke, apples boiled down into apple butter, and green beans strung and dried as "leather britches" all grew out of necessity.

Southerners have pickled watermelon rinds, made wine out of corn cobs, stewed mudbugs, killed spring lettuce with vinegar and bacon grease, and sautéed dandelion greens, thereby creating America's most diverse indigenous cuisine, appreciated all the more because of the hardships from whence it has come.

FRED W. SAUCEMAN
East Tennessee State University

John Egerton, *Southern Food: At Home, on the Road, in History* (1987); Lu Ann Jones, *Mama Learned Us to Work: Farm Women in the New South* (2002); Joe Gray Taylor, *Eating, Drinking, and Visiting in the South: An Informal History* (1982).

Soul Food

ORIGINS. Popularized in the 1960s, the term *soul food* is a political construct, a renaming and reclaiming of the traditional foods of African Americans, the foods of historical privation, by African Americans. Common usage of the term escalated in the late 1960s when soul music was in vogue and Black Power was touted.

Chicken and fish rolled in meal or batter and deep fried, greens and cowpeas boiled with pork and served with pot liquor, okra cooked to a low gravy, sweet potatoes baked to a golden brown, and cornbread in many varieties form the basis of a quasi-ethnic cuisine whose roots are, arguably, as African as they are American. Maize and sweet potatoes were taken from America to Africa by Portuguese traders in the 16th century, and peas of the black-eyed type have been eaten in Africa for some 400 years. Even specialized local cuisines with identifiable European roots, such as French cooking in Louisiana, have been greatly influenced by African taste in such things as the heavy use of red pepper and the creation of dishes like gumbo based on ingredients, such as okra, that came from Africa. In fact, the black presence may explain why foods like maize and cowpeas, which can grow anywhere in America and were taken into the American frontiers, remain staple foods only in the South, aside from those areas of the Southwest where they were staple foods of Native Americans. Some scholars see Native American influences in soul food as well.

POPULARIZATION. In March 1970 *Vogue* published an essay by Gene Baro that took notice of the newest food fad sweeping the land, observing that "the cult of soul food is a form of black self-awareness and, to a lesser degree, of white sympathy for the black drive to self-reliance. It is as if those who ate the beans and greens of necessity in the cabin doorways were brought into communion with those who, not having to, eat those foods voluntarily now as a sacrament."

Baro was not the first to plumb the deeper meaning of this exotic cuisine. In November 1968 Craig Claiborne, the Mississippi-born *New York Times* restaurant critic, had written a column praising the chitlins and champagne offered at Red Rooster's in Harlem, and soon the droves descended, tongues wagging, upturned noses sniffing out the heady scent of long-simmered swine intestines. *Esquire* had taken notice of the soul food craze eight months earlier. *Seventeen* magazine ran a feature soon after Claiborne's article. *Time* followed in March 1969, *McCall's* in September of the same year. Most articles purported to be soul food primers for the trend-conscious white consumer.

Some were condescending. "The big question is why soul food is so popular," observed an unnamed writer for *Time*. "It is cheap, simple fare that reflects the tawdry poverty of its origins. Soul food is often fatty, overcooked, and underseasoned. Considering the tastelessness of the cuisine, the soul food fad seems certain to be fairly short-lived. For many Negroes, it is long since over; it ended, in fact, as soon as they could afford better food." An African American advertising copywriter observed, "White men are too much. Here we are, trying to live the way they do, and what happens? They get themselves beads and shades and go out and dance the boogaloo."

By 1970 at least 15 soul food cookbooks had been published, including *Cooking with Soul* by Ethel Brown Hearon, *A Pinch of Soul* by Pearl Bowser, and the *Soul Power Cookbook* from the Lane Magazine Company. Most of the books included an explanatory essay of some sort. "Soul food grew in the way that soul music grew—out of necessity, out of the need to express the 'group soul,'" wrote Bowser. "Originally, of course, the need was to keep alive in spite of the paucity of scraps and the sometimes unsavoriness of the leftovers. Somehow, in transforming such things as animal fodder into rich peanut soup or wild plants into some of our favorite and tastiest vegetable dishes, there grew a pride—a pride in ingenuity and a pride in producing 'our own thing.'"

Some African Americans dismissed it all as a matter of misplaced sentimentality. "In the sixties, the young people in the cities were missing something they thought was in the South," said Edna Lewis, the grand doyenne of African American chefs. "They coined the term soul food and nobody challenged it."

By 1972 soul food was moving upscale as restaurants like Atlanta's Soul on Top o' Peachtree opened downtown. But, like the fondue fad of a few years before or the Cajun craze that would dawn some years later, soul food was soon banished to the back of the national cupboard. By October 1973 Soul on Top o' Peachtree closed. According to an article in the *Atlanta Constitution*, "Although the restaurant promised to be a fashionable place to purchase barbecue, greens, pig feet, and other 'soul food' dishes, the best selling meal in the house had an Italian flavor." Said proprietor Willie Stafford, "We had a $1.35 special on spaghetti and meatballs. We sure sold a lot of that stuff."

In *Native Son*, originally published in 1940, Richard Wright describes a pilgrimage from Chicago's wealthy white suburbs to the south side of the city where expatriate black southerners had been making their home since the early years of the Great Migration. Along for the ride are the black protagonist, Bigger Thomas, and two young whites, Jan, an earnest, clueless Communist, and his girlfriend, Mary, daughter of Bigger's employer. "Say Bigger, where can we get a good meal on the South Side?" asks Jan. "We want to go to a *real* place," says Mary. "Look Bigger. We want one of those places where colored people eat, not one of those show places," insists Jan. Bigger ponders this for a moment and then offers, "Well, there's Ernie's Kitchen Shack." And soon they're barreling down South 47th Street in search of honest-to-goodness, skillet-fried chicken.

NOUVEAU. In the new millennium, when the term *soul* affectionately may describe a talented country-western singer or may be employed by a theater company to convey that their hot new show is nurturing, satisfying, and comforting, the label has lost some of its relevance. The African American culinary frontier has expanded so that *soul* no longer wholly characterizes the cultural and social choices made by people of color in this country.

Of course, the traditional dishes and recipes of old can still be found—slowly cooked and highly seasoned greens, beans, and other fresh vegetables; macaroni and cheese; sweet potatoes in many forms; pork in all its manifestations; chicken; hot bread; sweet tea; cobbler; and so on. But the make-do nature of soul food has been morphing in recent years. In a time of rising middle-class values and improving social conditions, it was perhaps inevitable that a "new" style of southern and soul cooking would emerge—leaner cuts of meat, lighter styles of cooking and seasoning, an emphasis on health and nutrition.

But unlike New Southern Cuisine, with its emphasis upon comparatively exotic ingredients and innovative cooking methods, the Soul Food Revival, as the trend has been called, in a more realistic sense, exemplifies culinary freedom. Contemporary African American cooks are liberated from the association with the survival foods of the slave kitchen. Many restaurants now prefer terms like *home-style*, *southern-style*, even *Mama's cooking*. Many have moved uptown. At home, dinner often resembles the healthier, more vibrant cooking of African American farm cooks, such as that of cookbook author Edna Lewis.

In her 1988 book *In Pursuit of Flavor*, Lewis dared to step outside the narrow confines of soul food and redefined the African American woman in the kitchen. She revealed a culinary grace not often associated with the culture, cooking sweet potatoes with lemon, boiling corn in the husk, seasoning with fresh herbs.

Lewis and her peers dismissed the idea that poverty food defined African Americans. They emancipated a generation of new African American cooks. As a consequence, new African American cooking may have lost its "soul" but not its spirit of experimentation and originality.

MARGARET JONES BOLSTERLI
University of Arkansas

TONI TIPTON-MARTIN
Austin, Texas

JOHN T. EDGE
University of Mississippi

Sheila Ferguson, *Soul Food: Classic Cuisine from the Deep South* (1993); Eugene D. Genovese, *Roll, Jordan, Roll: The World the Slaves Made* (1976); Jessica B. Harris, *The Welcome Table: African American Heritage Cooking* (1995); Bob Jeffries, *Soul Food Cookbook* (1970); Bruce F. Johnston, *The Staple Food Economies of Western Tropical Africa* (1958); Helen Mendes, *The African Heritage Cookbook* (1971); National Council of Negro Women, *The Black Family Reunion Cookbook: Recipes and Food Memories* (1993); Curtis Parker, *The Lost Art of Scratch Cooking: Recipes from the Kitchen of Natha Adkins Parker* (1997); Carolyn Quick Tillery, *The African-American Heritage Cookbook: Traditional Recipes and Fond Remembrances from Alabama's Renowned Tuskegee Institute* (1997); Joyce White, *Brown Sugar: Soul Food Desserts from Family and Friends* (2003), *Soul Food: Recipes and Reflections from African-American Churches* (1998); Sylvia Woods, *Sylvia's Family Soul Food Cookbook: From Hemingway, South Carolina, to Harlem* (1999), *Sylvia's Soul Food* (1992).

Aunt Jemima

Although the brand that Aunt Jemima represents has never been based in the South, this controversial spokes-character and cultural icon was originally based on a freed slave named Nancy Green, born in Montgomery County, Ky., in 1834.

In 1889 Chris Rutt and Charles Underwood of St. Joseph, Mo., bought the Pearl Milling Company and developed the first ready-mix pancake flour. After hearing a performer wearing blackface, an apron, and a bandana headband sing a tune called "Old Aunt Jemima" at a vaudeville show, Rutt decided that he had found the perfect name for his and Underwood's new pancake mix. The following year they suffered financial difficulties and sold their formula to R. T. Davis and the Davis Milling Company. Davis, looking for a unique way to advertise his newly acquired product, discovered the warm and friendly Nancy Green working for a judge in Chicago and decided to bring the character of Aunt Jemima to life. The famous original Aunt Jemima image, painted by A. B. Frost, was based on Green's likeness.

At the 1893 World's Columbian Exposition in Chicago, Davis Milling constructed the world's largest flour barrel, and Nancy Green, as the vaudeville-inspired Aunt Jemima, demonstrated the pancake mix, making and serving thousands of pancakes and selling over 50,000 orders for the mix. Fair organizers were so impressed with Green in her role of Aunt Jemima that they declared her the "Pancake Queen." For the next several years Davis and Green

Aunt Jemima pancake mix advertisement, c. 1950 (Library of Congress, Washington, D.C.)

traveled the country promoting the pancake mix, their imminent arrival in towns often well advertised and highly anticipated. Nancy Green played the role of Aunt Jemima for 30 years, until her death in a car accident in Chicago in 1923.

In 1926 Davis sold his company to Quaker Oats, and in 1933 Quaker decided to bring Aunt Jemima back to life. They hired Anna Robinson, "a large, gregarious woman with the face of an angel," who traveled the country promoting the character until 1951. Her popularity continually increased, and from the mid-1950s until the late 1960s Disneyland boasted its own Aunt Jemima–themed restaurants. Aylene Lewis portrayed the character at the Aunt Jemima Pancake House from 1955 to 1962 and at the Aunt Jemima Kitchen from 1962 to 1969. Pancakes were no longer just for breakfast.

Over the decades, dozens of women donned Aunt Jemima's bandana in promoting and demonstrating the pancake mix across the country, but the product's packaging changed little. Aunt Jemima always wore the bandana and apron, and in person she spoke in dialect, sang songs, and told tales about the Old South. A typical 1920s advertisement portrays Aunt Jemima as a slave woman standing in the doorway of her cabin admiring a tall stack of pancakes. The copy reads, "Doesn't it make you think of Mark Twain's boyhood, and of Aunt Jemima, too, in her plantation cabin?" Unsurprisingly, African Americans objected to the stereotype, claiming that it was a glorification of slavery and a painful reminder of the occupational segregation that relegated a large percentage of black women to domestic service. Eventually the name "Aunt Jemima" came to represent something derogatory, akin to a female Uncle Tom.

In 1989, in an attempt to quell cries of racism and calls to discontinue use of their trademark character, the Quaker Oats Company modernized the image of Aunt Jemima from the stereotypical plump and jolly *Gone with the Wind* mammy character to a slimmer, lighter-skinned woman who wears pearl earrings and has a perm. Nevertheless, today's made-over Aunt Jemima continues to invite debate and controversy. While some argue that antipathy toward the character is no longer warranted, others continue to consider the character a symbol of racial prejudice and social injustice.

JAMES G. THOMAS JR.
University of Mississippi

Ronnie Crocker, *Houston Chronicle* (5 April 1996); Grace Elizabeth Hale, *Making Whiteness: The Culture of Segregation in the South, 1890–1940* (1999); Marilyn Kern-Foxworth, *Aunt Jemima, Uncle Ben, and Rastus: Blacks in Advertising, Yesterday, Today, and Tomorrow* (1994); M. M. Manring, *Slave in a Box: The Strange Career of Aunt Jemima* (1998); Diane Roberts, *The Myth of Aunt Jemima: Representations of Race and Region* (1994).

Barbecue, Carolinas

When two Carolinians meet for the first time, typically they exchange three important pieces of information: church attended, basketball team embraced, and kind of barbecue eaten. Religion and sports affiliations may be minor differences, but barbecue styles are schisms. One commonality exists: barbecue is pork. The differences come down to a few essential points: which part of the pig contributed the meat, how finely is the meat chopped, and what barbecue sauce was sprinkled into it as it was chopped.

In eastern North Carolina, in the belt centered around Wilson, barbecue means meat from the whole pig. The slow-cooked meat is chopped fine, almost minced, and dressed with a sauce made from vinegar and red pepper. The flavor is as distinctly eastern Carolina as are tobacco sheds.

In western North Carolina, around Lexington and Shelby, the meat comes from the shoulder. It is chopped more coarsely, almost shredded, then dressed with a sauce made from vinegar, red pepper, and a little tomato, usually from ketchup. In South Carolina, there are pockets, centering around Columbia, that use a mustard-based barbecue sauce, but in most of South Carolina, one will find variations of the same two styles that prevail in North Carolina.

Barbecue in the Carolinas rarely if ever involves sauce on the meat as it cooks. Cooks may use a dry rub, or maybe a simple wet mop dabbed on the meat to keep it from drying out. The meat is the key, slow-cooked to sweet succulence, then dressed simply with dashes of vinegary sauce. Sandwiches are usually topped with coleslaw, often mixed with more barbecue sauce. Plates often come with some form of stew as a side dish, Brunswick stew in North Carolina, barbecue hash in some parts of South Carolina. Hush puppies are often elemental, and the iced tea is sweet.

There has been a lot of migration among these styles, of course. Cities like Charlotte and Raleigh have eastern- and Lexington-style restaurants and devoted fans of each. The 20th century saw Carolinians moving from farms to towns for factory and mill jobs, and their barbecue styles followed.

But why did the eastern and western areas of the state evolve such distinct styles? One finds little conclusive evidence, but theories abound. The eastern part of the state was settled much earlier, so its sauce style may date to a colonial era preference for sour, piquant tastes. In a 1995 issue of *Food History News*, Clarissa Dillon sites 18th-century letters and other written references from several spots in the South that describe barbecue as a cooked pig basted with wine, lemon juice, and spices—with never a mention of tomatoes. Kay Moss,

of the Schiele Museum in Gastonia, N.C., suggests that tomatoes came late to the American diet, after the eastern barbecue style had become established. Moss found an 18th-century recipe from the Stockton family that specified pork, basted only with butter and pepper, but most early versions she has found describe a sauce of wine, lemon juice, sage, red and black pepper, and salt.

For the more modern Lexington-style barbecue, a firm genealogy dates to about 1920. Bob Garner tells the story of how a man named Jess Swicegood opened a barbecue stand in Lexington. A teenager named Warner Stamey took a job helping Swicegood. Stamey later sold barbecue in Shelby and Lexington and eventually opened Stamey's in Greensboro. Among other claims to fame, Warner Stamey is believed to have been the first person to add hush puppies, a fish camp standard, to the chopped barbecue plate. Stamey trained his brother-in-law, Alston Bridges, who opened a restaurant in Shelby that still bears his name. Another employee was Red Bridges (no relation to Alston but the source of endless confusion in the barbecue world), whose descendants still run Bridges's Barbecue Lodge in Shelby. And in the 1950s, Stamey employed a young Wayne Monk, who is now the best-known restaurant owner in pit-crazy Lexington, site of the annual Lexington Barbecue Festival.

In the Carolinas the barbecue business *is* a business. Church barbecues and family reunion pig pickin's are still held (though nowadays they are often catered), and people do cook barbecue at home in small batches, usually involving a half-shoulder—a Boston butt—cooked in the oven or on a kettle grill. But true barbecue requires hours of slow-cooking over a wood fire, a hot, smoky affair, and most Carolinians leave the work to restaurants. People are as loyal to their favorite places as they are to their college teams, and routes to the beach are chosen based on which restaurant one wants to pass. Landmark barbecue restaurants such as the Skylight Inn in Ayden, Allen & Son in Chapel Hill, and Parker's in Wilson are fixtures of their part of the culinary South.

KATHLEEN PURVIS
Charlotte Observer

Jim Auchmutey and Susan Puckett, *The Ultimate Barbecue Sauce Cookbook* (1995); Rick Browne and Jack Bettridge, *Barbecue America: A Pilgrimage in Search of America's Best Barbecue* (1999); John Egerton, *Southern Food: At Home, on the Road, in History* (1987); Lolis Eric Elie, *Smokestack Lightning: Adventures in the Heart of Barbecue Country* (1996); Bob Garner, *North Carolina Barbecue: Flavored by Time* (1996); John Thorne and Matt Lewis Thorne, *Serious Pig: An American Cook in Search of His Roots* (1996).

Barbecue, Memphis and Tennessee

When it comes to Memphis barbecue, it's all about the pig—preferably pulled and piled on a sandwich, topped with sauce and slaw, and served with a glass of sweet tea. Some Memphis restaurants offer beef brisket, smoked chicken, even the rare "vegetarian" barbecue (a Portobello mushroom sandwich at Central BBQ), but those dishes are like the Filet-O-Fish on a McDonald's menu, a post-

script to the main attraction—the pulled pork sandwich, which is the state's very own Big Mac.

Memphis proclaims itself the center of the barbecue universe. It is likely one of the few cities on the planet where one can consume barbecue for breakfast (at the more than 10 Tops locations, which open at 9 A.M. or earlier). "Once you get 50 miles away from Memphis, there's no such thing as barbecue," said Nick Vergos, part of the city's first family of barbecue, whose father, Charlie Vergos, opened the "world famous" Rendezvous in the early 1960s. Veteran restaurateur Walker Taylor, who has been serving barbecue at the Germantown Commissary for more than 25 years, casts a wider net. "You can get good Memphis-style barbecue in a one-hundred-mile radius," said Taylor, who jokingly referred to this territory as "The Ring of Fire."

John Egerton offers yet another view of the state's barbecue boundary, as the section of the state "that includes the area north of Jackson and around Dyersburg. It extends into parts of Arkansas and Kentucky," he said. "There are, of course, exceptions to the rule, but that's barbecue country to me."

In Memphis—home of the world's largest pork barbecue cooking contest, held on the banks of the Mississippi River every May—the passion for pig goes way back. According to a 1989 story in the *Commercial Appeal*, historian Ed Williams, with tongue in cheek, traced the region's first pig roast back to the 1500s: "When Hernando de Soto landed in Florida in May, 1539, he had with him six hundred men, two women,

Little Pigs Barbecue, Memphis, Tenn. (Courtesy Amy Evans, photographer)

three hundred and twenty-seven horses, and a herd of pigs. For two years, the Spaniards explored the southeastern United States, and the pigs multiplied. One night, in 1541, a surprise Indian attack set fire to the Spanish camp somewhere south of the Chickasaw Bluff, and most of the hogs were burned to death. It may have been the first time the smell of barbecue wafted over the Mid-South."

Leonard's, among the city's first barbecue restaurants, opened in 1922, borrowing cooking techniques from the area's African American backyard barbecuers who cooked in old bathtubs or in pits dug into the ground. "It all started around Brownsville, a hotbed for barbecue in the heart of an agricultural area," said Taylor, who turned his family's country store into the Germantown Commissary. "The reason people in that area cooked shoulder

was because it was cheap." The shoulder turned out to be a perfect fit for long, slow cooking over the embers of a hickory fire. "It's got that plate on the bottom, and a layer of skin that protected the meat," Taylor said. "It works like a piece of aluminum foil."

Shoulders were often cooked 8 to 12 hours before the meat was tender enough to pull off the bone, chop, and pile onto a sandwich. Cooking times vary widely now, as the average size of hogs has ballooned over the years. "We used to have a local slaughterhouse until about four years ago," Taylor said. "You would get a thirteen- to fifteen-pound shoulder that would sit nicely over the pit. Those days are over. Now, there are three or four major producers and shoulders are seventeen to twenty pounds."

The debut of the überhog is not the only recent development in the barbecue business. An increasing number of restaurants are turning to gas-powered cookers. They work on the same principle of cooking the meat at a low temperature for an extended period, with a separate burn box where smoldering wood smoke filters into the meat cooking on rotisserie racks. While advocates cheer this as a technological advance, barbecue purists are not convinced. In his 1996 book *Smokestack Lightening* Lolis Eric Elie describes "the mediocre barbecue we've endured in Memphis, meat with all the flavor of boiled cotton," to that produced by a seasoned pitmaster he finds in the country. "They say they have barbecue, but they don't have a thing in the world but baked meat with barbecue sauce on it," muses Billy Anderson of Anderson's Bar-B-Que in Lexington, Tenn.

Walker Taylor explains that the Germantown Commissary installed a Southern Pride cooker because the small kitchen couldn't handle the increasing volume of business with its traditional pit. "If I was only doing eight or ten shoulders a day, I would do it, but I would burn this place down if I cooked everything on the pit."

One of the city's most recognizable barbecue restaurants goes against the "low-and-slow" grain altogether and cooks its ribs over the direct heat generated by hardwood charcoal. "We don't call it barbecue. We call them charcoal-broiled ribs," said Nick Vergos, who runs the shipping part of the business, sending pork all over the country. "But then, is the guy who bakes his meat and puts sauce on it and calls it barbecue more barbecue than ours?"

Vergos's father's original restaurant served ham sandwiches and added ribs to the menu at the suggestion of a savvy meat salesman. "Mr. Fineberg brought my father some loin ribs and convinced him to try them," Vergos recounted the often-told history. "He had a waiter named Lil' John who said every barbecue he had ever eaten used vinegar. They didn't have any vinegar, but they did have pickles, so they used some diluted pickle juice to baste the meat."

The first batch didn't have much flavor, so the elder Vergos experimented with sprinkling the ribs with spices he had in the kitchen for his signature chili. And the dry-rub rack of ribs was born. For many, especially people outside the region, those dry ribs epitomize Memphis barbecue. Daisy May's BBQ USA in Manhattan touts its Memphis-style dry ribs, for instance.

Whether it's ribs or a chopped shoulder sandwich, sauce is used sparingly, or served on the side. The tomato-based sauces balance sweet and tangy and are often spiked with liquid smoke. Some barbecue restaurants in the Memphis area offer a hot sauce option, which is closer to the thin, vinegar-based sauces of North Carolina, but with a fiery kick.

Barbecue contest champion John Willingham writes in his cookbook, *John Willingham's World Champion Bar-B-Q*, "I am convinced that sauce was invented to cover up mistakes in cooking. . . . I, however, serve my sauces on the side only." Willingham, a Shelby County commissioner who operated a barbecue restaurant for several years, offers up his signature recipe that calls for tomato sauce, Coke, cider vinegar, chili sauce, steak sauce, lemon juice, dark brown sugar, soy sauce, and a host of spices.

Many restaurants have turned their sauces into side businesses. The Bar-B-Q Shop, which sells its sauce under the "Dancing Pigs" label, was singled out as having the country's best vinegar-based barbecue sauce during *Chili Pepper* magazine's 2005 Fiery Food challenge. Coleslaw, typically finished with a mayonnaise-based dressing, is the cool yang to the sauce's yin on a shoulder sandwich. Slaw preparations vary widely in texture and taste, from minced to shredded, and from sweet to the savory mustard slaw found at Payne's on Lamar—not to be confused with the Payne's on Elvis Presley Boulevard.

At Mary's Old-Fashioned Pit Barbeque in Nashville, pickles stand in for slaw. That shredded cabbage salad is an option, but costs extra. The pulled pork sandwich at Mary's shows its regional colors in another respect: it's offered on either the standard hamburger bun or on savory cornmeal cakes.

The atmosphere at restaurants in Tennessee barbecue country varies as much as coleslaw recipes. While some customers insist that the best barbecue is found at out-of-the-way holes-in-the-wall, full-service restaurants such as Corky's offer a casual dining experience and drive-through service. Many diners have made personal connections with the boisterous crew of waiters at the Rendezvous, where the minimum tenure of most members of the wait staff is 20 years.

After gnawing through racks of ribs or tackling wonderfully messy pulled pork sandwiches, diners face another challenge at the end of the meal. With the exception of the Rendezvous, which does not offer anything sweet, Memphis barbecue restaurants tempt customers with caramel cakes, banana pudding, fried pies, and, at the Germantown Commissary, fresh-baked coconut cream and lemon meringue pies, which have been made by the same woman for the past 18 years.

LESLIE KELLY
Memphis, Tennessee

John T. Edge, *Southern Belly: The Ultimate Food Lover's Companion to the South* (2000); John Egerton, *Southern Food: At Home, on the Road, in History* (1987); Lolis Eric Elie, *Smokestack Lightning: Adventures in the Heart of Barbecue Country* (2005); Jeffrey Steingarten, *The Man Who Ate Everything: Everything You Ever Wanted to Know About Food, but Were Afraid to Ask* (1999).

Barbecue, Texas

Like nearly everything else associated with the Lone Star State, Texas barbecue is stereotyped. The common assumption is that southern barbecue is slow-cooked pork and that Texas barbecue is slow-cooked beef. There is at least a grain of truth in that image—pork generally dominates barbecue in the Southeast, and beef often is the centerpiece of barbecue in the Southwest—but the history and culture of Texas (and its barbecue) are much more interesting and complex than the cowboy and beef cattle stereotype that throws such a long mythic shadow over all aspects of Texas, including its foodways.

Texas is a geographic and cultural crossroads, the site of a complex convergence of traditions where the Southeast meets the Southwest, where the southern plantations of east Texas encounter the ranches of south and west Texas, and where an ethnically diverse Texas culture shares an international border with Mexico. The music, food, and lifestyles of American Indians, Anglo Americans, African Americans, Mexican Americans, and numerous immigrant groups—Germans, Czechs, Cajuns, among many others—came to Texas from every direction, encountered each other, and for centuries have been sharing (and sometimes fighting over) land, legal systems, politics, music, and food. No place is more reflective of that convergence than central Texas, an area surrounding the state capital of Austin by about 75 miles in every direction that appropriately has been called the Texas Barbecue Belt.

The foodways that historically came together in Texas formed a rich mélange of regional cuisines, including most notably Mexican (or "Tex-Mex") food and barbecue. Because it has so many sources, Texas barbecue involves a wide array of meats (beef, pork, mutton, *cabrito* or kid goat, sausage, and chicken, among others), preparations (including dry rubs, wet mops, tomato-based sauce, vinegar-based sauce, and no sauce), woods (oak, hickory, mesquite, and more) and side dishes, drinks, and desserts that commonly go with it. Despite the many cultural sources and differences, all Texas barbecue traditions have one thing in common: meat (often beef) that has been slow-cooked over indirect heat and wood smoke, although sometimes

grilling directly over coals is a component of the slow-cooking process, especially in cowboy cooking. It is also a given that the social scene that revolves around the all-day cooking and eating is referred to as "a barbecue." Although barbecue has become a staple of Texas's restaurant industry, and barbecue cook-offs and eating contests are now widespread in Texas, barbecues also are often special cultural events such as family reunions and political gatherings. In 1860 Sam Houston spoke at "The Great American Barbecue," a major political rally, and nearly a century later, in 1941, Governor W. Lee "Pappy" O'Daniel threw a free barbecue on the grounds of the governor's mansion to celebrate his inauguration. Some 20,000 Texans showed up to consume 6,000 pounds of barbecued beef, in addition to mutton, chicken, a half ton of potato salad, and all the fixin's, plus one barbecued buffalo killed by Pappy himself for the occasion. U.S. president Lyndon B. Johnson held many barbecues for world leaders at his ranch on the banks of the Pedernales River in the central Texas Hill Country.

Barbecue came to Texas as part of the cultural baggage of southern Anglo Americans and African Americans who brought with them barbecue traditions that had been noted in the colonial South as early as the 17th and 18th centuries. In his 1705 history of Virginia, planter Robert Beverley discussed the "Barbacueing" that had been picked up from local natives, and George Washington later in the century wrote about attending and giving barbecues. The term itself—*barbecue* in English or *barbacoa* in Spanish—is a phonetic pronunciation of the Indian term *barbracot*, which refers to the raised wooden grill set up over a bed of coals to smoke and slow-cook meats in the Caribbean and on the North American mainland. Beginning in the 1600s, southern Anglo American colonists and African American slaves picked up this tradition from Indians in the New World and raised it to a culinary art and well-known social institution in the American South. While these barbecue traditions were developing across the South, Spanish and French adventurers in the part of colonial Spanish Mexico that would become Texas were contacting Indians who had included the grilling and smoking of meat in their traditions for centuries. When La Salle was establishing a French presence in Spanish Texas in the 1680s, he and his colleagues often hunted buffalo, then roasted and smoked the meat in pits, even commenting that the meat "had a much better taste" than that found in France. By the time Anglo Americans and their African American slaves left the South for Mexican Texas in the 1820s and 1830s, they took with them various barbecue traditions, many based on pork, a staple of the southern diet, including that of poor whites, slaves, yeoman farmers, and plantation owners alike. African Americans were often the cooks on plantations that dominated some areas of the South, including parts of east Texas, and African American barbecuing has remained a component of southern and Texas barbecue to this day.

By the end of the Civil War the Anglo Americans in Texas had merged their southern cow herding traditions with the vaquero ranching traditions of Spanish Mexico to form the American cowboy way of life based on driving surplus longhorn beef cattle to distant markets. Southern barbecue and Mexican *barbacoa* cooking traditions combined in outdoor cowboy cooking in pits and over coals. As a result of the proliferation of cattle in Texas and eventually across the nation, beef assumed a new importance, joining pork as a staple in many people's diets. Captain Flack, a famous frontier hunter, noted that it was common in mid-19th century Texas to hunt wild longhorn cattle along with deer, and that people would gladly use the meat. Adding to this mid-19th-century cultural mix were Texas's many immigrant groups, including large numbers of Germans and Czechs who settled in the central Texas region, bringing with them their traditions of sausage making and smoked meats.

Over the next 100 years the convergence of southern barbecue traditions with Texas's Spanish/Mexican-influenced cattle culture and European ethnic foodways led to the classic barbecue meal found in the central Texas Barbecue Belt in the early 21st century: slow-cooked and smoked beef brisket, sausage, and ribs, with a variety of sauces for pouring or dipping, plus the now-traditional side dishes of potato salad, coleslaw, pinto beans, pickles, and onions. Iced tea, soda, and beer are the usual drinks, and there is often a stack of squishy white bread slices with which to make a "sausage wrap" or a sliced beef sandwich or to use for sopping the plate. A few barbecue restaurants stubbornly still serve only meat, with no side dishes, reflecting their origins as meat markets and butcher shops in the 19th and early 20th centuries. Especially in the years since World War II, many meat markets serving leftover smoked meats as a sideline evolved into full-fledged barbecue restaurants with side dishes and sit-down dining. Although there are a few successful barbecue restaurant chains, most well-regarded barbecue places are mom-and-pop joints in the form of a roadside stand, a small house on a city street, or a sprawling suburban restaurant. The slow-cooking involved in most barbecue simply defies the approach that makes fast-food restaurants successful.

Three sites widely regarded as the holy trinity of central Texas barbecue joints are Louis Mueller's (pronounced Miller) Barbecue in Taylor, Kreuz (pronounced Krites) Market in Lockhart, and Cooper's Old Time Pit Bar-B-Que in Llano. All three are located in towns that think of themselves as the barbecue capital of Texas, and all three have family histories that have led to competing branches and sometimes family feuds that are of great interest to barbecue fans. They also reveal much about the German, meat market, and cowboy roots of Texas barbecue as it evolved beyond its predominately southeastern origins. Mueller's has a coarse-grained German "hot gut" sausage in addition to other meats; Kreuz's serves only meat on butcher paper (although it has added a few side dishes in recent years); and Cooper's enormous pits in the parking lot feature less smoking and more grill-

ing in the cowboy tradition of cooking directly over coals. The many Mikeska brothers, sometimes referred to as the first family of Texas barbecue, have run barbecue joints in towns sprinkled all over central Texas for several generations. Despite the tight family connection, the menus, sauces, and meats are different in every Mikeska restaurant, illustrating the many differences in barbecue wherever it is found from joint to joint, town to town, and region to region throughout Texas and the rest of Barbecue Nation. There are many disputes about Texas barbecue as a result of its diverse cultural roots, but there is no doubt that it is a beloved culinary tradition and a nearly sacred meal served at some of the most important moments in the private and public lives of Texans.

GEORGE B. WARD
Austin, Texas

T. Lindsey Baker, in *Juneteenth Texas: Essays in African-American Folklore*, ed. Francis E. Abernethy (1996); Robert Beverley, *The History and Present State of Virginia*, ed. Louis B. Wright (1947); Bill Crawford, *Please Pass the Biscuits, Pappy: Pictures of Governor W. Lee O'Daniel* (2004); J. Frank Dobie, *The Longhorns* (2000); David Hackett Fischer, *Albion's Seed: Four British Folkways in America* (1989); William C. Foster, ed., *The La Salle Expedition to Texas: The Journal of Henri Joutel, 1684–1687* (1998); Ernestine Sewell Linck and Joyce Gibson Roach, *Eats: A Folk History of Texas Foods* (1989); Jack Jackson, *Los Mesteños: Spanish Ranching in Texas, 1721–1821* (1986); Terry C. Jordan, *Trails to Texas: Southern Roots of Western Cattle Ranching* (1981); W. W. Newcomb Jr., *The Indians of Texas: From Prehistoric to Modern Times* (1961); Robb Walsh, *Legends*

Beans for sale at a farmers' market (Bill Tarpenning, photographer, United States Department of Agriculture)

of *Texas Barbecue Cookbook: Recipes and Recollections from the Pit Bosses* (2002).

Beans

Beans have been a mainstay of the southern table since long before European settlement. Fresh from the garden, dried, canned, or frozen, they have sustained the South for centuries.

The signature dish of the mountain South is a bowl of soup beans, with a wedge of hot cornbread and a slice of onion. Although most beans yield a flavorful soup, in southern Appalachia, pintos are the legume of choice, simmered in water and seasoned with pork. In times when meat was scarce, neighbors often passed hunks of pork among themselves to season their beans, until all the flavor was cooked out of this "community sinker."

Green beans, strung and broken into washpans on southern porches, are one of the most common side dishes all through the region. They, too, are typically cooked slowly, with pork side meat, until the beans are quite soft, usually about two hours. When new potatoes are freshly dug, cooks add them for the second hour. Half-runners and Kentucky Wonders are favorite varieties of green beans, staked in the garden with cane poles and tied with twine. The term *mess of beans* is used to describe the harvest and is a vague form of measurement that indicates roughly the amount of beans required to feed one's family. Before canning techniques were taught throughout the mountains by home demonstration agents, green beans were preserved for the winter by drying. The beans, left whole, were sewn onto threads and dried in the sun for about three weeks. These "leather britches," shuck beans, or shucky beans were then stored in covered containers for months. Cooking required a long soak in water and about six hours in simmering water on the stove before the proper tenderness was achieved.

Farther south, diners savor butter beans, particularly the speckled variety that William Faulkner supposedly reminisced about in Paris with fellow writer Katherine Anne Porter. Butter beans are related to limas but have a creamier flavor, hence the name. White navy beans, in a thick broth, are common cafeteria fare throughout the South.

Seasoned beans served over rice are basic to the coastal cooking of the South. A traditional Hispanic meal is Moors and Christians, featuring saucy black beans over boiled white rice. In Louisiana, cooking red beans and rice evolved into a Monday tradition, since that was washday and cooks could leave the beans relatively untended on the back of the stove while completing their housework. The dominant seasoning for a pot of red beans and rice is pork, in the form of ham, andouille sausage, or even Spanish-inspired chorizo. Either the stewed, spicy beans are cooked separately and served atop a plate of rice, or the rice is cooked in the bean liquid.

Diners all across the Deep South sit down to bowls of hoppin' John for good luck on New Year's Day. This dish is a blend of black-eyed peas and rice, again flavored by pork—ham hocks, side meat, or bacon. Brought to America on slave ships in the 17th century, black-eyed peas are actually beans (*Vigna unguiculata*) and are also commonly referred to as cowpeas, field peas, or

crowder peas. A hip-hop group, the Black Eyed Peas, finds this bean a symbol for their African American–inspired music.

In the novel and play *The Member of the Wedding*, by Georgia native Carson McCullers, a bowl of hoppin' John is the final test of a character's mortality: "Now hopping-john was F. Jasmine's very favorite food. She had always warned them to wave a plate of rice and peas before her nose when she was in her coffin, to make certain there was no mistake; for if a breath of life was left in her, she would sit up and eat, but if she smelled the hopping-john and did not stir, then they could just nail down the coffin and be certain she was truly dead."

Beans even show up on the southern dessert table, in the form of bean pies. Pinto beans in the Upper South and red beans in the Deep South are mashed, sugared, and baked in a crust, sometimes with pecans or other nuts added to the filling.

Storehouses of southern soil and sun, beans are nourishing, filling, and inexpensive, giving substance and variety to menus from the mountains to the marshes.

FRED W. SAUCEMAN
East Tennessee State University

John Egerton, *Southern Food: At Home, on the Road, in History* (1987); Ronni Lundy, *Butter Beans to Blackberries: Recipes from the Southern Garden* (1999), *Shuck Beans, Stack Cakes, and Honest Fried Chicken: The Heart and Soul of Southern Country Kitchens* (1991); Carson McCullers, *The Member of the Wedding* (1958).

Beaufort Stew/Frogmore Stew

The South Carolina Lowcountry, embracing the Sea Islands and the coastal plain, is home to a broad range of culinary traditions. Greatly influenced by French, English, African American, and Native American foodways, the variety is impressive and includes several seafood stews, of which Beaufort stew, also known as Lowcountry boil or Frogmore stew, is the most well known.

Taking its name from two of the oldest Sea Island communities, Beaufort and Frogmore, the stew typically calls for a rather simple recipe: combine several large boiling potatoes, a couple pounds of smoked sausage, half a dozen ears of corn, and two pounds of shrimp. Most recipes call for these ingredients to be boiled with certain seasonings, like crab boil, and the stew is normally served with hot sauce.

This stew is equally at home on Lowcountry townhouse tables and at the family reunions of people who have traditionally farmed and fished the Sea Islands. This is a clear indication of the sharing of traditions, or creolization, that took place during the era when rice plantations dominated the South Carolina coastal plain. Enslaved African Americans brought from Africa the skills and knowledge needed to grow rice, as well as culinary traditions that became intertwined with traditions of other ethnic groups.

Planters, slaves, and small family farmers all depended on one-pot meals prepared in large black iron kettles. Whether the dish contained potatoes or rice depended largely on availability and time of year. Quoting from the ante-bellum records of Hagley Plantation, Charles Joyner notes that between April and October each worker was allowed a pint of "small [rice] twice a week" and that "seafood ran a close second in popularity to pork among the Waccamaw slaves," who added "to their allowances of food by using their off times for fishing, crabbing, oystering, and clamming."

Even traditional dishes are subject to change and variation, and Beaufort stew is no exception. Although the long-standing prevalence of one-pot meals in American cooking points to antebellum origins, many argue that the nomenclature has been in use only since the middle years of the 20th century. Stories attempting to account for the stew's origins are numerous. They include tales of a fraternity cookout on a South Carolina beach and the last desperate attempt of an Army National Guard cook to feed the soldiers in his unit. Many scholars attribute the addition of link sausage to the influence of European butchery.

Numerous narratives clearly point to antebellum origins. Sabe Rutledge, who was born on a rice plantation just before the Civil War, told a researcher in the 1930s about two cooking pots maintained by her mother: "Boil all day and all night . . . cedar paddle stir with." Regardless of differences in nomenclature or recipe variations, one-pot meals have been a significant part of the American cooking heritage for hundreds of years.

The ingredients in Beaufort stew are boiled and then strained. The vegetables, shrimp, and sausage are removed from the pot and eaten only after this straining process is completed. This, when compared to other southern stews, presents a distinct difference in the method of consumption. It is commonly agreed that a Beaufort stew cooked long enough to thicken significantly becomes what folks generally refer to as a muddle.

SADDLER TAYLOR
McKissick Museum, Columbia, South Carolina

Charles Joyner, *Down by the Riverside: A South Carolina Slave Community* (1984), *Shared Traditions: Southern History and Folk Culture* (1999); Stan Woodward, *Southern Stews: A Taste of the South* (documentary film, 2002).

Benne

Benne is a South Carolina term for sesame. The oilseed *Sesamum indicum* is thought to have been brought to the United States from Africa during the period of the slave trade. The term itself seems to confirm the African origin of the plant as the word *bene* means sesame in the language of the Bambara peoples of Mali and among the Wolof of Senegal and Gambia. Sesame is among the herbs and spices listed in Egypt's Ebers papyrus (a voluminous record of ancient Egyptian medicine) and has long been used in the cooking of the southern part of the Mediterranean basin. The plant will tolerate high temperatures and drought. Most important, its oil has a nutty flavor and is resistant to rancidity.

Benne was noted in South Carolina records as early as 1730 as sesamum and appears in Thomas Jefferson's *Garden Book*. In the colonial period, sesame was much cultivated in personal gardens

by enslaved Africans along with other foodstuffs of African origin like okra, black-eyed peas, and watermelon. The British even contemplated cultivating the plant in the American colonies for its oil in hopes that its use would supplant that of imported olive oil.

In the South Carolina Lowcountry, the seeds are the major ingredients in a variety of dishes and turn up in almost every course of the meal from the benne crackers that accompany drinks to the benne brittle that may end the meal. Sarah Rutledge offers a recipe for benne-oyster soup in her 1847 *Carolina Housewife*. Finally, for many folks in the Carolinas, benne seeds are reputed to bring good luck.

JESSICA B. HARRIS
Queens College

Dorothea Bedigian, in *The Cambridge World History of Food*, ed. Kenneth Kiple and Kriemild Connee Ornelas (2000); Jessica B. Harris, *The Welcome Table: African American Heritage Cooking* (1995); Sarah Rutledge, *The Carolina Housewife* (1847); John Martin Taylor, *Hoppin' John's Lowcountry Cooking* (1992).

Biscuits

Biscuits have provided nourishment to generations of southerners, been a part of everyday family rituals, and become the symbols of regional tradition. North Carolina chef and author Bill Neal entitled a chapter of one of his books "The Pride of the South: Hot Biscuits." One of the first stories that legendary chef and food writer Edna Lewis told her friend Scott Peacock was of the northerner who came to the South and returned home. Someone asked him about the biscuits, and he explained, "Every time someone would start to bring biscuits to the table, they'd stop and say, 'I'm sorry but they're not hot enough' . . . and they'd disappear." Peacock saw this as an illustration of "the pride, even fanaticism, with which Southern cooks regard traditional breads."

Biscuits are quick breads, those not needing to rise before being baked. The term *bis coctus* is Latin, *biscuit* is Old French, and *bisquit* appeared in Middle English. Biscuits are likely European in derivation, although a British biscuit is a thin, crispy cracker or a cookie. Perhaps the first biscuits in the South were beaten biscuits, made with high-gluten flour and water, producing a dough that is beaten, or "broken," until it is spongy in texture. These baked biscuits are tender, as would be bread made with yeast. Beaten biscuits require considerable work, though, involving pounding of the dough with a mallet, skillet, or other heavy instrument, continually folding and flattening the dough. In 1877 the invention of a dough-kneading machine made the process less burdensome, although the machine was rare in parts of the South. Beaten biscuits almost disappeared from some regions of the South in the 20th century, but they did survive in the Upper South, often as an accompaniment to that region's cured country hams. Thinly sliced pieces of ham piled high on halves of a beaten biscuit are still a prized southern treat. Angel biscuits, sometimes called bride's biscuits, are also frequently served with country ham. These biscuits are made with both baking powder and yeast, making them

yeast rolls that have some of the character of beaten biscuits.

The standard biscuit of the South has been called a soda, baking power, or buttermilk biscuit, with all three of those ingredients important to most recipes. They are also known as raised biscuits. Commercial baking powder and baking soda were both available in the South by 1870, but even more important was the accessibility of flour from midwestern mills. The falling price of flour in the 1880s made it affordable to a wide range of southerners and promoted the southern turn to biscuits. The White Lily company soon began producing low-gluten flour, which was softer than that of the midwestern mills. Cooks have insisted ever since that it produces the best biscuits. Fat is another key element. Bill Neal's contemporary take on biscuit making suggests that vegetable shortening is the easiest fat to handle in biscuit dough, while butter produces the best flavor but weakest structure. "A biscuit without some little bit of lard will never taste truly Southern to me," he added. Many cooks produce "cat head biscuits," termed that because of the large size and rough exterior texture of the dough dropped onto the baking pan.

Biscuits became part of the standard southern breakfast—along with ham, eggs, grits, and redeye gravy. Some families ate biscuits three times a day, although cornbread remained typical bread for midday dinner. Biscuits on Sunday helped to make that a special day in the South. Bluesman B. B. King, son of a Mississippi sharecropper, remembers that "we always had buttered biscuits on Sunday mornings, with preserves that we put up ourselves." Biscuits were also often an accompaniment to Sunday chicken dinners after church.

The appeal of biscuits is partly seen in ways that people talk about them. African American writer James Weldon Johnson came south in the height of Jim Crow's racial oppression. Amidst many depressing experiences, he had breakfast at a café whose biscuits made a profound impression upon him. He found them "so light and flaky that a fellow with any appetite at all would have no difficulty in disposing of eight or ten." When finished, he felt that by eating in a homey café with good food, well run by African Americans, he had "experienced the realization of, at least, one of my dreams of Southern life." Kentuckian Martha Neal Cooke, in the 1950s, remembered from her childhood "silver dollar biscuits that would fog your glasses when you pulled them apart." John T. Edge has noted of Mississippian Queenie Dixon's bread: "Some say her biscuits are so light, they let you taste heaven."

Modernization has affected the production and consumption of biscuits. Comedian Jerry Clower saw the rise of store-bought, packaged biscuits as a sign that the world was going to hell in a breadbasket. In exuberant prose, he recounted, in one of his stories, his mama making cat head biscuits, wallowing the lard and flour in her hands. "Now them biscuits was fit to eat," he said, in his southern idiom. In contrast, the biscuits in little cardboard tubes, which you had to "whop on the side of the counter," were not. Nonetheless, working mothers in the South as elsewhere found packaged biscuit dough an acceptable substitute for homemade biscuits when they were marketed in the mid-20th century. Cookbooks soon offered recipes for "food processor biscuits" to save time in producing more authentic biscuits. Since the 1970s major chicken and hamburger fast-food chains in the South have served biscuits. A Hardee's franchise in North Carolina popularized a biscuit recipe that was popular with consumers, and Bojangles and Biscuitville are also popular outlets. As John Egerton has noted, fast-food biscuits have become in many communities "the new standard of what a biscuit is."

Southern singers have sung about biscuits, with "baking biscuits" given sexual implications by blues-singing women. Memphis Minnie warned, for example, "Don't let no outside women make no biscuits for your man." Since 1951 Sonny Payne has hosted his radio show, *King Biscuit Time*, from downtown Helena, Ark., kicking it off with "Pass the biscuits, because it's King Biscuit Time on KFFA radio!" And southern writers have written about biscuits. Terry Kay has a memorable biscuit-making scene in his novel, *To Dance with the White Dog*. Trying to duplicate his wife's recipe for biscuits, he is so unsuccessful that "he put one in front of the dog and the dog sniffed and looked up at him sadly and trotted away."

One southern sports team has made the biscuit a part of its name. The Montgomery Biscuits are a minor league baseball team, whose logo is a talking happy biscuit. They recently have partnered with Mary B's Biscuits and Alaga

Syrup. Mary B's Biscuits, manufactured by Hom/Ade Food, Inc., of Bagdad, Fla., are the best-selling fresh-baked frozen biscuit on the market, which is the latest expression of the continuing southern embrace of the biscuit. The product appeared on the market in 1998 and now can be purchased at 9,000 retail stores across the country. Whitefield Foods, Inc., headquartered in Montgomery, has manufactured Alaga Syrup since 1906. The Montgomery Biscuits have biscuits and syrup at the concession stands during their games, and a biscuit launcher fires Mary B's Biscuits into the bleachers between innings.

CHARLES REAGAN WILSON
University of Mississippi

John T. Edge, *A Gracious Plenty: Recipes and Recollections from the American South* (1999); John Egerton, *Southern Food: At Home, on the Road, in History* (1987); Edna Lewis and Scott Peacock, *The Gift of Southern Cooking: Recipes and Revelations from Two Great American Cooks* (2003); Bill Neal, *Biscuits, Spoonbread, and Sweet Potato Pie* (1990).

Black-eyed Peas

Black-eyed peas, *Vigna unguiculata* (*Vigna sinensis* is a synonym), are a variety of cowpeas and part of the *fabaceae* or pea family. Shelled black-eyed peas are kidney-shaped and have a dark eye in the center. The black-eyed pea's origins can be traced to east Africa, where cowpeas grow wild, and to India and other parts of Asia, where relatives of the black-eyed pea are found, including the Chinese bean or yardlong bean. Black-eyed peas came to the United States from Africa. The slave trade introduced them to the Caribbean and the continental U.S. as early as the 1600s.

Common names for black-eyed peas include blue-eyed beans, bung belly, chain-gang peas, China beans, cow beans, cowpeas, cream peas, field peas, and crowders. In northern and north-central areas of the United States, they are called black-eyed beans. In early America, black-eyed peas were also called cornfield peas, reflecting the practice of sowing them between rows of corn. Because English peas could not endure the warm climate, southerners used the word "peas" to describe the substitute they could successfully plant; hence the names southern peas and southern field peas.

George Washington experienced the difficulty of growing English peas first-hand when he tried to grow imported vetch and garden peas at Mount Vernon. In a 1796 letter to Thomas Jefferson, Washington expressed concern that peas from England could not survive the Virginia heat. The next year, he experimented with black-eyed peas. In a letter dated 15 July 1797 Washington wrote, "From the cultivation of the common black eye peas I have more hope and am trying them this year both as a crop, and for plowing in as a manure."

Early American farmers grew cowpeas as animal fodder and to improve soil. As for human consumption, black-eyed peas were often associated with slaves and the poor. Yet dishes containing black-eyed peas found their way to the tables of the rich, too. An entry on 3 August 1774 in Thomas Jefferson's garden book reads "black eyed peas come to table." Jefferson, in fact, grew several varieties of black-eyed peas at Monticello. Mary Randolph, daughter of a legislator and wealthy plantation owner, gave a recipe for field peas in her cookbook *The Virginia House-wife*, first published in 1824. Her recipe calls for the peas to be mashed, fried into a cake, and garnished with bacon.

In the beginning of the 20th century, agricultural scientist George Washington Carver increased the popularity of black-eyed peas through his work at the Tuskegee Institute in Alabama. Farmers often had to work with poor soil, and fertilizer was expensive. Though farmers knew manure would improve conditions, the poor could not afford to keep a large number of animals. Carver encouraged farmers to grow cowpeas, emphasizing their value as a nitrogen fixer. Carver also taught women how to cook cowpeas. He published four bulletins promoting their cultivation and use, highlighting nutritional benefits. In "Bulletin No. 5, Cow Peas," printed in 1903, Carver wrote, "As a food for man, the cow pea should be to the South, what the White, Soup, Navy, or Boston bean is to the North, East, and West: and it may be prepared in a sufficient number of ways to suit the most fastidious palate." Five years later, he published a new edition of the bulletin, noting a demand for information about cowpeas and the increase in production in various states. "Bulletin No. 35," published in 1917, contains 40 recipes, including croquettes, baked peas, creamed peas, griddle cakes, hoppin' John, pea coffee, and "cow pea custard pie."

Southerners traditionally eat black-eyed peas on New Year's Day for good luck. They are often boiled with salt pork or fatback. In some regions they are served with greens or cabbage, which symbolize dollar bills, and the black-eyed peas represent coins. In the Carolina Lowcountry, they are paired with rice in a dish called hoppin' John. In Texas, black-eyed peas are the main ingredient in a type of salsa or relish called Texas caviar, which is served with corn chips.

Some southern communities celebrate local ties to black-eyed peas. Athens, Tex., calls itself the "Black-Eyed Pea Capital" because commercial production of peas became the town's largest industry in the early 20th century. People in Harmon County, Okla., have held a black-eyed pea festival every August since 1987.

SHAUN CHAVIS
Boston University

Robert C. Baron, ed., *The Garden and Farm Books of Thomas Jefferson* (1987); Victor R. Boswell, in *The World in Your Garden*, ed. National Geographic Society (1957); Jane Carson, *Colonial Virginia Cookery* (1985); George Washington Carver, "Bulletin No. 5. Cow Peas" (1903), "Bulletin No. 13. How to Cook Cow Peas" (1908), "Bulletin No. 35. How to Grow the Cow Pea and 40 Ways of Preparing it as a Table Delicacy" (1917); Frederic G. Cassidy, ed., *Dictionary of American Regional English*, vol. 1 (1985); Frederic G. Cassidy and Joan Houston Hall, eds., *Dictionary of American Regional English*, vol. 2 (1991); John C. Fitzpatrick, ed., *The Writings of George Washington from the Original Manuscript Sources, 1745–1799*, vol. 35 (1940); Karen Hess, *The Carolina Rice Kitchen: The African Connection* (1992); Rackham Holt, *George Washington Carver:*

An American Biography (1946); Waverly Root and Richard de Rochemont, *Eating in America: A History* (1976); John Martin Taylor, *Hoppin' John's Lowcountry Cooking* (1992).

Bourbon Whiskey

Bourbon is a type or style of whiskey associated, in terms of production, with the Mid-South, and, in terms of consumption, with all of the southern states. The term *whiskey* refers to any spirit distilled from fermented grain and aged in hardwood barrels. Bourbon whiskey is such a spirit made from a mash of primarily corn, with smaller amounts of malted barley and either rye or wheat. The other major distinguishing characteristic of bourbon is that the barrels in which it is aged are heavily charred on their inside surface and used only once. This practice maximizes the filtering effect of the char and the extraction of sugars and flavors from the wood. The wood used for barrels is typically American white oak from Arkansas or Missouri.

The beverage known today as bourbon whiskey emerged in the mid-19th century, although the name was in use a few decades earlier. Its antecedents are the other whiskeys produced in America and Europe prior to the 19th century, as well as other aged spirits such as brandy.

The path to bourbon begins at the Cumberland Gap, the easiest point of passage through the Appalachian Mountains, where Kentucky, Tennessee, and Virginia meet. European settlement of that region began in earnest after the French ceded control of it to the British with the Treaty of Paris in 1763. The distillation of spirits from grain was a common activity on this frontier. Based on observations of Native Americans in the area, the new settlers quickly concluded that native corn (maize) was better suited to the region than wheat, rye, or other familiar Old World grains. One reason was that the new lands were heavily wooded and corn could be cultivated in fields from which stumps had not been removed. Corn also matured quickly in the Mid-South climate, so a crop could be harvested in about three months.

Farmers ate their corn and fed it to livestock. The only practical way to market surplus corn was in the form of whiskey. Many farmers had stills with which they processed their own corn and that of their neighbors who did not possess the skills or equipment. Millers also operated distilleries. On the frontier, whiskey functioned as virtual currency. Whiskey, along with flour and hemp, was one of the earliest and most successful frontier products sold in markets downriver.

The routine aging of bourbon began in the mid-19th century. Aging improves the taste of the whiskey significantly, enriching, mellowing, and polishing it. Whiskey is aged in 53-gallon (200-liter) barrels stored in large warehouses, also known as rickhouses, rackhouses, or barrel houses. During the warm days of summer, whiskey expands deep into the wood. In the cool nights it contracts, extracting various wood sugars and other flavors. This expansion/contraction is referred to as cycling. Humidity and air circulation are other factors that affect how whiskey ages. Two whiskeys made exactly the same way can taste very different when mature, because of differences in how they are aged.

Straight bourbon must be aged for at least two years. It usually is aged for four to six years and may be aged for 20 years or more. Because bourbon is aged only in new barrels, over-aging is possible.

The name *bourbon* comes from the Kentucky county of that name. Bourbon County was formed in 1785 when Kentucky was still a territory of Virginia. It was named in honor of the French royal family in gratitude for France's help during the Revolution. The original Bourbon County covered a vast area comprising 32 modern Kentucky counties. When the term *bourbon* first began to be used for whiskey, it described any whiskey made in that region. As the unique corn-based whiskey of the region grew in popularity, so did the name.

While bourbon whiskey can be made anywhere in the United States and has been made in states other than Kentucky, the beverage is most associated with Kentucky and today virtually all of it is produced there. With the exception of Tennessee whiskey, the other types of American whiskey (rye, corn, and blends) are mostly produced in Kentucky as well. The Kentucky Bourbon Festival is held each fall in Bardstown, Ky. Bourbon came to prominence with the opening of the western territories following the Civil War. Commercial-scale distilling developed during this period because of growing demand

from western markets and the improved ability to reach all markets by rail rather than water transport.

Today the definition of bourbon is a matter of federal law. The Standards of Identity for Distilled Spirits describe "bourbon whisky" as "whisky produced at not exceeding 160° proof from a fermented mash of not less than 51 percent corn . . . and stored at not more than 125° proof in charred new oak containers." To be called "straight" bourbon whisky it must "have been stored in the type of oak containers prescribed, for a period of 2 years or more." All whiskey sold in the United States must be bottled at not less than 80° proof (40 percent alcohol by volume). Although 80° is the most common proof, other proofs available are 86, 90, 100, 101, and 107.

"Degrees (°) of proof" is a way of describing alcohol concentration in an alcohol and water solution. For example, 100° proof describes a solution that is 50 percent alcohol and 50 percent water. The term evolved on the frontier, where various crude methods were used to determine the alcohol content of whiskey. A whiskey that passed these tests was said to be "proved."

Bourbon is the most popular type of American whiskey, but it is not the only type. The best-selling brand of American whiskey, Jack Daniel's Tennessee Whiskey, is not bourbon but a sour-mash whiskey. Tennessee whiskey is produced exactly like bourbon except it is filtered through sugar-maple charcoal before barreling. Other types of American whiskey are straight rye, straight corn, and American blended whiskey.

Bourbon whiskey plays a major role in southern culture, especially in cooking, hospitality, and literature. In the kitchen it shows up in recipes for many popular sauces and glazes, in sweet potato casserole and bread pudding, and in confections such as bourbon balls. It is the main ingredient in classic cocktails such as the mint julep, old-fashioned, whiskey toddy, and whiskey sour. Naturally, it is often paired with another iconic southern beverage, Coca-Cola.

In literature, bourbon whiskey figured prominently in both the works and life of William Faulkner. The image of a hard-drinking writer is hardly confined to the South, but if the writer is southern, the drink is likely bourbon. As Walker Percy wrote in his 1975 essay "Bourbon," "Bourbon does for me what the piece of cake did for Proust." Bourbon whiskey once was the most popular distilled spirit in the United States, but it began to fall from favor after World War II everywhere except the South, which is still known in the beverage industry as "the bourbon belt." Since the 1980s, bourbon and Tennessee whiskey have grown in international popularity.

Landmark distilleries such as Jim Beam, Jack Daniel's, Four Roses, Heaven Hill, Maker's Mark, Wild Turkey, Woodford Reserve, and Buffalo Trace are popular tourist attractions in Kentucky and Tennessee. The Oscar Getz Museum of Whiskey History is located in Bardstown, Ky.

CHARLES K. COWDERY
Chicago, Illinois

Gerald Carson, *The Social History of Bourbon: An Unhurried Account of our Star-Spangled American Drink* (1963); Charles K. Cowdery, *Bourbon, Straight: The Uncut and Unfiltered Story of American Whiskey* (2004); Henry G. Crowgey, *Kentucky Bourbon: The Early Years of Whiskey-Making* (1971); William Downard, *Dictionary of the History of the American Brewing and Distilling Industries* (1980); Gary Regan and Mardee Haidin Regan, *The Book of Bourbon and Other Fine American Whiskeys* (1995).

Brennan, Ella

(b. 1925) RESTAURATEUR.
Ella Brennan, matriarch of one of the most prominent restaurant families in the South, was born in New Orleans, La., on 27 November 1925. Early in her life, Brennan was introduced to outstanding food in her mother's home. She praises her mother as a great home cook who instilled in her children a love of local ingredients and traditions. At the age of 19, Ella Brennan began working with her brother, Owen Brennan, who had purchased a restaurant in the French Quarter. Instead of opting for college, Ella Brennan went to Europe, where she made a study of restaurant service, and New York City, where she worked briefly at the 21 Club.

Brennan's, the seminal family restaurant, specializes in French Creole dishes, served, contrary to expectations, by a family of Irish descent. It is still operated by a branch of the family. Since its opening in 1946, Brennan's has birthed a number of New Orleans offspring as well as restaurants in Houston and Las Vegas.

At Commander's Palace, the restaurant housed in a Victorian mansion in

New Orleans's Uptown neighborhood operated by the family since 1974, Ella Brennan serves what she calls Haute Creole cuisine—the sophisticated cooking of old Creole New Orleans, reinterpreted for the modern palate. An example of the dishes served at the flagship Brennan restaurant, now operated by the branch of the family aligned with Ella Brennan and her descendants, is bread pudding soufflé gilded with whiskey sauce.

Over the course of her career Brennan has exhibited a reputation for recognizing and developing restaurant talent. Among the now-famous graduates of her kitchen are Paul Prudhomme, who arrived in 1975, and Emeril Lagasse, who began his service in 1983. What's more, Brennan has worked with farmers and fishermen to cultivate local markets for their goods and provide her restaurants with the best possible ingredients. In her role as restaurateur, she has promoted the sociability of dining and the art of conversation. As the 21st century dawned, a new generation of the Brennan family, led by Ti Martin and Lally Brennan, stepped into the spotlight at Commander's, intent upon upholding the standards Ella Brennan set.

SCOTT R. SIMMONS
New Orleans, Louisiana

Ella Brennan and Dick Brennan, *The Commander's Palace New Orleans Cookbook* (1984); Pip Brennan, Jimmy Brennan, and Ted Brennan, *Breakfast at Brennan's and Dinner, Too* (1994); John Egerton, *Southern Food: At Home, on the Road, in History* (1987); Ti Adelaide Martin and Jamie Shannon, *Commander's Kitchen: Take Home the True Taste of New Orleans with More* than 150 *Recipes from Commander's Palace Restaurant* (2000).

Brown, Marion Lea

(1903–95) COOKBOOK AUTHOR. Writer, radio personality, textile designer, journalist, and editor, Marion Lea Brown, is best known for her two culinary works, *Marion Brown's Southern Cook Book* (1951) and *Marion Brown's Pickles and Preserves* (1955). Born in Petersburg, Va., Brown spent most of her adult life in Burlington, N.C., where she lived with her husband, Walter C. Brown, and two sons.

Marion Brown's Southern Cook Book remains an invaluable reference for culinary historians. Almost encyclopedic in its scope, and drawing on many community cookbooks, it chronicles a broad spectrum of historical and contemporary recipes, showcasing the state of southern cooking as it was in the mid-20th century. The book has been continuously in print for more than 50 years. Brown revised the book in 1968, updating and freshening the material for a contemporary audience.

Though Brown was not a professional historian, her understanding and use of materials available to her at the time make the cookbook an invaluable reference for historians, not so much for the actual historical recipes as for the selection of modern ones. Her collection of historical examples is telling and interesting; however, it is often drawn from such charming but historically unreliable works as Helen Bullock's *Williamsburg Art of Cookery* (1938). Of far more value for historians is Brown's keen eye for characteristically contemporary recipes, which is not merely exemplary of her own age, but is startlingly forward-looking. A good example is an early recipe for the vinaigrette-dressed black-eyed pea salad that was to become so popular toward the end of the century under such names as "Mississippi," "black-eyed pea," or even "redneck" caviar.

DAMON LEE FOWLER
Savannah, Georgia

Marion Brown, *Marion Brown's Pickles and Preserves* (1955), *Marion Brown's Southern Cook Book* (2001); Helen Bullock, *Williamsburg Art of Cookery* (1938, 1985); Damon Lee Fowler, *Classical Southern Cooking: A Celebration of the Cuisine of the Old South* (1995).

Brunswick Stew

Despite humble beginnings, Brunswick stew has been the subject of more public debate than any other southern stew. The stew is such a matter of pride that both Virginia and Georgia claim to be its birthplace. For years, stewmasters and their assistants from both states have competed in cook-offs at public festivals in an effort to settle the so-called stew war, and neither side has shown any willingness to relinquish its claim.

Historical markers found on U.S. Highway 1 in rural, south central Virginia proclaim Virginia's view and describe Brunswick stew in its most basic form: "According to local tradition, while Dr. Creed Haskins and several friends were on a hunting trip in Brunswick County in 1828, his camp cook, Jimmy Matthews, hunted squirrels for a stew. Matthews simmered the squirrels

with butter, onions, stale bread and seasonings, thus creating the dish known as Brunswick Stew. Other states have made similar claims but Virginia's is the first." Likewise, strategically located near Interstate 95, just outside of Brunswick, Ga., a concrete-filled, cast-iron stew pot is the backdrop for a plaque proclaiming coastal Georgia as the birthplace of Brunswick stew. Without a doubt, the signs give clear evidence of the ongoing stew war between Virginia and Georgia—although the war has spilled over to parts of Alabama, South Carolina, and Tennessee, and a great deal of North Carolina.

Matthews's recipe generally follows the pattern for other early stew dishes, such as those described in antebellum cookbooks that involve meat, sometimes marinated in vinegar, gently boiled in an iron pot with onion, seasonings, and butter. Gradually, the widespread domestication of animals such as sheep, hogs, chickens, and beef cattle eliminated the need to rely on the wild game common in early camp stews. Most contemporary recipes for Brunswick stew substitute pork, beef, or chicken for squirrel or other wild game, include several vegetables, and add seasonings that were missing in 19th-century versions.

While Virginia boasts ownership, the Georgia connections are also very strong. A book of antebellum recipes gathered by a Georgia homemaker, Annabella P. Hill, lists Camp Stew—Mr. B's Receipt. The recipe is virtually identical to contemporary Brunswick stew, including such vegetables as butter beans, corn, and tomatoes, while it calls for roughly equal quantities of squirrel and chicken meat.

It is important to note that Jimmy Matthews was African American. That fact, combined with the understanding that Native American cooking traditions also influenced these early camp stews, reminds us that Brunswick stew resulted from synthesis of shared food traditions.

Clearly, the stewmasters and crew members from the Brunswicks of Virginia, Georgia, and even North Carolina not only love the stew, but also cherish the ritual of stew making. The inconvenience of rising before dawn, the hard work of peeling potatoes and onions, and the hours spent pulling and pushing a five-foot paddle through an ever-thickening pottage become a labor of love. This sense of pride in the stew is effused with a strong sense of community service and camaraderie that strengthen the foundation of a tradition that remains an integral part of the community landscape.

SADDLER TAYLOR
McKissick Museum, Columbia, South Carolina

Annabella P. Hill, *Mrs. Hill's Southern Practical Cookery and Receipt Book* (1995); Elwood Street, *Brunswick County: The Home of the Stew* (1942); Stan Woodward, *Southern Stews: A Taste of the South* (documentary film, 2002).

Burgoo

Virginia sheep stew and Kentucky burgoo are unique among southern stews in their use of mutton or lamb, hinting at the historical importance of sheep in southern culture and diet. The inclusion of mutton is the major difference between burgoo and Brunswick stew. Otherwise, the two stews are quite similar, in both preparation and consumption.

While western Kentucky burgoo recipes are distinguished by this critical difference, many of them actually include other meats as well. Some recipes call for squirrel, veal, oxtail, or pork, bringing to mind jokes told by stewmasters that refer to "possum or animals that got too close to the pot." The storytelling and banter during the long hours of stew preparation are keys to strong social bonds that develop over a period of time. Kentuckians tell stories about the legendary Gus Jaubert, a member of Morgan's Raiders during the Civil War, who supposedly prepared hundreds of gallons of the spicy hunter's stew for the general's men.

The origin of the term *burgoo* is ambiguous. The term could be a corruption of the word *bulghur*, referring to a cereal porridge commonly fed to 17th-century English sailors, or a derivative of the Arabic word *burghul*, which refers to boiled cracked wheat. Another possibility stems from the French term *ragoût* (pronounced ra-goo), which is a heavy soup or thick stew. Nomenclature aside, the most striking characteristic of burgoo remains the inclusion of sheep as the primary meat ingredient.

While sheep raising is not commonly associated with the South, both the Spanish and English brought sheep to the New World during the earliest years of colonization. Early breeds such as Native Florida and Hog Island survive today. Domestic sheep production

Cooking burgoo for a benefit barbecue supper on the grounds of St. Thomas' Church, near Bardstown, Ky., 1940 (Marion Post Wolcott, photographer, Library of Congress [LC-USF33-030971-M3], Washington, D.C.)

increased dramatically in the Owensboro area after high tariffs on imported sheep were established in 1816. Both the topography and climate of western Kentucky were suited for the low-maintenance, grazing livestock. Able to survive on the most scant vegetation and capable of withstanding wide fluctuations in temperature, sheep were a natural fit.

Accomplished stew makers generally are men, sometimes dubbed "stewmasters" by their peers and stew consumers alike. The veneration of elders who carry closely guarded knowledge pertaining to "secret ingredients" and special techniques is an essential part of the burgoo tradition. The subsequent variety of burgoo recipes lends itself to a very localized sense of pride and distinctiveness from community to community. In no situation is this more evi-

dent than in the annual church parish picnic. During the summer, throughout western Kentucky, no less than 36 churches cook hundreds of gallons of burgoo. These picnics serve as fundraisers, homecomings, and community festivals. Most parishes have bumper stickers and signs proclaiming their barbecue and burgoo the region's "finest." Like other stews, burgoo is communal by nature, not only in preparation, but also in consumption. Through this sense of congregation, community stew makers come to identify with a particular tradition and proclaim a true sense of stew ownership.

SADDLER TAYLOR
McKissick Museum, Columbia, South Carolina

W. E. R. Byrne, *Tale of the Elk* (1995); Claudia Roden, *The Book of Jewish Food*

(1996); Reay Tannahill, *Food in History* (1973); Stan Woodward, *Southern Stews: A Taste of the South* (documentary film, 2002).

Cakes

To many southerners, the thought of favorite cakes brings to mind certain occasions. Weddings, holidays, "dinner on the grounds" church picnics, and funerals. Memories of fellowship hall tables laden with traditional southern sweets such as pineapple upside-down cake, Lane cake, coconut cake, and red velvet cake not only conjure tastes but also stories of the ladies who bake them. Some of these recipes are so linked to the baker that they become locally legendary. A church picnic becomes a silent yet fierce competition between cooks, and the event turns diners into unofficial judges, as it is not uncommon to see one plate with three types of coconut or caramel cake. Traditional favorites continue to evolve as ingredients become easy to find throughout the year and the price of expensive ingredients falls.

Early recipes were developed according to availability of products as well as economic status. While one family may have been able to prepare a dessert using store-bought tropical fruits like oranges or coconut, another family would need to send the kids out to gather pecans or black walnuts for free. The use of refined sugar as opposed to honey, molasses, or sorghum was also dictated by price and privilege. Location in the South drove recipes as well: someone living in Florida would have easier access to citrus fruits, while folks living in the mountains would be growing sweet potatoes and picking wild berries.

According to *The Williamsburg Art of Cookery—An Accomplished Gentlewoman's Guide*, published in 1742, "From christenings to funerals, cakes were most intimately associated with family and social life. There was a special cake for each happy or sad occasion." Early southern cakes were adapted from English recipes in order to use ingredients found specifically in the South. Because most southerners, rich and poor, had access to fresh dairy products such as milk, butter, and eggs, many delicious sweets made regular appearances at the dinner table as well as appearing for celebrations.

Humble cakes such as the pound cake—which uses a simple ratio of a pound of butter, a pound of sugar, a pound of flour, and a dozen eggs—are rich and delicious yet easy to mix and do not require a written recipe to remember. Leftover pound cake doubles as a delicious simple breakfast with coffee, and to this day even young southerners practice the ritual of smearing butter on a slice and toasting it for a morning meal. Pound cake is also one of those cakes that lasts a few days (because of the high fat content) and is something that a southern hostess can pull out in case someone happens to "drop by." Southern hospitality has reached mythical status partly because of the seemingly effortless ability of a woman to bring out a tray of sweets at any given moment. Pound cake is one of those foods that, dressed up with a dusting of powdered sugar or a light lemon flavored glaze, allows a hostess to appear to have spent all morning baking.

Another fruit cake is the stack cake. The method of making six or eight thin cake layers and spreading cooked dried apples between all the layers not only made the dessert look grand, it allowed a humble cake to soak up sweetness, moisture, and a rich flavor from the cooked apples. Two methods of preparing stack cake emerge from old records: one calls for a dough, rather than a batter, from which thin rounds are rolled and cut on a floured board and then baked, filled, and stacked. The other method directs the baker to pour batter into pie pans or cake rounds six or eight times to make that many thin layers. Dried apples, which carry the best flavor for this recipe, are cooked with cinnamon, cloves, and nutmeg to create a thick yet chunky applesauce. This sauce is spread between the cake layers and then the cake is stored, covered, for at least two days to allow the flavors to marry. The result is a flavorful and impressive cake that was most likely enjoyed during the colder months when fresh apples were not available.

More expensive and labor-intensive cakes, like Lane, Lady Baltimore, and Robert E. Lee cake, were made for special occasions, including weddings. While these three cakes are similar and are sometimes mistaken for each other, each has its own beginnings, and each has two or three distinct ingredients. The Lane cake was originated by Emma Rylander Lane of Clayton, Ala., and the original recipe was published in a little hometown cookbook entitled *Some Good Things to Eat* (1898). The cake layers are a basic yellow cake, and the filling is a boiled icing that includes raisins and "one wine-glass of good whiskey or brandy." The Lady Baltimore cake was born from Owen Wister's novel *Lady Baltimore*, set in Charleston, S.C., and published in 1906. In the novel Wister uses a character to describe the cake as "all soft, and in its layers it has nuts." The cake is indeed a white cake filled with raisins and nuts and with a meringue frosting. In the same manner, a Robert E. Lee cake, so named because it was made to honor General Lee, is a soft cake that includes lemon rind and juice. The icing that covers the cake is an egg white frosting, which takes its flavor from the juice of an orange or lemon. All three of these cakes emerged at about the same time, as reliable baking powder became available.

Modern southern bakers continue to use these recipes as a basis for their cakes. The availability of ingredients such as coconut and pineapple gave inventive cooks a way to dress up a humble skillet cake or yellow sponge cake. Cooking down sugar with butter creates a delicious caramel, and if one cooks this caramel in a cast-iron skillet, adds a single layer of pineapple rings with cherries in the center, tops it all with a simple yellow cake batter, bakes it, and turns it out on a decorative plate, the result is the favorite pineapple upside-down cake. Using the same method for making caramel, but allowing it to get to the soft-ball stage before mixing vigorously, gives the signature filling and frosting for the classic southern caramel cake. Layers of yellow cake filled and topped with seven-minute boiled icing and coconut create elegant and exotic coconut cake. Rich and mysterious, red velvet cake is actually a type of devil's food or chocolate cake that benefits from the addition of a little vinegar, copious amounts of red food coloring (one one-ounce bottle per recipe), and its signature cream-cheese frosting. The idea that red velvet cake originated in the South comes from the early use of beets in the recipe, which provided a less expensive sugar source and cast a red tone to the cocoa-filled batter.

While European pastries are now easy to find in southern towns, and it seems as if home bakers are harder to find, a quick survey of classic bakeshops reveals that most southerners continue to pine for the traditional flavors they grew up with. Perhaps youngsters now wax poetic about the caramel cake from Rhodes Bakery or the coconut cake from the Rich's Department Store bakeshop rather than their grandmother's cake.

ANGIE MOSIER
Atlanta, Georgia

Joseph E. Dabney, *Smokehouse Ham, Spoon Bread, and Scuppernong Wine: The Folklore and Art of Southern Appalachian Cooking* (1998); John Egerton, *Southern Food; At Home, on the Road, in History* (1993); Emma Rylander Lane, *Some Good Things to Eat* (1898); William Parks (publisher), *The Williamsburg Art of Cookery or Accomplished Gentlewoman's Companion* (1742); Linda Stradley, *I'll Have What They're Having— Legendary Local Cuisine* (2002); Owen Wister, *Lady Baltimore* (1906).

Catfish

There are some 2,000 species of catfish in the world, of which a couple dozen can be found in the United States, and, of these, about a dozen are native to the South. They can be roughly divided into three types: flathead, channel, and blue catfish. Flatheads and blues weighing upward of 150 pounds have been hauled out of southern waters. People in the South who live anywhere around a fishable body of water—whether it's a farm pond or the Mississippi River—have been eating catfish since time immemorial.

Catfish are omnivores in the true sense. They will eat practically anything, and this means they are easy to angle. A chicken liver or a ball of dough is sufficiently appetizing to entice a catfish to a hook. They grow to 18 inches in a year and, if left alone, will stay down near the bottom of whatever water they are in, living to old age and huge size. They were exploited first by Native Americans, followed by Americans of African and European descent. In the South the latter two groups tended to cook catfish in one way—bread it in cornmeal and fry it in hot grease in an iron skillet. Because of their omnivorous eating habits and preference for feeding close to the bottom, wild catfish have a musky flavor.

Once caught, and before being cooked, a catfish must be skinned. The time-honored method is to nail it to a board or tree by its head, make a slit around the gills with a knife, break off the dorsal and pectoral fins with pliers, and then use the pliers to grasp a loose

A mess of wild-caught catfish (Courtesy Wiley Prewitt Jr., photographer)

flap of skin from the incision and pull it down toward the tail. The skin should peel away from the fish like a tight piece of clothing coming off. Extreme care needs to be exercised when handling catfish: the spines at the tip of the dorsal and pectoral fins are bordered by a venom gland whose secretions can put a human being in severe pain lasting anywhere from 20 minutes to a couple of days, and hospitalization may be necessary if a fin breaks off in one's hand.

The catfish has proven adaptable to aquaculture, and it is the largest-selling farm-raised fish in the United States. Catfish can be easily trained to come to the surface for food, and if they are fed a diet of grain-based aquaculture feed, their meat will have a neutral flavor that will take on the taste of whatever spices are used in its preparation. The lion's share of the North American fish-buying public does not want the fish it consumes to have a strong flavor, and the adaptability of farm-raised catfish has been a marketing plus.

The catfish industry originated in the northwest quadrant of Mississippi below Memphis known as the Mississippi Delta. Four states now report catfish as a commercial crop, but still nearly half the nation's catfish are grown in the Delta. For more than a century, this huge, flat stretch of fertile Mississippi River bottomland was cotton country, but international competition virtually destroyed the market for North American cotton, beginning in the 1970s. Catfish saved many a Delta farmer's vast postplantation cotton land from the foreclosure auction block.

The Delta's soil holds water extremely well. The climate is warm, and a channel catfish (*Ictalurus punctatus*) can be grown to the market weight of a pound and a half in a year. A 15-acre pond can hold 50,000 fish. The pond-bank price in 2001 was hovering around 70 cents a pound, just as it had done over the past decade, and the fish sold for around five or six dollars a pound in supermarkets. A lot of it was selling. In the year 2000, some 600 million pounds were processed in the United States, according to the federal department of agriculture.

Like those from cotton cultivation before it, the profits from catfish farming are not widely distributed in the Delta. Workers in and around the ponds, and those in the processing plants, are generally from the same African American families that used to work the cotton fields. Wages are low, and the work is difficult, particularly for the women employed in the plants. The development of the catfish industry in the Delta has been marked by a series of labor-management conflicts.

Catfish farming is not cheap, nor is it for the faint-hearted. A modest eight ponds, each 15 acres, will cost nearly $500,000 to dig and stock, and then it will be 18 months until the first fish can be harvested—if they do not get sick and die or if a pond's oxygen level does not descend on a summer night past the critical level, suffocating all 50,000 fish in the pond. Nevertheless, in short order, catfish have gone from trash fish to preferred buys in supermarkets across the United States.

RICHARD SCHWEID
Barcelona, Spain

Linda Crawford, *The Catfish Book* (1991); Bruce Halstead, *Poisonous and Venomous Marine Animals of the World* (1988); Michael McCall, *The Catfish Journal* (August 1990); Richard Schweid, *Catfish and the Delta* (1992).

Chase, Leah Lange

(b. 1923) NEW ORLEANS CREOLE COOK AND RESTAURATEUR.

Leah Chase was born in Madisonville, La., where she grew up. The oldest of 11 children, Chase maintains that her mother hated to cook, except for baking bread. The Lange home nevertheless was the center of huge family feasts, and when those happened, everybody cooked. A typical Thanksgiving celebration would start with a glass of homemade strawberry wine and a bowl of gumbo. The meal itself would consist of fresh pork roast, wild game that Chase's father had killed, oyster patties, oyster dressing, and *petits pois*. Cakes and pies would round out the dinner.

Abandoning Madisonville for New Orleans, Chase bypassed Haspel Brothers' Sewing Factory, where well-raised Creole girls were expected to work, and struck out for the French Quarter. Within a short time she was hired at the Colonial Restaurant, where she worked under the tutelage of Bessie Sauveur. After marrying Edgar (Dooky) Chase II, she moved into his family's business, helping turn what had been a po' boy stand into the Dooky Chase Restaurant, one of the most prominent Creole restaurants in the country. Chase took her place in the kitchen, from which she has wielded great influence

Leah Chase, owner of Dooky Chase Restaurant (From *And I Still Cook* © 2003 by Leah Chase. Used by permission of Pelican Publishing Co., Inc.)

on what is considered today to be Creole cuisine.

Rudy Lombard, in *Creole Feast* (1978), states, "The single, lasting characteristic of Creole cuisine is the Black element. Black involvement in the New Orleans Creole cuisine is as old as gumbo and just as important." Lombard further describes Creole cuisine as a "creative improvisation," with the Creole chef relying "heavily on experience, combined with the full use and development of all five senses."

Leah Chase is the kind of Creole chef Lombard describes. She is self-taught and rarely measures an ingredient. She has strong opinions about the basics of Creole cooking and does not hesitate to pronounce, "That's not Creole." The gumbo at the Dooky Chase Restaurant is what Leah Chase calls

typical Creole gumbo: it contains crab, shrimp, chicken, two kinds of sausage, veal brisket, ham, and the perfect roux. "Not a real dark roux," she says. "That's more Cajun." But she maintains the roux must be the perfect color and texture and that the cook had better stand by her pot to make that happen. "Don't give me that sticky, gooey stuff."

Chase has other rules: onions and seasonings must be cut fine—they cannot float; beans cannot float either—they have to be creamy; okra has to be cooked down, cabbage has to be smothered; a good dose of paprika makes gravy glow; onions and garlic and green peppers had better be there; and only the best ingredients will do—Vaucresson's *chaurice*, the best smoked sausage, lean ham, and lean veal brisket. Creole desserts are pretty basic fare: bread puddings, pound cakes, and apple or custard pies. Under Chase's hand, as one might expect, even bread pudding gets a kick. She tosses in a glass of rum to "pep it up."

Leah Chase played a significant role in the civil rights movement in New Orleans, as her restaurant became a gathering spot for activists. She has continued to play a role since then as a community leader. Her influence on Creole cooking meanwhile spread beyond the city in the 1970s, when she became the focus of articles in regional and national publications. She has been honored repeatedly as a "Queen of Creole Cooking."

After Hurricane Katrina inundated much of New Orleans and left Dooky Chase sitting in five feet of floodwater, the restaurant was temporarily closed. But after a collective effort of fund-raising, Dooky Chase reopened.

CAROL ALLEN
Paris, France

Carol Allen, *Leah Chase: Listen, I Say Like This* (2002); Nathanial Burton and Rudy Lombard, eds., *Creole Feast* (1978); Leah Chase, *And I Still Cook* (2003), *The Dooky Chase Cookbook* (1990), *Down Home Healthy: Family Recipes of Black American Chefs* (1994); Brian Lanker, *I Dream a World: Portraits of Black Women Who Changed America* (1989).

Chess Pie

The origins of the name *chess pie* are hard to trace, primarily because the dish does not appear in southern cookbooks before the 20th century. Some of the earliest printed references to the pie were penned by Sister J. M. Mangus of Roanoke, Va., in *The Inglenook Cook Book* in 1906 and in a cookbook published by the Fort Worth Women's Club in 1928. Food writers have offered several playful explanations for the unusual name. First, because of their high sugar content, chess pies were stored at room temperature in pie safes or storage cabinets called pie chests. When the *t* was dropped from chest, the pie was called ches' pie. Another explanation suggests the pie is so simple that when a southern cook was asked to name it, the reply, "it's just pie," became "it's jes pie," and the "jes" became "chess."

The cheese etymology seems a likely explanation, because in old cookbooks, cheesecakes and pies that were sometimes made with cheese, sometimes without (referring to cheese in the textural sense), are often included in a single category. A number of cheeseless "cheese" pastries in *Housekeeping in Old Virginia* (1879) are made with egg yolks, sugar, butter, milk, and lemon juice—very much like chess pie filling. While the pie could have grown out of a British cheesecake tradition, it probably also developed in response to the increased availability of both refined sugar and dairy products. During the 1930s sorghum and molasses were replaced by refined white sugars, and rural electrification made refrigerators more common and dairy products more widely available.

The chess pie is a relatively recent addition to the dessert repertoire of southern families. Since the 1930s this simple pie-confection has been made with four basic ingredients: milk, sugar, eggs, and butter. Traditional cooks sometimes added vanilla, cinnamon, and cornmeal or flour before stirring the mixture together and baking it in a pie crust. Chess pie is a custard or transparent pie that became so popular it spawned chess cakes, chess bars, and chess cookies.

With the rise of celebrity restaurant chefs at the end of the 20th century, chess pies became a symbol of new southern cooking. One such chef and food writer, Bill Neal, prefaces a chess pie recipe in his book *Southern Cooking*, by saying: "In Tennessee, as many as six or seven of these pies, once baked and cooled, are stacked on each other and sliced as a cake. Elsewhere, they are offered singly, with a little whipped cream." Basic chess pies have been expanded to assume many different forms, including chocolate chess pies. The December 2001 issue of *Southern Living* magazine featured recipes for tangerine, grapefruit, lemon-lime, and orange chess pies. A new generation of chefs use chess pies as the foundation for innovative confections that feature allspice, cumin, curry, ground white pepper, pecans, coconut, and rich pastry crusts. To this mixture they add garnishes of meringue, mint leaves, and fresh fruit. Mississippi pastry chef Martha Foose dishes up sweet-tea chess pie.

Chess pie has strong associations with the notions of home and comfort. And in her book *Queen of the Turtle Derby and Other Southern Phenomena* writer Julia Reed discusses the importance and uniqueness of southern cooking, specifically invoking the chess pie as a unique staple of the South's cuisine and culture.

MARK F. SOHN
Pikeville College

FRANCES ABBOTT
University of Mississippi

Sarah Belk, *Around the Southern Table* (1991); Craig Claiborne, *Craig Claiborne's Southern Cooking* (1987); John Egerton, *Southern Food: At Home, on the Road, in History* (1987); Bill Neal, *Bill Neal's Southern Cooking* (1989), *Biscuits, Spoonbread, and Sweet Potato Pie* (1996); Mark F. Sohn, *Southern Country Cooking* (1992).

Chicken, Fried

Columbus brought chickens to America in 1493, and they have graced American tables—particularly in the South—ever since. Southern fried chicken is probably the single most popular and uni-versally consumed food ever to come from this region of the country. It appeared in the earliest cookbooks. Mary Randolph's *Virginia House-wife* (1824) recommended a method strikingly similar to that commonly used today: cut-up pieces of chicken dredged in flour, sprinkled with salt and pepper, and fried in hot fat.

There are, of course, numerous variations on the basic technique. Some cooks insist on frying chicken in lard, but others prefer vegetable oil; some say pan frying in an inch or so of fat is best, while others choose deep frying instead; some use only flour to coat the chicken pieces, but others add cornmeal or milk or egg; some restrict seasonings to salt and pepper, while others go for spicier or more pungent tastes, such as hot sauce, garlic, red pepper, or lemon; some seek a dry, crisp, crunchy exterior, and others pour gravy or cream sauce over the finished product.

Chicken gravy is, in some circles, a classic accompaniment. The gravy is made from the dregs in the frying skillet, supplemented by a mixture of flour and either milk or water and seasoned with salt and pepper. Spooned onto potatoes or rice or biscuits, chicken gravy offers a savory flavor that southerners have known and loved for generations.

The standard explanation for the origins of fried chicken suggests that the wide availability of fowl in the colonial era and the cooking techniques of African slaves combined to produce "fried" chicken, and cooks of African descent have long been recognized as among the region's best fryers. But rarely do

Mrs. McLelland cooking fried chicken for Sunday dinner, Escambia Farms, Fla., 1942 (John Collier, photographer, Library of Congress [LC-USF34-082651-C], Washington, D.C.)

southerners reach consensus on a definitive version of the dish. Virtually the only aspect of southern fried chicken that no one debates is the best way to eat it: with the fingers, the only practical means of separating the crisp skin and tender meat from the bone. "Finger lickin' good" became a motto of Colonel Harland Sanders's Kentucky Fried Chicken when the Corbin, Ky., entrepreneur launched a fast-food chicken business in 1956.

Following in the wake of Sanders, numerous fast-food franchise outlets now dispense the popular finger food in cities and towns throughout the nation and the world. The volume of fried chicken sales is such that the raising of chickens has become a major agricultural industry in the South.

Purists bemoan that mass production yields an inferior fowl, one that is oversized and lacks the leanness, tenderness, and taste that young pullets had when they scratched in southern yards and received ample rations of cracked corn as they approached frying size. Noting the mid-20th-century trend toward larger, less flavorful fowl, Ralph McGill of the *Atlanta Constitution* declared a preference for "barnyard subdebs, rarely more than ten to twelve weeks old and weighing from a pound and a half to two pounds."

Even as chicken raising and chicken cooking have become increasingly industrial, the southern affinity for fried chicken has not waned. Fried chicken has come to be appreciated as both symbol and sustenance. As such, the dish remains proudly provincial. In his 1982 book *American Taste* Jim Villas of North Carolina observed: "Let's not beat around the bush for one second. To know about fried chicken, you have to have been weaned and reared on it in the South. Period."

What is more, fried chicken is the stuff of song, as in "Fried Chicken," a single cut in 1957 by Hank Penny, that featured a song called "Rock of Gibraltar" on the B-side. It is also the stuff of tragicomedy. "Last time I was down South, I walked into this restaurant," wrote Dick Gregory in his memoir, *Callus on My Soul*. "This white waitress came up to me and said, 'We don't serve colored people here.' I said, 'That's all right, I don't eat colored people. Bring me a whole fried chicken.' About that time, these three cousins came in. You know the ones I mean, Ku, Klux, and Klan. They said, 'Boy, we're givin' you fair warnin'. Anything you do to that chicken, we're gonna do to you.' So I put down my knife and picked up that chicken and kissed it."

JOHN EGERTON
Nashville, Tennessee

John T. Edge, *Fried Chicken: An American Story* (2004); Damon Lee Fowler, *Fried Chicken: The World's Best Recipes from Memphis to Milan, from Buffalo to Bangkok* (1997); Ronni Lundy, *Shuck Beans, Stack Cakes, and Honest Fried Chicken: The Heart and Soul of Southern Country Kitchens* (1991); Page Smith and Charles Daniel, *The Chicken Book* (1975); *Southern Living* (September 1995); Psyche A. Williams-Forson, *Building Houses out of Chicken Legs: Black Women, Food, and Power* (2006).

Chitterlings

Many aspects of contemporary African American and southern white cuisine have their roots in the eating habits of the Old South. Many of the principal foods and dishes use pork products. These dishes include fatback, pigs' ears, pigs' feet, pork chops, and chitterlings. Chitterlings, or chitlins, are the small intestines of hogs, cooked in batter. Studies of early African American eating habits suggest that such foods as chitlins came into the diet because of the necessity for rural, poverty-ridden southerners to use every bit of food available. When a hog was slaughtered, no edible part was wasted. In the book *Chitlin Strut and Other Madrigals* novelist and essayist William Price Fox of South Carolina asks the question, "Who will eat a chitlin?" He answers, "You take a man and tie him to a stake and feed him bread and water and nothing else for seven days and seven nights, and then he will eat a chitlin. He won't like it, but he will eat it." Fox perceives the consumption of chitlins as a badge of impoverished circumstances, emerging as a staple in the southern diet out of necessity as opposed to preference.

To prevent spoilage, chitlins were prepared and eaten soon after the hog was killed. The common method of preparation was to clean the intestines carefully, soak them in water for a day, parboil them, and only then to fry them in batter. Viscera have been part of the staple diets of other cultures, including the Eskimos and people in Central Europe and the Balkans. They have been found to be nutritious and a good source of iron. Southerners have disdained the eating of viscera at times, and some people who eat chitlins have attempted to hide them behind names such as "Kentucky oysters." Not all southerners are ashamed of the uncommon food, however.

White, rural southerners of the 20th century celebrated chitterlings as both cultural emblem and nourishment. Active chitterling eating clubs like the Royal Order of Chitlin Eaters of Nashville, Tenn., and the Happy Chitlin Eaters of Raleigh, N.C., emerged by the middle of the century. The traditional song "Chitlin Cookin' Time in Cheatham County" indicates the importance of chitlins to regional identity:

> There's a quiet and peaceful county
> in the state of Tennessee.
> You will find it in the book they call
> geography.
> Not famous for its farming, its
> mines, or its stills,
> But they know there's chitlin cookin'
> in them Cheatham county hills.
>
> When it's chitlin cookin' time in
> Cheatham county,
> I'll be courtin' in them Cheatham
> county hills.
> And I'll pick a Cheatham county
> chitlin cooker.
> I've a longin' that the chitlins will fill.

African Americans with roots in the rural South also claimed a specific cultural meaning for chitlins. Because of the restriction imposed on cuisine by life at the bottom of the white power structure, African American cooks fashioned a cuisine of their own, reinventing traditional foodways in an African-influenced manner, and claimed chitterlings as distinctly African American.

Chitterling imagery infuses African American cultural forms. The informal circuit of juke joints and clubs patronized by African Americans has long been called the Chitlin Circuit. Bluesman Mel Brown, a veteran of the circuit, titled his early 1970s greatest-hits album *Eighteen Pounds of Unclean Chitlins and Other Greasy Blues Specialties*. In his novel *Invisible Man* Ralph Ellison invokes chitterlings as both a chosen cultural icon and a liability. The protagonist imagines a scene wherein he accuses Bledsoe, a pompous but influential educator and leading citizen of a small southern town, of a secret love of chitterlings: "I saw myself advancing upon Bledsoe . . . and suddenly whipping out a foot or two of chitterlings, raw, uncleaned, and dripping sticky circles on the floor as I shake them in his face, shouting: 'Bledsoe, you're a shameless chitterling eater! I accuse you of relishing hog bowels! Ha! And not only do you eat them, you sneak and eat them in *private* when you think you're unobserved! You're a sneaking chitterling lover!'"

When soul food came into vogue in America during the late 1960s and early 1970s, chitlins were privileged as an authentic cultural marker. But not all African Americans embraced chitterlings as a badge of identity. In 1968 Eldridge Cleaver mused, "You hear a lot of jazz about soul food. Take chitterlings: the ghetto blacks eat them from necessity while the black bourgeoisie has turned it into a mocking slogan. . . . Now that they have the price of a steak, here they come prattling about Soul Food."

Today, chitlins endure as an element of southern culinary culture. Each fall in Salley, S.C., as many as 20,000 people gather to celebrate chitlins at the Chitlin' Strut festival. The one-day event features the crowning of Miss Chitlin' Strut, the frying and eating of five tons of chitlins, and the Chitlin' Strut contest itself. The "Chitlin' Strut" is a dance with twisting gyrations reflecting, some participants say, "the way chitlins make you feel."

KAREN M. MCDEARMAN
FRANCES ABBOTT
University of Mississippi

Eldridge Cleaver, *Soul on Ice* (1968); Ralph Ellison, *Invisible Man* (1952); William Price Fox, *Chitlin Strut and Other Madrigals* (1983); Bob Jeffries, *Soul Food Cookbook* (1970); Julian H. Lewis, *Negro Digest* (April 1950); *Southern Living* (November 1979); Calvin C. Schwabe, *Unmentionable Cuisine* (1979).

Claiborne, Craig

(1920–2000) FOOD WRITER, EDITOR. Born in Sunflower, Miss. (population 500), Craig Claiborne cherished childhood memories of beaten biscuits, churned clabber, hot cornbread, and chicken barbecues tended by his father. Another memory, that of his mother's monogrammed silver spoon, used to stir so many sauces that "the lip, once a perfect oval, [was] worn down by an inch," had special significance. Forced by financial setbacks to move to Indianola and open a boardinghouse in 1924, his mother used her ability to "divine" ingredients, reproducing countless dishes from Creole snapper to Brunswick stew, to keep the family solvent and make Miss Kathleen's one of the most "genteel" and well-regarded establishments in the Mississippi Delta. John Dollard rented a room in her home while researching his classic study of southern race relations, *Caste and Class in a Southern Town.*

Shortly after graduating from the University of Missouri in journalism (June 1942), Claiborne enlisted in the navy, having "never sampled a glass of wine" nor eaten anything more exotic than jellied consommé. By the end of his tour of duty, however, he had tasted Moroccan lamb couscous and French pastries in Casablanca and had visited cafés and bistros throughout Europe. Following a brief stint in advertising and publicity in Chicago, another year in Europe, and reenlistment in the navy at the outbreak of the Korean War, he finally decided to fuse his interests in food and writing and enrolled in the Lausanne Professional School of the Swiss Hotel Keepers Association.

Claiborne settled in Manhattan and worked a series of part-time jobs, including bartending in upstate New York and acting as a receptionist at *Gourmet* magazine. Eventually he moved into an editor's position. In 1957 Claiborne met and was interviewed by Jane Nickerson of the *New York Times*, who was looking for someone to replace her as food editor at the paper. Despite the tradition of women filling the post, Claiborne became the paper's food editor upon Nickerson's resignation in 1957. During his 29 years at the *Times*, Claiborne pioneered a new system for restaurant reviews by concluding each review with a rating on a four-star scale after repeated visits. His new work revolutionized the place of restaurant reviews in American newspapers, moving them from the arena of advertising to important food criticism. After his retirement from the *Times* in 1986, he continued to travel, lecture, and write books. He authored numerous recipes and more than 20 books.

Shortly before the publication of his now-classic *New York Times Cook Book* in 1961, Claiborne began to test and prepare recipes with Pierre Franey, former chef of Manhattan's Le Pavilion restaurant. Working together in Claiborne's East Hampton home, the two concocted recipes that enriched the food pages of the *Times* and served as the basis for a series of cookbooks. Claiborne died in January 2000 at the age of 79.

In addition to his regular column, cookbooks, and a dining guide to Manhattan, Claiborne published *A Feast Made for Laughter* (1983), a memoir complete with 100 favorite recipes. Listed next to the *oeufs à la chimay* is, of course, a recipe for cheese grits.

ELIZABETH M. MAKOWSKI
University of Mississippi

Craig Claiborne, *Best of Craig Claiborne: 1,000 Recipes from His New York Times Food Columns and Four of His Classic Cookbooks* (1999), *Cooking with Craig Claiborne and Pierre Franey* (1985), *Craig Claiborne's A Feast Made for Laughter* (1982), *Craig Claiborne's Gourmet Diet* (1980), *Craig Claiborne's Kitchen Primer* (1993), *Craig Claiborne's Southern Cooking* (1992), *The New York Times Cook Book* (original edition, 1972; revised edition, 1990); Bryan Miller, *The New York Times* (24 January 2000); Jim Villas, *Gourmet* (April 2000).

Coca-Cola

William Allen White once called it "the sublimated essence of all that America stands for," and an anonymous but no less fervent admirer called it "the holy water of the American South." The "it," as the latest in a long line of slogans proclaims, is, of course, Coca-Cola.

John S. Pemberton, known as "Doc," like most pharmacists of his era, concocted Coca-Cola in 1886 primarily as a hangover cure. It has subsequently been many things to many people—to Robert Winship Woodruff, its high priest for nearly 60 years, it was "a religion as well as a business." Pemberton first made Coke, its nickname from early on, in Atlanta, and Coca-Cola men have bestrode that city ever since. Pemberton was pleased soon after his invention to sell the rights to the beverage for $1,750 to another Atlanta pharmacist, Asa Candler. Candler was even more pleased in 1919 to sell the Coca-Cola Company for $25 million. It was the biggest financial deal, until then, in the history of the American South. (Candler sold only part of his bounty; earlier, in 1899, thinking that consumption of the drink would be limited largely to soda fountains, he had disposed of practically all the bottling rights to it for one dollar. The drink had first been bottled back in 1894 by Joseph Biedenharn in

Vicksburg, Miss.) The prime mover in the 1919 transaction was the banker Ernest Woodruff. His son Robert (1889–1985) took over the company in 1923. "Asa Candler put us on our feet," one Coca-Cola executive would say years afterward, "and Bob Woodruff gave us wings."

Dwight D. Eisenhower once speculated that his good friend Bob Woodruff might be the richest man in the United States. Atlanta's Emory University, on whose predecessor campus Woodruff had spent less than a year as an undergraduate before being invited to leave, would over the ensuing years be endowed, by him and his family, with some $150 million of Coca-Cola largess.

Until World War II, when the Coca-Cola Company construed it to be its patriotic duty to get Coke to every thirsty American serving abroad, the drink was chiefly marketed in the United States. Soon it was universal. Asa Candler had briefly flirted with the idea of Coca-Cola cigars and Coca-Cola chewing gum at the turn of the century, but until the 1950s the company was strictly a one-product enterprise. Then it began to diversify. Orange juice, other soft drinks, eventually even wines, and most recently films (Columbia Pictures) have merchandised under Coca-Cola's auspices around the world. The placid liquid that Doc Pemberton had first mixed in a backyard, three-legged iron pot (stirring it with an oar) had become the foundation of a multibillion-dollar industry.

In 1985 Coca-Cola chairman Roberto Guizueta announced that, for the first time in 99 years, the drink's taste formula would be changed, leading to much hoopla and to criticism from some for yet another change in a southern tradition. The company relented in the face of the public pressure and continued marketing "classic" Coke. However, despite (or perhaps because of) the overwhelming public demand for a return to the "classic" Coke taste, Coca-Cola currently comes in a variety of flavors such as Cherry Coke, Vanilla Coke, and Coca-Cola with Lime, as well as in low-calorie and caffeine-free formulas. As of 2006, the Coca-Cola Company operates in over 200 countries and produces over 400 brands. It is undoubtedly the most ubiquitous consumer product in the world.

E. J. KAHN JR.
The New Yorker

Frederick Allen, *Secret Formula: How Brilliant Marketing and Relentless Salesmanship Made Coca-Cola the Best-Known Product in the World* (1994); Bob Hall, *Southern Exposure* (Fall 1976); Constance L. Hayes, *The Real Thing: Truth and Power at the Coca-Cola Company* (2004); E. J. Kahn Jr., *The Big Drink: The Story of Coca-Cola* (1951); Kathryn W. Kemp, *God's Capitalist: Asa Candler of Coca-Cola* (2002).

Coons and Possums

These days, if southerners consider raccoons and opossums at all, they think of them as little more than ruined piles of fur along the highways or noises around the garbage can at night. There was a time, however, when folks accorded these creatures almost mythic status and prized them as game and food animals. The words of a song collected in 1920s

Mississippi by folklorist A. P. Hudson evokes those days when

> Old Blue treed,
> I went to see.
> There sat the 'possum on a 'simmon tree.
> He grinned at me,
> I looked at him.
> I shook him out,
> Blue took him in.
> I took him home and baked him brown,
> Placed them taters all around.

In the heavily farmed and settled South of the 19th and early 20th centuries, when species like white-tailed deer and wild turkey dwindled into memory, coons and possums remained available and familiar game. Through that long association coons and possums became symbols of a rural South where hunting was commonplace and foodways were closely tied to the land.

The lore of the South is crowded with references to coons and possums. Some people kept coons as pets despite the havoc they could cause in a household, and even today older folks may compare an overly active or curious person to a pet coon. Hunters respected the coon as game, and a coonskin cap was long the mark of an accomplished woodsman. In a more obscure tradition, hunters preserved the S-shaped penis bones from large boar coons as trophies, charms, or even toothpicks. The wide mouth of the possum and its 50 teeth (more than in any other North American land mammal) engendered the phrase "to grin like a possum," as its practice of feigning death when fright-

ened produced the charge of "playing possum." As the only marsupial native to North America, the possum inevitably inspired fantastic tales about its biology. Some folks insisted that the male used his forked penis to copulate with the nostrils of the female, who later blew the baby possums into her pouch through her nose. Others believed that the baby possums formed on the ends of their mother's nipples like fruit. Strangely enough, the notion that possums are immune to snakebite is partly true. Though susceptible to the neurotoxins from cobras and coral snakes, for example, when subjected to venom from common southern vipers such as copperheads, water moccasins, and rattlesnakes, possums survive with no apparent damage.

Snakebites have been the least of their problems as both possums and coons endured consistent hunting pressure in the rural South that last peaked during a spike in fur prices in the late 1970s and early 1980s. While trappers probably took the greatest number of animals, hunting with dogs is the most recognizable method of capturing coons and possums. Early on, coon hunting evolved into a more specialized pursuit than possum hunting. Hunters used hounds like redbones, bluetick, or treeing Walkers that showed a special ability for coon hunting. Coon hides were always valuable, and coon hunts themselves are sometimes quite rigorous, involving the traversing of hills or swamps, walls of briars, and cold water, all in darkness. Good coon dogs and their owners could achieve a level of local celebrity that possum hunting seldom offered. Almost any canine might develop into a good possum dog, and hunters generally did not have to travel far to find their quarry. Though few hunters would have shunned the possum as game, they considered it less of a challenge and always more common than the coon.

For the actual chase, both coon and possum hunters went out at night with one or perhaps a few hounds. They searched areas like the margins of agricultural fields, wooded streams, or river bottoms and stands of mast-producing trees that offered a chance of striking game. With coons, the hunt's duration depends upon how long the animal runs before taking refuge in trees, holes, or caves. Coons often end the chase in some of the tallest trees available. In early times, hunters might simply cut down the tree to get at the coon; in later years they used torches or flashlights to "shine" enough of the animal to shoot. Possums, on the other hand, usually go up the first available tree or sapling, making them more accessible to those with few resources, like children or the very poor. Sometimes people could indeed simply shake the animal out like the hunter in "Old Blue." Hunters also took advantage of possums' habit of feigning death as a way to bring them home alive; they might then pen and feed the animals for days or weeks to improve the quality of the meat or just to save them for a special occasion.

For many hunters the meat was just as important as the hide. If hunters took more than they needed, they could always sell or trade the excess. A big coon might weigh 20 pounds, and a large possum, 7 or 8. While they grow larger in the northern states, the coons and possums in the South offered a significant addition to any rural kitchen. Folks relished them in part because both animals accumulate large amounts of fat during late summer and early fall when food is abundant. Now that modern medicine associates fat with so many health problems and we get much of ours from drive-through windows, it is difficult to appreciate the importance of fat in the diets of earlier southerners. Edible animal fat was valuable, and in the autumn a quarter of the body weight of healthy coons and possums might be fat. John Audubon and John Bachman noted the anticipation that proceeded a 19th-century possum hunt and pronounced the animal an "excellent substitute for roast pig." While hunters almost always took the pelts from the more valuable coons, people often scalded and even singed the fur from possums during times when the fat was more important than the skin.

In a nod to that older preparation, Louisiana biologist George H. Lowery Jr. enlivened his 1974 biology text with a possum recipe. He suggested stuffing the body cavity of a scalded and scraped possum with a combination of its own browned, chopped heart and liver, onion, bread crumbs, boiled egg, spices, and a dash of Tabasco. Most published recipes for both possums and coons are somewhat less elaborate and follow a fairly standard formula. They call for skinning the animal, removing the glands or lymph nodes under the legs, trimming away most of the once-prized fat, and parboiling before seasoning, covering, and baking. Baking time varies, but averages around two hours at 300° to 375°, depending on the size of the animal. Cooks often call for the addition of the traditional sweet potatoes or some other root vegetables during the last hour of cooking. Some folks barbecue the meat after parboiling, especially that of coons. Barbecued coon is not uncommon at large-scale game dinners sponsored by hunting clubs or churches where cooks grill other types of less oily game. The dark, rich meat of coons holds up well to a spicy sauce and is less threatening to timid modern diners than is the plain baked animal. Many southerners still enjoy coon hunting, even though the pelts are worth very little, and thus the animals still find their way onto the table. Hunters seldom kill and eat possums today. People associate possums with rural poverty and reject them perhaps because they are too common, too easy to hunt, and too greasy—the same reasons they were once so valuable.

Certain groceries and fish markets still carry coons and possums in season, and trappers and hunters sell them to those who know where to look. For the interested, a call to local wildlife conservation officials can probably put one in touch with trappers and hunters who can fill any order. Buyers should be aware, however, that the skinned carcasses of the animals are very difficult to distinguish from that of a housecat. At one time, passing off stray cats as coons or possums was such a standard practical joke that most buyers refused to pay unless the carcass had a foot attached

for positive identification. Determined cooks who choose to purchase rather than hunt their own will also encounter an interesting facet of American wildlife law that makes coons, possums, and other furbearers the only truly wild game legally sold in the United States. Around the turn of the 20th century legislatures criminalized the sale of game like deer and quail as part of general wildlife conservation efforts but made allowance for furbearers. Nowadays the laws of individual states vary but many continue to allow licensed trappers and hunters to sell furbearer carcasses for food. Recent interest in game in upscale American restaurants is misleading, as animals and birds typically marketed as "game" in the United States are grown on farms and do not live in the wild. Furbearers may be the nonhunting cook's only chance at purchasing truly wild southern game.

WILEY C. PREWITT JR.
Lodi, Mississippi

John James Audubon, *The Quadrupeds of North America* (1856); Burkhard Bilger, *Outside* (July 2001); Jerry Clower, *Stories from Home* (1992); Billy Joe Cross, *Cooking Wild Game and Fish Mississippi Style: A Treasury of Unique Recipes for the Sportsmen* (1976); George A. Feldhamer, Bruce C. Thompson, and Joseph A. Chapman, eds., *Wild Mammals of North America: Biology, Management and Conservation* (2003); Arthur Palmer Hudson, *Journal of American Folklore* (April–June 1926); T. A. Long, *The Rugged Breed: True Adventures of Coon Hunters and Their Dogs* (1965); George H. Lowery Jr., *The Mammals of Louisiana and Its Adjacent Waters* (1974); Keith Sutton, *Hunting Arkansas: The Sportsman's Guide to Natural State Game* (2002); Keith and

Theresa Sutton, *Duck Gumbo to Barbecued Coon: A Southern Game Cookbook* (2001); Leon F. Whitney and Acil B. Underwood, *The Coon Hunters Handbook* (1952).

Corn

Stephen Vincent Benét, in *Western Star*, wrote a significant quatrain about one group of early settlers and their contact with corn:

And those who came were resolved
to be Englishmen,
Gone to world's end, but English
everyone,
And they ate the white corn-kernels,
parched in the sun.
And they knew it not, but they'd not
be English again.

Indeed, the parched corn and the seed corn that various Indian tribes gave to colonists saved their lives and changed their diets, habits, and culture. Corn became the most important crop in the South and throughout the country, feeding families and their livestock and thus establishing and sustaining a new way of life in a new land. Indians throughout what would become the United States, as well as Mexico and Central and South America, had grown corn, or maize, for thousands of years, selectively improving it from a coarse grass with a few kernels into a strong stalk with primitive ears bearing more kernels. Maize was not then grown in Europe. Early European settlers in America understood the value of this crop and further developed it through their traditional farming practices to produce enough grain to feed their livestock and their large families. Even-

tually, there would be enough surplus to sell, but corn, in the early days, anchored a subsistence way of life.

Corn involved the entire farmstead. Horses, mules, or oxen provided the power for turning the soil, harrowing, laying off rows, cultivating, and hauling the harvest to barns and cribs. The whole family, adults and children, often worked in the fields, cultivating, hoeing, cutting tops, and pulling fodder for livestock feed, as well as harvesting, shucking, shelling, and grinding the corn. This subsistence way of life also depended on additional livestock—milk and beef cattle, hogs, sheep, chickens, ducks, geese, and turkeys—all eating corn. The manure they produced was spread over the fields as fertilizer. Corn that shattered in the field or traveled through the digestive system of the domestic animals fed the wild birds and other game that also supplemented the family's diet.

Imaginative cooks made a variety of dishes from the product—cornbread, muffins, fritters, roasting ears, corn pudding, pickled corn, hominy, grits, mush, and coating for fried meat and fish. However, a steady diet of corn brought on pellagra with diarrhea, loss of appetite, ulcers of the tongue and skin, depression, sluggishness, fever, and delirium, because corn does not contain vitamin B (niacin). Fortunately, southerners also grew a variety of beans that provided niacin.

The carbohydrates in the corn made it a potent source of alcohol when distilled after a fermenting process. Whiskey became a transportable trade item as well as a social one. Cornhusks not consumed by livestock could be braided into chair seats or horse collars, and even fashioned into attractive dolls. Cobs made a functional bowl for tobacco pipes and served a useful purpose in outhouses. They also became stoppers for jugs, and, soaked in fat or oil (later kerosene), they were useful in starting fires. Cornstalks were made into toys for children. Corn husking was an excuse for parties, with music, dancing, and sometimes a jug of whiskey from last year's crop.

By 1849 the South had 18 million acres planted in corn, as compared to 5 million in cotton. Corn's reproductive return is greater than that of any other cereal crop, with one grain producing anywhere from 500 to 4,000 kernels. With new varieties of hybrid seed corn and better methods of cultivation and use of fertilizers, corn became a major crop for domestic use and export. In 2002, 9.5 billion bushels of corn, at an average of 127.6 bushels per acre, and 102.4 tons of silage were grown in the United States. Products made from corn syrup and carbohydrates are used in numerous foods that we consume every day. In addition, there are more than 500 industrial uses of corn, which makes its way into automobile paint, plastics, tires, textiles, library paste, gunpowder, baby powder, sandpaper, soap, surgical dressings, insecticides, shoe polish, embalming fluids, rubbing alcohol, deodorants, mattresses, varnish, brake fluid, adhesive tape, and fireworks.

The crop that had been essential to subsistence living in the early days of the South is now a major crop with innumerable uses at home and abroad.

LOYAL JONES
Berea, Kentucky

Samuel R. Aldrich and Earl R. Leng, *Modern Corn Production* (1966); Joseph E. Dabney, *Smokehouse Ham, Spoon Bread, and Scuppernong Wine: The Folklore and Art of Southern Appalachian Cooking* (1998); Betty Fussell, *The Story of Corn* (1992); Nicholas B. Hardeman, *Shucks, Shocks, and Hominy Blocks* (1981); Janice B. Longone, *Mother Maize and King Corn: The Persistence of Corn in the American Ethos* (1943); Paul Weatherwax, *Indian Corn in Old America* (1954).

Cornbread

Ground corn provided the staff of life for Native American societies throughout the Western Hemisphere before the arrival of Europeans, and later southerners followed their example. The Indians called their breads *suppone* and *appone*, and *pone* became the term in the South for cornmeal bread. Made from meal, salt, water, and bear or hog grease, these early pone breads might be called ashcake, from being baked in fireplace coals; hoecake, bread literally baked on a hoe; johnnycake, an adaptation of "journey cake" (a pocket bread), or corn dodgers, which were originally cooked in boiling water that caused the bread tidbits to bounce around.

"Second generation" cornbreads came later, with additional ingredients, such as flour, baking powder, baking soda, eggs, and buttermilk. They are sometimes called batter cakes, eggbread, or corn cakes. Cracklings, the crispy

Student cafeteria helper at Bethune-Cookman College in Daytona Beach, Fla., with a large tray of cornbread she has prepared for luncheon, 1943 (Gordon Parks, photographer, Library of Congress [LC-USW3-016880-C], Washington, D.C.)

morsels remaining after the rendering of lard, were also added to cornpone. Later cornmeal breads included corn light bread, griddle cakes, and corn muffins and corn sticks, the latter baked in their own special iron pans. Hushpuppies, a traditional accompaniment to fried fish, are balls of cornmeal, with such other ingredients as onions, eggs, sugar, milk, or self-rising flour. Observers first noted hushpuppies around World War I, with the fish camps near St. Marks, Fla., south of Tallahassee, the likely point of origin. The name famously comes from cooks' tossing the bread to barking dogs to quiet them.

Spoonbread is perhaps the highest culinary attainment of cornbread. Redding S. Sugg Jr. called it "the apotheosis of cornbread," and Bill Neal referred to it as "an elegant soufflé; the fabled spoonbread, a mainstay of the aristocratic southern table." John Egerton has described it as a "steaming hot, feather-light dish." The Native American porridge called suppone may be the ancestor of spoonbread, but southerners did not add butter, milk, and eggs until after the Civil War. The term was not used in print until 1906, and the dish was most common in the Upper South.

Cornbread is a prime expression of the popularity of quick breads in the South. Wheat was the most popular grain throughout much of North America by the 19th century, but it was a rarity in most of the South until the latter part of that century. Southern mills did not grind high-gluten wheat, and people in the South continued to rely on the ground cornmeal they had used since frontier days. Cornbread did not keep well from one day to the next, so the daily preparation and serving of hot, fresh bread became the norm. Cornbread ingredients long represented a southern distinctiveness. Food writers have noted that northerners were more likely to use yellow cornmeal and southerners white cornmeal, with people from nonsouthern areas more likely to add sugar and flour.

John Egerton sees philosophical meanings in the evolution of cornbread from its Native American origins to the high-styled spoonbread. A correctly baked dish of spoonbread "can be taken as testimony to the perfectibility of humankind," whereas a hot and crispy hoecake testifies to "another kind of perfection, an enduring strength that has not been improved upon in four centuries of service to hungry people." An examination of contemporary regional cookbooks suggests that cornbread continues to be a common dish in the South and less so across the nation. This conclusion reinforces what Sallie F. Hill wrote in *The Progressive Farmer's Southern Cookbook* (1961): "To try to cook without cornmeal in the South is a lost cause."

CHARLES REAGAN WILSON
University of Mississippi

John T. Edge, *A Gracious Plenty: Recipes and Recollections from the American South* (1999); John Egerton, *Southern Food: At Home, on the Road, in History* (1987); Damon Lee Fowler, *Damon Lee Fowler's New Southern Kitchen: Traditional Flavors for Contemporary Cooks* (2002).

Country Captain

Country captain—also, chicken country captain—is a spicy dish of chicken simmered in a tomato-based curry sauce, usually served with plain white rice. Different recipes call for onions, garlic, raisins, and almonds, and the cooking time varies from kitchen to kitchen. Shrimp is also cooked "country captain" style.

Legend places the origin of the dish in Savannah, Ga., but nearly every seaboard city from Baltimore to Savannah lays claim to it. It does not appear in printed Georgia cookbooks until the 20th century, and neither Henrietta Stanley Dull (*Southern Cooking*, 1928) nor Harriett Ross Colquitt (*The Savannah Cook Book*, 1933) mentions it. One of the earliest printed recipes was from Philadelphia-based Eliza Leslie (*Miss Leslie's New Cookery Book*, 1857). Leslie credited British sea captains trading between the East and West Indies with the introduction of the dish; other legends credit local sea captains. One version of the story recognizes a particular British captain who brought the dish from Bengali, India, where he had been stationed, to friends in Savannah. Savannah was then an important shipping port for the spice trade, and the dish may have been named for officers in India called "country captains." As this legend has it, the enthusiasm of these friends catapulted the dish onto the permanent menu of Savannah and the country kitchens of Georgia.

The Georgia connection was cemented in the 1940s, when Mrs. W. L. Bullard served country captain to President Franklin D. Roosevelt and General George S. Patton during a visit to Warm Springs, Ga. Roosevelt visited the town's naturally heated mineral springs regularly as treatment for his polio-related paralysis, and country captain became a fixture in his Warm Springs diet. His love of the dish helped to rekindle its popularity and raise it to the southern classic status.

Despite the lack of hard evidence about its origins, the dish remains firmly planted in the southern repertory. Today's country captain retains curry and Indian spices as the dominant seasonings but evidences southern appropriation as well, with the addition of regional favorites like bacon, chicken fried in grease, and garden vegetables.

DAMON LEE FOWLER

Savannah, Georgia

FRANCES ABBOTT

University of Mississippi

Alan Davidson, *Oxford Companion to Food* (1999); John Egerton, *Southern Food: At Home, on the Road, in History* (1987); Damon Lee Fowler, *Classical Southern Cooking: A Celebration of the Cuisine of the Old South* (1995); John F. Mariani, *Encyclopedia of American Food and Drink* (1999); Patricia Bunning Stevens, *Rare Bits: Unusual Origins of Popular Recipes* (1998); John Martin Taylor, *The New Southern Cook: 200 Recipes from the South's Best Chefs and Home Cooks* (1995).

Country Ham

Country ham is a 19th-century southern term for a pork delicacy that has been known and loved in Asia and Europe for more than 2,000 years. It is the hind quarter of a hog that has been cured with salt, (often but not always) colored and flavored with wood smoke, and hung up to age through a summer or longer.

The first British colonists who came to Virginia brought pigs with them, and they also brought knowledge of the ancient technique of preserving meat by covering it with salt. The necessary combination of winter cold for slaughtering and summer heat for curing was ideally found in the colonies of Virginia, Maryland, and North Carolina, and ever since, country hams have remained popular in those states and their westward extensions, particularly Kentucky and Tennessee. Virginia's renowned Smithfield hams and the prime products of western Kentucky and other places in the region are unsurpassed by the best that France, Italy, and other nations have to offer. Trigg County, Ky., holds an annual festival to honor its history as a notable center of country ham production. Each October the Trigg County Country Ham Festival, started in 1977, brings in tens of thousands of people from all over the country to sample the county's famous hams and witness the awarding of a first prize for the year's best country ham.

Modern food technology has developed short-cut methods of duplicating the appearance of genuine country ham, but not its taste. As a result, many commercial "country" hams on the mar-

*Wife of tenant farmer cutting piece of ham in smokehouse near Pace, Miss., 1939
(Russell Lee, photographer, Library of Congress [LC-USF34-032054-D], Washington, D.C.)*

ket today have been artificially cured, smoked, and aged and do not have the rich aroma and flavor of hams produced by traditional processes. Diligent inquiries in rural areas of the Upper South can, however, still turn up hams that are in every way equal to those that came from the smokehouses of the region more than 300 years ago.

Ideal country hams are produced from year-old hogs that weigh at least 300 pounds and have been fattened on corn or peanuts. Such hams will weigh 25 to 30 pounds when butchered and about 20 percent less when properly cured and aged. As soon as a hog has been butchered in cold weather, the hams are rubbed down with a dry mixture of salt and other additives, usually sugar and saltpeter. Then they are completely covered in a bed of salt for four to six weeks, after which they are washed off and trimmed, and finally hung by their hocks in a dark smokehouse, there to take on a deep nut-brown appearance and a distinctive flavor from the enveloping hickory smoke. The hams must remain suspended to sweat through the hot summer months. A bare minimum of nine months is needed to complete the entire curing, smoking, and aging process; a full year, or even two years, is considered more nearly ideal.

Many variations on this basic method are favored from one ham maker to the next. Some mix a large amount of sugar with the salt and call their hams "sugar cured" (though sugar is actually not a preservative); some make smoke with oak or sassafras; some skip the smoking stage altogether, claiming it has no effect on flavor. But for the salt and the aging through the "summer sweats," there are no satisfactory substitutes and no alternatives, modern technology notwithstanding.

When a ham is ready to eat, it may be baked in the oven, boiled on top of the stove, or sliced and fried. (It could also be eaten raw, as is common in Italy and Spain, but southerners generally are leery of raw pork, even if it has been properly cured.) Fried ham yields a rich bonus in the form of redeye gravy, produced by adding a little water to the frying skillet. In whatever form it is prepared, country ham is as old as the South itself.

Country ham has featured frequently in a number of forms of cultural expression, reifying the importance of the dish to southern life. Mississippi-born comedian and author Jerry Clower chose *Country Ham* (1974) as the title for one of his albums containing stories and jokes about rural southern life. Also focusing on a depiction of southern country communities, North Carolina novelist Reynolds Price places country ham and southern foodways at the heart of his fictional scenes of community and family in *Good Hearts* (1988). Narrating a main character's attendance at a family meal in her country home, he writes: "It was Mama's usual light lunch—the turkey with cornbread dressing and cranberry sauce, country ham, snaps and little butterbeans she'd pulled up last

July, spiced peaches . . . every mouthful made the only way, from the naked pot upward by hand." A meal including country ham embodies the spirit of rural southern family and community in this context.

Evidence of the importance of country ham to southern culture also emerges in an investigation of country ham in the lyrics of southern musicians. Georgia native Cledus T. Judd penned the song "Bake Me a Country Ham" (2004). In the song, the singer meets a woman who offers to do something to make his day better. He responds to her offer in his chorus:

Let the sweet smell fill the air,
Serve it to me in my underwear.
I'm tired of eating imitation Spam:
Could you bake me a country ham?

Images of country ham appear in contemporary southern hip-hop music—another significant contemporary southern musical genre. The Kentucky-based rap sextet Nappy Roots regularly celebrates country heritage through lyrical tributes to the symbols of rural southern life. Their 2002 album *Watermelon, Chicken, and Gritz* speaks to the joys and restrictions of a southern country experience. Rapper Ron Clutch lyricizes: "Candied yams, chitlins, greens, and smoked country ham / Chicken wings, cornbread, Gran in the kitchen throwin' down." County ham connects Nappy Roots with several generations of family, with southern home space, and with southern identity itself. The significance of country ham to southern tradition thus continues to materialize in the artistic expression of multiple southern communities.

JOHN EGERTON
Nashville, Tennessee

FRANCES ABBOTT
University of Mississippi

John T. Edge, *Southern Belly: The Ultimate Food Lover's Companion to the South* (2000); John Egerton, *Side Orders: Small Helpings of Southern Cookery and Culture* (1990), *Southern Food: At Home, on the Road, in History* (1987); Sam Bowers Hilliard, *Hog Meat and Hoecake: Food Supply in the Old South, 1840–1860* (1972); Jeanne Voltz and Elaine J. Harvell, *The Country Ham Book* (1999).

Crawfish

Known provincially as "crayfish," "crawdads," or "mudbugs," crawfish are related to shrimp and lobster. Their average length is four inches, and they are most active at night. There are over 500 species in North America, where the vast majority make their home in fresh water, although they are sometimes kept as pets. The crawfish is widely farmed in Louisiana (nearly 120,000 acres of lakes within the state produce 50,000 or so tons of live crawfish a year), where it consists primarily of two species, the Red Swamp (*Procambarus clarkii*) and the White River (*Procambarus acutus*), which are harvested from November through June.

The crawfish, while abundant across the South, is a culinary icon in Louisiana. As Cajun legend has it, the crawfish followed the Acadians south to the bayous of Louisiana when they were exiled from Nova Scotia in the 1700s; enormous lobsters when the journey began, the crawfish diminished in size as they traveled deeper into the heat and humidity of the Deep South. In reality, however, American Indians were the first in the region to harvest and eat the diminutive creatures. The Indians placed reeds baited with deer meat in ponds and streams, periodically pulling them up to see if any crawfish were attached. Using this primitive fishing method, they would harvest crawfish by the bushel. White immigrants to the area primarily used crawfish as fish bait until the 1920s and 1930s, and the crawfish did not begin to be widely consumed outside of southern Louisiana until the 1960s.

Today, chiefly during spring and summer months, crawfish can be found on restaurant menus, at roadside stands, and at backyard boils. Standard preparation of crawfish consists of boiling them whole, with various seasonings and spices as well as vegetables, such as potatoes and corn, and sometimes with another meat, such as sausage. The Cajun and Creole cuisines of Louisiana have made famous many unique dishes comprised of the tail meat of crawfish, including crawfish étouffée, crawfish bisque, the crawfish po' boy, and crawfish pie. Also, crawfish boils are a standard social event throughout southern Louisiana. Most often, crawfish are eaten while standing, usually at a makeshift crawfish table crafted of plywood, with a hole in the middle; the hole accommodates a garbage can, into which the shells are tossed as the crawfish are peeled and eaten (generally about five

Louisiana mudbugs (PDphoto.org)

pounds of whole crawfish per person make a meal). A hotly debated point among crawfish consumers is whether to "suck the head." Sucking the head is necessary to obtain the spicy juices within. Many refrain from this tradition, considering it crass and unpalatable, while others maintain the practice, avowing the head is the best part.

The crawfish has become a major part of southern culture through annual local festivals like the Breaux Bridge (Louisiana) Crawfish Festival (Louisiana is the self-proclaimed "Crawfish Capital of the World") and the Texas Crawfish & Music Festival. Events at these festivals usually consist of crawfish-eating contests, crawfish étouffée cook-offs and demonstrations, Cajun dance contests, zydeco music, and the always-popular crawfish races. Inevitably, Hank Williams's paean to the crawfish and to Cajun living, "Jambalaya," is heard again and again:

> Jambalaya, a-crawfish pie and-a file gumbo,
> 'Cause tonight I'm gonna see my machez a mio.
> Pick guitar, fill a fruit jar and be gay-oh,
> Son of a gun, we'll have big fun on the bayou.

RENNA TUTEN
MARY MARGARET MILLER
JAMES G. THOMAS JR.
University of Mississippi

Ella Brennan and Dick Brennan, *The Commander's Palace New Orleans Cookbook* (1984); Rima and Richard Collin, *New*

The deviled egg, an iconic southern hors d'oeuvre (Courtesy Angie Mosier)

Orleans Cookbook (1987); John Egerton, Southern Food: At Home, on the Road, in History (1987); Howard Mitcham, Creole Gumbo and All That Jazz: A New Orleans Seafood Cookbook (1978); Paul Prudhomme, Chef Paul Prudhomme's Louisiana Kitchen (1984).

Deviled Eggs

Few covered-dish dinners in the South are without a plate of deviled eggs. Hostesses have been making them since the 1920s, when hors d'oeuvres began to be fixtures at luncheons and showers. Deviled eggs are among the easiest to prepare and least inexpensive of such dishes, being simply halved hard-boiled eggs whose yolks have been removed and mashed with other ingredients and then stuffed back into the cavities of the whites. Mustard is perhaps the ingredient that changed stuffed eggs to deviled ones. Although deviled foods had long been popular with the English, who had embraced them in India, the Underwood company purports to have coined the term *deviled* in the United States for its canned spiced ham product that contains mustard.

In their most basic form, deviled eggs include only mayonnaise, mustard, salt, and pepper blended with the egg yolks, though some cooks have been known to use softened butter rather than mayonnaise. Sweet pickle heads the list of other common additions, which also include curry powder, crumbled crisp bacon, crabmeat, pimiento, and horseradish.

As noted in *Damon Lee Fowler's*

New Southern Kitchen, "No matter how sophisticated the crowd professes to be, they will go after deviled eggs like cats after cream, leaving latecomers to hover around that empty plate with a look of wistful disappointment. I unashamedly admit that there has been more than one batch that never made it out of my kitchen."

Deviled eggs grew in popularity to such a degree that plates specifically designed with elliptical depressions to accommodate the slippery eggs were mass produced and became popular bridal shower gifts in the 1940s, 1950s, and 1960s. "No southern bride, rich or otherwise," John Martin Taylor writes, "was without the funny piece of china with its 24 egg-shaped indentations to hold the stuffed eggs. Often the plate was relegated to the back of a shelf, but it would always come out for parties." These days, china egg plates are in short supply, but pressed-glass ones are still widely available.

John T. Edge has written on the multiplicity of approaches to deviled eggs in today's southern restaurants: "At Sally Bell's Kitchen in Richmond, Virginia, they do it by the book, boiling the egg whites to a springy turn and mashing the yolks with a bit of mustard, a smidgen of relish, and a dusting of paprika, before wrapping each egg half in its own pouch of wax paper."

In 2004 the Southern Foodways Alliance hosted the Deviled Egg Recipe Competition. The five finalists, spanning the nation from New Orleans to New York City, discussed the significance of deviled eggs in their family histories and shared recipes, which included innovations such as capers, onion, anchovies, black olives, and garlic.

DONNA FLORIO
Birmingham, Alabama

FRANCES ABBOTT
University of Mississippi

John T. Edge, *Attaché Magazine* (April 2003); Debbie Moose, *Deviled Eggs: 50 Recipes from Simple to Sassy* (2004); Moreton Neal, *Remembering Bill Neal: Favorite Recipes from a Life in Cooking* (2004); Helen Siegel, *The Totally Eggs Cookbook* (1997); Marie Simmons, *The Good Egg: More than 200 Fresh Approaches from Soup to Dessert* (2000).

Dull, Henrietta Stanley

(1863–1964) COOKBOOK AUTHOR.
Born in 1863 on a plantation in Laurens County, Ga., Henrietta Stanley married S. R. Dull and had a family of six children by the time she was 30. She expected to live a quiet life as a mother and homemaker, but her husband's failing health made it necessary for her to take up a career outside the home.

Dull seems to have migrated toward cooking naturally. She began her long career in food by baking for her neighbors, an enterprise that eventually expanded to a catering business. Her reputation grew when the Atlanta Gas Light Company hired her in 1910 to teach homemakers about cooking on new gas ranges. Her teaching expanded to such prominent venues as Macy's department store in New York. In 1920 she began writing a cooking column for the home economics page of the *Atlanta Journal Sunday Magazine*.

Repeated requests for printed recipes led Dull to compile her columns under a single cover. In 1928, when she was 65, she published *Southern Cooking*, a work that set the standard for southern cookbooks for the rest of the century. It remained in print until after her death in 1964, selling more than 150,000 copies (and is still available in a facsimile edition).

In 1945 Dull stepped down from the newspaper, but her mark on the history of southern cooking had been made. *Southern Cooking* remains a critically important work for food historians, forming a definitive bridge between the 19th and 20th centuries. Known for their concise, no-nonsense brevity and illuminating clarity, the book's more than 1,300 recipes give a sharp picture of a cuisine in transition. Dull brought a cuisine still rooted in the land and wedded to its own traditions into the urbanized, international age of the 20th century.

DAMON LEE FOWLER
Savannah, Georgia

Henrietta Stanley Dull, *Southern Cooking* (1928; with introduction by Damon Lee Fowler, 2006); Damon Lee Fowler, *Classical Southern Cooking: A Celebration of the Cuisine of the Old South* (1995).

Fast Food

Fast food is the antithesis of traditional southern foodways. Traditional southern food is, almost by definition, cooked and consumed slowly, preferably in the presence of one's friends and family. The image of a traditional southerner speeding down a highway munching on a burger and fries from a paper sack is so alien that until recently it was inconceivable. The fast-food phenomenon, at least initially, was seen by many southerners not as a new convenience, but as an abomination.

Fast food is a misnomer and does not actually delineate a class of food items. Rather, it is a category of restaurants partially defined by its offerings, but, just as important, by its "quick" service and minimal dining setting without table service. The restaurant industry prefers the term *quick-service restaurant*, divorcing the concept entirely from the food items offered. Strictly speaking, many traditional southern restaurants fulfill the bare requirements of speed and service, but the implicit tie to specific items tends to exclude barbecues, fish camps, and buffets from being called fast-food restaurants. This partially explains the scarcity of classic fast food in the South during the product's early years, but the lack is also attributable to the region's low frequency of eating outside the family environment, low travel index, and low average incomes.

This is not to say that fast food was unknown in the South. Colonel Harland Sanders created the Kentucky Fried Chicken business in Kentucky, though he did not initially see it as a business that would create freestanding restaurants. He first franchised his chicken as a menu item in cafeterias and other restaurants. His success was so great that some analysts predicted in the late 1950s that chicken, not hamburgers, would dominate the fast-food market in the future. By the late 1960s, Minnie Pearl, the Grand Ole Opry comedian famous for her hats and homespun humor, secured commitments for 1,400 locations of Minnie Pearl's Fried Chicken. Though her chicken chain ultimately did not take flight, numerous southern franchises did, including Popeyes Chicken & Biscuits of New Orleans, La.; Church's Chicken of San Antonio, Tex.; and Bojangles' Famous Chicken 'n' Biscuits of Charlotte, N.C.

Three important hamburger chains originated in the South. Krystal, founded in 1932 on the corner of Seventh and Cherry Streets in Chattanooga, Tenn., is the second-oldest fast-food chain in the United States and the oldest in the South. It was originally so popular that by necessity it became a pioneer in the "to go" industry. Now a southern cultural icon, Krystal today operates over 400 restaurants in 11 states—all in the South. Burger King, the nation's second-largest burger chain, was founded in Miami, Fla., in 1954, though the company never had a strong regional identity. Hardee's, founded in 1960 in North Carolina, however, continues to have a strong regional affinity, though many of its 2,200 locations are now outside the region, especially in the Midwest. Hardee's pioneered fast food in hundreds of smaller and medium-sized southern towns and to this day continues to hold a special image in those smaller communities.

Critical for fast-food success in the South was the introduction of the breakfast biscuit sandwich and its widespread diffusion, especially through the Hardee's franchise system. The breakfast biscuit played a particularly important role in making fast-food acceptable among older southerners. Thousands of aging southern wives, growing tired of baking two or three biscuits for breakfast each morning, discovered that palatable, inexpensive biscuits could be purchased down the street at a local fast-food outlet such as Hardee's, Biscuitville, or Mrs. Winner's. Thus many older southerners first entered a fast-food store to have a morning biscuit breakfast, not to purchase a Big Mac. Possibly more important was the social impact of this lifestyle change, as tens of thousands of these folks discovered their friends were doing the same thing. Impromptu breakfast clubs became a regular part of the rural and small-town social schedule for the generally aging population. Certainly traditional cafés also often had morning tables set aside for this purpose, but the low cost, large parking lots, and suburban locations of fast-food stores gave them an advantage in the battle for the breakfast market among this demographic group. An interesting sidelight to this phenomenon is the increasing number of wives who meet their women friends at a different location after they send their husbands down to have breakfast with the "boys."

Beef consumption generally is lower in the South than elsewhere in the nation. An analysis of the top 50 quick-service restaurants nationally reveals that almost half of the 14 fast-food chains headquartered in the region are primarily known for their chicken menu items. Fried-fish restaurants, though few in number, tend more likely to be headquartered in the region as well. Hamburger-based chain restaurants are today found throughout the South, but are more prominent in urban areas or regions where nonsoutherners tend to congregate. In one sense the spread of hamburger fast-food outlets throughout the South could be used as a surrogate measure of the nationalization of the region's culture.

RICHARD PILLSBURY
Folly Beach, South Carolina

John A. Jakle and Keith A. Sculle, *Fast Food: Roadside Restaurants in the Automobile Age* (2002); Richard Pillsbury, *From Boarding House to Bistro: The American Restaurant Then and Now* (1990); Michael Roark, in *The Taste of American Place: A Reader on Regional and Ethnic Foods*, ed. Barbara G. Shortridge and James R. Shortridge (1998).

Fish, Rough

Rough fish, coarse fish, gross fish, and *commercial fish* are some of the inclusive terms that describe numerous species seldom intentionally caught by recreational anglers despite their economic value and importance as food fish. Commercial fishermen traditionally use nets and other specialized tackle to capture fish such as buffalo, gar, and paddle fish for the table. In general, the commercial fisheries of the southern river systems are not widely known. Their patrons are often rural folk or the poor, and the popularity of many river species has declined in recent decades. Nonetheless, untold thousands of pounds of commercial species are caught and marketed as food every year.

Before the refinement of aquaculture in the 1950s and 1960s, commercial fishermen were the major source for southern catfish. While some southerners still prefer wild-caught catfish, and fishermen still sell them, the pond-raised product has taken most of the trade. Buffalo, on the other hand, are not farmed and are available only through the commercial fishery or one's own efforts. Bigmouth and smallmouth buffalo, members of the sucker family, commonly weigh 20 to 30 pounds and can reach around 50. Buffalo were always important food fish for the people who lived near rivers and larger streams. They became a particularly appreciated, cheap, consistent source of protein for farm laborers in the South, both before and after the Civil War. Like all suckers, buffalo are very bony except for the rib sections. Thus, in addition to common methods of frying, people sometimes process buffalo in jars— somewhat like salmon or tuna. The cooking process softens the small bones, with cooks using the canned buffalo, like salmon, for croquettes. Today, one can still purchase fresh buffalo in some grocery stores and fish markets in the South and find it fried in some of the region's fish houses. Other suckers, including the various redhorse species, are important in some areas, usually during their spawning season, when fishermen net or gig them. Like buffalo, their flesh is considered excellent but bony, and cooks usually fry them very well done to break down the small bones.

The gar species, including the longnose, the shortnose, and the alligator, have also been important commercial fish. All of the species are quite palatable, except for their eggs, which can be extremely poisonous. Unfortunately, the alligator gar is very rare these days, except in its extreme southern range.

A longnose gar (Courtesy Wiley Prewitt Jr., photographer)

Able to tolerate brackish water, the alligator gar is still taken in some of the lower rivers and coastal water of the Gulf of Mexico, with specimens reaching up to 10 feet long. The shortnose and longnose are much more common and much smaller, although the longnose commonly reaches five feet. Many people enjoy gar once they hull them out of their armorlike skin. Some commercial fishermen report that the demand for them is second only to that for catfish. Many gar are destined for the fryer, as are most fish in the South. There is also a tradition of smoked gar and gar balls. The latter is probably the most often cited preparation for gar. Cooks usually describe it as a simple fish fritter or fish cake made of minced or ground gar mixed with cornmeal, seasonings, egg, and buttermilk and deep fried much like a hushpuppy.

Like the alligator gar, the Atlantic sturgeon and its Gulf subspecies are hard to find today, though it and other sturgeon species once made up an important fishery. After decades of unregulated harvest, large sturgeon became rare catches even by the 1930s. In her *Freshwater Fishes in Mississippi*, Fannye A. Cook reported that one C. C. Charbonneau took a six-foot sturgeon—a youngster by the standards of the Atlantic sturgeon—from the Pearl River in 1933, providing "the chief food for seventy-five persons at a fish fry." These days, the small but common shovelnose sturgeon is the only species taken by commercial fishermen in some numbers.

The general depletion of sturgeons, not only in the South but worldwide, has led to more pressure on the paddlefish, another traditional commercial species. Also known as spoonbill, or boneless cat (because of its cartilaginous skeleton much like a shark's), the paddlefish has only one relative, an enormous species in the Yangtze River system of China. The American species of paddlefish is native to the Mississippi drainage and neighboring coastal rivers. Fishermen usually take the paddlefish in gill nets, trammel nets, or hoop nets, and specimens of a hundred pounds are not unknown. Fishermen and fish eaters have always highly regarded paddlefish as food, but the use of its roe as a substitute for sturgeon caviar has led to some outrageous overexploitation. Occasionally, game and fish officials confront gangs of poachers who net thousands of pounds of spoonbills just for the eggs that they can sell on the black market. Legally fished paddlefish roe brings a good price and is said by some to be the equal of sturgeon roe in quality.

For the mainstream culture, the rivers of the South, their fish, and their fishermen remain a mystery. The fish, if they are known at all, connote the foodways of the rural poor to some and raise fears of pollution to others. Tiny fish markets and fish peddled from the backs of pickups put off those accustomed to their food in plastic wrap and Styrofoam. The inland commercial fishery endures nevertheless and offers consumers an alternative to farmed fish with a variety of species available almost nowhere else.

WILEY C. PREWITT JR.
Lodi, Mississippi

Fannye A. Cook, *Freshwater Fishes in Mississippi* (1959); Jens Lund, *Flatheads and Spooneys: Fishing for a Living in the Ohio River Valley* (1995); Lawrence M. Page and Brooks M. Burr, *A Field Guide to Freshwater Fishes* (1991).

Fish Camps

While in many areas of the South *fish camp* refers to a campsite or lodge reserved for fishing expeditions, fish camp restaurants are local seafood houses, found in abundance in the Carolinas and well-established throughout the Deep South, specializing in deep-fried fresh- and saltwater seafood.

Although restaurants calling themselves fish camps can be found from Tennessee to Texas, a high concentration of fish camps can be found in the western half of the Carolinas. In Gaston County, N.C., there are half a dozen within a one-mile radius of one another, with another five or six less than a 10-minute drive away. Lineberger's Fish Fry, a long-established restaurant in Gaston County, typifies the fish camp. As the name implies, this fish camp, like many others, began as a site at one of the local fishing spots, in this case the Catawba River, where in the 1930s Luther Lineberger set up vats of hot lard and offered to fry up the fresh catches of his fellow fishermen. Lineberger and a few other competing entrepreneurs began offering side dishes to go with the fish and in a short time replaced their frying sheds with clapboard-and-screen restaurants. These fry houses with dirt floors and long tables soon evolved into modern family restaurants, but their name and their cuisine remained the same.

Western Carolina camps are distinctive in that, unlike the calabash restaurants of the Carolina coast, they serve freshwater fish, particularly catfish, and unlike typical catfish houses found in Alabama, Tennessee, and elsewhere, they also offer saltwater seafood. Catfish, flounder, and shrimp tend to be the most popular items and are always accompanied by the trinity of slaw, hushpuppies, and french fried potatoes—all in large quantities at a low price. Menus are kept simple, as is the decor. And while a few fish camps serve alcohol, the majority serve nothing stronger than sweet tea or Coca-Cola. Most restaurants are family owned and operated and use traditional recipes and serving philosophies. Harold Stowe, the longtime proprietor of Stowe's Fish Camp in Belmont, N.C., argues that the success of his family's fish camps lies in their "family-oriented atmosphere" and the fact that they "treat everybody the same . . . all classes of people, all races . . . are treated the same." (The popularity of Stowe's Fish Camp has also been helped by its salt-and-pepper catfish, a dish Harold Stowe says his wife Betty invented.)

Recently the seemingly contradictory phenomena of the growing popularity of fast-food restaurants and an increase in dietary concerns over fried food have resulted in a decline of fish camp patronage in much of the South, a decline echoed in the 1999 cancellation of Gaston County's long-running festival, the Fish Camp Jam. Nevertheless, as long as southerners believe, as historian Joe Gray Taylor has observed, that "God made fish to be fried," fish camps will continue to serve up whole orders of

flounder, half orders of perch, and all-you-can-eat salt-and-pepper catfish.

STEPHEN CRISWELL
*University of South Carolina
Lancaster*

Kenneth S. Allen, *Charlotte* (June 1998); John T. Edge, *Gourmet* (May 2000); Sam Bowers Hilliard, *Hog Meat and Hoecake: Food Supply in the Old South, 1840–1860* (1972); Joe Gray Taylor, *Eating, Drinking, and Visiting in the South: An Informal History* (1982).

Goo Goo Clusters

The Standard Candy Company heralds the Goo Goo Cluster as "A Good Ole Southern Treat." Often advertised as "the South's favorite candy" and "the Goodest Bar in town," the Goo Goo Cluster has been a candy staple in Nashville, Tenn., where it originated, and throughout the South for almost a century.

First created by William H. Campbell in 1912, the Goo Goo Cluster is a combination of caramel, marshmallow, peanuts, and pure milk chocolate. (Later the company began making Goo Goo Supremes, which substitute pecans for peanuts.) Though the packaging and distribution techniques have changed with modernization and company expansion, the ingredients, cooking methods, and essential southern identity have remained the same.

The Goo Goo Cluster's name has been a curiosity since its origin. One account says that Campbell settled on the name because his son, only a few months old at the time, uttered those words when first introduced to the new candy. Another version suggests that

Campbell was struck with his son's first utterance and decided it was an appropriate name. Whatever the true version, Standard Candy Company has long contended that a Goo Goo is the first thing a southern baby requests.

Since 1968 the *Grand Ole Opry* has been singing the praises of the Goo Goo to those in attendance and thousands more over WSM radio. So closely associated with the *Opry* is the candy that some have suggested *Goo* stands for *Grand Ole Opry. Opry* announcer Grant Turner long let listeners know how to order the candy by mail, encouraging them further with the familiar slogan: "Go Get a Goo Goo. . . . It's Good."

TOM RANKIN
Duke University

Steve Almond, *Candyfreak: A Journey through the Chocolate Underbelly of America* (2005); Margaret Loelo, *Wall Street Journal* (8 December 1982); John F. Persinos, *Inc.* (May 1984); Tim Richardson, *Sweets: A History of Candy* (2002).

Woman preparing gravy in a sharecropper cabin, 1938 (Russell Lee, photographer, Library of Congress [LC-USF34-031226-D], Washington, D.C.)

Gravy

Gravies moisten and flavor the foods they accompany, and in traditional southern kitchens they are usually thickened with flour and occasionally with cornmeal. Southern gravies are called pan gravies because they are made in a skillet with drippings from fried food, but a specific definition of pan gravy does not allow for the great variety of sauces that reflect the nature of southern cooking. Southerners enjoy many different types of gravy that go with a range of dishes and meals.

Brown gravy is prepared with beef drippings and often served over beef and potatoes. At Ajax Diner in Oxford, Miss., a locally cherished sandwich called the Big Easy, named in honor of onetime Ole Miss quarterback Eli Manning, is made with layers of chicken-fried steak, mashed potatoes, and butter beans, topped with thick brown gravy.

Chicken gravy is made from the pan drippings of fried chicken. In his song "Lazy Bones" Savannah-born composer Johnny Mercer writes, "Long as there is chicken gravy on your rice / Ev'rything is nice," illustrating one of the ways in which chicken gravy is incorporated into southern meals.

White gravy, also called cream gravy or breakfast gravy, is an all-purpose gravy boiled with milk or cream, served over biscuits for breakfast or chicken-fried steak for dinner. When crumbled sausage and drippings from the pan are added, it is commonly called sawmill or sausage gravy. Texas country singer Guy Clark celebrates the marriage of chicken-fried steak and white gravy in his song "Texas Cookin'": "Get them steaks chicken fried / Sho' do make a man feel happy / to see white gravy on the side." Particularly when called sawmill gravy, this variation is commonly conceived of as a subsistence food for the poor. Just a few scraps of meat and a small amount of milk are enough to make the concoction. Even the name may suggest poverty, as a possible reference to the limited diet of coffee, biscuits, and gravy once consumed by backwoods sawmill workers.

Some southern cooks make gravies with a white roux, a boiled but not browned mixture of butter and flour, which becomes a thickening for white sauce. Redeye gravy is a ham gravy made when the drippings of fried country ham, loosened with cola, coffee, or water. Legend of dubious authenticity implicates Andrew Jackson in naming this gravy. He supposedly ordered a whiskey-drinking cook to bring him ham with gravy "as red as your eyes." More likely, the name *redeye* comes from the deep red color of the juice from country ham. In the *Louisville Courier-Journal* in 1948, Allan M. Trout wrote: "The most nourishing liquid in the world is the gravy that fried ham gives up. . . . There is abundant life in ham gravy. It will put hair on the hairless chest of a man, or bloom into the pale cheeks of a woman. Breast-fed babies whose mothers eat ham gravy are destined to develop sturdy bodies and sound minds. . . . But ham and gravy is a lopsided combination. The gravy always gives out before the ham. . . . That, sir, is why we cannot bottle ham gravy to sell to gravy lovers. A surplus of ham gravy cannot be attained."

Another variety, popular in Appalachia, is chocolate gravy, sweet gravy prepared with cocoa and poured over biscuits for breakfast. This gravy is stirred with milk and occasionally cream. Chocolate gravy also enjoys a rich history in the cooking of the Arkansas Ozarks, although its origins are unknown.

Less-known, but still notable, gravies include egg gravy thickened with eggs, baloney gravy stirred in the pan drippings of fried baloney, and squirrel gravy cooked with fried squirrel and served for breakfast in place of sausage gravy. More obscure still are gravies made with wild game, pig's feet, and oysters. Once, no meal—whether breakfast, lunch, or dinner—was complete without gravy to compliment the food, and for many people that remains true.

In all its varieties, gravy holds a central place in the culture of the American South. Songwriters and performers comment on the importance of gravy to cultural identity in their lyrics and titles, from the North Georgian Skillet Lickers' old-time fiddle song "Soppin' the Gravy," to Jelly Roll Morton's "Low Gravy," to jazz pianist and composer Duke Ellington's "Ain't the Gravy Good?"

Gravy shows up in a range of literary creations as well. It appears in the family dinner scenes over pork chops in Shirley Abbott's 1983 memoir and historical exploration, *Womenfolks*, about several generations in her Arkansas farm family. James Agee documents the connection between gravy and a sense of home place in *Let Us Now Praise Famous Men* (1939). In recording the lives of sharecropping families in Hale County, Ala., Agee comments on the importance of food, although scarce, to the sensory experience of home. Describing one home amidst the constant consumption of biscuits and gravy from pork, he writes: "There is even in so clean a household as this an odor of pork, of sweat, so subtle it seems to get into the very metal of the cooking-pans . . . yet this is the odor and consistency and temper and these are true tastes of home."

MARK F. SOHN
Pikeville College

Jane Carson, *Colonial Virginia Cookery* (1968), *The Women's Day Encyclopedia of Cookery* (1966); John Egerton, *Southern Food: At Home, on the Road, in History* (1987); Ronni Lundy, *Shuck Beans, Stack Cakes, and Honest Fried Chicken: The Heart and Soul of Southern County Kitchens* (1991); William Woys Weaver, in *Food in Change: Eating Habits from the Middle Ages to the Present Day*, ed. Alexander Fenton and Eszter Kisban (1986).

Greens

Joining cauliflower, Brussels sprouts, and broccoli, greens are members of the genus *Brassica*. Among the many species and hybrids of *Brassica* greens, southern greens include, but are not necessarily limited to, beet tops, collard greens, rapini (also known as broccoli de rabe or broccoli rabb), chard, kale, rape, Swiss chard (or chard), dande- lion greens, mustard greens (or curly mustard), wild mustard (also known as old field mustard), summer mustard, turnip greens, cress (also known as creasy, creecy, or creasy greens or dry land creases), watercress, winter cress, old hen and chicken, plantain (or plantin), hen pepper, mouse ears, purslane, speckled breeches, old sage, wild lettuce, greenbrier sprouts, poke (also known as poke sallet, poke salad, pokeweed, and polk), crow's foot, wild tung grass, chochanna (*Kochvni*), fiddleheads, chicory, bear lettuce (or bear lettice), dock, narrow leaf dock (or nar dock), marsh marigold dock, shonny, Uncle Simpson's lettice, groundhog salit, stagger weed, Old King cure-all, lady's fingers, lamb's-quarters (also known as lambsquarters or pigweed), lamb's tongue, sissle, red worms, sorrel, sheep sorrel, and branch lettuce. Many of these greens occur naturally or are farmed in the South and appear commonly on the southern table.

The inclusion of vegetables, particularly those homegrown, in the southern diet reflects the economic disadvantage under which the region labored for much of its past and into the present; as meat was an expensive food item, southerners had to rely more heavily on nutrition from vegetables. The climate and geography of the South offer greens a long growing season (from early spring until late fall or early winter), which fosters its elemental addition to subsistence gardening.

The peoples of the South also affected the important role greens play within southern foodways. The Native Americans residing in the South included native greens in their culinary repertoire and incorporated new greens brought from abroad in their agriculture. Just as the Native Americans received knowledge of greens of the Old World from European settlers, they, in turn, taught the "new" southerners about the greens native to the New World, such as poke sallet. Last, but definitely not least, African slaves carried some of their native greens (e.g., collard greens) to the South. The method most commonly used in preparing greens derives from African culinary techniques and was crafted by the slaves cooking in southern kitchens.

Makers of greens in restaurants and homes in the South traditionally begin preparation by cleaning the greens thoroughly, as the leaves tend to collect dirt and sand. After browning or parboiling some pork (often ham hock, salt pork, or bacon), the cook places the greens in a large pot with enough water to cover them and simmers the greens with the chosen pork product, onions, garlic, and other seasonings until the greens are well cooked and the water reduced; depending upon the cook, this can take anywhere from 45 minutes to several hours. Southern greens are frequently served with hot pepper sauce and vinegar and a slice of cornbread to soak up the potlikker.

Potlikker, the liquid remains at the bottom of a pot of greens, holds a special place in southern history. Huey "the Kingfish" Long brought potlikker national attention by sparking a 1931 debate with Julian Harris, news editor of the *Atlanta Constitution*, on whether crumbling or dunking was the better

A shopping cart full of greens soon to be sold at a farmers' market, Oxford, Miss. (Courtesy John T. Edge, photographer)

method for soaking cornpone in potlikker. Senator Long also carried potlikker into the national and historical spotlight by including a long-winded treatise on potlikker in a 15½-hour filibuster speech.

Politics aside, potlikker serves as a folk remedy for many ailments plaguing southerners. The intuition of early folk doctors regarding how to employ greens medically coincides roughly with scientifically informed contemporary treatments. Studies in the 1930s revealed that collard and turnip greens contain high amounts of vitamins A, B, and C; folk medicine has long utilized greens as a spring tonic. Because greens are iron rich and high in fiber, folk healers prescribe them to battle anemia and constipation. Greens are also known to help with rheumatism, a sore throat, and a waning libido.

Southern folklore has much to say about nonmedicinal effects of greens too. If consumed in too great a quantity, greens are prone to make a man become feisty and ill-tempered. Greens bring good luck and fortune, which explains the southern tradition of eating greens on New Year's Day. Another southern myth pertaining to greens speaks to the precautions of the diet of recent mothers: if mothers with newborns eat turnip greens, their babies will die, suggesting a possible link between eating greens and the resulting toxicity of breast milk. Regarding the planting and harvesting of collard greens, a folktale warns that if the farmer lets the collards go to seed during the year they are planted, someone in the family will die; this correlates with the adage "waste not, want not" in the often poor and hungry South.

As greens hold such an important place in southern culture, many southerners celebrate them with local festivals. Harlan, Ky., in June, honors the town's favorite food with its Poke Sallet Festival. Likewise, one September weekend each year, Ayden, N.C., pays homage to collard greens. The people of Ayden are so passionate about their collards that they produced a volume of poetry dedicated to these lauded vegetables, *Leaves of Greens: The Collard Poems*.

Southerners also praise their greens through song. Probably the most famous piece of music featuring greens is Tony Joe White's "Polk Salad Annie," which Elvis Presley recorded in 1970.

Blues anthems eulogizing greens include "Good Old Turnip Greens," "Collard Greens," "Mustard Greens," and "Them Greasy Greens," each with renditions during the civil rights movement, when African Americans coined the term *soul food* and embraced the ethnic cuisine it described (of which greens were an important component) as a symbol of pride and solidarity. Though he never recorded a song specifically about greens, jazz pianist Thelonious Monk flaunted his southern heritage by often wearing a collard leaf as a boutonniere.

With growing interest in ethnic and regional foodways, greens are gaining national celebrity on network cooking shows. Southern cuisine was once epitomized by fried chicken and barbecue, but now other important staples are starting to taste the limelight.

BROOKE BUTLER
University of California, Davis

B. A. Botkin, *Treasury of Southern Folklore* (1977); James W. Byrd, *Tennessee Folklore Society Bulletin* (1966); John Egerton, *Side Orders: Small Helpings of Southern Cookery and Culture* (1990); Evan Jones, *American Food: The Gastronomic Story* (1975); Kay K. Moss, *Southern Folk Medicine: 1750–1820* (1999); Newbell Niles Puckett, *Folk Beliefs of the Southern Negro* (1968); Joe Gray Taylor, *Eating, Drinking, and Visiting in the South: An Informal History* (1982); Jackie Torrence, *The Importance of Pot Liquor* (1994).

Greens, Collard

Collard greens grow throughout the South and, probably as much as any other food, serve as a culinary Mason-Dixon line. Some claim greens kept

Sherman's scorched-earth policy from totally starving the South into submission; many today can testify to surviving Depression winters with greens, fatback, and cornbread. Southern childhood memories often focus on collard greens: either the pleasant, loving connection of grandma's iron pot and steaming potlikker, or the traumatizing effects engendered by the first whiff of the unmistakable odor for which greens are famous. Writing in the *Charlotte Observer* in 1907, Joseph P. Caldwell explained, "The North Carolinian who is not familiar with pot likker has suffered in his early education and needs to go back and begin it over again." Particularly among rural and poor southerners, collard greens have endured as a dietary staple.

Sometimes defined as headless cabbages, collards are best when prepared just after the first frost, though they are eaten year-round. They should always be harvested before the dew dries. When being prepared, they are "cropped," then "looked," then cooked; that is, cut at the base of a stalk, searched for worms, and then cooked "till tender" on a low boil, usually with fatback, or neck or backbone, added. The resultant "mess o' greens," topped with a generous helping of vinegar, can easily make a meal in itself. If they are summer greens (and much tougher), the tenderizing could take two hours or more of cooking; after first frost, it may take less than an hour. A whole pecan in the pot should eliminate the pungent and earthy smell. Potlikker, the juice left in the pot after the greens are gone, is a southern version of nectar from the gods and is valued both as a delicacy—particularly when sopped with cornbread—and for its alleged aphrodisiacal powers. Greens combine well with black-eyed peas and hog jowl in the South's traditional New Year's Day meal. To ensure good fortune, one should either eat lots of greens or tack them to the ceiling. In fact, a collard leaf left hanging over one's door can ward off evil spirits all year long.

Nutritionally, collards are a good source of vitamins A, B_6, and C, as well as calcium, iron, thiamine, and niacin. They seem to have unique laxative qualities, though the resultant gas is often troublesome. Folk legends claim a fresh collardleaf placed on the forehead should cure a headache. The same remedy can be applied to nervous afflictions plaguing women, though it works best on such cases when the leaf is still wet with dew and the woman just rising. The roots bound on arthritic joints ease pain, and a poultice prepared from collard leaves has been recommended as a cure for cancers on the face, boils, and festering sores.

Though collard greens are grown year-round throughout the South and Southwest (Indians call them *quelites*), they are most prevalent in the Deep South and the eastern plains of North and South Carolina. The exporting of collards to displaced southerners in the Northeast has become a big business in the three leading collards-producing states. From the last week of October through May, eight firms from Georgia and the Carolinas ship a thousand tons of whole, fresh collards a week to the major northeastern metropolitan areas. The greens are cut and banded, then packed in bundles on ice, about 25 pounds per box or 20 tons a truckload.

In 2001, 7,500 acres of collards, with a cash value of over $17 million, were harvested in Georgia. South and North Carolina, numbers two and three in production respectively, each cultivate about a third as much as Georgia annually, although Burch Farms in Faison, N.C.—with 1,200 acres—has become the region's leading producer for export. Exported greens are hybrids, but the most popular varieties grown for southern consumption are heirlooms.

Collards are usually grown for utilitarian purposes, but southerners have been known to decorate a particularly brilliant plant as a Christmas tree (some grow as tall as six feet). Thelonious Monk, the great jazz musician born in Rocky Mount, N.C., wore a collard leaf in his lapel while playing New York club dates. Greens were first officially celebrated in 1950, when the North Carolina playwright Paul Green led a "Collards and Culture" symposium in Dunn, N.C. According to the late Sam Ragan, Green "urged us all to move out of the commonplace and bring a new dimension to our collard lives."

Flannery O'Connor's Ruby Hill, in "A Stroke of Good Fortune," takes a less favorable view of greens. When her brother, home from the European Theater, asks her to cook him some, she complies grudgingly: "'Collard greens!' she said, spitting the word from her mouth as if it were a poisonous seed."

After William Faulkner was awarded the Nobel Prize for Literature in 1950, a fellow Oxonian wrote Sweden's King

Gustav IV: "I'll bet William didn't tell you what a big coon and collards eater he is. Now, I told William to carry some delicious coon and collards to you. If he had I am sure you would have given him a larger prize."

Collard greens are celebrated in three annual festivals—in Port Wentworth, Ga.; Gaston, S.C.; and Ayden, N.C. A new world's record for eating collards was established at the 2002 Ayden festival when Daniel Mitchell of Deep Run, N.C., ate eight pounds in 30 minutes and kept them down long enough to claim his prize.

ALEX ALBRIGHT
East Carolina University

Alex Albright and Luke Whisnant, eds., *Leaves of Greens: The Collard Poems* (1984); "Collard files," Folklore Archives, English Department, East Carolina University, Greenville, N.C.; John Egerton, *Southern Food: At Home, on the Road, in History* (1993); Greenville, N.C., *Daily Reflector* (8 September 2002); Flannery O'Connor, in *The Complete Stories* (1971); Sam Ragan, *The Pilot* (12 July 1984); *The State* (July 1984).

Greens, Turnip

Turnip greens, or *Brassica campestris*, are the tender leaves of a white turnip. The variety of turnip typically grown for the harvesting of its greens is the Seven Top, though there are more than 40 turnip cultivars in the United States. Turnip greens are slightly sweet if gathered when the plant is young (about 5 to 7 weeks); they develop a somewhat bitter and shaper flavor when harvested from an older plant.

The turnip originated in Europe, where the root and its greens have been cultivated for over 4,000 years. Turnip greens are a favorite green of Appalachia, a region whose ancestry is thought to be made up predominantly of Lowland Scots and Ulstermen. Because of their isolation, people in the Appalachians had cooking methods for greens different from those of most other southerners, who traditionally simmer greens with a piece of pork for 45 minutes to several hours. Folks in the Appalachians commonly parboil their turnip greens and then fry them with fatback or other pork products; some cooks scramble eggs along with the greens while frying.

Turnip greens are richer in vitamins and minerals than most vegetables, including the root from which they stem. They contain significant amounts of vitamins A, B, and C, as well as riboflavin, calcium, beta carotene, iron, folic acid, and other beneficial nutrients. Because of the nutritive composition of turnip greens, they have long served as a folk-healing remedy for such ailments as rheumatoid arthritis, colorectal cancer, atherosclerosis, and emphysema. Turnip greens are also known to absorb fats in the stomach, aiding in digestion.

The first weekend in June residents of Easton, Tex., celebrate their local foodways with their Heritage Turnip Green Festival, which features the town's annual Turnip Green Softball Tournament. Likewise, Nashville, Tenn., pays homage to turnip greens each fall with a special weekend devoted to the leafy greens at the city's farmers' market;

highlights include a turnip greens eating contest, music, and free samplings of turnip greens and other favorite southern foods.

BROOKE BUTLER
University of California, Davis

John K. Crellin, comp. and ed., *Plain Southern Eating: From the Reminiscences of A. L. Tommie Bass, Herbalist* (1988); Joseph E. Dabney, *Smokehouse Ham, Spoon Bread, and Scuppernong Wine: The Folklore and Art of Southern Appalachian Cooking* (1998); Newbell Niles Puckett, *Folk Beliefs of the Southern Negro* (1968).

Grits

Grits are—or is, as the case may be— a by-product of corn kernels. Dried, hulled corn kernels are commonly called hominy; grits are made of finely ground hominy. Whole-grain grits may also be produced from hard corn kernels that are coarsely ground and bolted (sifted) to remove the hulls.

Writing in the *New York Times* on 31 January 1982, Mississippi-born Turner Catledge provided a succinct history of grits in the South:

Grits is the first truly American food. On a day in the spring of 1607 when sea-weary members of the London Company came ashore at Jamestown, Va., they were greeted by a band of friendly Indians offering bowls of a steaming hot substance consisting of softened maize seasoned with salt and some kind of animal fat, probably bear grease. The welcomers called it "rockahominie."

The settlers liked it so much

they adopted it as part of their own diet. They anglicized the name to "hominy" and set about devising a milling process by which the large corn grains could be ground into smaller particles without losing any nutriments. The experiment was a success, and grits became a gastronomic mainstay of the South and symbol of Southern culinary pride.

Thus, throughout its history, and in pre-Columbian times as well, the South has relished grits and made them a symbol of its diet, its customs, its humor, and its good-spirited hospitality. From Captain John Smith to General Andrew Jackson to President Jimmy Carter, southerners rich and poor, young and old, black and white have eaten grits regularly. So common has the food been that it has been called a universal staple, a household companion, even an institution.

Grits cooked into a thick porridge are so common in some parts of the South that they are routinely served for breakfast, whether asked for or not. They are often flavored with butter or gravy, served with sausage or ham, accompanied by bacon and eggs, baked with cheese, or sliced cold and fried in bacon grease. Mississippi-born Craig Claiborne, the late *New York Times* food writer, loved grits and published elegant recipes for their preparation.

Some historians assert that neither hominy nor grits were universally eaten in the South prior to the Civil War, but most food scholars conclude that Indian corn in all its myriad forms— grits, hominy, roasting ears, succotash (usually a combination of corn kernels and lima beans), and various kinds of cornbread—sustained the pioneers and their succeeding generations from the beginning of European settlement on the Virginia coast.

Stan Woodward's film *It's Grits* (1978) chronicled national and regional attitudes toward the dish. Grits enjoyed a surge of national popularity during the early part of the Carter administration but have since returned to their status as a distinctly regional food. One noted foreign visitor who took a liking to grits was the Marquis de Lafayette, hero of the American Revolution. So much did he enjoy eating the dish during his return visit to the United States in 1824–25 that he took a substantial supply back to France for himself and his friends.

The last 30 years have seen renewed interest in grits. It has become a part of southern creative expression, as when bluesman Little Milton says, "If grits ain't groceries / Eggs ain't poultry / And Mona Lisa was a man." Jimmy Carter's presidency in the 1970s led to media interest in grits as a southern icon and the film *My Cousin Vinny* included a humorous scene of a couple from the Bronx eating the mysterious (to them) grit. By the mid-1980s a new generation of renowned southern chefs, including Bill Neal from North Carolina and Frank Stitt from Alabama, began serving sophisticated dishes with grits, such as Stitt's grits soufflé with fresh thyme and country ham. South Carolina cookbook author John Martin Taylor helped popularize stone-ground grits, and smaller producers of artisanal grits grew into successful businesses, including Old Mill of Guilford (North Carolina), Falls Mill (Tennessee), Logan Turnpike Mill (Georgia), Adam's Mill (Alabama), Anson Mills (South Carolina), and War Eagle Mill (Arkansas).

JOHN EGERTON
Nashville, Tennessee

Marilou Awiakta, *Selu: Seeking the Corn Mother's Blessing* (1993); John T. Edge, *Saveur* (November 2003); John Egerton, *Side Orders: Small Helpings of Southern Cookery and Culture* (1990); Betty Fussell, *The Story of Corn* (1992); John Martin Taylor, *Hoppin' John's Lowcountry Cooking* (1992).

Mr. B's Gumbo Ya-Ya
(Courtesy NewOrleansOnline.com)

Gumbo

Gumbo, a regional specialty found most readily in south Louisiana and neighboring areas, is a soup or stew based on local ingredients, served with rice. There are many varieties of gumbo, and individual cooks or families often have their own special heritage recipes. Gumbo often consists of a seasoned mixture of two or more types of meat and/or seafood, usually in a roux-based sauce or gravy.

This heady, aromatic dish is a hybrid product of varied cultures. Its name comes from Africa—*ngombo*, the Bantu word for okra, and okra remains a primary ingredient in one family of gumbo recipes. Another variation, filé gumbo, contains filé powder (ground sassafras leaves) as thickener and unique flavoring agent borrowed from Native Americans. In southwestern Louisiana prairie country, chicken and sausage gumbo has no okra or filé powder but is thickened with a dark roux and flavored with more pepper than other varieties.

Meats used in gumbo may include chicken, duck, squirrel, or rabbit, along with seasoning meats such as sausage or ham (but rarely beef, pork, or lamb stew meat), sometimes in combination with oysters. Seafood gumbo may include shrimp, crab, or oysters, but not often finfish. It commonly includes okra—and often tomatoes, too, in the New Orleans area. Onions, parsley, and pepper season gumbo, and often a dark roux enriches flavor and color.

Gumbo is sometimes called the "national dish of Louisiana." Countless observers, both outsiders and locals, have seen gumbo as a metaphor for south Louisiana, with its ingredients and cooking reflecting the varied ethnic history and geography of the state. It is today a standard item on restaurant menus. The ingredients found in gumbo support the popular local belief that it is a dish that allows the cook to combine small amounts of various ingredients on hand, none of which would be sufficient for a family meal, into a single large dish, which can be extended with the addition of rice.

In Louisiana, gumbo comes in several forms, most notably Creole, Cajun, chicken and gumbo z'herbes. First, there is *Creole*. The word began as a description of offspring of European settlers (in Spanish, *criollo*) and then evolved into meaning homegrown (as in "Creole" tomatoes). Creole cooking, as a style, is that practiced in the areas in and around New Orleans by European and African immigrants and their descendants. Then there is *Cajun*, a shortening of the word *Acadian*, which refers to French settlers of the Nova Scotia region who, displaced by the English, finally settled in southwest Louisiana in the late 18th century.

As with any kitchen dispute, there are as many theories as there are cooks, but the usually accepted difference between a Cajun and a Creole gumbo lies in the roux. Browning flour in fat (slowly, slowly, stirring all the while) creates a roux, and in Cajun gumbos this is a necessary thickener. Creole gumbos rely mainly on vegetable aids for thickening, with a much thinner roux if one is used. Cajun gumbos have more pepper and other spices.

Gumbo nearly always begins with what some chefs call the holy trinity of vegetables—onion, celery, and bell pepper. These are seasoned and sautéed, and the seasonings might include salt, black pepper, cayenne pepper, thyme, garlic, green onions, parsley, bay leaves, and basil. In okra gumbo, tomatoes are usually added. A typical filé gumbo contains the above seasonings, plus chicken or other fowl and its stock, oysters and oyster water, and a seasoning pork— ham, andouille, a smoked sausage, or tasso (dried and smoked meat, in this case, pork). A seafood gumbo contains okra, tomatoes, all the above seasonings, possibly a flavoring pork, and shrimp (with stock from boiling their shells) and hard-shelled crabs (also with stock). Crabmeat may be added.

Many variations on the recipes above are possible, and some people use both filé and okra. Rice always accompanies gumbo, and some cooks sprinkle filé over each bowl served rather than add it to the pot. Some cooks add a serving of potato salad in place of rice.

Two other gumbo families exist. Gumbo z'herbes is very similar to what is called greens and potlikker in other southern kitchens. When seasoning meat is left out, gumbo z'herbes becomes an ideal Lenten soup, and the number of greens in a Good Friday gumbo z'herbes can correspond to the number of apostles. Chicken gumbo is associated with Mardi Gras celebrations in southwestern Louisiana, where masked revelers have traditionally visited farmhouses, chasing live chickens and gathering other ingredients for a communal evening gumbo meal and dance. Every New Orleans cookbook includes a gumbo recipe, illustrating the endless variations of the dish. A few of the many famous gumbo recipes can be found in *The Original Picayune Creole*

Cook Book (1906) and *Chef Paul Prud-homme's Louisiana Kitchen* (1984).

The word *gumbo* does have other meanings. Gumbo mud is black, sticky, and best created by the Mississippi River. Gumbo, or "Gombo" French, is a patois of French and African languages once spoken by blacks in New Orleans and surrounding areas. Gumbo, meaning a mixture of many ingredients, also is used in a Cajun saying: "Gumbo ya-ya," roughly translated as "Everybody talks at once."

The blended, diverse nature of gumbo itself makes the concept ripe for use as a metaphor in southern art. A number of southern musicians have written songs signifying the importance of gumbo, including Billie and Dede Pierce's "Billie's Gumbo Blues." Gumbo often makes an appearance in southern literature. In *A Night in Acadie* (1897) by Kate Chopin references to gumbo as a symbol of cooking and social gathering in Louisiana and as a metaphor for social diversity and cultural blending abound. In Ernest Gaines's 1993 novel *A Lesson before Dying*, gumbo marks the communion between two of the central characters, Grant, a schoolteacher, and Jefferson, a man sentenced to die for murder. In a central scene, Grant forges a relationship with Jefferson in prison by convincing him to eat some of the gumbo that Miss Emma has made for him. Grant tells Jefferson, "It would mean so much to her if you would eat some of the gumbo. . . . Will you be her friend? Will you eat some of the gumbo? Just a little bit? One spoonful?" Jefferson responds with a nod,

signaling the growing bond between the two men. In this text, as well as others, gumbo signifies the merger of diverse ideas and forces and the development of a common language between southerners.

CAROLYN KOLB
New Orleans, Louisiana

C. PAIGE GUTIERREZ
Biloxi, Mississippi

Rima and Richard Collin, *New Orleans Cookbook* (1987); John Egerton, *Southern Food: At Home, on the Road, in History* (1987); C. Paige Gutierrez, *Cajun Foodways* (1992); Howard Mitcham, *Creole Gumbo and All That Jazz: A New Orleans Seafood Cookbook* (1978); Paul Prudhomme, *Chef Paul Prudhomme's Louisiana Kitchen* (1984); Lena Richard, *New Orleans Cookbook* (1998); Lyle Saxon, ed., *Gumbo Ya-Ya: A Collection of Louisiana Folk Tales* (1945); *The Picayune's Creole Cook Book* (1906).

Hash, South Carolina

In South Carolina, hash ("barbecue hash" in some places) takes the place of honor held by Brunswick stew in Georgia and Virginia and burgoo in Kentucky. Like both Brunswick stew and burgoo, South Carolina hash is widely regarded as an accompaniment to barbecue. Like other stews, hash has a long history and holds an important place as a food of congregation. By the colonial period, hash was a stew made from small pieces of roasted meat of any kind, cooked down with onions, herbs, and vinegar water.

Served over rice (or sometimes grits), hash varies in terms of specific ingredients from one cook to the next. Broadly speaking, there are three major hash types in South Carolina, corresponding to the state's primary geographic regions. Hash from the Lowcountry consists of several de-boned hogsheads, supplemented with organ meats like pork liver, cooked in a stock that favors tomato and ketchup. Vegetables can include onions, corn, and potatoes. Hash from the midlands consists primarily of higher-quality cuts of pork, onions, and a mustard-based stock. Finally, Upcountry hash is largely beef-based, with no dominant ketchup, vinegar, or mustard-based stock. This hash most resembles the camp stews or hunter's stews of the early 19th century. Its ingredients are normally limited to beef, onions, butter, and a variety of seasonings.

Any mention of stew ingredients yields opportunities to discuss issues of socioeconomic class, since most stew recipes ultimately come from rural folk traditions. The transformation of very common ingredients into exceptional stews is a theme integral to the story of hash making.

Hash makers from communities throughout South Carolina—much like the burgoo makers of Owensboro and other Kentucky towns—have developed recipes that are a source of immense local pride. Hash consumers tend to be loyal to a certain hash maker or at least develop preferences for certain types of hash. In general, folks who prefer mustard-based hash do not consider ketchup- or vinegar-based hash to their liking and vice versa. In addition, the consistency of the hash is a defining characteristic. In this regard, hash can

be separated into two basic categories: hash with meat that has been processed in a grinder and hash with meat that has been "pulled." The latter results in hash with a stringy, more irregular consistency—much different from hash cooked with ground meat.

While many hash makers still cook in the large, cast-iron pots that have been a part of the cooking tradition for generations, some have opted to go with similarly sized stainless steel or aluminum pots. The quality of the hash produced in such pots is at issue for many hash makers. Some feel that hash produced in cast-iron pots over a wood-fed fire is of the best quality. Similar sentiment is found among many who make burgoo, Brunswick stew, bogs, and muddles.

While many rural fire departments, agricultural clubs, and other civic orga-nizations cook hash several times a year for community fund-raisers, the most prolific producers of South Carolina hash are locally owned barbecue restau-rants, many of which developed from family "shade tree" cooking traditions. These families traditionally cooked barbecue and hash for reunions or celebratory occasions like the Fourth of July, but found that demand was high enough to warrant a full-time venture.

Whether through restaurants, clubs, or churches, groups of all sizes—from families to whole communities—are involved in the hash making process. Over time, people maintain, adapt, and reform these local traditions. Hash mas-ters, like their stewmaster contempo-raries in neighboring states, typically go to great lengths to retain the uniqueness of both their recipes and their cooking techniques.

SADDLER TAYLOR
McKissick Museum, Columbia,
South Carolina

STAN WOODWARD
Greenville, South Carolina

Karen Hess, *The Carolina Rice Kitchen: The African Connection* (1992); Annabella P. Hill, *Mrs. Hill's Southern Practical Cookery and Receipt Book* (1995); Mary V. Huguenin and Anne M. Stoney, eds., *Charleston Receipts* (1950); Charles Joyner, *Down by the Riverside: A South Carolina Slave Community* (1984); Sarah Rutledge, *The Carolina Housewife* (1847); John Martin Taylor, *Hoppin' John's Lowcountry Cooking* (1992).

Hearn, Lafcadio

(1850–1904) JOURNALIST, AUTHOR, ILLUSTRATOR.
On 27 June 1850 Patricio Lafcadio Tessima Carlos Hearn was born to a Greek mother and an Irish father, a surgeon in the British army, on the Greek island of Lefkas. His parents divorced and abandoned Hearn, who was subsequently raised in Great Britain by a great aunt and then by a guardian. At 19 Hearn moved to Cincinnati and worked as a newspaper reporter, embarking on a career that eventually led him to New Orleans. From 1877 until 1888 Hearn worked as a journalist and correspondent reporting for local New Orleans publications, as well as *Harper's Weekly, Cosmopolitan, Scribner's,* and other national magazines. Hearn became a prolific writer and illustrator of stories about the unique vices, traditions, and cultural expressions of New Orleans. His romantic and imaginative articles instilled readers in the United States and Europe with an image of New Orleans that continues to shape the world's view of the Crescent City.

While Hearn lived in New Orleans, he also collected local songs for a New York music critic, opened the short-lived 5-Cent Restaurant, and collected recipes of local dishes from homes he visited. Hearn published these recipes in 1885 as *La Cuisine Créole,* which became the earliest published collection of New Orleans and Louisiana recipes. "'La Cuisine Créole' (Créole cookery)," Hearn writes in the introduction, "partakes of the nature of its birthplace— New Orleans—which is cosmopolitan in its nature, blending the characteristics of the American, French, Spanish, Italian, West Indian and Mexican. In this compilation will be found many original recipes and other valuable ones heretofore unpublished, notable those of Gombo filé, Bouille-abaisse, Court-bouillon, Jambolaya, Salade à la Russe, Bisque of Cray-fish à la Créole, Pousse Café, Café brule, Brûlot, together with many confections and delicacies for the sick, including a number of mixed drinks." *La Cuisine Créole* made a permanent contribution to Creole cuisine and a lasting impact on American culture. Hearn's work in *La Cuisine Créole* continues to serve as an invaluable record of the history of Creole food, New Orleans, and Louisiana.

After making, and writing, history in New Orleans, Hearn moved to Japan, taught English, changed his name to Koizumi Yakumo, married a Japanese woman who was the daughter of a samurai, learned Japanese, and continued his voluminous writing and illustration. As had been the case with his work in New Orleans, Hearn's critics accused him of "exoticizing" Japan for his readers. However, Hearn secured a place in history after publishing numerous volumes in Japanese, particularly Japanese fairy tales, for which he is eminently famous. Hearn died on the Japanese island of Honshu on 26 September 1904.

SCOTT R. SIMMONS
New Orleans, Louisiana

Lafcadio Hearn, *Lafcadio Hearn's Creole Cook Book* (reprint ed., 1990); S. Frederick Starr, *Inventing New Orleans: The Writings of Lafcadio Hearn* (2001).

Hill, Annabella Powell

(1810–1878) COOKBOOK AUTHOR.
Born in Madison County, Ga., in 1810 to Virginia natives Major John Edmonds and Annabella Burwell Dawson, Annabella Powell Edmonds married Edward Young Hill in December 1827. The Hills lived in Monticello, Ga., until 1845, when Edward, a judge, was elected to the superior court and the family moved to La Grange, Ga. The Hills figured in the politics of the Baptist church in Georgia and helped found at least one girls' academy. Judge Hill died in December 1860, on the eve of the Civil War. After the war, economic hardship forced Annabella Hill to sell her property in La Grange and move to Atlanta, where she became principal of the lottery-funded orphan's school from around 1868 until shortly before her death in 1878.

Annabella Hill began writing a cookbook sometime in the late 1850s or early 1860s. Published in 1867 as *Mrs. Hill's New Cook Book*, it proved to be a seminal work, one that could almost be called the southern *Fanny Farmer* of its day. It enjoyed numerous editions through the remainder of the 19th century and is frequently referenced in later cookbooks. Since 1995, it has been reprinted in a facsimile edition

Hill's cookbook stands today as a critical link in the chain of southern food history. In addition to being one of the only printed records of antebellum cooking in Georgia, it clearly illustrates the complicated cross-pollination among diverse cultures that shaped southern cooking. Comprehensive and encyclopedic in its scope (there are more than 1,100 culinary and medicinal recipes), unparalleled in its detail, and invaluable for its rare crediting of borrowed material, *Mrs. Hill's New Cook Book* is in many ways a telling portrait in recipes, not only of one woman, but of a place and era that have been for too long distorted by romance and legend.

DAMON LEE FOWLER
Savannah, Georgia

Damon Lee Fowler, *Classical Southern Cooking: A Celebration of the Cuisine of the Old South* (1995); Annabella Powell Hill, *Mrs. Hill's New Cook Book* (1867).

Hines, Duncan

(1880–1959) CRITIC, ENTREPRENEUR.
Although today his name is widely recognized as a cake mix brand, Duncan Hines was in fact influential in shaping the qualitative experiences Americans expect from their restaurant meals.

Born in Bowling Green, Ky., on 26 March 1880, Hines was raised near there by his grandparents after his mother's death in 1884. From his grandmother he learned to appreciate southern cooking and the importance of sanitary cooking methods. He attended Bowling Green Business College (1896–98), then moved west. He worked for several employers before relocating to Chicago in September 1905. From there he worked for the next 33 years as a traveling salesman.

In that profession, as Hines traveled from one town to another, he had a keen interest in where he dined. Aware of the problem of restaurant food poisoning and unsanitary roadside meals, he noted dining facilities that were clean and served excellent food. Between 1905 and 1934 Hines secured a reputation for discovering superior restaurants; for him, detecting them was both a preventive measure and a hobby. In 1934 a Chicago newspaper heard of Hines's expertise and published an article about him. Soon people by the thousands began calling and writing him, all wanting to know where quality restaurants could be found in specific cities.

Responding, Hines compiled a list of 167 superior restaurants in 30 states and sent it with his 1935 Christmas cards. The response to this card was so overwhelming that he compiled an expanded list, and in June 1936 self-published his first book, *Adventures in Good Eating*, a national restaurant guide. By March 1938 the book was selling so well that he quit his sales job and became his own publisher.

Hines received new attention in December 1938, when a *Saturday Evening Post* article about his avocation made him an overnight national celebrity. The reasons for Hines's sudden fame and widespread acceptance were twofold: his writings were widely needed, and he would not accept payment for a listing in order to preserve the perception of his impeachable independence and his public credibility. Because of his impartiality and the accuracy of his recommendations, Americans flocked to he restaurants he favored; by the mid-1940s he had become the nation's most trusted name in the food industry.

Hines moved back to Bowling Green in April 1939, conducting his operations from there and announcing that restaurants that wanted his recommendation would have to implement his suggestions. Many restaurants, aware of the good fortune his favor could bring, complied with his wishes—which were soon copied in other establishments as well. By the conclusion of World War II, America's expectations for quality restaurant dining had been permanently altered.

In October 1949 Hines and businessman Roy Park inaugurated Hines-Park Foods, Inc., which eventually produced over 250 items that were personally approved by Duncan Hines for consumption. Wanting a brand name that would produce instant success, Procter and Gamble bought the exclusive rights to Duncan Hines's name in August 1956, compensating him with a percentage of each case of cake mix it sold. Hines died of cancer on 15 March 1959.

LOUIS HATCHETT
Henderson, Kentucky

John T. Edge, *Oxford American* (September/ October 2000); Louis Hatchett, *Duncan Hines: The Man Behind the Cake Mix* (2001), *Kentucky Living* (May 1999); Duncan Hines, *Duncan Hines' Food Odyssey* (1955); Harvey Levenstein, *Paradox of Plenty: A Social History of Eating in America* (1993); David M. Schwartz, *Smithsonian* (November 1984).

Hot Tamales

In Latin America, hot tamales are as ubiquitous as sandwiches. This also holds true in, of all places, the Mississippi Delta. The history of the hot tamale in this area reaches back to at least the early part of the 20th century. Reference to the Delta delicacy appears in the song "They're Red Hot," recorded by legendary bluesman Robert Johnson in 1936. But how and exactly when were hot tamales introduced to what has been called "the most southern place on earth"? More important, why have they stayed? There are as many answers to these questions as there are tamale recipes. In restaurants, on street corners, and in family kitchens throughout the Delta, this old and time-consuming culinary tradition remains vibrant in the 21st century.

Many hypothesize that tamales made their way to the Mississippi Delta in the early 20th century when migrant laborers were brought in from Mexico to work the cotton harvest. The basic tamale ingredients—cornmeal and pork—were easily adapted by the African Americans who shared the fields. Others maintain that the Delta's history with tamales goes back to the U.S.-Mexican War 100 years earlier, when soldiers from Mississippi traveled to

Hot tamale cart, Mississippi Delta
(Courtesy Amy Evans, photographer)

Mexico and brought tamale recipes home with them. Others still argue that tamales have always been in the Delta as part of the area's Native American agriculture based in maize, serving as a portable food for war parties and field workers for millennia.

Today, African Americans are the primary keepers of the tamale-making tradition in the Delta, a position enhanced by their interaction with Mexican migrant laborers. Through slavery and sharecropping, tamales have proved to be a viable support system—financially and nutritionally—to rural communities throughout the area. The same is true in the contemporary Delta. Tamale stands and stories abound, underscoring the endurance of this particular foodway in this part of the American South.

In the Mississippi Delta, no two people make hot tamales exactly the same. Pork is traditional. Some cooks use beef, while others prefer turkey. Some boil their meat, while others simply brown it. Some people use masa, while most prefer the rough texture of cornmeal. Most wrap in corn shucks, while a few have turned to less expensive parchment paper. Some season the tamale in just one way, while many will season the meat and the meal, as well as the water used to simmer the rolled bundles. Some eat theirs straight out of the shuck, while others smother them in chili and cheese. As it turns out, there are as many stories about how Deltans acquired tamale recipes as there are ways of making them. (Incidentally, in the Delta vernacular, the singular is, indeed, *tamale*, not the Spanish *tamal*.)

Whatever its origin, the hot tamale has been a staple of Delta communities for generations. Tamales have persisted in the Delta because of family tradition, public demand, and simple necessity. African Americans discovered a warm and hearty food that could be easily transported to a cotton field and kept warm while they worked. They also discovered the economic opportunity of selling tamales between harvests when the cold weather kept them out of the fields. To this day, many residents claim that the best time to eat a hot tamale in the Delta is during the winter months. But a good craving is hard to deny, and people sell and eat tamales year-round.

Oddly enough, the Delta tamale has begun a return to its Mexican origins. For generations, Delta tamale makers have used cornmeal in lieu of the traditional masa harina, a fine corn flour especially for tamale making. But today, with globalization and the Internet, many tamale makers now have easy access to traditional tamale ingredients. Tastes seldom change in the Delta, however. The small, rough, corn-textured, beef-filled hot tamale is still the preference of Delta connoisseurs. This version is also smaller in size than most traditional tamales found in Latin America. Tastes in the Delta have also influenced the tamale's color. In keeping with Robert Johnson's song, "They're Red Hot," many Delta hot tamales are, in fact, bright red in color. This vibrant visual is the result of spices added in all stages of tamale preparation and cooking. The result is a true red-hot icon of Mississippi Delta foodways.

AMY EVANS
University of Mississippi

Rick Bayless, *Authentic Mexican: Regional Cooking from the Heart of Mexico* (1987); John Egerton, *Southern Food: At Home, on the Road, in History* (1987); Betty Fussell, *The Story of Corn* (1992); Jeffrey M. Pilcher, *¡Que vivan los tamales! Food and the Making of Mexican Identity* (1998).

Hushpuppies

Hushpuppies (or hush puppies, hush-puppies) are small balls, ovals, or crescents of fried cornmeal batter that traditionally accompany fried fish and, in areas of the Carolinas, barbecue.

The basic recipe for hushpuppies calls for cornmeal or a mixture of cornmeal and flour; eggs; milk, buttermilk, or water; baking powder and/or soda; salt; and onions mixed well and spooned or rolled into balls and dropped into hot oil or lard, preferably grease in which fish have been frying. Variations on this recipe are many. Some cooks omit the onions; many add sugar. Still others add chopped pickles, fresh corn, hot sauce, or fines herbes. Shapes also vary from hand-rolled balls, to spooned crescents, to ovals created by a hand-cranked device that drops batter into the fryer.

The origins of both this southern side dish and its name are uncertain. As early as the 18th century in New Orleans cooks prepared lightly sweetened balls of cornmeal called croquettes (or beignets) de maïs. However, the usually unsweetened cornmeal fritters found today in fish camps, catfish houses, calabash restaurants, and other seafood eateries around the South may be a more recent creation. The name *hushpuppy* may give some clue as to the dish's origins. According to legend, someone—fishermen, hunters, plantation cooks—troubled by dogs impatiently whining to be fed, dropped a concoction of cornmeal and flour into a deep-fat frying vat and tossed the golden brown nuggets that resulted to the dogs, crying "Hush, puppies!" As *The Yearling* author Marjorie Kinnan Rawlings puts it, "the dogs, devouring them, could ask no more of life, and hushed." Chef Marvin Woods, in his version of this story, sets it during the Civil War. Others give the tale a later setting and ascribe the creation of hushpuppies to workers monitoring cane syrup vats in Florida, a group of Maryland women hosting a combination fish fry and quilting bee, or an African chef in an Atlanta restaurant.

The basic motif of this story has even found its way into corporate America: The Hush Puppies shoe company claims that a salesman, Jim Muir, stumbled on the name while dining with a friend in Tennessee. When the friend quieted his restless hounds by throwing them fried hushpuppies, Muir thought that the name "hushpuppies" would fit his new line of casual shoes designed to "quiet" tired "dogs."

Regardless of their origins, by the middle of the 20th century and continuing through the present, hushpuppies, along with coleslaw and french fries, have become the expected side dishes to go with fried fish. As Rawlings, in her *Cross Creek Cookery*, puts it, "Fresh caught fish without hush puppies are as a man without a woman, a beautiful woman without kindness, law without a policeman."

STEPHEN CRISWELL
University of South Carolina
Lancaster

Marion Brown, *Marion Brown's Southern Cook Book* (1968); John T. Edge, *Southern Belly: The Ultimate Food Lover's Companion to the South* (2000); John Egerton, *Southern Food: At Home, on the Road, in History* (1987); Damon Lee Fowler, *Classical Southern Cooking: A Celebration of the Cuisine of the Old South* (1995); Sam Bowers Hilliard, *Hog Meat and Hoecake: Food Supply in the Old South, 1840–1860* (1972); Marjorie Kinnan Rawlings, *Cross Creek Cookery* (1975); Marvin Woods, *The New Low-Country Cooking* (2000); Sylvia Woods and Christopher Styler, *Sylvia's Soul Food* (1992).

Jack Daniel Distillery

Lynchburg, Tenn. (pop. 361), the seat of a dry (Moore) county in the Cumberland foothills, is the home of the nation's oldest registered distillery.

In the 1860s Jack Newton Daniel chose Lynchburg's Cave Spring Hollow as the site for his whiskey-making business. Using cold spring water stabilized at a year-round 56° and all but free of iron and other trace minerals, a "yeasting back" process (retaining some of the mash from previous runs to use as a starter), charcoal leaching, and oaken-cask warehousing, Daniel produced a distinctive Tennessee whiskey that by the turn of the century was winning international acclaim.

Inheriting the business from his uncle in 1907, Lem Motlow was forced to turn to the mule and harness trade (he opened Lynchburg Hardware in 1912) during Prohibition, but he resumed distillery operations soon after repeal. When Motlow died in 1947, the prosperous distillery passed to his four sons.

Continuity, an unshakable commitment to traditional brewing standards and methods, marks the history of Jack Daniel Distillery. In 1946 when the war-effort ban on whiskey production was lifted on condition that processors use inferior grades of grain, Daniel preferred to reopen a year later rather than compromise quality. Today, burning rick yards producing the hard sugar-maple charcoal through which the whiskey is slowly mellowed still dot the hollow; white oak barrels continue to be used for aging. Although twist caps have replaced cork stoppers, the "square shooter" bottle chosen by Jack Daniel in 1895 continues to be the company trademark.

The "Black Jack" bottle—a southern icon (Charles Reagan Wilson Collection, University of Mississippi, Oxford)

Owned now by Brown-Forman, Inc., the Jack Daniel Distillery avoids a corporate image and stresses in its advertising the timeless character of its small-town operations. Ad copy has immortalized the Lynchburg General Store, Miss Mary Bobo's Boarding House (where Mr. Jack took his noonday meals), and the Moore County Court House, built in 1884.

Although consumer profiles note that the average Jack Daniel drinker is an upwardly mobile, college-educated urban male, it is clear that he still finds a place in his heart for a little southern town that has not changed much and for a whiskey that "hasn't changed at all."

ELIZABETH M. MAKOWSKI
University of Mississippi

Jeannie R. Bigger, *Tennessee Historical Quarterly* (Spring 1972); Ben A. Green, *Jack Daniel's Legacy* (1967); Peter Krass, *Blood and Whiskey: The Life and Times of Jack Daniel* (2004); Jim Murray, *Classic Bourbon, Tennessee, and Rye Whiskey* (1998).

Jambalaya

Jambalaya is a rice-based dish containing an assortment of meat and vegetables prepared in a single cooking vessel. American food critics and cultural commentators frequently identify jambalaya as a quintessentially Cajun or Creole dish, exemplifying the best of Louisiana's versatile culinary traditions. To less provincial gourmets, however, jambalaya appears to be little more than a Gallicized variation of paella. Yet, jambalaya may be the product of mutually reinforcing culinary traditions introduced into Louisiana from two different continents.

The adoption of a Spanish dish by Louisiana's Gallic community should not be surprising. The Pelican State was a Spanish possession for four decades in the late 18th century, and, throughout its history, Louisiana has maintained close ties with the Spanish communities of the Caribbean Rim.

The date of paella's introduction into Louisiana remains a matter of speculation—the documentary record being silent on the subject, but it probably dates from the late 18th century. Underlying this claim is the fact that traditional consumption of the dish is concentrated in the areas settled by Hispanic immigrants in the late 18th century. For example, Gonzales, Louisiana's self-proclaimed jambalaya capital, lies near the colonial era Isleño (Canary Island) settlement of Galveztown.

The rural jambalaya tradition differs in some notable aspects from its urban counterpart in New Orleans. In rural south Louisiana, jambalaya is brown, because the rice constituting the body of the dish absorbs the sauce in which it is cooked. Jambalaya is traditionally cooked in a cast-iron pot. Cast-iron pots achieve very high cooking temperatures, resulting in more complete caramelization of natural sugars in meats and vegetables—and thus a brown sauce. In New Orleans, however, jambalaya is red because of the heavy use of tomatoes. The use of tomatoes is considered one of the hallmarks of Creole cuisine.

New Orleans jambalaya is possibly an offshoot of jollof rice, a West African delicacy. Jollof rice is quite similar to paella in that its ingredients include whatever happens to be available. Tomatoes, however, are a key ingredient. Like paella and jambalaya, the entire dish is prepared in a single cooking vessel. The result is strikingly similar to New Orleans jambalaya.

RYAN A. BRASSEAUX
CARL A. BRASSEAUX
Lafayette, Louisiana

Rima and Richard Collin, *New Orleans Cookbook* (1987); John Egerton, *Southern Food: At Home, on the Road, in History* (1987); Howard Mitcham, *Creole Gumbo and All That Jazz: A New Orleans Seafood Cookbook* (1978); Paul Prudhomme, *Chef Paul Prudhomme's Louisiana Kitchen* (1984); Lyle Saxon, ed., *Gumbo Ya-Ya: A Collection of Louisiana Folk Tales* (1945); *The Picayune Creole Cook Book* (1906).

Jefferson, Thomas

(1743–1826) GARDENER, EPICURE. We venerate Thomas Jefferson for his role in the founding of the republic, for his having penned the Declaration of Independence, and for his prodigious intellect, among many other reasons. He is also celebrated as gardener and epicure of Monticello.

During his term as American ambassador to the court of Louis XIV (1784–89) he became entranced with fine wines and the royalist cuisine of France, developing ruinously extravagant tastes. He toured the great vineyards and financed the apprenticeship of his servant James Hemings as a chef during those years. In *The Negro Chef Cookbook* (1960), Leonard E. Roberts writes that after returning home "[Hemings] and Jefferson concocted the great continental cuisine of France and made some of our most glamorous American dishes. At Monticello and the White House, they introduced ice cream, macaroni, spaghetti, savoye, cornbread stuffing, waffles, almonds, raisons, vanilla, and many more dishes and foods to America." But Jefferson never "abjured his native vittles," and he is perhaps responsible, at least in part, for the extraordinarily successful melding of classical French cuisine with the best elements of Virginia cookery, including the transforming presence of the enslaved cooks in the kitchens of the gentry, who imbued everything they cooked with the aromas of Africa.

While Jefferson indulged himself by hiring a French chef at the President's House, no white hand ever "stirred the pots" at Monticello. Jefferson would not have been able to maintain his baronial style of living without the hundreds of slaves who tended the gardens, did the cooking, and met his every need. Beginning with James Hemings, all the cooks at Monticello had had at least some French training: Peter Hemings was trained by his brother James; Edith Fossett (Edy), said to have been Jefferson's favorite cook, debuted under Honoré Julien, George Washington's onetime French chef, at the President's House.

A great deal of the culinary lore of Monticello has been preserved in writing, beginning with myriad receipts and culinary observations kept by Jefferson in his own hand, as well as manuscripts kept by his granddaughters, which contain receipts from the cuisine of the royal court of France alongside ones for African stews entitled "Gumba," for example. Miraculously, much of that lore reached his kinswoman Mary Randolph, whose brother, Thomas Mann Randolph, married Jefferson's daughter, Martha. Mary Randolph may very nearly be thought of as the amanuensis of the culinary legacy of Monticello; her work, *The Virginia House-wife* (1824), the earliest known southern cookbook, was enormously popular and influential down through most of the century. In the opinion of many, it remains to this day the finest work to come out of the American kitchen. But Jefferson knew that gardening and subsistence farming were the very basis of life and of Epicureanism. His passion for gardening continued to the end of his days.

KAREN HESS
New York, New York

Edwin Morris Betts, ed., *Thomas Jefferson's Farm Book* (1999), *Thomas Jefferson's Garden Book, 1766–1824* (1999); James M. Gabler, *Passions: The Wines and Travels of Thomas Jefferson* (1995); Mary Randolph, *The Virginia House-wife* (1824).

King Cakes

King cakes, rich briochelike delicacies, make their appearance on 6 January, or Twelfth Night, and herald the beginning of the Carnival season in New Orleans. Like the French *gateaux des rois*, king cakes (at one time the term was used only in the plural even after the custom of smaller individual cakes had been abandoned) hold the surprise of a bean, ring, or, most often today, a plastic baby, often said to represent the baby Jesus. In France, the winner (the person who finds the surprise in his or her cake) becomes the king or queen of the next party—with an older aristocratic tradition specifying that the king provide funding for a ball, and the queen, the ballroom. In some early New Orleans Mardi Gras krewes, a slice of cake holding a golden bean was given to the young lady chosen as queen. More democratically, at least one other group of men found their queen through her lucky choice of the slice with the concealed favor. Today's winner of the baby must bring the next king cake.

King cakes are made throughout southern Louisiana during Carnival season. Not until the 1980s did they find their way into Mobile and other Gulf Coast locales celebrating the season. Even today, in buying a king cake outside Louisiana, one finds the plastic baby gingerly taped to the package, rather than unseen within the cake.

Flavors and designs differ from one bakery to another, with the plastic babies coming in brown and beige and slightly different sizes, though one inch is the most common length. During the 1980s and 1990s, one bakery would avail itself of as many as 50,000 babies per season. The centerpiece of a party, a coffee break, or any other cause for festivity, king cakes are always decorated with coarse sugar in green, purple, and gold—the colors of Mardi Gras. Ingredients include flour, yeast, butter, and eggs. The consistency is much like that of challah bread, but newer versions include fruit and cream cheese.

SUSAN TUCKER
Tulane University

Peter S. Feibleman, *American Cooking: Creole and Acadian* (1971); John D. Folse, *The Encyclopedia of Cajun and Creole Cuisine* (2004); Mary Land, *New Orleans Cuisine* (1969).

Krispy Kreme

In the window of Krispy Kreme stores, a lit "Hot Doughnuts Now" sign signals to passersby that the company's signature "Original Glazed" doughnuts—each containing 200 calories, 12 grams of fat, and 22 grams of carbohydrates—are freshly made and ready for eating. Southern humorist Roy Blount Jr. once wrote that "when Krispy Kremes are hot, they are to other doughnuts what angels are to people. They're not crispy-creamy so much as right on the cusp between chewy and molten." Krispy Kreme was founded in 1937 in Winston-Salem, N.C., by a young entrepreneur named Vernon Carver Rudolph. Today, Krispy Kreme turns out an estimated 7.5 million doughnuts a day and over 2.7 billion doughnuts a year. This southern company has become a nationally (and to some extent, internationally) recognized corporate entity that has truly turned doughnuts into dollars.

Born in 1915, Vernon Rudolph entered the doughnut business at age 18, selling doughnuts door to door for his uncle Ishmael Armstrong, a grocery store owner in Paducah, Ky. After selling his store in 1933, Armstrong bought a doughnut shop and its special doughnut recipe from a Frenchman named Joe Le-Beau, who had come to Kentucky from New Orleans. Armstrong moved the business to Nashville, and his nephew followed to help. In 1935 Vernon's father, Plumie Harrison Rudolph, obtained a loan with which Vernon bought the Nashville shop from his uncle, and he and his father went into business together, opening a shop in Charleston, W.Va., in 1936. A year later, Vernon's father and a salesman opened up a shop in Atlanta on Ponce de Leon Avenue, and Vernon headed to Winston-Salem.

Rumor has it that Vernon chose the North Carolina city because earlier,

Krispy Kreme, "America's Favorite Doughnut" (Courtesy James G. Thomas Jr., photographer)

standing on a corner in Peoria, Ill., he pulled a pack of Camel cigarettes out of his shirt pocket and decided that a city that was home to such a large, national manufacturer (Camels being a product of Winston-Salem-based R. J. Reynolds) would be an ideal place to set up his business. At age 22, Rudolph and two friends traveled to Winston-Salem with a new green Pontiac, $200 between them, a few pieces of doughnut equipment, and the secret doughnut recipe. Once in town, the men found a rental space across from Salem College, spent their last $25 on the first month's rent, and ate, slept, and borrowed on credit until the store got off the ground. Working 18-hour days, Rudolph and his friends soon had eight Krispy Kreme shops in five southern states.

During World War II, Rudolph was drafted and sent to Fort Bragg as a private. Because of the death of his wife, Ruth, in an automobile accident in 1944, however, Rudolph served only 18 months before returning to Winston-Salem and his business. After opening another shop in Greenville, S.C., in 1946, Rudolph incorporated the retailers into the Krispy Kreme Company. (He remarried that same year.) In 1947 the Krispy Kreme Corporation was formed as a separate legal entity to manufacture dry mixes for production and sell doughnut manufacturing equipment and bakery supplies.

From this point forward, Krispy Kreme's equipment department continued to invent and construct improved equipment for the standardized production of "America's Favorite Doughnut." In 1951 the first "all-new model shop" appeared in Greensboro, N.C., complete with off-street parking, a loading dock, steel tiles for improved sanitation, and tiled floors. During the 1950s Krispy Kreme introduced the coffee bar to its stores, developed a research lab, and also introduced the Krispy Kreme Fundraising Program (a program that allowed schools and community groups to raise money through the sale of doughnuts). By 1957 Krispy Kreme had shops and franchises in 20 states, and an automatic doughnut-cutting table had replaced hand-cutting of the doughnuts, cutting around 500 doughnuts an hour. In 1959 the first three standardized shops opened, featuring the now-famous green-tiled, gabled roofs, standardized production equipment, coffee bars, showcases for displaying doughnuts, outdoor signs, color schemes of aqua and white, and large windows through which customers could view the doughnuts' production (also known as the Doughnut Theater). During the 1960s the process of doughnut production (which included proofing, frying, glazing, and screen loading) became completely automated. By 1963 Krispy Kreme included wholesale and retail plants, franchised plants, production under private labels for grocery and

bakery chains, a plant producing mixes, and plants manufacturing doughnut-producing equipment.

In 1973 Vernon Rudolph died. Three years later, Krispy Kreme Doughnut Corporation became a wholly owned subsidiary of Beatrice Foods Company of Chicago. Because the change was unsuccessful, a group of franchise owners leveraged a buyout in 1982, making Krispy Kreme once again an independent corporation. Krispy Kreme headquarters remain in Winston-Salem. In 1997 Krispy Kreme donated 15 cubic feet of corporate records and related artifacts (including Krispy Kreme uniforms, coffee mugs, cooking utensils, and an original Ring King Junior automated doughnut maker) to the Smithsonian Institution's National Museum of American History.

Krispy Kreme went public on the stock market in April 2000, with over 3 million shares. In 2001 the company opened its first store outside the United States, in Mississauga, Ontario, Canada. In 2002 baseball slugger Hank Aaron opened a Krispy Kreme franchise on Evans Street in Atlanta, and as of May 2005 Krispy Kreme has 360 U.S. retail stores—covering virtually every state—as well as stores in Mexico, Canada, the United Kingdom, Australia, and South Korea.

MARGARET T. MCGEHEE
Emory University

John T. Edge, *Donuts: An American Passion* (2006); Louise Skillman Joyner, *A Man and an Enterprise: The Story of Krispy Kreme and Its Founder, Vernon Carver Rudolph* (1977, 1992); Krispy Kreme Corporation Records, Archives Center, National Museum of

American History, Smithsonian Institution; Krispy Kreme website: http://www.krispykreme.com; David Taylor, *Smithsonian Magazine* (March 1998).

Lagasse, Emeril

(b. 1959) NEW ORLEANS CHEF.
Born 15 October 1959 in Fall River, Mass., Emeril Lagasse developed a love of food at an early age through his mother and later during his teens working in a Portuguese bakery. This passion inspired Lagasse to forgo a music scholarship to the New England Conservatory of Music and attend Johnson and Wales University's culinary school instead.

Upon graduation, Lagasse worked in France, New York City, Boston, and Philadelphia. Before long his path crossed with New Orleans restaurateur Ella Brennan, who was looking for a successor to Paul Prudhomme at Commander's Palace. Brennan brought Lagasse to New Orleans and immersed him in the local food culture. Lagasse took the helm at Commander's Palace in 1982 and ran the kitchen until 1990, when he left to open his own namesake restaurant on lower Tchoupitoulas Street. Lagasse found almost immediate success with his first restaurant and his "New New Orleans" cooking, featuring "kicked up" versions of old favorites like barbecue shrimp. Lagasse also became the host of a television cooking show called *The Essence of Emeril* on a new national network known as the Food Network. This show evolved into a live hour-long, one-man performance known as *Emeril Live*.

Lagasse evolved off the air as well—opening two more restaurants in New Orleans (Nola and Emeril's Delmonico), and others in Las Vegas, Orlando, Miami, and Atlanta. He maintains "Emeril's Homebase" in New Orleans, which houses restaurant operations as well as cookbook and recipe development and testing, the emerils.com website, and a storefront for his signature products.

SARAH O'KELLEY
New Orleans, Louisiana

Emeril Lagasse, *Emeril's Creole Christmas* (1997), *Emeril's New New Orleans Cooking* (1993), *Emeril's Potluck* (2004), *Emeril's There's a Chef in My Family* (2004), *Emeril's There's a Chef in My Soup* (2002), *Emeril's TV Dinners* (1998), *Every Day's a Party* (1999), *From Emeril's Kitchens* (2003), *Louisiana Real and Rustic* (1996), *Prime Time Emeril* (2001).

Lewis, Edna

(1916–2006) CHEF, COOKBOOK AUTHOR.
In her quiet yet self-assured way, Edna Lewis was one of the first people to generate respect and acceptance for southern cooking as true American cuisine. Born in Freetown, Va., the granddaughter of freed slaves, she went on to become a celebrated chef in New York in the late 1940s and 1950s, when there were few, if any, other black or female chefs working in the city.

One of eight children, she thrived on the land, helping to grow, gather, hunt, and harvest everything her family and neighbors put on their tables. In the morning she watched when the women gathered fresh vegetables and fruits still covered with dew. She helped hand-feed and raise chickens so they would be just the right size and age in the spring, when fried chicken was a seasonal favorite. Fried chicken is one of Lewis's signature dishes, the cooking medium composed of fresh-rendered lard and churned butter flavored with a slice of smoked ham. The children participated in all the farm work. She helped plant the crops and shuck the corn and observed as her aunt made sweet hominy from whole kernels or ashcakes from fresh-ground cornmeal baked in the hearth.

Lewis recounts in her writings family conversations around the dining room table. They would talk about the quality of their food, how it was cooked, and how it could be made better. Special dishes like baked Virginia ham and caramel layer cake were made for celebratory events like Emancipation Day or Revival Week at Freetown's church.

During the Depression, Lewis moved to New York, where she felt free from racism for the first time. She took on several different jobs, from typist at the Communist Party offices to live-in housekeeper. She even tried her hand at window dressing. She and her friends cooked for each other; and her southern dishes were always a favorite. Two friends, Karl Bissinger, fashion photographer, and John Nicholson, window designer, convinced her to become a partner and cook at their new restaurant, Café Nicholson on East 58th Street, in 1948.

The plan was to keep the food simple, using only the best seasonal ingredients. There would be no menu; diners would eat whatever was being served that day. The choices included herb roasted chicken, filet mignon, fish, salad, and chocolate mousse or pears and cheese. The recipes were not necessarily southern, but they proved Lewis's unique skill in intensifying the ingredients' inherent flavors. The small restaurant became a mecca for celebrities; writers, artists, performers, and politicians packed the place every day. Edna Lewis's composure and self-assurance belied her youth, and with her regal appearance, patience, and humor, she gained the respect of all she met. She was as much a draw at Café Nicholson as her food.

In 1952 Lewis left Café Nicholson and again took up a variety of occupations, from pheasant farmer to private caterer to lecturer at the African Halls of the American Museum of Natural History. As a chef, she had a lasting impact on the cuisines of Fearrington House in Pittsboro, N.C., and Middleton Place in Charleston, S.C. In the early 1970s she met Judith Jones, an editor at Alfred A. Knopf, who encouraged her to write down her recipes and her memories of home in her own words. The result was *The Taste of Country Cooking*, the first of several cookbooks Lewis authored.

In 1992 Lewis retired from her last job as a chef, at Gage and Tollner in Brooklyn, but she continued cooking and promoting the flavor and value of traditional southern food. In 1999 Lewis was named Grande Dame of Les Dames d'Escoffier International and received the Southern Foodways Alliance's Lifetime Achievement Award. Her last cookbook, *The Gift of Southern Cooking: Recipes and Revelations from Two Great*

American Cooks, was written with her friend and collaborator, Scott Peacock, with whom she lived in Decatur, Ga.

BAILEY BARASH
Atlanta, Georgia

Rand Richards Cooper, *Bon Appétit* (November 2001); Gwendolyn Glenn, *American Visions* (February–March 1997); Edna Lewis, *In Pursuit of Flavor* (1988), *The Taste of Country Cooking* (1976); Edna Lewis and Scott Peacock, *The Gift of Southern Cooking: Recipes and Revelations from Two Great American Cooks* (2003); Edna Lewis and Evangeline Peterson, *The Edna Lewis Cookbook* (1989); Kate Sekules, *Food and Wine* (November 1998).

Maque Choux

Maque choux (sometimes rendered *maquechoux*) is a traditional Cajun dish of stewed corn. Sweet corn kernels are "shredded" as they are removed from the cob by means of several lenthwise strokes of a sharp knife. The pulp and "milk," the starch-rich liquid inside the kernels, is recovered by scraping the corncob with the knife's blade after most of the kernels have been removed. Shredding the kernels allows for faster cooking, as it permits quicker chemical reactions that transform corn starches into sugars. The corn pulp and milk contribute to maque choux's legendary creamy richness.

Meats and seafood—including chicken, tasso, smoked sausage, andouille, shrimp, and crawfish—are sometimes added to the recipe as flavoring agents and as protein supplements, creating a heartier dish. When incorporated into maque choux, meats are usually browned and removed from the pot. Onions, bell pepper, and corn are then sautéed in a small amount of vegetable oil until the onions begin to wilt. Diced tomatoes and liquid are then added. Cajun cooks have traditionally added water to the mixture, but some incorporate milk or cream to increase the density and richness of the dish. In restaurants, stock and cream are often used in place of water. If meat or seafood is included in the recipe, it is generally returned to the mixture during this segment of the cooking process. The maque choux mixture is then covered and simmered for approximately two to three hours. The dish is generally seasoned with salt, black pepper, and ground cayenne. Although it may contain meat or seafood, maque choux is usually served as a side dish.

As one would suspect, the dish has Native American origins. Early European explorers noted that Native American tribes residing along the lower Mississippi River consumed a dish known to the French as *sagamité*. Frenchmen accompanying Pierre Le Moyne d'Iberville through present-day Iberville Parish in 1699 recorded that the Bayougoula women prepared three varieties of *sagamité*: maize stewed in bear oil, succotash, and fried cornmeal. Iberville's companions evidently preferred the first variety—the progenitor of the modern Cajun maque choux— for, in another encounter with the Bayougoula, the Canadians prepared a repast of "*sagamité* with plums."

Like other French-speakers already established in the colony, the waves of Acadian exiles who settled in southern Louisiana between 1764 and 1788 incorporated *sagamité* into their culinary repertoire in the late 18th century. Wheat, cabbages, and turnips constituted the staples of the predispersal Acadian diet, but wheat would not grow in their hot, humid adopted homeland, and cabbages and turnips were marginal winter crops. As a consequence, the exiles were compelled to make readily available corn the mainstay of their diet. At the dawn of the 19th century, C. C. Robin, a Frenchman touring the Acadian settlements in the Opelousas and Attakapas regions in present south-central Louisiana, observed that "the use of corn is universal both among the poor and the rich. Corn is prepared here in an infinite number of ways." Robin indicates that finely ground corn was eaten with milk in a manner reminiscent of modern Cajun cornbread, while "corn broken into larger grains and cooked with a larger quantity of water is called *sagamité*. It is believed that this last method is the healthiest, and it is especially refreshing."

Sagamité may have been healthy and "refreshing," but it was unquestionably bland, and foodways expert C. Paige Gutierrez notes that, in the late 20th century, elderly Cajun informants in the Breaux Bridge area did not recall the original dish fondly. It is thus hardly surprising that Louisianans embellished the original dish by adding onions. This variation is popularly known as maque choux, a term whose linguistic origins are unknown. William A. Read's important linguistic studies indicate that, during the mid-20th century, the term *maquechoux* was employed "in French Settlement, in Pointe Coupée, and in

the [Cajun] Southwest." The dish, however, appears to have been unknown in the Cajun communities of the Acadian Coast and Bayou Lafourche region. Although consumption of the dish appears to have been initially widespread in Louisiana's French Triangle, only the Cajuns, descendants of Louisiana's Acadian immigrants, continued the dish's culinary evolution by adding additional seasoning and protein supplements.

Cajun cooks originally employed only freshly picked corn, and thus maque choux was available on a seasonal basis, usually in early summer. Cajuns presently consume less savory forms of maque choux year-round through the utilization of canned or frozen corn. Although maque choux is considered a Cajun dish, particular components of the ingredient list, namely bell pepper and tomato, appear to have been influenced by cooks in south Louisiana's Afro-Creole community.

RYAN A. BRASSEAUX
CARL A. BRASSEAUX
Lafayette, Louisiana

Marcelle Bienvenu, Carl A. Brasseaux, and Ryan A. Brasseaux, *Stir the Pot: The History of Cajun Cuisine* (2005); John D. Folse, *The Encyclopedia of Cajun and Creole Cuisine* (2004).

Mickler, Ernest Matthew

(1940–1988) COOKBOOK AUTHOR. Ernest Matthew Mickler, author of *White Trash Cooking* (1986) and *White Trash Cooking II: Recipes for Gatherin's* (first published as *Sinkin' Spells, Hot Flashes, Fits, and Cravins* [1988]), found his way to southern food writing first through travel and later through academic training.

Born in Palm Valley, Fla., and shaped by memories of his mother's cooking, Mickler recounts her work as a formative part of his life and work. When she wasn't pumping gas, "she was cooking up a big dinner of fried chittlins, a mess of turnip greens, enough hoe cakes for a Bible story, a wash pot full of cabbage stew and two large Our Lord's Scripture cakes."

Relieved to graduate from high school, Mickler traveled around as part of a singing-songwriting duo. Settling back in Florida, he befriended Memphis Wood, art director of Jacksonville University. Mickler earned a B.A. from Jacksonville and then a Master of Fine Arts from Mills College in Oakland, Calif. After earning his M.F.A., Mickler spent several years in an art community in Mexico, where he assembled his first book before returning to Florida.

White Trash Cooking became a surprise best-selling cookbook after its rocky road to publication. Mickler connected with its eventual publisher, the Jargon Society, while working as a caterer in Key West, Fla. Quizzing party guests about possible publishing connections, Mickler met Anthony G. Woolcott, a British publisher, who knew Jonathan Williams of the Jargon Society. The Jargon Society of Winston-Salem, N.C., originally published *White Trash Cooking* with a $1,000 advance to Mickler and an initial print run of 5,000 copies. In 1986, Ten Speed Press secured the rights to Mickler's second book, *White Trash Cooking II* for a $150,000 advance.

The Jargon Society, seeking to capitalize on the early success of *White Trash Cooking*, submitted a check and copy for an advertisement to *The New Yorker*. *The New Yorker* returned the ad, and, later, a spokesman for the magazine explained the rejection: "We thought the title might offend our readers." *The New Yorker* failed to recognize the sincere sensibility present in Mickler's work.

In grounding his work, Mickler makes the distinction between "white trash" and "White Trash," with the latter distinguished by genuine kindness, pride, and manners. White Trash were Mickler's people. For Mickler, the distinction is cultural rather than economic. *The New Yorker* and publishers that passed over the work missed the warmth and kindness that Mickler brought to the food and to his people.

Harper Lee, author of *To Kill a Mockingbird*, calls *White Trash Cooking* an important "sociological document" and "a beautiful testament to a stubborn people of proud and poignant heritage." Mickler's recipes produce good food and his writing and photographs respect his subjects.

After Mickler's death in 1988, his sister, Trisha Mickler, organized his remaining notes and several of his photographs to publish the final work in the White Trash series, *More White Trash Cooking* (1998). The University of Florida, Gainesville, houses Mickler's collected papers as part of the George A. Smathers Special Collections.

BRIAN FISHER
Oxford, Mississippi

John T. Edge, *Oxford American* (Winter 2006); Ernest Matthew Mickler, *White Trash Cooking* (1986); *New York Times*, 22 September 1986.

Mint Julep

The mint julep, along with white columns, moonlight, jasmine, and magnolias, is part and parcel of the patrician southern myth. A volume devoted solely to its history asserts, "Wherever there is a mint julep, there is a bit of the Old South. For the julep is part ceremony, tradition, and regional nostalgia; and only by definition liquor, simple syrup, mint, and ice. It is all delight. It is nectar to the Virginian, mother's milk to the Kentuckian, and ambrosia to southerners anywhere."

The origin of what may be the South's most famous drink—excepting only Coca-Cola—has as many claimants as Homer's birthplace: Virginia, Maryland, New England, Georgia, Kentucky, and Louisiana. It may be all of these locales, for wherever whiskey was drunk in the Federal period (and it was drunk enthusiastically almost everywhere), it was natural that it should be drunk with the local plant that imparted a most delectable flavor to the rough distillation of those days.

Actually, credit for the julep (the word deriving from Middle English meaning "a sugar syrup") belongs to Virginia. Its first recorded use was there. In 1797 the American Museum described the Virginian who upon rising "drinks a julep made of rum, water, and sugar, but very strong." The mint was added a few years later. Describing life on a James River plantation in his *Travels in the United States* (1803), John Davis noted the early morning mint julep.

Mint was as widespread as alcohol in America, and the drink spread to Maryland (made, as in Virginia, with rye whiskey), to New England (made with rum), to Kentucky (made with the corn whiskey that was ancestor to bourbon), to New York (made with anything, even gin), and to Louisiana (made with brandy). Recipes for the drink were wildly varied, sometimes full of fruit to the point of resembling a salad, often with rum ladled on top of other liquors, sometimes with bourbon lending additional flavor to apricot or peach brandy.

As tastes changed in post-Prohibition America, the drink became simpler but no less ceremonial. It has been praised by historians—C. J. Latrobe, Frederick Marryatt, and W. H. Russell—and used for atmosphere by O. Henry, Margaret Mitchell, and a thousand other writers of fiction. It has truly passed into the realm of cliché, but this concoction of bourbon whiskey, sugar, mint, and ice retains both its charm and its good taste.

RICHARD B. HARWELL
Athens, Georgia

William Grimes, *Straight Up or on the Rocks: The Story of the American Cocktail* (2001); Richard B. Harwell, *The Mint Julep* (1975); Soule Smith, *The Mint Julep: The Very Dream of Drinks* (1949); Joe Gray Taylor, *Eating, Drinking, and Visiting in the South: An Informal History* (1982); Jerry Thomas, *How to Mix Drinks* (1862).

MoonPies

The MoonPie, long marketed as "the original marshmallow sandwich," had humble beginnings at the Chattanooga Bakery in Chattanooga, Tenn. Although its precise origin is not known, the MoonPie is believed to have been created in 1918 or 1919. Legend has it that a traveling salesman stopped by the bakery and suggested that a snack consisting of two cookies with marshmallow in between and covered with chocolate would sell. At that time, the bakery reportedly produced more than 200 different items; so successful was this one suggestion that it now is the only snack produced by the company.

Since their invention MoonPies have had broad appeal throughout the South and have been a favorite snack food for both children and adults. Consisting of a quarter inch of marshmallow sandwiched between two cookies about four inches in diameter, MoonPies have been coated with chocolate, banana, coconut, or vanilla frosting. Many companies have attempted to imitate the MoonPie and capitalize on the snack's popularity, but any discerning southern palate can distinguish the real taste.

In 1969 the bakery introduced a Double Decker pie, featuring two layers of marshmallow sandwiched between three cookies and then covered with flavored frosting. This version can be found primarily in convenience stores. With increased interest and new distribution techniques, the MoonPie has moved beyond its traditional southern territory and is now available in nearly all parts of the country. The Moon-

The only thing better than a MoonPie is a MoonPie with an ice-cold RC Cola
(Courtesy James G. Thomas Jr., photographer)

Pie Cultural Club is a Charlotte, N.C., group dedicated to spreading "the story of the MoonPie" and establishing "club chapters throughout the civilized world."

Nevertheless, over the years, washing down a MoonPie with an ice-cold RC Cola has become a much-revered southern tradition, with the MoonPie Bakery selling t-shirts picturing the pair accompanied by the tagline, "You Wouldn't Understand . . . It's a Southern Thing!" On the third Saturday of every June, the town of Bell Buckle, Tenn., even holds the Bell Buckle RC and MoonPie Festival, where MoonPie kings and queens are crowned, a MoonPie toss is held, and the world's largest MoonPie is cut and served to the crowd. And Oneonta, Ala., hosts the annual World Championship MoonPie Eating Contest.

Today, MoonPies can be purchased in 25 leading grocery store chains across the South and nation, at countless other retail outlets, and from vending machines in many places. The MoonPie has become a cultural icon, its distinctive logo a nostalgic image of the South. Folk artist Howard Finster so loved the MoonPie that he painted his take on the logo and donated it in 1999 to the Chattanooga Bakery.

THOMAS RANKIN
Duke University

Ron Dickson, *MoonPie Handbook* (1985); David Magee, *MoonPie: Biography of an Out-of-this-World Snack* (2006); William E. Schmidt, *New York Times* (30 April 1986).

Moonshine and Moonshining

In the American idiom, any rum, brandy, or sugar spirit, but especially whiskey, may be called *moonshine* when distilleries are unregistered and liquor untaxed. Grose's 1785 *Dictionary of the Vulgar Tongue* referred to "white brandy smuggled on the coasts of Kent and Sussex, and gin in the north of York-shire" as *moonshine*. Presumably, moon-lit nights struck a profitable balance of dark and light for smugglers running contraband past British tax gaugers. Transplanted moonshining and its tax-evading wiles were some of the earliest imports to the American colonies. Despite a common belief that illicit distill-ing is dead or dying, strong traditions of distilling America's primal craft spirit continue, especially in the southeastern states.

A typical shot of the storied scamper juice checks in around 100 proof, but some rustic specimens creep up to a volatile 160. Proof originally denoted a spirit's ability to dampen gunpowder yet sustain a flame. By U.S. standards, it is exactly twice the spirit's alcohol content at 60° Fahrenheit. More docile commer-cial spirits are generally 80 proof, more than half water. Because moonshine can induce a swift drunkenness more profound than that offered by its city cousins, downing it as if it were vodka or bourbon constitutes a grave error. For this reason, it has been christened *popskull, stagger soup*, and *busthead*. Other terms of endearment include *ton-sil varnish, mule, panther piss, squirrel whiskey, tiger's milk, confederate chloro-form, block and tackle, bug juice, forty rods, field whiskey, hillbilly pop, radiator whiskey, mountain dew, firewater*, and, simply, *wet goods*.

Moonshine is made by fermenting sugar, fruit, or converted grains with yeast in water to form a low-ethanol *wash, mash*, or *beer*. The mash is then heated in a still that condenses ethanol vapors in a chilled copper coil called a *worm*. To maximize the perception of aromatic molecules and tame its fire, white liquor should then be filtered, cut with pure water, and aged, but little ever is. Among white lightening connois-seurs, corn whiskey remains the most esteemed of indigenous spirits, even when regional or class preferences favor applejack, peach brandy, rye, or the table sugar–based *splo* one is apt to find in cities (so named for the 'splosion it causes in drinkers' heads).

Moonshine's quality and reputation suffered a ruinous decline during the national prohibition against alcohol (1920–33) when artisan distillers putting out small-batch spirits for steady local markets were displaced by novice op-portunist distillers making bad hooch, by scurrilous bootleggers selling out-right poison, and, finally, by interstate whiskey syndicates that introduced sugar as a major ingredient to cash in on a sustained liquor-guzzling frenzy. Passed-down recipes for poor-quality sugar-based shine outlasted Prohibition and predominate today, perpetuating a regrettable tradition of *sellin' whiskey*, liquor to be made fast and sold fast. Sugar's new cheapness and widespread availability in the early 20th century introduced fantastic profit margins to what had been largely a way for entrepreneurial farmers to concentrate their crops' value. "Sugarhead" whiskey's popularity and profitability nearly struck a deathblow for handmade all-grain whiskeys and pure-fruit brandies.

The tradition of bootlegging was partly responsible for the birth of southern stock car racing, as liquor haulers raced to escape the law on back roads and competed with each other to test the speed and skill of drivers. Driving skills born out of outlaw need soon found a popular audience and were formalized in the public forums of Daytona Beach and eventually NASCAR. In the 1958 film, *Thunder Road*, actor Robert Mitchum dramatized the life of bootlegger Luke Doolin, who returns from the Korean War to take over his family's moonshine business as a runner. The film reinforces the historical connection between driving culture and moonshining and posits a specific version of masculinity associated culturally with that environment.

Three trends have led to a general increase in moonshine quality since the 1980s. The first is renewed academic interest in the study of the South. A new swell of multiethnic southerners embraces moonshine as a distaff badge of authenticity. For them, drinking regional whiskeys is a way to explore "southernness" by quaffing deeply of their communal heritage.

More important, skilled home beer brewers and winemakers have pushed their hobbies into the realm of distilling through the Internet, where they have learned about ingredients and recipes and about advances in still design. They are learning from each other how to recreate small-batch, handmade liquors and how to design their own equipment. Informed by brewers' curiosity and openness, their new-style moonshining centers on sharing information rather than the brutal and violent secretiveness that characterizes old-school moonshine syndicates.

Benign neglect plays its role, too. Distilling without permits remains illegal in the United States, but budget constraints and shifting priorities have led federal agencies to turn a blind eye toward moonshiners "making" for themselves and friends. Some distillers are even going into legitimate business by dusting off family moonshine recipes, applying for permits, and selling, well, not exactly *moonshine* since they are paying taxes on it, but a spirit every bit as authentic as those first distilled on American soil.

MATTHEW B. ROWLEY
Philadelphia, Pennsylvania

John C. Campbell, *The Southern Highlander and His Homeland* (1921); Jess Carr, *The Second Oldest Profession: An Informal History of Moonshining in America* (1972); Irvin S. Cobb, *Red Likker* (1929); Joseph Earl Dabney, *More Mountain Spirits* (1980),

Mountain Spirits: A Chronicle of Corn Whiskey from King James' Ulster Plantation to America's Appalachians and the Moonshine Life (1974); Pete Daniel, *Standing at the Crossroads: Southern Life in the Twentieth Century* (1986); John Kearins, *Yankee Revenooer* (1969); Esther Kellner, *Moonshine: Its History and Folklore* (1971); Horace Kephart, *Our Southern Highlanders* (1913); Mark Edward Lender, *Drinking in America: A History* (1987); David W. Maurer, *Kentucky Moonshine* (1974); Wilbur R. Miller, *Revenuers and Moonshiners: Enforcing Federal Liquor Law in the Mountain South, 1865–1900* (1991); Derek Nelson, *Moonshiners, Bootleggers, and Rumrunners* (1995); Michael Nixon and Michael McCaw, *The Compleat Distiller* (2001); Robert A. Pace and Jeffrey W. Gardner, *Tennessee Anthropologist* (Spring 1985); Matthew Rowley, *Moonshine!* (2007); Ian Smiley, *Making Pure Corn Whiskey* (2003); Eliot Wigginton, ed., *The Foxfire Book* (1972); J. W. Williamson, *Hillbillyland: What the Movies Did to the Mountains and What the Mountains Did to the Movies* (1995).

Muddle

While central and eastern North Carolina have claimed Brunswick stew as a native favorite, the fish or chicken muddle has an equally strong historical precedent in the state. According to oral tradition, the fish muddle has ties to Native American culture. Prominent along the Roanoke River in the northeastern part of the state, the muddle is a close cousin to the fish chowders, perloos, and chicken bogs of neighboring South Carolina. The traditional muddle recipe was far from complex: fish, onions, potatoes, and basic seasonings. Despite these humble origins, some contemporary recipes include ingredients like white wine, leeks, celery, and fresh tarragon. In *Tar Heels: A Portrait of North Carolina*, Jonathan Daniels made a keen observation regarding the typical fish muddle recipe when he said of it, "the ingredients of which vary with what you have got."

Historically, muddles are cooked when the fish are "running." After they are caught, the fish—rockfish were common—are cleaned and cooked right on the riverbank, in large cast-iron pots. Unlike Brunswick stew or burgoo, these stews are cooked down to a thick mush or porridge. Similarly to bogs and perloo (from the French *pilau*), rice or potatoes provide the thickening agent in a muddle. In direct contrast, most fish chowders, like the catfish chowder of Sea Island Gullah tradition, do not include rice and have a much thinner consistency.

Muddles have more similarities with other regional stews, however, than differences. A muddle is a communal dish, a food of congregation. Easily prepared for large groups of people, muddles are typically a fixture at political rallies, church homecomings, festivals, and community gatherings. The social connections are so strong that, like the term *barbecue*, *muddle* is used to refer to the gathering as well as the dish itself.

Recently, because of a severe drop in the rockfish population, chicken has come to be a popular replacement for the traditional fish. The practice of cooking the muddle on riverbanks in large cast-iron pots has largely faded as well. This mirrors the decline in backyard "shade tree" hash preparation in South Carolina. While no longer as common on the small family farms and riverbanks of South and North Carolina, both chicken bog and fish muddle remain staple culinary delights at festivals, stump meetings, family reunions, and church homecomings throughout the region.

SADDLER TAYLOR
McKissick Museum, Columbia, South Carolina

Jonathan Daniels, *Tar Heels: A Portrait of North Carolina* (1941); Lettie Gay, ed., *Two Hundred Years of Charleston Cooking* (1930); Annabella P. Hill, *Mrs. Hill's Southern Practical Cookery and Receipt Book* (1995).

Mullet

Two species of this highly edible fish are found in the waters of the South, the striped or black mullet, *Mugil cephalus*, and the white mullet, *Mugil curema*, members of a large family of fish (*Mugilidae*) consisting of some 100 species distributed worldwide. Colonists brought to this country their taste for the European varieties and quickly found the fish of New World waters equally delectable and suitable for salting for both home consumption and as an item of trade. Especially plentiful on the coast of North Carolina, they were caught there with large haul seines after 1760. Typically, camps were set up on the barrier islands where a gang of men, black and white, would build conical huts of rushes over a pole frame. The camps would become active in the late summer and early fall following a wind shift known as a "mullet blow." A lookout platform would be erected, and when a school of mullet was spotted, a boat containing the seine would be launched and rowed around the school, playing out the net. With both ends of the net back on shore, the crews would haul the nets, pulling the net full of mullet onto the shore for salting and packing. In later days, manpower was replaced by the use of tractors, and the mullet fishery has remained an annual tradition on the Carolina coast. Beginning in the 1870s, mullet were first iced for shipping and became the basis of a lucrative fishery based in Carteret County, N.C.

By the 1880s Carteret County fishermen had begun to fan out in search of untapped supplies of mullet, and many of those fishermen relocated to the Gulf Coast, especially to the area around Cortez, Fla. There, the mullet—a highly adaptive fish equally at home in salt, brackish, or fresh waters—were and are plentiful and have become something of a cultural marker from Florida westward along the Alabama shore. Considered a "trash" fish by some, mullet are highly prized by many others for their nutlike flavor. Typically they are eaten fried or smoked, the latter being sometimes referred to as barbecued. The roe or egg sack of the female mullet is considered a prized delicacy fried and served with scrambled eggs, although much of it is now sent to Japan where it is consumed as karasumi. Mullet gizzards are also prized.

In addition to its culinary uses, mullet has recreational and metaphoric applications. Before Hurricane Katrina, the Interstate Mullet Toss was held annually at the Flora-Bama Lounge, which straddled the Florida-Alabama state line; and the annual Boggy Bayou Mullet Festival is still held at Niceville, Fla. In Carteret County, N.C., cross-water rivals Beaufort and Morehead City high schools battle annually for the football trophy known as the Mullet Bucket, which is in fact a wooden bucket that a local restaurant fills with hamburgers and that the winning team gets to keep until the outcome of the next year's game. Writer Michael Swindle has also identified the characteristics and distribution of folks he calls "Mulletheads," meaning aficionados of the fish rather than the 19th-century usage meaning a fool. More mysterious are the origins of the name of the notorious "mullet" haircut worn by Billy Ray Cyrus and many a southern male. The verb *mullet*, meaning to curl or dress the hair, has been documented as early as 1932.

J. MICHAEL LUSTER
Arkansas Folklife Program, Arkansas State University

John Egerton, *Southern Food: At Home, on the Road, in History* (1987); Ben Green, *Finest Kind: A Celebration of a Florida Fishing Village* (1985); Mark Larson and Barney Hoskyns, *The Mullet: Hairstyle of the Gods* (1999); John Michael Luster, "Help Me to Raise Them: The Menhaden Chanteymen of Beaufort, North Carolina," Ph.D. dissertation, University of Pennsylvania (1994); A. J. McClane, *McClane's Field Guide to Saltwater Fishes of North America* (1978); Diane Roberts, *Oxford American* (January/February 1999); Michael Swindle, *Mulletheads: The Legends, Lore, Magic, and Mania Surrounding the Humble but Celebrated Mullet* (1998).

Neal, Bill

(1950–1992) CHEF, COOKBOOK WRITER.

Before the 1980s fine dining in the South was usually practiced in private homes. Bill Neal took that distinctive cuisine out of the home and brought it into the restaurant he founded and those founded on the inspiration of his idea.

Neal grew up in the country near the small rural mill village of Grover, N.C. His father, Frank, gave up farming to manage the local textile mill, but his paternal grandfather maintained the family farm. Neal spent afternoons and summers helping with chores and absorbed a love of gardening and an appreciation of farm-fresh food that lasted a lifetime.

After high school in Blacksburg, S.C., Neal won a full academic scholarship to Duke University, where he met his future wife and business partner, Susan Moreton Hobbs, of Brookhaven, Miss. On school vacations, the two of them honed their palates in the classic French Quarter restaurants of New Orleans, where Neal was first introduced to haute cuisine.

Later Neal taught high school English for a year before enrolling in graduate school at the University of North Carolina at Chapel Hill. There he and Moreton financed his studies by catering for his English literature professors. A trip to France, where quality of food is a national obsession, inspired Neal to change career paths, and he abandoned academia for cooking.

With a year of apprenticeship behind

him, Neal became *chef de cuisine* at the Villa Teo, a fine dining establishment in Chapel Hill. In 1976 he and Moreton opened their own place, Restaurant La Résidence. Modeled after a rural French bistro, the restaurant attracted national attention and garnered a host of culinary awards.

Further travel in France convinced Neal that cooking and eating locally grown fresh produce and meats warranted a revival in the United States. He believed that Americans, particularly southerners, were ready to change their habits and reverse the fast-food trend of the times if given the opportunity. The popularity of his first book, *Bill Neal's Southern Cooking*, an effort to raise consciousness about the South's unique culinary legacy, proved him right.

In 1982 Neal opened Crook's Corner, with partner Gene Hamer. The time was ripe for the diner-style restaurant's concept: a menu that featured creatively rendered traditional southern fare, an interesting wine list, and knowledgeable servers who guided diners to appropriate pairings. Rave reviews from the *Washington Post* and the *New York Times* attracted patrons from all over the South and beyond, making Crook's perhaps the best-known restaurant in North Carolina, and even the Southeast, at the end of the 20th century.

Before his death at age 42, Neal wrote three more books, *Good Old Grits* (with David Perry), *Biscuits, Spoonbread, and Sweet Potato Pie*, and *Gardener's Latin*, as well as countless magazine articles. He also edited a new edition of *The Kentucky Housewife* and a collection of newspaper columns by garden writer Elizabeth Lawrence, published as *Through the Garden Gate*. Moreton recalls anecdotes about his life in her memoir, *Remembering Bill Neal*.

Crook's Corner remains a beacon of the American regional food movement and a model for a new generation of southern restaurateurs. Neal's signature recipe, his version of Charleston's traditional breakfast dish, shrimp and grits, appears on menus from Houston to Baltimore. The two restaurants he founded are still in operation in Chapel Hill today.

Neal taught and inspired a generation of chef/restaurateurs who went on from Crook's and La Résidence to open their own eateries all over the South. Kevin Callahan, a former cook at Crook's Corner and present owner of Acme Food and Beverage Company in Carrboro, N.C., articulates his influence: "Bill came along when dining out in the South meant a trip to a steak house, a Chinese restaurant, or a country club. He was the first person I knew to claim that southern food, the kind of food served at family reunions, deserved respect. That attitude had an effect on what it meant to work in a restaurant. Bill showed us all that it was worthwhile work. Today we all stand on his shoulders."

CHARLES REAGAN WILSON
University of Mississippi

Bill Neal, *Bill Neal's Southern Cooking* (1985), *Biscuits, Spoonbread, and Sweet Potato Pie* (1990); Moreton Neal, *Remembering Bill Neal: Favorite Recipes from a Life in Cooking* (2004).

Okra

Okra came to the American South from Africa, with evidence suggesting that it originated in Ethiopia. The West African term, *ukru ma*, became *okra* after slaves brought the plant through the Caribbean to southern plantations. Thomas Jefferson's *Notes on the State of Virginia* (1785) mentioned the growing of okra in the state, and Mary Randolph's *Virginia House-wife* (1824) gave some of the earliest published recipes for its use.

Southerners have boiled, fried, steamed, and pickled the okra pod. They have cooked the plant's leaves and flower buds and eaten them as greens. Civil War era southerners ground okra seeds and used them as a coffee substitute when coffee beans were unavailable. Okra is cooked in soups and stews, with gumbo a major okra-based southern dish. If a southerner with a predilection for both ancestor worship and cooking decided to form a First Families of Vegetables society, okra would be a charter member. Thomas Jefferson recorded planting it and originally reported its cultivation in Virginia before 1781. It had reached Louisiana shortly after 1700.

Okra (*Hibiscus esculentus*) is a member of the mallow family (*Malvaceae*), as are cotton, hibiscus, and hollyhocks. The okra pod is a tapering, five-sided capsule containing numerous round seeds, and its best-known feature is its gummy, mucilaginous juice.

The word *okra* is *nkru* is the Ashanti language of West Africa; Accra, the name of the capital of Ghana, comes from the same root word. In Bantu, the language family of southern Africa, it is called *ngombo*, from which our word *gumbo* comes; *gumbo* and *okra* have been used interchangeably to refer to the vegetable.

Probably okra was first cultivated in Africa, and from there it spread to India (where it is called "lady fingers"). It was recorded in Egypt in the 13th century. Okra could have come to the South with Africans, either directly or via the West Indies, or it could have been brought in by European colonists who knew that it would grow in a warm climate. It is planted in early spring and matures in about eight weeks. Southern agricultural specialists tried to breed out okra's prickly outer surface with the Clemson Spineless variety but were unsuccessful.

Okra has vitamins A and C, and a 3.5-ounce serving has about 29 calories. This, of course, does not apply to that favorite southern dish, fried okra, in which the cornmeal-salt-pepper coating and the bacon drippings in the frying pan add to the calorie count. Okra can be pickled, stewed with tomatoes, or—best of all—used as the thickening base for gumbo, a rich stew of seafood or meat.

Okra, like the peanut, has a myriad of uses: southerners have used it to staunch bleeding, substitute for plasma, make a coarse cloth or paper, adorn dried flower arrangements, produce seed necklaces, clean metal, unstop drains, increase milk yield of cows. Raw okra will also adhere to the nose and forehead for a speedy Halloween mask.

Okra has diverse symbolic meanings. In the Southern Horoscope the okra sign governs those born between

DELTA STATE
FIGHTING OKRA!

The Fighting Okra, the unofficial mascot of Mississippi's Delta State University (Courtesy James G. Thomas Jr., photographer)

December 22 and January 20. Okra is a "slippery sign" and those born under it are warned: "Although you appear crude, you are actually very slick on the inside. Okra have tremendous influence. An older Okra can look back over his life and see the seeds of his influence everywhere. Stay away from MoonPies." In the Yoruba beliefs of Africa, okra is used to lower fevers and aid in childbirth. According to Denise Fonseca, a cultural historian examining similarities in the Yoruba culture as it appears in Brazil and Louisiana, okra can be a "ritual offering for several gods who are linked to the libido, to male and female sexuality, to the relationship between men and women and to fertility." And, indeed, the poet and playwright Ntozake Shange, in her work *from okra to greens/a different kinda love story* uses okra to denote the female in a feminist discourse on sexual conflict.

CAROLYN KOLB
New Orleans, Louisiana

Edwin Morris Betts, ed., *Thomas Jefferson's Garden Book, 1766–1824* (1999); Alphonse Pyramus de Candolle, *Origin of Cultivated Plants* (1884); Carroll Lane Fenton and Herminie B. Kitchen, *Plants We Live On: The Story of Grains and Vegetables* (1971); Sonia L. Nazario, *Wall Street Journal* (21 January 1983); Dick Raymond and Jan Raymond, *The Gardens for All Book of Eggplant, Okra, and Peppers* (1984); Andrew F. Smith, *Souper Tomatoes: The Story of America's Favorite Food* (2000); Eileen Tighe, *Woman's Day Encyclopedia of Cookery* (1966).

Onions, Vidalia

Vidalia onions may be one of the great agricultural marketing success stories of the 20th century. In 1931 Mose Coleman of Toombs County, Ga., discovered that the onions he had harvested were sweet rather than hot. The onions were so popular that Coleman was able to demand $3.50 for a 50-pound bag, an unheard of price during the Depression. Other farmers started cultivating sweet onions, which took on the name of the nearby town of Vidalia. By the 1940s the onions had such a strong following that Georgia built a farmers' market in Vidalia, and visitors to the area spread word of the unusual crop around the country. A national marketing push was undertaken in the 1970s, giving the sweet onions a nationwide reputation. Vidalias are now grown in 20 Georgia counties and are a $50 million crop. Economic experts value related sales at roughly $150 million.

The onion itself is a granex, a hybrid between the Texas grano and the Bermuda onion. The grano is mild but not particularly sweet, while the Bermuda is a sweet onion with a flat shape. In early years of Vidalia production, cross-breeding yielded onions that were somewhat squatty, but not consistently so. Growers have refined the onion into a slightly flat shape, so it is easily identified in the market.

Vidalia proponents contend that their onions cannot be grown successfully anywhere else, but onion experts disagree. "The soil type in the Vidalia area exists throughout the coastal plain throughout the Southeast," says Bill Randle of the University of Georgia. "It's sandy without significant sulfur contamination. You could probably grow a similar onion in it." Supporting this theory, sweet onions are grown not only in the South, but in other regions of the country as well. Texas grows 1015 Super-Sweets; Hawaii, Maui Sweets; Michigan, AmeriSweets; and California, Sweet Imperials.

Leonard Pike, who developed the Texas 1015 sweet onion, suggests that while soil is a factor, breeding is key. "Genetics is the primary thing that makes [an onion] sweet," Pike says. "Region has something to do with it, but not as much as people tell you. Stress will make onions pungent, or if the soil is high in sulfur. We can grow pungent and very mild side by side."

Vidalias are harvested in the spring, but they are successfully held in cold storage, making them available throughout the year for their many devoted fans.

DONNA FLORIO
Birmingham, Alabama

Barbara Bacheller, *Lilies of the Kitchen* (1986); Fred Griffith and Linda Griffith, *Onions, Onions, Onions, Onions* (1994); Marian Morash, *The Victory Garden Cookbook* (1982); William Woys Weaver, *Heirloom Vegetable Gardening* (1997).

Oranges

When Columbus brought orange seeds on his second voyage (1493) to the New World and planted an orchard near Isabella, a town in the Caribbean on the north coast of Santo Domingo, the orange already had a long history of uses, lore, and meaning, stretching far back to the fruit's probable origins in Southeast Asia. The orange moved through India into the Middle East, and from there the Arabs brought the orange to northern Africa and, eventually, to Spain. The English word *orange* originates in the Spanish *naranja*, derived from the Sanskrit *naranga*, "fragrant." Europeans valued the orange for its medicinal uses learned from the Arabs, and European explorers planted oranges as "scurvy prevention stations" (as John McPhee calls them) to ensure their crews a source of vitamin C. The first oranges incorporated into European foodways were *Citrus aurantium*, the "sour orange," but by 1635 the sweet orange, *Citrus sinesis*, spread as a highly valued confection.

The Spanish settlement at St. Augustine in Florida had a sweet orange grove as early as 1579, and the English conquerors of the city were shipping oranges back home by the 1770s. By the time the United States acquired Florida in 1824, settlers had planted commercial orange groves south from St. Augustine, along the St. Johns River, and in the Tampa Bay area. The industry faced a

Miss America 1954, Evelyn Ay, posing in front of an orange tree, Winter Haven, Fla. (Florida State Archives)

cycle of booms and busts in the decades after the Civil War, with up to as many as 5 million boxes shipped just before the devastating freeze of 1894–95.

Before mass marketing and distribution, the orange was a luxury item. The orange found in a child's Christmas stocking represented the exotic Orient of the nativity story, and the availability of fresh oranges in winter, when all other fruits were sweet memories, helped put them at the center of Christmas symbolism and foodways.

The age of mass marketing oranges and orange juice began in 1908, when a cooperative, the California Fruit Growers Exchange, launched an expensive advertising campaign for its label, Sunkist. The advertising words and pictures stressed the healthful benefits of eating oranges and of drinking a glass of orange juice for breakfast. The colorful magazine and newspaper ads offered free recipe books and Sunkist recipe cards. Learning from California, Florida growers' cooperatives joined the mass marketing of oranges. When food scientists perfected the process of concentrating and freezing orange juice, just after the Second World War, Florida's industry boomed. Aggressive advertising persuaded Americans that their day "could not begin without a glass of Florida sunshine."

The incorporation of oranges into southern foodways is—exceptional of dishes like ambrosia and beverages like orange wine—largely an invention of these advertising campaigns and of the recipes created by large producers to make use of the fruit and its juice. The influx of Cuban refugees beginning in the 1960s and the growing popularity of Caribbean foodways in Florida and other places with large Caribbean immigrant populations have brought folk culinary uses of the orange, such as the long marination of pork and beef in sour orange juice, into the commercial mainstream.

Today Florida produces 70 percent of the oranges grown in the United States, 90 percent of which are processed into juice—the primary source of vitamin C for the majority of Americans. Florida oranges are exceptionally juicy compared to their thicker-skinned California cousins, which are generally considered better for eating rather than drinking. Once exotic and expensive, the orange is now among the most popular of all fruits consumed in the United States, coming in a close third behind the banana and the apple.

JAY MECHLING
University of California, Davis

John McPhee, *Oranges* (1967); Jay Mechling, in *Rooted in America: Foodlore of Popular Fruits and Vegetables*, ed. David Scofield Wilson and Angus Kress Gillespie (1999).

Oysters

In the United States oysters are harvested on both the east and west coasts and along the Gulf of Mexico. Louisiana consistently ranks as one of the nation's top oyster-producing states, providing between 25 and 40 percent of the nation's total oyster output. *Crassostrea virginica* (Eastern or American oyster) is the species found along the Atlantic seaboard and the Gulf. Oysters vary in appearance and taste between specific southern places. Oysters from Apala-

chicola, Fla., are generally plump and sweet, with a hint of copper flavor. These oysters have a greenish, deep shell. Oysters from Breton Sound, La., grow wild in reefs and vary in saltiness according to the season, becoming sweetest in the spring, when the marshes are flooded with fresh water.

Today, naturally grown oysters are almost nonexistent, but seeding programs using existing oyster beds have created a successful and healthy industry. Young oysters, known as "spats," are used to seed the beds. It takes about three years for an oyster to mature. During that period the seed oysters may be transplanted several times to waters of varying salinity and food supply in order to stimulate growth. Since oysters filter their food through the water, factors such as water temperature, salinity, and mineral content can affect the taste. By the same token, oysters are susceptible to biotoxins in the water. State and federal agencies monitor and approve oyster beds that are safe for commercial harvesting.

The old rule of thumb was to eat oysters only in months with the letter *r* in their name, because in colder weather oysters would not spoil as quickly. Today, however, refrigeration keeps them fresh, and oysters can be harvested year-round. While raw oysters may be dangerous for certain at-risk groups, oysters have numerous health benefits. They are high in calcium, iron, vitamin B_{12}, and zinc. Their reputation for being an aphrodisiac has not hurt either. When former governor of Louisiana and septuagenarian Edwin Edwards proclaimed his intent to have a

Shucking oysters at New Orleans's Remoulade Restaurant (Courtesy NewOrleansOnline.com)

are but a few other ways to serve the shellfish. Two of the best-known recipes for oysters came from New Orleans. Jules Alciatore, son of the founder of Antoine's Restaurant, created Oysters Rockefeller, named for John D. Rockefeller. This dish consists of baked oysters on the half shell with spinach and a rich sauce. Arnaud Cazeneuve of Arnaud's Restaurant created a dish of baked oysters on the half shell with shrimp, garlic, and shallots. He named the dish Oysters Bienville for Jean Baptiste Le Moyne, Sieur de Bienville, the founder of New Orleans. Locals in Wilmington, N.C., remember a Carolina oyster roast at Henry Kirkum's place during World War II. At this and other roasts, cooks practiced the traditional Wilmington preparation of roast oysters dating back to colonial times. Now Uncle Henry's Oyster Roast and Seafood Restaurant, run by sons and grandchildren of the original Henry, preserves the tradition. Around World War II, oysters were as common to the coast as country ham and fried chicken were to the inland, but now they are becoming scarce, and roast oysters harder to find.

child with his significantly younger wife, the Louisiana Oystermen's Association asked Edwards to appear in a promotional piece.

Oysters can be purchased in the shell by the bushel (75 pounds) or sack (100 pounds). Shucked oysters are sold by weight, volume, or count, either frozen, canned, or in plastic containers. "Shucking" is the process of removing an oyster from its shell. Preferably, one would use an oyster knife, which has a strong steel blade designed for prying open the hinged end of the shell.

Purists argue that the only way to consume oysters is raw on the half shell, perhaps with a bit of fresh lemon juice, horseradish, or cocktail sauce. Fried oysters, oyster dressing, oyster pie, smoked oysters, and oyster shooters

The southern love of oysters surfaces in a number of different forms of cultural expression. In Roy Blount's *Book of Southern Humor* (1994) in the poem "Song to Oysters," for example, he jests:

I like to eat an uncooked oyster.
Nothing's slicker, nothing's moister.
Nothing's easier on your gorge
Or, when the time comes, to
    dischorge.

The oyster functions as a metaphor for love and sexuality in the recordings of a number of southern musicians, including Fats Waller's "You're Not the Only Oyster in the Stew" and "Oysters and Wine at 2 A.M." sung by the Old South Quartette. Finally, writers of fiction have used the oyster as symbol of a distinctly southern landscape and home space. In Ellen Glasgow's 1913 novel *Virginia*, while eating a lunch of oysters, a mother and daughter have a pivotal exchange about family status, marriage, and class in restricted southern society. In his first novel, *Oyster*, writer Henry Biguenet depicts the oyster-fishing bayou country of 1950s Louisiana. In the story, two rival oyster-fishing families struggle against the invasion of the petroleum industry, which damages the oysters that constitute their livelihood, and the text chronicles their personal decline as it mirrors the decline of the natural world of oyster fishing upon which they rely.

AIMÉE SCHMIDT
Decatur, Georgia

FRANCES ABBOTT
University of Mississippi

John Egerton, *Side Orders: Small Helpings of Southern Cookery and Culture* (1990); M. F. K. Fisher, *Consider the Oyster* (1941); John F. Mariani, *The Dictionary of American Food and Drink* (1983); Joan Reardon, *Oysters: A Culinary Celebration with 185 Recipes* (1999).

Oysters Rockefeller

The celebrated New Orleans French-Creole dish of oysters, each baked on its half shell beneath a sauce of puréed greens and seasonings, was first served in 1889 at Antoine's in the city's French Quarter, where it continues to appear on the menu as *huitres en coquille à la Rockefeller*. According to brochures and other printed documents issued over the years by the restaurant's owners, the Alciatore family, the "Rockefeller sauce" was the same used at Antoine's before 1889 in its specialty of snails, known as *escargots bourgignonne*. As the 20th century approached, diners at Antoine's began showing an obvious preference for Louisiana oysters, prompting the owners to place them lightly on their shells, which rested on a bed of rock salt, lightly oven-brown the topping, and serve them with something similar to the bourgignonne sauce. At the time, John D. Rockefeller (1839–1937) was considered the wealthiest man in the country. Because of the sauce's richness, Jules Alciatore, a son of the restaurant's founder who then held the title of proprietor, named the dish for the American industrialist, although Rockefeller himself never visited Antoine's.

Over the decades, millions of orders for oysters Rockefeller have been served at the restaurant. The recipe has never been divulged, although many have speculated that it contains watercress, chervil, scallion, celery, garlic, butter, and the anisette liqueur produced in New Orleans under the brand name Herbsaint. Countless variations on the original dish, many of them containing spinach, also have appeared in scores of other restaurants in New Orleans and elsewhere. The popularity of oysters Rockefeller also has inspired other New Orleans chefs to improvise on the Antoine's original. Perhaps the most durable variation has been oys-

ters Rockefeller soup, which was introduced in the late 1980s by Brigtsen's
proprietor-chef Frank Brigtsen.

GENE BOURG
New Orleans, Louisiana

Roy L. Alciatore, *Centennial Souvenir of
Restaurant Antoine* (1940); Hermann B.
Deutsch, *New Orleans Item* (4 April 1940).

Panfish

Panfish can mean almost any small fish
caught for personal consumption. However, in the South the term often refers
to some members of the sunfish family
(*Centrarchidae*). The family is vast and
includes such familiar species as bluegill, redbreast, and white crappie and is
widespread across the South, with rep-
resentatives in almost every corner of
the region. Often brightly colored, they
have relatively short, compressed bodies
and appear round or oval when viewed
from the side, contributing to the names
of some species like the dollar sunfish
and the pumpkinseed. Local names for
sunfish are as numerous as the places
anglers find them and have many variations on perch and bream (in the South
pronounced "brim"), two fish to which
they are not related and to which they
are only vaguely similar. Confusion is
easy, as a redear sunfish may be a shell-
cracker in Georgia, while in Mississippi
it could be a chinquapin, and a white
crappie could be a white perch in Tennessee and a *sac-à-lait* in Louisiana.

No matter their names, sunfish
usually afford young southerners their
first fishing experience. From streams,
farm ponds, reservoirs, or oxbows,
children often take their first sunfish

with the simplest tackle and bait, traditionally a cane pole and crickets, worms,
or minnows. Before the days of effective pesticides, anglers sometimes used
roaches purchased from grocery stores
and warehouses that maintained traps
to control the insects. On light tackle
all the members of the sunfish family
are great fighters, although this is only
part of their appeal. Overwhelmingly,
this is a catch-and-eat fishery, with most
sunfish species so prolific that fisheries
biologists encourage large limits that
typically range from 25 to 50 per person
per day. Some species like the bluegill
and crappie can reach several pounds,
but fish of a few ounces to a pound
and a half comprise the bulk of most
catches.

Anglers and cooks alike praise the
eating qualities of sunfish. Like the
simplicity in catching them, their cleaning and preparation can be an exercise
in the fundamental skills of preparing
wild foods. Successful anglers traditionally used a spoon, knife, or a specially
manufactured tool to scale, or scrape
away the scales, prior to slicing off the
head and removing the entrails from the
body cavity. The generally smaller size
of the fish makes them ideal for cooking
whole. Today, some folks fillet their fish,
particularly larger species like white
and black crappies, often with electric
knives. Old-timers insist on whole fish
as some contend the intact skin and
bones add a large measure of flavor. The
flesh of these fish is white and usually
firm and delicate, especially when fresh.
Cooks usually coat the washed and
dried whole fish or fillets with cornmeal
or corn flour seasoned with salt and

pepper prior to frying. Families sometimes keep the egg cases from spawning females and fry them along with the fish. Traditionally, they constituted a boneless tidbit for children. The thin, rounded shape of whole sunfish lends itself well to both pan frying and deep frying. There are reports of baked and broiled sunfish and even chowders, stews, and gravies made from boned fish.

Today, in the South, one can still spark an argument over whether the bluegill or the crappie is the better eating fish. Because they can almost never be legally purchased, sunfish are one of those special wild foods that can only be gathered and shared among family and friends. At a time when anglers routinely release many types of recreationally caught fish, sunfish remain standards in many home fish frys.

WILEY C. PREWITT JR.
Lodi, Mississippi

Byron W. Dalrymple, *Hunting for the Pot, Fishing for the Pan* (1981); Lawrence M. Page and Brooks M. Burr, *A Field Guide to Freshwater Fishes* (1991); *Sportsman's Guide to Game Fish* (1968); Keith Sutton, ed., *Arkansas Wildlife: A History* (1998); .

Peaches

Mountain folks love their apples, and Florida has its oranges, but a case can be made for peaches as the iconic fruit of the American South. As Ronni Lundy notes, "Few fruits are as purely associated with the South as sweet, dripping peaches." Camille Glenn wrote that peach ice cream is "one of the favorite summer desserts in the South, if not *the* favorite." Lundy adds that "the best

cobbler of all, bar none, is peach, where the oozing sweetness of the gold and crimson slices cozies up just perfectly to the two types of crust." Writer Melissa Faye Greene waxes poetic about another favorite peach delicacy, peach pie, noting that a "Georgia peach, a real Georgia peach, a backyard greatgrandmother's orchard peach, is as thickly furred as a sweater, and so fluent and sweet that once you bite through the flannel, it brings tears to your eyes." Contemporary cookbooks update the peach with new recipes. John Martin Taylor has one for zesty peach compote with ginger ice cream and gingersnaps, and Damon Lee Fowler tells how to prepare pecan-crusted goat cheese with warm peach chutney.

The peach (*Prunus persica*) that gives such culinary delight is not indigenous to the South, but it does go back a long way in regional history. It is native to China and found its way to Europe in the first century B.C. The Spanish introduced peaches to the South in the 16th century, but the quality was at first poor. They were fed to hogs in the colonial era but became so numerous that colonists assumed they were natural to the region. "Here are likewise great Peach-Orchards," Thomas Glover wrote about Virginia in 1676, "which bear such an infinite quantity of Peaches that at some Plantations they bear down to the Hoggs fourty bushels in a year." Colonial settlers also used peaches to make mobby, a strong drink that they then distilled into brandy. Then, as now, people dried peaches for cooking through the winter. Quality improved to such an extent that Thomas Jefferson

Grown in every state across the South, peaches are a sweet summer treat (Courtesy Mike Corbin)

had more than three dozen varieties of peaches at Monticello by the early 19th century. New varieties introduced from China in that century, especially the Chinese Cling, became the progenitors of modern peaches in the South.

The peach has also been at the center of much southern cultural expression. Country music legend Jimmie Rodgers sang "When It's Peach-Picking Time in Georgia," and bluesman Guilford "Peach Tree" Payne sang the "Peach Tree Blues" in 1923. Writer Dori Sanders grew up on her family's peach farm in Filbert, a small community in York County, S.C. Her father, a former sharecropper, bought the land in 1915, making it one of the oldest African American farms in the area. It specializes in growing Georgia Bells and Elberta peaches, which the family still sells at a roadside stand nearby. Sanders's novel *Clover* (1990) and her other writings often make use

of the peach farm setting. South Carolina is one of the South's leading producers of peaches, but most states in the region produce the fruit. No state is more associated with peaches than Georgia. The Georgia Peaches was a prominent minor league baseball franchise in the 20th century, and Georgia-born baseball player Ty Cobb was known as "the Georgia Peach," although his ornery personality made for a tarter version of the fruit. Today, tourists in Atlanta can buy peach-shaped salt-and-pepper shakers, a prime symbol of the state's cultural identity.

CHARLES REAGAN WILSON
University of Mississippi

Mike Corbin, *Family Trees: The Peach Culture of the Piedmont* (1998); John Egerton, *Southern Food: At Home, on the Road, in History* (1987); Ronni Lundy, *Butter Beans to Blackberries: Recipes from the Southern Garden* (1999).

Peanuts

Sitting by the roadside on a summer day,
Chatting with my mess-mates, passing time away,
Sitting in the shadows, underneath some trees.
Goodness, how delicious, eating goober peas.

Peas, peas, peas, peas,
Eating goober peas.
Goodness, how delicious,
Eating goober peas.
—Traditional verse, but often attributed to "A. Pindar"

Whether you call them goobers, goober-peas, pinders, pindas, monkey nuts, earthnuts, ground peas, or ground nuts, and whether you like them raw, parched, roasted, boiled, fried, candied, served as a spread on bread with blackberry jelly, or dropped by the bagful into your favorite cola soft drink, they are still just peanuts.

Peanuts are actually not a nut at all, but a legume, one that apparently originated in South America. And contrary to what is imagined by many nonsoutherners, they do not grow on trees. The seed pods actually develop and mature underground—thus the name *ground peas.* Uncultivated ancestors of the peanut plant can still be found in parts of Bolivia and Argentina. The peanut was first introduced into Europe, Africa, and other parts of the world by European traders in the 15th and 16th centuries. And it was from Africa, where the nuts were called *n-guba,* and through African slaves via the islands of the Caribbean, that peanuts were first brought to America north of Mexico, and thence into the Southeast, where they stuck like, well, like peanut butter.

While it is clear that African slaves in the colonial South ate peanuts, it is not clear just *how* they ate them. In all likelihood, the peanuts were eaten raw, shelled and boiled (like peas), or dried and roasted—in the shell or not. And that generally is how they were prepared and eaten by southerners at least until the end of the 19th century. They were also widely grown and used as a favorite fodder for fattening and "sweetening" hogs before the slaughter.

Another early method for preparing peanuts was to grind the roasted nuts into a stiff paste, which then was dissolved in boiling water. The resulting gruel was mixed with additional ingredients, including cinnamon or other spices, and served as a beverage. The 18th-century American botanist William Bartram, who tromped the woods and streams of the Southeast during the late 1700s in search of interesting plant specimens (and, coincidentally, observing and reporting on regional culture), declared that peanuts ground and mixed with pulverized sassafras root-bark makes a laudable substitute for chocolate. Ground peanuts were also commonly used as a thickener in soups and stews, as an ingredient in cookies and cakes, and in breads.

During the American Civil War, peanuts increased in their popularity as never before. Not only did they provide both armies with an easily acquired and portable foodstuff that did not easily spoil, but also oil rendered from them could be used for frying and baking, for lubricating machinery, as fuel for lamps, and as a medium for medicinal concoctions. The height of the peanut's importance in the South, either as a food or as an economic factor, did not, however, come until later.

When the boll weevil first entered the United States, about 1890 in Texas, and a few years later, about 1906, in Oklahoma, people little noticed it. But by the mid-1920s, the all-important southern cotton crop had been devastated by the blossom-boring insect from Mexico. Many southern farmers turned to peanuts for their economic salvation. The lowly peanut flourished in sandy southern soil, and the peanut in its many variants soon became one of the most favored products of southern agriculture and one of the most favored snack foods in America.

Before the late 1800s, peanut butter was generally a locally made product, one that was peddled door to door in the urban neighborhoods of the Northeast. However, by the early years of the second decade of the 20th century, peanut butter had become a national sensation. It is not clear who assembled the first peanut butter and jelly sandwich, or when, but peanut butter and jelly quickly become constant and lasting companions in the kitchens of America. Peanut butter manufacturing became, and remains, a major part of the national food industry.

Also in the early 1920s, an African American genius from Tuskegee, Ala., named George Washington Carver single-handedly brought peanut product development to levels that no

Jimmy Carter, peanut farmer
(Courtesy Jimmy Carter Library)

one before him could have imagined. Among the hundreds of uses for peanuts that he developed were peanut candies of many kinds, peanut-flavored ice cream and cakes, peanut flour, peanut hay for feeding livestock, peanut milk, multiflavored peanut soft drinks of several varieties, peanut face and skin creams, peanut inks, and a myriad of other edible and nonedible creations.

Whether toasted, roasted, parched, or candied (as in Cracker Jacks), by the 1920s cooked peanuts packaged and sold in small bags or boxes had become the favorite vendor snack in all of America. Bags of peanuts in the shell were an integral part of hometown and major league baseball games, traveling circuses, carnivals and fairs, community street fairs and festivals, high school football games, and shops and marketplaces in towns large and small. That tradition continues today in most southern communities and beyond. In the rural South, especially in the Piedmont South, roadside boiled peanut stands are a common stop for travelers and locals alike.

In 1976 a southern peanut farmer named Jimmy Carter was elected president of the United States, and Georgia peanuts instantly became an international sensation. Southerners in the 21st century continue, in record numbers, to grow—and to consume—peanuts. Peanuts, as much as kudzu, cotton, and fried chicken, are a quintessential southern icon.

FRED C. FUSSELL
Buena Vista, Georgia

Andrew F. Smith, *Peanuts: The Illustrious History of the Goober Pea* (2002); Jasper Guy Woodruff, *Peanuts: Production, Processing, Products* (1973).

Pecans

Pecans are the edible nuts produced by the pecan tree, *Carya illinoinensis*, a large deciduous tree native to the south central United States and portions of Mexico. The native range is bounded by Davenport, Iowa, to the north, Schleicher County, Tex., to the west, and Cincinnati, Ohio, to the east, extending in the form of scattered occurrences south into central Mexico. Cultivated pecans have been introduced to a zone stretching from North Carolina to parts of California. The name is Algonquian, indicating a nut too hard to crack by hand, and was not species specific. Early Spanish explorers encountered pecans in Texas and referred to them as *nueces* and *nogales*, the Spanish words for walnuts. Both George Washington

and Thomas Jefferson were interested in the cultivation of pecans, but it was Antoine, a slave gardener at Oak Alley plantation upriver from New Orleans, who is credited with first successfully grafting pecan trees, in 1846. Louisiana soon became known as the cradle of improved pecan production not only through the development of such cultivars as the Centennial, Moneymaker, Frotscher, Rome, and Mire, but also because of New Orleans's importance as a market town and distribution point for pecans from Mississippi and Texas.

New Orleans is also noted as the home of the pecan praline, a candy of sugar and pecans adapted from French prototypes made with almonds. Today, pralines are popular across the South, with chewy versions more popular to the east and crispy versions more popular in Texas and Mexico. In addition to these and other pecan candies—including the famous pecan log developed by the Georgia-based Stuckey's chain—pecans are most frequently used in sweet and savory snacks, fruitcakes, and pecan pie. Pecan pie may have been developed in the latter part of the 19th century, and there are claimants from both Louisiana and Texas for the original recipe, but it was only with the development of Karo brand corn syrup in 1903 that the pecan pie known today became possible. John Egerton points out that it was only beginning in the 1940s that the recipe became a staple in southern cookbooks. Today, Georgia is the nation's leading producer of pecans from cultivars, and Texas leads in the combined harvest of cultivars and seedlings. Pecan groves are agricultural icons throughout the American South.

J. MICHAEL LUSTER

Arkansas Folklife Program, Arkansas State University

John Egerton, *Southern Food: At Home, on the Road, in History* (1987); H. Harold Hume, *The Pecan and Its Culture* (1912); Jane Manaster, *The Pecan Tree* (1994); Darrell Sparks, *Pecan Cultivars: The Orchard's Foundation* (1992); H. P. Stuckey and Edwin Jackson Kyle, *Pecan Growing* (1925).

Pepper Vinegar

Pepper vinegar is vinegar containing pickled capsicums, or chili peppers. It is commonly used as a table condiment in eateries throughout the South and Southwest. Pepper vinegar adds intense piquancy to a bowl of pot beans but can be used to enhance the flavor of a variety of other meat and vegetable dishes. Commercially produced pepper vinegars come with a flip-top or shaker spout to prevent the peppers from escaping. The remaining peppers can be "topped off" with vinegar once the liquid has been depleted.

To make pepper vinegar at home simply pack peppers into a clean Mason jar or other glass container with a lid, such as an olive jar. Fill the container about half to three-fourths full, top off with vinegar, and close. Let it rest in the refrigerator for at least three days before consuming. The result is a pepper-flavored vinegar sauce suitable for a variety of savory dishes.

A variety of vinegars is appropriate for making pepper vinegar at home. Readily available vinegars such as dis-tilled white vinegar, white wine vinegar, or cider vinegars produce a flavor reminiscent of commercially produced pepper vinegars. Adding noniodized salt or a clove of garlic is optional for flavoring pepper vinegars but not required for achieving a satisfying result. Dark, sweet, or flavored vinegars (such as balsamic vinegar) are not desirable.

Among the best kinds of pepper to use in pepper vinegar is the "bush" pepper, which is green when young, then turns yellow, then orange, and finally matures to red. Bush peppers are mild when young and green and grow hotter as they become red. They are tiny peppers, about one inch long. Cracked peppercorns also produce a type of pepper vinegar, but it has a very different flavor altogether.

LUCY NORRIS

New York, New York

John Egerton, *Southern Food: At Home, on the Road, in History* (1987); Lucy Norris and Elizabeth Watt, *Pickled: Vegetables, Fruits, Roots, More—Preserving a World of Tastes and Traditions* (2003); John Martin Taylor, *The New Southern Cook: 200 Recipes from the South's Best Chefs and Home Cooks* (1995).

Peppers, Hot

Peppers are an ancient food in the Americas, and the remains of wild peppers dating back to 7000 B.C. have been found in human coprolites—fossilized excrement—uncovered 150 miles south of Mexico City. There is further evidence that hot pepper is one of the oldest of cultivated New World plants, believed to have been first grown as far

Fresh jalapeño peppers (Ken Hammond, photographer, United States Department of Agriculture)

spread, after Columbus, to the rest of the world. Although they are today consumed with fervor in Asia and Africa, hot peppers were unknown on those continents until they were carried there by Spanish and Portuguese explorers. Flourishing in the soils of both Asia and Africa, they were in short order embedded in the cuisine. By the time those selfsame Europeans were trafficking slaves in the opposite direction, peppers were so entrenched in the societies of West Africa that slaves were said to have brought seeds with them to ease the culinary hardships of their servitude. One South Louisiana commercial hot sauce, Tabasco, dates to the 1860s.

What is it about peppers, particularly the hot and pungent varieties, that has drawn people for so long? There are a variety of answers. Peppers add flavor to bland food and limited diets, and they serve in regions without refrigeration to disguise something that might be slightly off-flavor. In addition, they have a high content of vitamins A and C. Another attraction of peppers is that they cause an intense physical stimulation that passes rapidly, leaving no unpleasant marks or aftereffects.

Capsicum has played a role as a medicine for centuries. It was used by the Mayans and Aztecs of pre-Columbian Mexico to help ease bronchitis, throat ache, and gum pain. A cayenne or other hot red pepper in a cup of lemon or sassafras tea is often used by Cajuns in southern Louisiana to treat a cough or cold. And capsaicin, the ingredient in hot peppers that makes them hot, is used in a topical ointment

back as 3500 B.C. in Mexico. Here the pepper being discussed is of the genus *Capsicum*, a hot and sweet pepper as opposed to *Piper*, denoting the black pepper that came to Europe via Marco Polo's 13th-century travels in Asia.

There is no record of *Capsicums*, either hot or sweet, in any place outside the Americas until Christopher Columbus brought them to Spain. By the time Europeans arrived in the Americas, *Capsicum* peppers were being grown and eaten by indigenous populations up and down the American continent. The first written reference to them occurs in the journal of Columbus's first voyage, where he touted them as the equal of black pepper. Peppers drew the attention of Europeans right away, and it took very little time for them to to treat shingles, as well as to ease arthritis and joint pain.

The use of *Capsicum* as a weapon has an equally long history. The Incas burned peppers because the smoke held back—temporarily—the Spanish invaders, and nowadays capsaicin is the principal active ingredient in many of the disabling sprays women carry in their purses to ward off an attacker. As recently as 1964, the U.S. Army was conducting tests using capsaicin as a possible weapon.

RICHARD SCHWEID
Barcelona, Spain

Jean Andrews, *The Domesticated Capsicums* (1985); Barbara Pickersgill, in *The Domestication and Exploitation of Plants and Animals*, ed. Peter J. Ucko (1969); Ralph Roys, *The Ethnobotany of the Maya* (1931); Richard Schweid, *Hot Peppers: The Story of Cajuns and Capsicum* (1987).

Persimmons

The small orange-red fruit of the wild persimmon tree, *Diospyros virginiana*, is native to North America and edible only when fully ripe, after the first frost. Many consider persimmons completely ripe only after they have fallen from the tree. Cultivated varieties native to China and Japan were introduced into the gardens and yards of the southern states after 1870. Native persimmons are used in breads, beer, jams, puddings, pies, cakes, cookies, and ice cream, and eaten as fresh fruit.

Persimmons were used in food and beverages by the Cherokee and other Native Americans, who introduced them to early European settlers. Persimmon beer was referred to colloqui-ally as a "possum toddy." The unripe fruit is notoriously inedible but has been chewed by some as a toothache cure. The bark of the persimmon tree has been used in a concoction for sore throat and in other astringent medicinal applications. In the Ozarks, the one to six large, flattened seeds found in the fruit have been used to predict weather. The seeds are cracked open and examined for the image of a knife, a fork, or a spoon, which predicts variously cold, mild, wet, or dry weather and also offers signs of luck. The wood of the persimmon tree is used for golf clubs, shuttles, shoe lasts, and tool handles. It is considered unlucky (and wasteful) to burn persimmon wood. Persimmons grow primarily in the southeastern United States from Maryland to Texas; a second species, the Texas persimmon, *Diospyros texana*, spreads southward into Mexico.

J. MICHAEL LUSTER
Arkansas Folklife Program, Arkansas State University

Steve Brill, *The Wild Vegetarian Cookbook* (2002); Joseph E. Dabney, *Smokehouse Ham, Spoon Bread, and Scuppernong Wine: The Folklore and Art of Southern Appalachian Cooking* (1998); The Mary Celestia Parler Collection, University of Arkansas Library; Vance Randolph, *Ozark Superstitions* (1947); Robert A. Vines, *Trees of East Texas* (1977); Eugene Walter, *Hints and Pinches: A Concise Compendium of Aromatics, Chutneys, Herbs, Relishes, Spices, and Other Such Concerns* (2001).

Pickling

Pickling is the process of preserving foods with either a vinegar or salt brine and with spices and/or sugar. Varieties of foods are appropriate for pickling: vegetables, meat, and fruit. Done properly, pickling is a safe way to save foods for future consumption during times when certain foods may be scarce or out of season. Although a variety of pickles can be purchased commercially, canning homemade pickles remains an important part of the southern culinary heritage, and many families work to keep their recipes alive. Community groups, churches, and extended families are known to get together to make batches of pickles to share and swap. An annual family reunion or summer holiday may be set aside for recreating a cherished pickle recipe. Pickles, often regarded as cucumber dills, come in many forms. In the South, for instance, pickled okra and pickled green tomatoes are regional favorites.

Okra crops thrived in the South's warm climate and became overabundant, producing throughout a long growing season. Pickling okra was born out of a need to prevent pods from spoiling. As pickling became more common to southerners, the taste of pickles grew more desirable. Pickling okra is also an ideal way to preserve the pods without intensifying the sliminess often associated with cooked okra. Ideally, okra pods should be pickled young in vinegar brine with the addition of a single hot red chili pepper and scant pickling spices. Recipes vary throughout the South depending on local preference or family tradition.

Tomatoes are also among the crops that thrived in the warm southern climate. Tomatoes are at their most abundant in the late summer but continue to bear fruit throughout early fall. When tomatoes are green, they are bitter and hard, unlike the flavorful ripe, red tomato. Those qualities made them ideal for pickling, which also allowed people to make use of green tomatoes that were harvested before the first frost. Green tomatoes are also best pickled in vinegar, salt, and spices.

Other types of pickles common in the South include sweet hot pickled cucumber, pickled watermelon rind, pickled beets, pickled jalapeños or other peppers, pickled eggs, and pickled pigs' feet and snout.

LUCY NORRIS
New York, New York

Barbara Ciletti, *Creative Pickling: Salsas, Chutneys, Sauces, and Preserves for Today's Adventurous Cook* (2000); David Mabey and David Collison, *The Perfect Pickle Book* (1995); Lucy Norris and Elizabeth Watt, *Pickled: Vegetables, Fruits, Roots, More— Preserving a World of Tastes and Traditions* (2003); Linda Ziedrich, *The Joy of Pickling: 200 Flavor-Packed Recipes for All Kinds of Produce from Garden or Market* (1999).

Pies

Cash-strapped Europeans developed pies in order to make the most of ingredients. Early pie crusts completely enrobed the filling and were much harder and denser than the ones we know today, which aided in preserving an interior product that might otherwise spoil. Primitive pies were most likely filled with meat and vegetables as opposed to sweets and fruit fillings. Hand pies were an easy pocket food or workman's lunch. The crust allowed a worker or traveler to place a pie in a coat pocket and be off. Early American settlers desperately needed to stretch their ingredients, and the practice of fabricating a pastry dough from soft flour and just a little fat made a very humble meal seem fancy.

Southern pies take on their own personality. Favorite pies of the South not only use indigenous ingredients as fillings, but have a signature ingredient in the pastry dough as well. *The American Woman's Cook Book*, published for the Culinary Arts Institute in 1942, goes so far as to list a recipe, for "Southern pie crust" in the ingredient roster of distinctly southern recipes, such as pecan pie and sweet potato pies. The "southern" distinction comes from the use of lard as the fat for the pastry. Pork products were in abundance, since many rural southerners killed and processed hogs, so lard was the fat of choice. While butter was the chosen binder in European pastry, pork fat lent a distinct, flaky quality to a southern pie crust. Later, Crisco shortening would elbow its way into southern crusts as an alternative to keeping rendered pork fat on hand. While some bakers swear by a Crisco crust, many purists will fashion their pastry only with lard. Others, though, like a mix of both—half shortening, half lard. Even the folks at Crisco knew they might have a hard time converting southern cooks to their product, so they decided to launch an ad campaign in the 1970s that was sure to make an impact. Those who can remember Crisco's spokeswoman of the day will have a difficult time forgetting country superstar Loretta Lynn's catch phrase, "It'll do you proud ever time."

Soft wheat flour is another essential ingredient of a flaky crust. Southern brands such as White Lily and Martha White are the brands of choice for pie crusts. The texture of southern baked goods is distinct, and chefs and cookbook writers give a nod to the brands of the South, admitting that the actual brand of flour can make or break an authentic regional dish. Celebrated baker and author Rose Levy Beranbaum, in her *Pie and Pastry Bible*, very distinctly says to use either White Lily or Martha White flour when listing ingredients for typically southern desserts.

Martha McCulloch-Williams, in her 1913 work *Dishes and Beverages of the Old South*, begins her chapter on pies with this advice: "The Philosophy of Pie Crust: Pie crust perfection depends on several things—good flour, food fat, good handling, most especially good baking. A hot oven, quick but not scorching, expands the air betwixt layers of paste, and pops open the flour-grains, making them absorb the fat as it melts, thereby growing crisp and relishful instead of hard and tough." The evolution of pie crusts, from hard wrap for the preservation and protection of food to fine pastry art, could be one reason fledgling bakers laugh at the notion that something is "easy as pie." With so much riding on a successful pie crust, young brides and homemakers practiced diligently to perfect their pastry in hopes of becoming a heralded home baker one day. Without question, perfect pie crust is one of the most difficult tasks to master in the kitchen.

Fillings that define southern pies would be those that are in season and indigenous, such as fresh apples, black-berries, and blueberries, and those—whether fruits, nuts, or vegetables—that have been "put up" for the winter. Some pie fillings may be made from simple brown sugar, molasses, or custards, and the most famous southern pie may very well be the pecan pie. Florida is some-times left out of southern food discus-sions, but key lime pie is a favorite, and no one would argue that its home is, geographically at least, as southern as one can get.

Chess pie is a very old recipe most likely brought from England and is the product of cooks wanting to make cheese curd pies. English lemon curd pie filling is quite similar to lemon chess pie. The origin of the name *chess pie* may have come from shortening "cheese (curd)" pie. There are some colorful stories that explain the origin of the name, however, and they make the story of the simple chess pie a bit more inter-esting. Some say that because this pie was made from eggs, butter, sugar, and not much else, it needed to be kept in a "pie chest" and thus became "chess pie." Others say that it is simply from some-one asking, "What kind of pie is this?" and the cook replying, "Oh, it's jes pie." Regardless of where the name came from, chess pie represents a pie that can be made from ingredients that most folks keep on hand: butter, eggs, sugar, and a little flour. Sometimes cornmeal is added, and to make the chess pie a little more special, lemon or chocolate might be stirred into the mix.

Florida's key lime pie is arguably one of the nation's most recognized regional dishes. Hailing from Key West, the

southernmost point in the continental United States, this creamy pie is the daughter of necessity in that an inven-tive cook needed to come up with a creamy pie without using milk. Until the Overseas Highway opened in the 1930s to connect the Florida Keys to the main-land, fresh milk and ice were not readily available. Cooks relied on canned con-densed milk, which had been invented by Gail Borden in 1856. Sweetened condensed milk and the tart juice of the key, or Persian, lime, which grows in abundance on Key West, are the main ingredients of this favorite pie. Cooks and eaters alike argue about different as-pects of the confection—cooked or un-cooked filling, graham cracker or pastry crust, meringue or whipped cream on top. The debate will no doubt go on, but all agree that not a drop of green food coloring should ever be added to the filling. The key lime lends a lovely, pale yellow tone to the smooth pie, and that is exactly as it should be.

Apple pie is not a distinctly southern pie, but in the hands of a southern cook it becomes decidedly southern by way of an iron skillet. While southerners love a traditional apple pie, made with tart June apples, perhaps their favorite is made from the same apples, dried for the winter months, sealed in an envel-ope of pastry dough, and fried golden brown in a shallow pool of oil. Pie thus becomes breakfast, dessert, or a snack to be wrapped in wax paper and tucked into a worker's lunch bucket or a trav-eler's shoe box meal. These fried pies are best when served straight from the skillet but are enjoyable even hours after they have been cooked. Many farm-wives and deft cooks have picked up a few extra dollars by frying up a number of pies, sliding them into glassine envelopes, and stacking them by the cash box at farm stands, meat-and-three restaurants, hardware stores, and service stations. Southern fried pie may be the original "impulse buy."

Sweet potato pie is similar in appearance and texture to pumpkin pie, but contains less sugar, because sweet potatoes possesses their own sweetness, which imparts a distinct flavor. Sweet potatoes are easy to grow. Forget about one for a while and a new plant will sprout, leaves and all, without any soil in sight. Because the sweet potato is so abundant and easy to store for weeks and, in the right conditions, months at a time, it is one of the most important vegetables grown in the South. African Americans can be credited with many recipe origins because a similar vegetable grows in Africa and was a staple for numerous healthy and sustaining stews. The sweet potato variety used for a traditional southern pie has been traced to Central and South America. Peeled, cooked until soft, and mashed with eggs, butter, and sugar, the sweet potatoes make a filling that is thick and rich. Mixed with spices such as cinnamon and nutmeg, the pie takes on an exotic quality and has become a favorite at harvest and holiday time.

Perhaps the most distinctly southern pie is the pecan pie. Native to Texas but growing all over the South and as far north as Iowa and New York, pecan nuts are generally thought of as a southern ingredient. Corn syrup, eggs, and copious amounts of butter make up the filling of a pecan pie. While pecans can be quite expensive in modern markets, the pecan pie was actually a very inexpensive pie to make in the day when most southern homes had a pecan tree in the vicinity. Children were sent out to gather the pecans that fell, and when mixed with the farm dairy products and corn syrup that were in every southern cupboard, the nuts produced a rich dessert. Today, southern cooks and pastry chefs play with the ingredients here and there, adding chocolate and additional varieties of nuts. Some may think a "bourbon pecan pie" is a new-fangled chef's trick, but one can bet that the recipe was born long ago in either Tennessee or Kentucky, where a splash of the region's finest was added for character.

Scott Peacock in *The Gift of Southern Cooking* recalled a session of pie baking with southern food queen and co-author Edna Lewis: "I noticed that Miss Lewis didn't make her pies too sweet, and I appreciated for the first time the special quality that lard lent to pastry crusts: a crisp flakiness that shattered beautifully, far better than butter or shortening doughs. But as a young chef, prone to make showy dishes when cooking for public occasions or even just for friends, I learned from Miss Lewis's desserts something more fundamental about cooking: that is, a great dessert—a great dish—doesn't have to be fancy. It can be as simple and homey as a blackberry pie, if it is made with integrity and if every part of it, both pastry and filling, is the best of its kind."

ANGIE MOSIER
Atlanta, Georgia

Rose Levy Beranbaum, *The Pie and Pastry Bible* (1998); Ruth Berolzheimer, ed., *The American Woman's Cook Book* (1942); Joseph E. Dabney, *Smokehouse Ham, Spoon Bread, and Scuppernong Wine: The Folklore and Art of Southern Appalachian Cooking* (1998); John T. Edge, *Apple Pie: An American Story* (2004); Edna Lewis and Scott Peacock, *The Gift of Southern Cooking: Recipes and Revelations from Two Great American Cooks* (2003); Martha McCulloch-Williams, *Dishes and Beverages of the Old South* (1913, 1988); Linda Stradley, *I'll Have What They're Having—Legendary Local Cuisine* (2002).

Pimento Cheese

Pimento cheese, a spread of grated cheese, pimientos, and seemingly infinite variations, was first popularized in the South. It has been a staple of picnic baskets, lunchboxes, and afternoon snacks for nearly a century.

The pimiento is a long, red, heart-shaped vegetable native to the Americas, which takes its name from the Spanish word for "pepper." While most closely associated with olives, ham loaf, and pimento cheese, the little pepper is versatile: one member of its family is used to make paprika, and another variety of the pimiento tree yields allspice.

The moment of convergence of the pimiento and cheese remains as much of a mystery as when the spelling of "pimiento cheese" began to drift toward the colloquialized "pimento cheese." Some sources suggest that already-prepared pimento cheese was featured in southern grocery stores as early as 1915. Pomona Products Company founder George Reigel, of Griffin, Ga., began canning Sunshine Pimentos in 1916, making it even easier for home cooks to whip, mash, stir, and blend their own versions of the spread.

Pimento cheese may have been a special treat for southerners, since the sharp cheddar cheese that was used to make it was store-bought and not produced by the family. As cheese became more widely available, and commodity cheese became a part of southern households, pimento cheese was a wallet-friendly part of southern meals. It keeps well for several days, making it even more practical.

There are as many recipes for pimento cheese as people who make it, but its essence is constant: cheese, pimentos, and a binding agent (most commonly either store-bought or homemade mayonnaise). Most agree that only sharp cheese will do for perfect pimento cheese. Variations come from a number of "secret" ingredients, including sugar, the Worcestershire sauce called for in Elvis's favorite recipe, onions, garlic, jalapeño peppers, Tabasco, and cream cheese.

Modern southerners probably use food processors or a fork to blend their pimento cheese, leaving the Mouli graters of their youths behind; but pimento cheese heaped in a sandwich, stuffed in a rib of celery or a tomato, spread on an apple, topping a baked potato or hamburger, or spooned straight out of the crock is still an important part of their cuisine. It is enjoyed at the Master's Golf Tournament in Augusta, Ga., and by North Carolina writer Reynolds Price, who dubs it the "peanut butter of [his] childhood."

Memory makes pimento cheese truly

Shrimp po' boy (Kurt Coste, photographer, NewOrleansOnline.com)

distinctive: almost every southerner has a story to tell about the spread, whether it is a warm remembrance of Mother's recipe or a diatribe about how the stuff is no good at all. A purely southern invention, pimento cheese remains a vital piece of the region's culinary puzzle.

KENDRA MYERS
University of Mississippi

Daniel N. Lapedes, ed., *McGraw-Hill Encyclopedia of Food, Agriculture, and Nutrition* (1977); Becky Mercuri, *Sandwiches That You Will Like* (2002); H. S. Redgrove, *Spices and Condiments* (1933); Southern Foodways Alliance, *Pimento Cheese Invitational* (2003); James Villas, *Gourmet* (November 1999).

Po' Boy

Researchers and food historians have yet to discover the precise origins of the po' boy, or poor boy, the hefty sandwich sold in scores of restaurants and food stands in and around New Orleans. Most agree, however, that this classic of New Orleans's multifaceted cuisine—made with a distinctive, traditional French-style bread and a variety of fillings—first appeared in the city's blue-collar neighborhoods around 1920. True to its name, the po' boy provided low-cost sustenance for generations of the city's working classes. From the 1920s to the 1940s a typical sandwich could be had for as little as five cents if it contained such modest ingredients as inexpensive cold cuts or french fried potatoes moistened with gravy and a few bits of roast beef. During the same era, a dime or 15 cents might produce a thick filling of hot beef or cold ham slices, fried shrimp or oysters, or even trout and soft-shell crab. One more nickel would pay for most po' boy lovers' beverage of choice—root beer or some other soft drink.

A milestone in the po' boy's history occurred in 1922, when two brothers from Raceland, La., Benny and Clovis Martin, opened their first sandwich shop in New Orleans's French Quarter at the corner of Ursulines and Decatur Streets, across from the French Market. Nine years later the Martins moved their po' boy business into a much larger building at 2000 St. Claude Avenue. From 1929 to 1973 Martin Bros. Poor Boys was New Orleans's prime purveyor of the authentic sandwich. A stone's throw away on Touro Street was Gendusa's Bakery, where the bread was made to the brothers' specifications—a 32-inch loaf with a cottony, low-gluten texture inside a thin, but crunchy, crust. Loaves with rounded-off ends replaced the more traditional pointed ones, to reduce the amount of bread waste. The Martins offered some 20 sandwich fillings, the most popular being fried shrimp, fried oysters, ham, and thin-sliced roast beef in a light, but assertively seasoned, gravy. "Dressed" has always meant the addition of lettuce, tomato slices, mayonnaise, and perhaps a few slices of dill pickle.

The po' boy provided the inspiration for two more classic New Orleans sandwiches—the "loaf," 12 or more inches of buttered, toasted French bread stuffed with fried oysters or shrimp, and the "peacemaker," a buttery fried-oyster po' boy that a husband traditionally brought home to appease his wife after a "night out with the boys." By the mid-20th century, the po' boy's popularity in New Orleans cut across all socioeconomic lines. The beginning of the twenty-first century saw hundreds of restaurants and sandwich shops in New Orleans and its suburbs trying to meet the demand, with a multitude of fillings that included frankfurters, meatballs with tomato sauce, fried catfish, hamburger patties, and beef brisket, among many others.

GENE BOURG
New Orleans, Louisiana

Rima and Richard Collin, *New Orleans Cookbook* (1987); John Egerton, *Southern Food: At Home, on the Road, in History* (1987); Alex Martin, *New Orleans Times-Picayune, Dixie Magazine* (29 November 1981); Bunny Matthews, *New Orleans Times-Picayune, Dixie Magazine* (29 November 1981); Becky Mercuri, *Sandwiches That You Will Like* (2002); Gregory Roberts, *New Orleans Times-Picayune* (February 23, 1986).

Poke Sallet

Poke sallet is a dish of cooked greens prepared from the young leaves and tender shoots of the pokeweed plant, *Phytolacca americana*, a native annual found throughout the eastern United States westward to Minnesota and south to Mexico, distinguished by its red stalks and dark purple berries. The dish is also spelled "poke salot," "poke sallit," and "poke salad," among other variations. The name derives from the Algonquian word *pocan*, indicating a plant that yields a red dye, and *sallet*, an early dialect term for a mess of cooked greens as distinguished from a raw salad.

Pokeweed is one of the first spring greens to appear, and the shoots and first leaves are gathered when the plant is less than eight inches high. As the plant matures, the leaves, like the berries and especially the large tap root, become highly toxic, and the leaves and/or shoots must be parboiled two to three times with changes of boiling water to eliminate the toxicity. Shoots can be prepared like asparagus. The leaves have a flavor similar, but superior, to spinach and are usually parboiled and then fried, with or without batter, and seasoned with vinegar, pickle juice, pepper sauce, or other condiments, and often accompanied by eggs. They are sometimes combined with other wild greens such as lamb's quarters, dock, wild mustard, or dandelions. Some cooks also parboil, peel, and fry the stalks in bacon grease in a manner similar to the preparation of okra.

Pokeweed has seldom been deliberately grown, although Dr. John Bowers of the University of Arkansas did experiment with cultivation in the 1950s, and at least one company currently offers seed for sale. Also beginning in the 1950s, at least two commercial canneries, Bush Brothers of Tennessee and Allen Canning Company of Arkansas, offered canned poke sallet to the market for those who valued not only its delicate flavor but also its reputation as a spring tonic. The market was reportedly especially strong in California among Depression era southern out-migrants and their descendants, but Allen Canning Co. canned its last poke sallet in April 2000.

Poke sallet is rich in iron and vitamin C. Additionally, the leaves, berries, stalks, and roots of the plant have been used in a variety of traditional medicinal applications to treat ailments including rheumatism, neuralgia, bruises, burns, boils, warts, and hair loss. The berries produce a red dye or ink used by the Algonquians, generations of children, and Alabama self-taught artist Jimmy Lee Sudduth. Singer and songwriter Tony Joe White, a native of West Carroll Parish, La., had a top-10 pop hit with the oddly spelled "Polk Salad Annie," a record that is still celebrated in the local community of Oak Grove with an annual Poke Salot Festival.

J. MICHAEL LUSTER
Arkansas Folklife Program, Arkansas State University

Lee Allen, *A Field Guide to Edible Plants: Eastern and Central North America* (Peterson Field Guides, 1977); Steve Brill, *The Wild Vegetarian Cookbook* (2002); Joseph E. Dabney, *Smokehouse Ham, Spoon Bread, and Scuppernong Wine: The Folklore and Art of Southern Appalachian Cooking* (1998); John Egerton, *Southern Food: At Home, on the Road, in History* (1987); Steven Foster and James A. Duke, *A Field Guide to Medicinal Plants: Eastern and Central North America* (1990); Gerald Klingaman, University of Arkansas Cooperative Extension Service *News* (2 May 2003).

Pots and Skillets

References to kettles, shaped metal vessels, can be found as early as the 17th century. One description of a pot is a vessel that grows narrower toward the top, whereas a kettle is described as growing toward the top. Pots or kettles with three legs were often used over coals from a fireplace as boiling vessels to prepare meat or vegetable meals.

Cast-iron stew pot (Alfred Harrell, photographer, Library of Congress [NV-SI-217], Washington, D.C.)

They could be either open or lidded, and when there was a lid, it was sometimes modified with a rim so it could hold coals to provide heat on top, supplementing the usual coals below the pot.

After pots and kettles had long been used for cooking on open fire sites and fireplace hearths, the Dutch oven was developed early in the 18th century. The cast-iron Dutch oven, or bake kettle, had three legs on the bottom, a rimmed lid, and a bail on the side ears of the pots. Compared to earlier vessels, it had a wider diameter and shallower depth, which allowed for baking breads and desserts.

Similar cast-iron ovens have been used for about three centuries. They have the same three legs on the bottom, a tight-fitting rimmed lid, and two ears on the upper sides of the oven for use of hooks or bails for lifting. It is a versatile vessel for browning, steaming, stewing, frying, warming, and baking.

Skillet-type vessels have been known as posnets, spiders, frying pans, or even, for a Dutch oven, skillet-with-a-lids. Posnets are small, rounded-bottom saucepans with three legs and a long handle on the side to allow placement in the fire area. These vessels, often called skillets, provided a pan to stew or heat food by setting the vessel over coals on the fireplace hearth. A spider usually was a flat-bottom, low-sided pan, with three legs to support it over coals, and a long handle on the side to facilitate placing the spider over coals on the hearth. The shape of the pan, with three long legs, led to the name *spider*. Various sizes and different lengths of legs made the spider a very usable vessel. The frying pan, a similar vessel with a flat bottom, shallow sides, and no legs, which can be used with or without a lid, is a standard cooking vessel today. It is widely used in kitchen ovens, on stove tops and camp stoves, and over campfires.

Pots, kettles, and skillets have been associated in the South with family and communal events central to the region's character. Pots made it possible for Louisiana Cajuns to cook their jambalaya and Georgians to make their Brunswick stew. Pots, kettles, and skillets have been essential cooking implements for Fourth of July cookouts, autumn tailgating at football games, and fried chicken and catfish cooking at political rallies. Appalachian stack cakes were traditionally cooked in iron skillets and served at the Christmas table. Lodge, the nation's leading cast-iron manufacturing company, based in South Pittsburg, Tenn., manufactures cookware in the traditional manner, although today consumers can purchase iron cookware already seasoned with oil and baked in order to achieve what the company calls "that prized heirloom finish."

JOHN G. RAGSDALE
El Dorado, Arkansas

Linda Campbell Franklin, *300 Years of Kitchen Collectibles* (2003); Suzanne Goldenson with Doris Simpson, *The Open-Hearth Cookbook* (1982); John G. Ragsdale, *Dutch Ovens Chronicled* (1991).

Pralines

Unlike the near disappearance of rice calas (deep-fried rice fritters) from New Orleans cuisine, the popularity of praline (pronounced *prah*-leen in Louisiana and *pray*-leen in Georgia and parts east) candy has never waned. Throughout the South, the praline is considered a beloved sweet. Eaten alone, as a topping for ice cream, or mixed into icing, it has enjoyed steady and enthusiastic, though more celebratory than daily, consumption by natives and tourists alike.

A patty with the basic flavor of caramelized sugar tinged with the slight bitterness of pecans, the praline of the American South looks little like the sugared almonds or hazelnuts of ancient origin. A French version, later called by the Creoles *les amandes risolées dans du sucre*, reached the peak of its popularity in the 1600s at the court of Louis XIV, where they were made by a chef employed by the Maréchal du Plessis-Praslin, whose name they were given, in the shortened form, *praline*. In French confectionery, the praline remains a cooked mixture of sugar, almonds, and vanilla. Often ground to a paste, this mixture is most likely to be found as a pastry or candy filling.

Oral tradition holds that both the Ursulines and later emigrés fleeing the French Revolution contributed to the appearance of the praline in the Louisiana territory. Louisiana cooks used pecans and, at first, only brown sugar to make their pralines. Although little written evidence exists, the praline is said to have been sold on the streets of antebellum Mobile and New Orleans by free women of color as well as slaves. Today it is possible to find pralines whose origin is claimed by cities from Pensacola, Fla., to Midland, Tex. The recipe remains 90 percent sugar, nuts, vanilla, and butter, with variations in the type of sugar added, the occasional substitution of peanuts or coconut, the choice of cream or milk as an additional ingredient, and the presence of other embellishments, such as chocolate and coffee. Devotees are usually divided between the creamy praline, favored in the Gulf South, and the sticky praline, favored in Texas.

SUSAN TUCKER
Tulane University

Rima and Richard Collin, *New Orleans Cookbook* (1987); John Egerton, *Southern Food: At Home, on the Road, in History* (1987); *The Picayune's Creole Cook Book* (1922).

Preserves and Jellies

The process of preserving fruit with sugar, well known in 17th-century Europe and certainly familiar to the colonizers of the New World, was not widely practiced in the South during the colonial period. Despite the proximity of a robust sugar industry in the

Caribbean Islands, sugar remained an expensive commodity in the colonial South. Moreover, in a society facing the daily challenge of carving out an existence in a new land, the labor-intensive production of preserves, marmalades, jams, and jellies took a backseat to more pressing activities. Orchard fruits, though abundant, were primarily cultivated to produce cider and brandy. While the colonists enjoyed fresh and wild fruits in season, apples, which could be successfully stored without spoilage, were the fruit most commonly consumed during the winter months.

During the Revolutionary War sugar became scarce, and Britain's reluctance to normalize trade relations with the new United States after the conflict kept the price of sugar relatively high. There is ample evidence, however, that by the beginning of the 19th century the art of making preserves and jellies was alive and well in the southern states. Fertile soil and a long growing season, coupled with a slave population that swelled into the millions during the first half of the 19th century, provided the necessary conditions for the rise of the plantation system and a class of wealthy agrarians who possessed the leisure and the means to enjoy the pleasures of the table. Cookbooks published during the antebellum period contain detailed entries for the preparation of preserves and jellies from a staggering variety of fruits. The classic proportions of a pound of sugar to a pound of fruit (or a pint of juice) are invariably called for, but techniques vary widely depending on the properties of the specific fruit, certain recipes even calling for drying

the fruit in the sun for several days midway through the cooking process. Calves feet and isinglass were used to enhance the jellying of low-pectin fruits or in jellies made from blossoms, teas, or coffee. Sometimes currant or quince jelly was added to the kettle to the same end. Stoneware containers were the receptacle of choice for the cooked jelly, usually sealed with brandy-soaked paper.

While antebellum cookbooks were generally penned by educated southern plantation mistresses, it is not clear how much preserving the authors personally undertook. More likely they trained and supervised slaves to perform the hot and laborious task of preserving fruit over open fires in the heat of summer. This conclusion is supported by the 1881 publication of a cookbook by former slave and San Francisco pickle maker Abby Fisher. *What Mrs. Fisher Knows about Old Southern Cooking* contains recipes for, among other things, the assortment of jellies and preserves for which Abby Fisher received a medal at the 1880 San Francisco Mechanics Institute Fair, jellies and preserves that she perfected in the pre-Emancipation kitchens of the South.

The Mason jar, which made the preservation of fruits and vegetables more reliable and economical, appeared in 1859, just in time for the outbreak of the Civil War. That development, coupled with the need to furnish troops in the field with nonperishable rations, boosted food preservation during the war years, at least in the North. Ironically, the predominantly agricultural South was ill equipped to feed itself or its troops, since most of its acreage produced inedible cash crops. Several years into the war, with the naval blockade in place, sugar had become virtually unobtainable in the South, except for the brown sugar produced in Louisiana. With the fall of Vicksburg, that too disappeared and, with it, any possibility of making jellies or preserves.

After the Civil War, hunger and poverty were widespread in the South. Any southerner who owned a plot of land cultivated a garden and canned its surplus to augment the precarious food supply. Anybody with a fig tree in the yard or access to a blackberry bramble learned how to preserve fruit so that nothing would be wasted. No longer the hallmark of prosperity, largesse, or a large household staff, home preserving in the post–Civil War era was first and foremost a subsistence endeavor. Tellingly, cookbooks published after the Civil War include recipes utilizing native fruits that grow uncultivated, such as roselle, persimmon, muscadine, crabapple, and papaw.

When the Great Depression left the national economy in a shambles, the architects of the New Deal encouraged Americans to provide for their own needs. During this era, the Ball Brothers Company, manufacturers of glass jars for preserving and canning, developed a small, efficient canning unit that the Works Progress Administration used to establish community canning centers, helping to defray the labor and expense of canning in individual households with a collective approach. During World War II, subsidized by a number of emergency relief agencies, many more of these centers were established, logical extensions of the "Victory Garden." By 1946 there were 3,600 community canning centers in the United States, most in the South, with a high concentration in the Piedmont region.

After the war, the demand for food, and its price, fell. Almost all the community canning centers outside the South closed, as the nation entered a period of prosperity. Those that remained open in the South, where poverty continued to be a fact of life and the centers still provided an invaluable service, were supported primarily by county governments or school systems.

The consolidation of the canning industry in the 1950s and 1960s closed most small commercial canning and preserving companies in this country as well as all but a handful of community canning centers. Preserves and jellies made by large manufacturers are available today in supermarkets throughout the South at prices most southerners can easily afford. Be that as it may, southerners still make preserves and jellies at home, when the fruit is ripe and the days are hot, preserving the season's bounty for a chillier day, and at the same time preserving the taste and the memory of who they are and where they come from.

ANN CASHION
Washington, D.C.

Mary L. Edgeworth, *The Southern Gardener and Receipt Book* (1859); Stephen Klein, *Community Canning Centers* (1977); Elaine M. McIntosh, *American Food Habits in Historical Perspective* (1995); Lucy Norris and Elizabeth Watt, *Pickled: Vegetables, Fruits, Roots, More—Preserving a World of Tastes* and *Traditions* (2003); Rafia Zafar, *Gastro-nomica* (Fall 2001).

Prudhomme, Paul

(b. 1940) NEW ORLEANS CHEF.
Cajun food and recipes can be found in restaurants and cookbooks from Peoria to Paris, and Paul Prudhomme is credited with taking the food of Acadiana to every corner of the globe. Born 13 July 1940, in the small south Louisiana town of Opelousas, Prudhomme learned the basics of cooking in his mother's kitchen. At the age of 17, he opened his first restaurant, Big Daddy O's Patio, in Opelousas. For a decade he moved from restaurant to restaurant, cooking as far afield as Colorado. His mastery of cooking techniques, cooking concepts, and multileveled layering of flavors propelled his career and earned him the position of executive chef at Commander's Palace restaurant in New Orleans in 1975. Rather than embrace the traditional Creole cuisine of New Orleans or fall back on his Cajun roots, Prudhomme helped create a vibrant new New Orleans cuisine, infused with flavors from other cultures while at the same time building on the best of local ingredients and traditions. His work at Commander's revolutionized the New Orleans restaurant industry and inspired many other New Orleans chefs and restaurants.

In July 1979 Prudhomme and his wife, K. Hinrichs, opened K-Paul's Louisiana Kitchen, in the French Quarter of New Orleans. K-Paul's food quickly became popular, with lines of guests waiting for hours to get a spot

Chef Paul Prudhomme, the most celebrated champion of New Orleans cuisine (Paul Rico, photographer, courtesy Chef Paul Prudhomme's Magic Seasoning Blends)

at one of the restaurant's community dining tables. His most famous dish, blackened redfish, was a filet of Gulf of Mexico redfish, seasoned with herbs and spices, seared in a hot cast-iron skillet until the exterior was nearly black and a crust had formed. With an award-winning restaurant as a launch pad, as well as a pleasant disposition and a desire to share the food of his home, Prudhomme was a natural as the unofficial spokesman for Louisiana food. In an era before name chefs were considered celebrities, he was one. Prudhomme appeared on national television, wrote best-selling cookbooks, starred in instructional cooking videos, and created a line of seasoning blends called Magic Seasoning Blends, which are sold in all 50 states and in 35 foreign countries. (He has, at various times, also claimed to have invented the turducken—a chicken stuffed inside a duck stuffed inside a turkey.) As a result of his efforts, Prudhomme has shared the foods of Acadiana with the rest of America and the world.

Although he has operated New York and San Francisco outposts, Prudhomme today owns only one restaurant, K-Paul's in New Orleans. The menu changes daily and usually features several blackened items, but Prudhomme never forgets his roots. He keeps traditional favorites from Acadiana on the menu for guests who have never had a bowl of chicken-and-sausage gumbo or a side dish of candied sweet potatoes.

SCOTT R. SIMMONS
New Orleans, Louisiana

Brett Anderson, *New Orleans Times-Picayune* (12 June 2005); Paul Prudhomme, *Chef Paul Prudhomme's Fork in the Road: A Different Direction in Cooking* (1993), *Chef Paul Prudhomme's Louisiana Kitchen* (1984), *Chef Paul Prudhomme's Louisiana Tastes: Exciting Flavors from the State That Cooks* (2000), *Chef Paul Prudhomme's Pure Magic* (1995), *Chef Paul Prudhomme's Seasoned America* (1991), *Kitchen Expedition* (1997), *The Prudhomme Family Cookbook: Old-Time Louisiana Recipes by the Eleven Prudhomme Brothers and Sisters and Chef Paul Prudhomme* (1987).

Puddings

While the English term *pudding* has been applied to dishes as varied as meat-based Yorkshire pudding (or the southern delicacy liver pudding, aka liver mush) to any dish served as dessert (as in the British "pudding course"), in the cuisine of the American South, pudding has generally referred to boiled or baked sweet desserts, whose basic ingredients usually include milk or cream, butter, eggs, and sugar. To these ingredients are added fruit, spices, nuts, and other flavorings.

Mary Randolph, in her 1824 cookbook *The Virginia House-wife*, notes that many puddings are baked in a crust; while Annabella P. Hill in her 1872 *Southern Practical Cookery and Recipe Book* argues that true puddings are baked "without crusts . . . usually in deeper vessels . . . served hot and eaten with sauces." Many classic southern pies apparently began as puddings. For example, Randolph's recipe for transparent pudding is, as Karen Hess has pointed out in her commentary on *The Virginia House-wife*, identical to a 1736 published recipe for lemon cheesecake.

Varieties of puddings are as numerous as the ingredients found in southern gardens, orchards, or pantries. Southern recipe collections include peach, lemon meringue, persimmon, sweet potato, arrowroot, plum, almond, curd, cherry, apple, pumpkin, and rice puddings, as well as a cranberry-based "winter's pudding" and a number of puddings with such colorful names as Henrietta pudding (a nutmeg and brandy concoction), Tot Fait (a New Orleans soufflé pudding), "nice boiled pudding," "poor man's pudding," and "The Queen of Puddings." These latter three are versions of bread pudding, possibly the most common and, in certain parts of the South, the most popular type of pudding. Versions of bread pudding range from haute cuisine, such as the Creole bread pudding soufflé served at New Orleans's Commander's Palace, to rather modest fare such as crumb pudding (a pudding made with leftover biscuits) or a soda cracker–based pudding mentioned in Randolph's recipe collection. Bread puddings made with cornbread can also be found in many southern recipe collections, but more common on the tables of early European settlers in the South were variations on the cornmeal-based Indian pudding. While many scholars note that the "Indian" in the name of this dish refers to Indian corn rather than its creators, it is likely that some form of this dish was enjoyed by indigenous Americans before the arrival of Europeans. John Egerton notes in *Southern Food* that "among the Indians themselves the dish was called sagamite, and some colonists, particularly in New England, called it hasty pudding." Egerton notes that while Indian pudding was popular enough in the 1800s to warrant recipes for multiple versions in Randolph's *Virginia House-wife*, by the late 1900s this pudding was rarely found on tables in the South.

One of the most popular puddings in the South and one more commonly associated with southern foodways in general is banana pudding. Bill Neal points out that this dessert is technically a "trifle" rather than a pudding and labels it "rather pedestrian"; however, Egerton names banana pudding his "all-time favorite dessert," a sentiment likely shared by countless other southerners, including Sylvia Woods—known as the Queen of Soul Food—who labels the dish "the queen of puddings." Joe Gray Taylor, in his *Eating, Drinking, and*

Visiting in the South, points out that in the antebellum South, "Bananas were imported into Charleston and New Orleans in great numbers," becoming one of the most popular imported fruits among southerners. Pedestrian or not, the pudding southern cooks created with this tropical fruit combined with vanilla wafers and the basic egg, milk, and sugar mixture of most puddings has delighted generations of southerners across racial, economic, and social lines.

STEPHEN CRISWELL
University of South Carolina Lancaster

John T. Edge, *A Gracious Plenty: Recipes and Recollections from the American South* (1999); John Egerton, *Side Orders: Small Helpings of Southern Cookery and Culture* (1990), *Southern Food: At Home, on the Road, in History* (1993); Annabella P. Hill, *Mrs. Hill's Southern Practical Cookery and Recipe Book* (1872, 1995); Bill Neal, *Biscuits, Spoonbread, and Sweet Potato Pie* (1990); Mary Randolph, *The Virginia House-wife* (1824, 1985); Joe Gray Taylor, *Eating, Drinking, and Visiting in the South: An Informal History* (1982); Sylvia Woods, *Sylvia's Family Soul Food Cookbook* (1999).

Quail

Perhaps no other game bird has been more closely connected with the southern farm environment and culture than the bobwhite quail. Unlike many game species, the bobwhite, *Colinus virginianus*, prospered as the cotton culture spread across the South in the 19th and early 20th centuries. Farm families hunted and trapped the birds for home use and to sell as a regular part of their agricultural production. Quail, known in the South as partridges, "pottiges," or simply birds, became an obsession for natives and for many outsiders who ventured south to hunt them. Former president Jimmy Carter remembered that bobwhites were a topic of great interest in the gathering places of his boyhood home of Plains, Ga., and that there was "no facet of their existence that was not thoroughly analyzed."

The bobwhite retained the aura of a special food in the South even though it became quite common. The wild bird has a delicate, white-fleshed breast with slightly darker legs and in prime condition weighs only about 6 ounces. Bobwhites have a dressed weight of about 3.5 ounces, and one antebellum writer aptly described birds bound for the table as "a great dainty." The tiny birds seem to have always been in demand in the South.

The prolific Memphis writer Nash Buckingham wrote numerous stories involving quail from the 1920s to the 1950s, and one of his more famous hunting tales, "Bobs of the Bayou Bank," began with a demand for quail by his wife, who had promised a meal of them to her bridge club. Memphis bridge matrons and sharecroppers shared an equal enthusiasm for the culinary qualities of quail. As Georgia outdoor writer Charles Elliott wrote of the pursuit of the birds, "Everyone participated, from the gallused country lad with a single-barrel shotgun to the affluent citizen."

In the preparation of quail, the classes in the South had their differences. Alabama author and newspaper editor Johnson J. Hooper in his 1856 hunting manual *Dog and Gun* advised gentlemen hunters to hunt the quail without nets, traps, or resorting to ground shooting, unlike "the commune vulgus who kill him foully and serve him more foully, to wit: in hog's lard." Hooper's objection points to the almost universal practice in southern kitchens of frying skinned quail with a simple coating of salted and peppered flour. Often a brown flour gravy was concocted, and cooks might smother the fried birds or serve biscuits and gravy on the side. This treatment of quail, already ubiquitous before the Civil War, remained such a common ritual that growing up in the 1970s some folks cannot remember eating them any other way until notions of saturated fat caused cooks to experiment with baking.

Hooper's hunting manual was meant to emulate those of the elite Englishmen that he admired, and, like them, he probably preferred his birds plucked and roasted. Upper-class sportsmen have often appropriated the hunting and eating of quail through the written word. None has done better at that in recent years than French-born hunter Guy de la Valdéne, longtime resident of the quail plantation country of north Florida and a man very serious about the preparation of his game birds. He offered some stern critiques on the southern practices of frying quail and grilling them in bacon. His own cooking suggestions include roasting plucked, never skinned, birds with such accompaniments as "shallots, pitted grapes, cherries" or "calf brains" that do not overpower the mild flavor of the quail.

In cookbooks across the South one can find a good many complicated recipes for baked and broiled quail that imply the festive atmosphere a meal of bobwhites can engender. The recipes also reflect the historical commercial importance of quail for restaurants and their typically more complex cooking schemes. The trade in bobwhites at the turn of the 20th century was enormous, with one famous statistic showing around 500,000 birds shipped from Alabama alone in the winter of 1905. By the 1950s, organized statewide game law enforcement had eliminated most outright sales of birds in the Deep South but not commercial demand. With state-issued propagation permits, growers raised quail to supply the restaurant trade and folks who had no inclination to hunt for themselves. Quail growers are scattered across the South today, and the pen-raised bobwhites they provide are one of the few commercially farmed species of southern game.

The hunting and eating of wild quail is still perceived by outsiders and natives alike as a very southern thing. These days, mainly because of habitat changes that favored other game species, the natural population of bobwhites has declined precipitously. In many areas, hunting is nonexistent or carried on with semidomesticated birds. Parts of Texas still contain healthy populations, and remnant coveys are scattered across the Southeast, while there are robust populations in the highly managed and manipulated quail plantations of south

Georgia and north Florida. In the South as a whole, however, the wild quail is almost a memory.

WILEY C. PREWITT JR.
Lodi, Mississippi

Nash Buckingham, *Mark Right!* (1936); Jimmy Carter, *An Outdoor Journal* (1994); Guy de la Valdéne, *For a Handful of Feathers* (1995); Charles Elliott, *Prince of Game Birds: The Bobwhite Quail* (1974); William Elliott, *Carolina Sports by Land and Water Including Incidents of Devil-Fishing, Wild Cat, Deer, and Bear Hunting, Etc.* (1846); Johnson J. Hooper, *Dog and Gun: A Few Loose Chapters on Shooting, among Which Will Be Found Some Anecdotes and Incidents* (1856); Walter Rosene, *The Bobwhite Quail: Its Life and Management* (1969).

Ramos Gin Fizz

The frothy, pearly white cocktail known as the gin fizz was born in New Orleans some time around 1888. That was the year the drink's creator, Henry C. Ramos, came down the Mississippi River from Baton Rouge and bought the Imperial Cabinet saloon at the corner of Gravier and Carondelet streets. There, Ramos began serving his now-fabled libation, made with dry gin, milk or cream, seltzer water, powdered sugar, orange-flower water, lime juice, lemon juice, egg white, and vanilla (although some purists claim vanilla was not an original ingredient). A frequent sight at the Imperial Cabinet was a bartender vigorously blending the gin fizz's ingredients with a cocktail shaker. In 1907 Ramos moved his business to The Stag, a saloon on Gravier Street across from the old St. Charles Hotel. At The Stag the cocktail's popularity grew even more. During the 1915 New Orleans Carnival season, the huge demand for gin fizzes reportedly was keeping The Stag's 35 "shaker boys" busy all the time, and customers had to wait an hour or more to be served. In 1919 the advent of federal Prohibition (banning the sale or production of alcoholic beverages) so angered Ramos that he revealed the recipe for the gin fizz, assuring his brainchild's survival long after Prohibition ended in 1933. Two years later, the resurgence in New Orleans's affection for the cocktail prompted the Roosevelt Hotel (formerly the Grunewald Hotel, now the Fairmont Hotel) to trademark the term *Ramos Gin Fizz*. The Fairmont's bar (paradoxically named for another New Orleans–born drink, the Sazerac) claims to serve the only authentic version of Ramos's creation.

GENE BOURG
New Orleans, Louisiana

Stanley Clisby Arthur, *Famous New Orleans Drinks and How to Mix 'Em* (1937); John F. Mariani, *The Dictionary of American Food and Drink* (1994).

Ramps

In southern Appalachia, the ramp, or wild mountain leek, is both a welcomed sign of spring renewal and a mark of shame. Members of the Eastern Band of the Cherokee Nation remember being sent home from school when teachers detected the scent of ramps on their breath. According to mountain folklore, ramps will keep away a cold, the flu, and the neighbors. They are eaten raw with soup beans, parboiled, or fried in bacon grease. Often they are mixed with scrambled eggs or fried potatoes.

Cherokees have foraged for *Allium tricoccum* for generations. Before refrigeration, ramps were often canned, and Cherokees who remember those days say they smelled through the jar. The vitamin C packed in the leaves and bulbs of ramps provided a much-needed variation in diet. Modern medical science has given credence to the Cherokee belief in the therapeutic properties of ramps. In addition to being rich in vitamins, ramps contain a fatty acid used in the treatment of hypertension, and they are said to be effective in increasing production of high-density lipoproteins, believed to combat heart disease by reducing blood serum levels of cholesterol.

Cherokee folk wisdom teaches that ramps thin and cleanse the blood. In the winter, ramps were used in decoctions to treat coughs and colds, and in the summer, the juice of the strong, warm-weather bulbs was blended into poultices to relieve the pain and itching of bee stings. All those healthful properties are counterbalanced, though, by what Cherokees describe as the natural affinity between ramps and pork fat.

In southwest Virginia, the word *ramp* became a term of derision, used in reference to the Melungeons, persons of mixed African, European, Native American, and Mediterranean ancestry, primarily located in southern Appalachia, particularly northeast Tennessee and southwest Virginia.

Despite its sullied reputation, the ramp has made it into white-tablecloth restaurants such as Blackberry Farm in the Smoky Mountain community of Walland, Tenn., where the chef pickles ramps and uses them as a garnish for salads, freezes the lightly blanched bulbs so that they can be served out of season, makes a pesto from the tops, and prepares a ramp compound butter.

With ramps becoming a gourmet table item, the push is on to cultivate them commercially, but like the independent mountain people who have been picking them for so long, the plants do not lend themselves to easy manipulation. This long-lived perennial takes six to seven years to reproduce by seed, so farmers can't simply plow up fields and sow ramps. Nevertheless, scientists at North Carolina State University are encouraging cultivation of ramps so that native plant populations will be allowed to regenerate and multiply.

The plant is elevation sensitive and thrives in cool, shady areas with damp soil and an abundance of decomposed leaf litter or other organic matter. New leaves emerge in March or April and then die back as the weather gets warmer. Once the leaves have died back, usually in June, a flower stalk emerges. The flower blooms in early summer, and seeds develop in late summer. These seeds eventually fall to the ground and germinate near the mother plant.

While pickling is a common method of preservation, in Graham County, N.C., the Smoky Mountain Native Plants Association extends the shelf life of the ramp by drying it for a product called ramp meal. This combination of ramp and corn originated among 19th-century bear hunters, who mixed dried ramps and cornmeal to make cornbread in their camps. In the fall of 2000

the association took up the cause as a way to help people earn extra money through the growing and selling of native Appalachian plants, to preserve those plants for future generations, and to provide education about native plant species.

Growers and foragers bring newly harvested ramps to a common kitchen where a staff of local workers washes each individual leaf and bulb, dries and processes the ramps, and hand-packages every bag of meal. The product is available in differing strengths. The milder version contains only the green part of the plant. "Real rampy" is a spiked-up combination of green stalk and white bulb for heartier tastes. The cornmeal itself is always the white variety, milled from locally grown heirloom corn.

Many communities in the Appalachian region hold springtime festivals to honor the ramp. As the Cherokee language literally describes them, ramps are "a smelly business but good."

FRED W. SAUCEMAN
East Tennessee State University

Anthony Cavender, *Folk Medicine in Southern Appalachia* (2003); Fred W. Sauceman, in *CrossRoads: A Southern Culture Annual,* ed. Ted Olson (2005).

Randolph, Mary

(1762–1828) AUTHOR OF *THE VIRGINIA HOUSE-WIFE* (1824). Born into the aristocratic and endlessly intermarried Randolph clan, Mary Randolph was Thomas Jefferson's second cousin and his daughter Martha's sister-in-law. She was born in 1762, the daughter of Anne Cary Randolph and Thomas

Mann Randolph, and married her first cousin, David Meade Randolph, in 1782.

Long accustomed to the privilege afforded a First Family of Virginia, the couple apparently enjoyed an elegant home in Richmond that was known for its lavish entertainments. When a series of economic setbacks forced them to sell the house in 1804, Randolph opened a kind of upscale boardinghouse. By all accounts the accommodations and the food were excellent, and Randolph was even reputed to be "the best cook in Virginia"—no mean accomplishment for a woman belonging to a class where most of the cooking would have been done by servants.

After retiring to Washington in 1819, Randolph began to compile a cookbook from her long experience as a housekeeper. Published in 1824 as *The Virginia House-wife* (the hyphen was dropped in later editions), it is believed to be the first printed record of southern cooking. Randolph died four years later, in 1828, and was buried in a family cemetery on the grounds of Arlington House, which later became Arlington National Cemetery.

Mary Randolph's enduring contribution to southern food is incalculable. Her cookbook remained in print for almost half a century, wielding an influence that was felt as far away as Georgia and New Orleans.

DAMON LEE FOWLER
Savannah, Georgia

Karen Hess, *Martha Washington's Booke of Cookery* (1981); Mary Randolph, *The Virginia House-wife* (1824).

Rawlings, Marjorie Kinnan

(1896–1953) FOOD WRITER.

In February 1942 Scribners published Marjorie Kinnan Rawlings's *Cross Creek*, her "autobiography" of the remote hamlet in north Florida that she had learned to call home. This remarkable book cemented her place as one of the finest regional writers to emerge in the 1930s. Moreover, it showed her readers another of her talents, for the longest chapter in the book, "Our Daily Bread," revealed her skills as a cook and entertainer and demonstrated her flair for recounting the delights of dining. Indeed, "Our Daily Bread" proved so popular with readers that Rawlings determined to produce a cookbook that would provide recipes and menus as well as offer accounts of the delectable meals for which she had become justifiably famous among her friends. In August 1942, just six months after the appearance of *Cross Creek*, Scribners published *Cross Creek Cookery*.

Cross Creek Cookery has been called "not a cookbook in the traditional manner, but . . . [rather] a mouth-watering, evocative, and charmingly conversational discussion of cooking at Cross Creek." An examination of "Our Daily Bread" and *Cross Creek Cookery* reveals Rawlings as a regionalist who uses food—its gathering, its preparation, and its ingestion—as a tool to explore the life and customs of her particular region.

Rawlings's life at Cross Creek honed her culinary skills and taught her the finer points of the art of cooking. In "Our Daily Bread" she begins her cook's tour of north Florida with an examina-

Marjorie Kinnan Rawlings at work (Florida State Archives)

tion of the various meanings and guises of bread in Cross Creek country. Her description of local vegetables follows, and such delights as pokeweed, mustard greens, turnip greens, and collard greens are scrutinized. Then Rawlings introduces by turns "Florida fruits" and meats prepared at the Creek—she calls these her "most exotic dishes," and she includes turtles and crabs, blackbirds and limpkins in this category—and a few other dishes that do not fit into any clear classification. The chapter concludes with a long anecdote about Fatty Blake's "doings at Anthony," an event that included the serving of squirrel pilau and Brunswick stew.

The immediate success of *Cross Creek* and especially its chapter "Our Daily Bread" was the impetus for the writing of *Cross Creek Cookery*. Rawlings noted that "eight out of ten letters about Cross Creek ask for a recipe, or pass on a recipe, or speak of suffering over my chat of Cross Creek dishes." Clearly, there was a ready market for a book of recipes based upon "Our Daily Bread." In addition, the conditions prevailing in 1942 created a potential readership for such a book. Rawlings recounts the receipt of letters from American military men in many parts of the world: "Always there was a wistful comment on my talk of food; often a mention of a boyhood kitchen memory."

Cross Creek Cookery begins and ends with anecdotal chapters called "To Our Bodies Good" and "'Better a Dinner of Herbs.'" However, Rawlings prefaces the book with an overview by listing what she calls "Cross Creek Menus." These enticing menus include breakfasts featuring "very small crisp-fried Orange Lake bream" and "kumquat marmalade" and "camp dinners" consisting of "fried fresh-caught Orange Lake fish (bream, perch, or bass), hushpuppies, cole slaw, coffee [and] any dessert any wife has thought to bring along or send, preferably lemon pie." The recipe chapters of the book move in an orderly way from soups, through luncheon dishes, vegetables, and potatoes, rice, and grits, to Florida seafoods, game and meats, and salads. The longest chapter, "Desserts," follows all of these, naturally, and the whole thing is concluded with a look at "Preserves, Jellies and Marmalades."

"Our Daily Bread" and *Cross Creek Cookery* reveal both an imaginative writer and an imaginative cook. That the two were merged as one in the person of Marjorie Kinnan Rawlings is to our benefit. Lovers of good prose, lovers of regional delineations, and lovers of good food continue to rejoice in these two documents and in their creator. Rawlings would be pleased at her continued appeal, for near the end of *Cross Creek Cookery* she tells us that "no greater offense can be given in the rural South than to refuse a meal." Rawlings offers her readers meals for the mind, and no one in his or her right mind will refuse the invitation to partake.

MICHAEL DEAN
University of Mississippi

Sally Morrison, *Cross Creek Kitchens: Seasonal Recipes and Reflections* (1983); Idella Parker with Mary Keating, *Idella: Marjorie Rawlings' "Perfect Maid"* (1992); Marjorie Kinnan Rawlings, *Cross Creek* (1942), *Cross Creek Cookery* (1942).

Red Beans and Rice

Beans and rice are combined in many cultures to form the most elemental of meals. In New Orleans red beans and rice is a meal that has been elevated to a Monday ritual and celebrated as such for generations. The meal is a simple and economical preparation of red kidney beans combined with aromatics, spices, and pork and then simmered until tender and served over a bed of cooked rice. Because red beans require minimal effort and only occasional tending while cooking, people made the dish on Monday, the traditional New Orleans washday. During the all-day process of washing clothes by hand, a cook could put a pot of red beans on to simmer, add a ham bone left over from Sunday dinner for flavor, and, with only occasional stirring, prepare a one-pot meal.

Red beans and rice has a long history in New Orleans. An early recipe for "Red Beans and Rice" (*Haricots Rouge au Riz*) appears in the 1901 edition of *The Picayune's Creole Cook Book* (originally published as *The Picayune*). More than a hundred years earlier, in the late 18th century, the meal was mentioned in local writings. It is possible that the earliest of traders, immigrants, and slaves brought the idea of combining beans and rice to New Orleans by way of the Spanish Caribbean. The essential ingredients of the meal may be basic, but cooks who arrived in New Orleans from many different cultures have had a hand in creating the dish known today. African, French, Native American, and Spanish cooks have used the abundant local flavorings and spices, as well as their own ingenuity and knowledge, to turn this simple dish into a spicy, full-flavored meal.

Although many New Orleanians would agree that red beans and rice is one of the city's most famous and favored dishes, the ingredients and preparation are the subject of heated debate. Nearly every local cookbook and family recipe box includes a recipe for red beans and rice, and each recipe is different. Some people want the consistency of the beans to be souplike, while others prefer it thick and creamy. Some cooks soak the beans overnight before boiling; others do not. Some people prefer sausage over ham hock, while others like red beans cooked only with salt pork, and still others only with pickled pork. Even the bread served with red beans and rice is controversial. Some people like a loaf of hot French bread, others prefer slices of French bread slathered with butter and toasted, and still others want cornbread. After the dish is served, diners can personalize the flavor of a plate of red beans and rice with a dash or two of hot sauce, a splash of vinegar, or even a shake or two of Worcestershire sauce.

No matter how red beans and rice is prepared, it is a beloved food in the Crescent City. Red beans and rice is mentioned in jazz, blues, and hip-hop songs. During Mardi Gras, rather than tossing traditional beads to revelers, some float riders throw coveted strands of plastic red beans and rice. New Orleans's favorite son, Louis Armstrong, signed his letters "Red Beans and Ricely Yours." Its familiar place among the most recognizable of New Orleans foods is understandable. People at any point on the social spectrum can enjoy a plate of red beans and rice at home or at any of the hundreds of local restaurants that serve po' boys and plate lunches.

SCOTT R. SIMMONS
New Orleans, Louisiana

Marcelle Bienvenu, ed., *The Picayune's Creole Cook Book Sesquicentennial Edition* (1987); Rima and Richard Collin, *New Orleans Cookbook* (1987); John Egerton, *Southern Food: At Home, on the Road, in History* (1987); Jeff Hannusch, *New Orleans* (March 1984); Sharon Tyler Herbst, *The New Food Lovers Companion* (2nd edition, 1995).

Restaurants, Atlanta

Atlanta, W. E. B. Du Bois wrote, is "south of the North, yet north of the South." Du Bois was not referring to food, of course, but his words could apply. The Deep South's largest metropolis attracts so many residents from outside the region that its taste buds do not know which way to turn. In 21st-century Atlanta, good bagels are as easy to find as good biscuits.

The city's size and vitality have engendered one of the South's finest dining scenes. In the years before and after the 1996 Olympics came to town, Atlanta erupted in restaurants as dining out became one of its favorite pastimes. At one point, two of the South's four Mobil five-star restaurants were within a mile of each other in the Buckhead neighborhood.

Other than geography, most of

the city's newer restaurants have little in common with traditional southern food. When the *Atlanta Journal-Constitution* named the city's top 50 dining establishments in 2005, only six could be said to feature the region's cookery prominently.

One of the best-known chefs in Atlanta personifies local attitudes. Scott Peacock, from Alabama, celebrated the South's culinary heritage in his cookbook collaboration with the late Edna Lewis. The spirit lives on in his restaurant, Watershed, where buttermilk fried chicken is one of the main draws. Guenter Seeger, on the other hand, who closed his heralded namesake restaurant in 2006, brought an uncompromising drive for quality from Germany. While he used many of the indigenous ingredients, he was no fan of southern cooking. "Fried chicken?" he once said. "I don't get anything out of it."

Even before the most recent boom times, Atlanta sometimes abjured its native victuals, as one of Thomas Jefferson's critics said of him. In the 1970s, Calvin Trillin poked fun at the tendency of boosters in places like Atlanta to steer visitors to revolving restaurants in the sky with overpriced continental menus. When a friend returned from Atlanta having dined at such a place, Trillin lamented that no one had told her about the more authentic pleasure of cornbread and pot likker at Mary Mac's Tea Room.

Fortunately, such traditional cooking thrives in cafés and meat-and-threes across the Atlanta area—at standbys like Thelma's, the Colonnade, and Son's Place. The native fare may seem a little harder to find in the forest of taquerias and Thai noodle shops, but it is still there.

Truth be told, Atlanta's greatest contributions to everyday dining can be found out in that sprawl. Two of the most successful fast-food chains in America, Waffle House and Chick-fil-A, originated in the Atlanta suburbs after World War II. And one of their roadside precursors stands as perhaps the city's most beloved eatery: the Varsity, an art deco landmark near the Georgia Tech campus that has been slinging chili dogs and onion rings since 1928. In a city of cars and long commutes, it is only fitting that the fondest memories would twine around a place that bills itself as the world's largest drive-in.

JIM AUCHMUTEY
Atlanta Journal-Constitution

Jim Auchmutey, *Atlanta Journal-Constitution* (22 November 1998); Meredith Ford, Fall Dining Guide, *Atlanta Journal-Constitution* (6 October 2005); John Kessler, *Atlanta Journal-Constitution* (5 February 2006); Calvin Trillin, *American Fried* (1974).

Restaurants, Charleston

Among Charleston's landed classes in the 18th century, dining outside the home was almost exclusively a social affair. In a colonial trading port still in the thrall of the British aristocracy, a wide variety of social clubs—organized around cultural, ethnic, and sporting affiliations (horse racing and Madeira wine collecting were among the most popular)—dominated city recreational life and created the only real opportunities to dine in public.

Early in the 19th century proto-restaurants developed within the city's taverns, a few of which began to offer a free dish or small meal, largely as an enticement to potential drinkers. Tavern or pub fare would account for the majority of restaurant meals for the next century and a half. Although the category *restaurant* begins to appear in city directories in the mid-19th century, poverty was the defining feature of Charleston's post–Civil War culinary landscape, and dining out was not customary. The single afternoon meal, cooked at home, prevailed in Charleston up until the post–World War II era, when more than a few Charleston families still took time out of the work day to convene for a mid-afternoon dinner.

The à la carte restaurant, where the diner is able to choose from a range of dishes, emerged from the example of the French brasserie in the mid to late 19th century, as the growing steamship trade brought a wave of new hotels and new influences (as well as tourists) to Charleston, as it had to New Orleans a little earlier. City directories record exponential growth in the number of restaurants listed in the first half of the 20th century. As in other cities of the East Coast, the local produce of the Charleston area was shoehorned into a dominant French idiom, while the food served in homes remained remarkably regional and distinct.

With the emergence of fast-food chains and after a decade of increasing prosperity in the 1980s, Charlestonians began to warm to the concept of dining out. Restaurants sprung up to meet the demand and to serve an ever-increasing flow of tourists visiting the city. In the early 1990s restaurants like Magnolia's, on East Bay Street, took their inspiration from the city's architectural sophistication and historical richness. The cuisine of Charleston's past was co-opted by a more eclectic modern restaurant idiom that began to spread from other cities around the country. Shrimp and grits, a classic Lowcountry dish, became postmodern—tweaked with cream and seasoned with nonnative ingredients like French shallots and tasso ham. Over the course of the decade, improvements in the speed of refrigerated transport brought ever more exotic ingredients, like passion fruit from Hawaii and fresh foie gras from New York, to the region. Chefs at restaurants like Charleston Grill and McCrady's, in the later 1990s, attempted to fuse the techniques of an even more esoteric global cuisine (influenced by French and Spanish chefs) with the ingredients and icons of Lowcountry cuisine, resulting in dishes like caramelized fig-stuffed hush puppy with cabernet-braised pig's feet and olive oil-poached game hen with foie gras foam.

MATT LEE
TED LEE
Charleston, South Carolina

John Egerton, *Southern Food: At Home, on the Road, in History* (1987); Jane Kronsberg, *Charleston: People, Places, and Food* (1997); Margaret Moore, *Complete Charleston: A Guide to the Architecture, History, Gardens and Food of Charleston and the Low Country* (2005); Jane Stern, *Cooking in the Lowcountry from the Old Post Office Restaurant: Spanish Moss, Warm Carolina Nights, and Fabulous Southern Food* (2004); John Martin Taylor, *Hoppin' John's Lowcountry Cooking* (2000); Marvin Woods, *The*

New Low-Country Cooking: 125 Recipes for
Coastal Southern Cooking with Innovative
Style (2000).

Restaurants, Nashville

Granny White Pike, a well-traveled
road in Nashville, is named for Lucinda
"Granny" White, whose early 1800s inn
and tavern was a popular stopover on
the stagecoach route south. It is a fitting
symbol for Nashville's restaurant history,
which is distinguished by hospitality
and straightforward home cooking.
Nashville's largely Protestant population
of European and African descent and its
multifaceted identity as the Tennessee
state capital, a center of commerce, and
the home of country music inform its
restaurant history.

Nashville's downtown hotels have accommodated much of the meeting and
eating of locals and visitors for the past
200-plus years. The Talbot and St. Cloud
in the early 1800s and later the Duncan, Tulane, Andrew Jackson, and Noel
hotels served as the homes away from
home for state politicians, city fathers,
and businessmen. Catering to a mostly
middle-class, white, male clientele, they
typically offered basic accommodations
and hearty meat-and-potatoes fare.

The opening of the elegant Maxwell
House Hotel just after the Civil War and
the Hermitage Hotel shortly after the
beginning of the 20th century added
new elegance to the hotel mix, appealing
to a population eager for a more refined
culture. Banquets and entertaining were
no longer proprietary to the aristocratic
plantations. Those who could afford to
celebrated special occasions and holidays at the swank hotels serving enormous feasts including every possible
meat and game, oysters from the Gulf,
and plenty of sweets.

The lasting restaurant recipes
claimed by Nashville are simple concoctions replicated on menus even
today. In the late 1800s restaurateur
Xavier Faucon created the delicious
Faucon salad of iceberg lettuce with
blue cheese dressing, hard-cooked egg,
and crumbled bacon still on a handful
of restaurant menus. Kleeman's, widely
regarded as the best place in town to eat
in the early 20th century, served sliced
chicken on egg bread and apple pie à
la mode. Satsuma Tea Room, Varallo's,
Cross Keys, and other downtown restaurants emerged before World War II
and continued into the late decades of
the century.

By the 1920s Nashville's famous plate
lunch, the meat-and-three (a meat with
three side dishes), made its appearance.
Professional men working in town
were moving their families further out
in the suburbs; no longer able to go
home for midday dinner, they dined on
hearty plate lunches in unpretentious
surroundings. Hap Townes took over a
20-year-old restaurant business from his
father in 1946 and ran it until the late
1980s, serving cafeteria-style lunches to
patrons from all walks of life. Arnold's
Country Kitchen, Swett's, Sylvan Park,
Silver Sands, Wendell Smith, the Knife
and Fork, and numerous other popular
cafés continue turning out home-style
offerings like fried chicken, pork chops,
collard greens, black-eyed peas, cornbread, iced sweet tea, and sweet confections.

Local temperance laws kept mixed

drinks out of restaurants until 1967, but private men's clubs flourished. Many were civic in nature, representing various causes and groups, but always combining good eating and drinking with their stated purpose. Others were purely social. The 216 Club opened its doors in 1934, offering personal whiskey bottle storage and manly steakhouse cuisine to city leaders and businessmen. A short drive into North Nashville, Al Alessio's notorious Automobile Business Club nourished gamblers with hearty simple food, including a rich Roquefort salad dressing and Philadelphia pepper pot in midcentury. Jimmy Kelly's later opened in the fashionable Belle Meade neighborhood, continuing Nashville's clubby camaraderie among young socialites, couples, and families. Now in its third location, Jimmy Kelly's still serves hot corn cakes to patrons before their steaks arrive.

Tea rooms were, in the early 20th century, the acceptable restaurant venue for women to own, operate, and patronize. Satsuma, opened in 1918 by two home economists, continues to provide a daintified version of the plate lunch to a downtown lunch crowd. Hetty Ray's Tea Room offered smothered chicken, frozen fruit salads, and fancy parfaits in an elegant, serene atmosphere deemed appropriate for women.

Until segregation in public places was outlawed by the Civil Rights Act of 1964, African Americans were barred from eating in all Nashville restaurants and hotels that were not black-owned. African American men, nevertheless, worked out front as the white-gloved waiters in the dining rooms of private clubs, country clubs, hotels, restaurants, steamboats, and trains. And they were in the kitchens stirring pots and washing dishes. Barbecue joints were the only eating establishments owned and operated by African Americans patronized by the white community. A few plate lunch restaurants, like Swett's, open since 1954, offered neighborhood dining. Lunch counter sit-ins in downtown Nashville in the early 1960s helped bring about needed change. Today, African American chefs and proprietors like the Swett family lead the way in many Nashville restaurant kitchens.

Nashville shoppers enjoyed the new eateries in fashionable downtown department stores in the mid-20th century. The Cain-Sloan Iris Room fed a steady clientele of ladies light lunches as lovely models paraded through dressed in the latest fashions. The basement lunch counter of Fred Harvey's circus-themed department store, complete with carousel horses, served sliced chicken sandwiches and homemade apple pie reminiscent of Kleeman's.

Breakfast became an eat-out occasion for city dwellers at lunch counters and along well-worn highways. The most famous of the bunch, the Loveless Cafe, open since 1951, serves country breakfasts complete with secret-recipe skillet baked biscuits, homemade preserves, grits, and fried country ham and eggs to a never-ending hungry crowd.

Nashville has produced a remarkable number of chain restaurants characterized by unpretentious everyday cooking and plenty of it. Most notably, Shoney's made it big with the successful all-you-can-eat breakfast bar and boosted the salad bar craze. And, since its first store opened outside Nashville in 1979, the Cracker Barrel Old Country Store has become a familiar site along interstates in the South and Midwest—a 21st-century throwback to Granny White's home-cooked stopover for weary travelers.

MINDY MERRELL
Nashville, Tennessee

John Egerton and E. Thomas Wood, eds., *Nashville: An American Self-Portrait* (2005); Jane Stern and Michael Stern, *Roadfood* (2005), *Southern Country Cooking from the Loveless Cafe: Fried Chicken, Hams, and Jams from Nashville's Favorite Cafe* (2005).

Restaurants, New Orleans

New Orleans is arguably the most famous food center in the South. Blessed with a richness of natural resources—seafood from the Gulf, the bayous, the Mississippi River, and Lake Pontchartrain; rich soil for crops; and an abundance of wild game from swamps and woods—residents drew not only upon Louisiana's French (both Creole and Cajun) heritage but also upon Italian, German, Native American, and African cultures to create a distinctive cuisine. New Orleanians, it has been said, live to eat, and during the typical meal, diners often talk about what they ate yesterday and where and what they will eat tomorrow. Most meals are also complemented by a variety of alcohol, including several local concoctions such as the Sazerac and the Ramos gin fizz.

Throughout the 19th and 20th centuries, writers—not just of travel and dining guides, but also of novels, plays, and poetry—praised the unique virtues of the city's multilayered cuisine. As early as the 1850s, William Makepeace Thackeray was extolling the greatness of the food and drink in New Orleans, which he commended as the one city where "you can eat and drink the most and suffer the least." Because New Orleans was long hidebound with residents resisting change and, in many instances, professing to be blissfully unaware of goings-on in the rest of the country, the cuisine stayed very much the same. Only in the 1970s did noticeable change occur, with the advent of the first celebrity chefs—Paul Prudhomme, followed by others such as Emeril Lagasse and Susan Spicer—and the introduction of new cooking styles, as exemplified, for example, in nouvelle cuisine. Until that time, the city's restaurants never depended on the star power of any one person to attract diners. The mainstays of the typical Creole restaurant in the old days and, to some extent, even today, were the line cooks, who might be known by regular diners but received no publicity and little acknowledgment. Many of these cooks were black, and through the years several African American restaurants—Chez Helene and Dooky Chase, for example—took their place as noteworthy dining establishments.

By the time of the Louisiana Purchase in 1803, New Orleans was the site of coffeehouses and cafés where men gathered to drink and dine and discuss commerce and politics. Early eateries included the Café des Réfugiés, founded in 1791 as a gathering place for French settlers ousted from the West Indies by slave rebellions. The 1800s and early

1900s saw a flurry of restaurant development in a city already devoted to dining, either in the home or at some eatery. Antoine's was founded in 1840, Madame Begue's in 1863, Maylie's in 1876, Commander's Palace in 1880, Victor's in the late 1800s, Galatoire's in 1905, and Arnaud's in 1918. French and Creole cuisine dominated in these establishments, and each added its own distinct contribution to the cuisine of the city. Antoine's, for example, the first formal restaurant in New Orleans, was responsible for many new dishes, including oysters Rockefeller and *Pompano en Papillote*; Madame Begue introduced the *petit dejeuner*, which ultimately evolved into what we now know as brunch; Maylie's was noted for such dishes as *bouilli* (boiled beef) and the table d'hôte meal in which a set menu of several courses was routinely served to customers; and Galatoire's became the ultimate French bistro in America's most French city. However, a mainstay of the New Orleans food scene was, and to some degree continues to be, the neighborhood po' boy sandwich shop or seafood joint.

New Orleans is a city of culinary dynasties, with restaurants that have been in the same families for generations. Antoine's, one of the oldest dining establishments in the country, was founded by Antoine Alciatore and is now being managed by members of the fifth generation of his family. Galatoire's celebrated its centennial year in 2005, and four generations of that family have been active in its operation. Although Brennan's was a latecomer to the local restaurant scene, not founded until

1946, three generations have now been involved in the management of the many branches of that dynastic culinary empire.

Despite the inroads made by new young chefs, intent on introducing innovations such as nouvelle cuisine and dishes lower in fat, New Orleanians remain, for the most part, committed to the food of the past, whether it is found in fine restaurants, in neighborhood cafés, or in their own homes.

Hurricane Katrina, in August 2005, devastated New Orleans restaurants. Although the French Quarter was less damaged than most of the city, many famous restaurants there were affected. Antoine's, for example, employed a staff of 130 before Katrina, including chefs, waiters, wine stewards, bus boys, and dishwashers, and after the storm they scattered to an estimated 14 states. Many of the unskilled workers and others who had long worked for Antoine's lived in the totally flooded Lower Ninth Ward and East New Orleans, and they had no housing, poor health care, and few schools for their children in the aftermath of the storm, making returning there difficult to consider even months afterward. Antoine's also suffered from the inability of restaurant suppliers to stock their kitchen and of available contractors to do repairs. Hundreds of pounds of steaks and seafood spoiled, decomposing in freezers without electricity. As of November 2005, only 18 percent of the city's 3,700 pre-Katrina restaurants had reopened, according to the Louisiana Restaurant Association. Seafood was always a featured attraction of New Orleans restaurants, and devastation to oyster and shrimp beds made it difficult to provide adequate supplies.

By May 2006 the pre-Katrina restaurant work force of 133,000 had been reduced to 22,000, and only half of the city's restaurants had reopened. Many of these were neighborhood restaurants, those po' boy sandwich counters and local Creole restaurants that were as important to the city's food culture as its white-tablecloth establishments. One example was Willie Mae's Scotch House, in the Treme neighborhood, which is also home to another famous Creole place, Dooky Chase. Willie Mae Seaton has run the Scotch House for a half century. It is a double shotgun house that is her home and a 30-seat restaurant with a small bar that once served her famous cocktail of scotch and milk. The Southern Foodways Alliance spearheaded an effort, beginning in January 2006, to bring volunteer work crews for weekend work parties repairing Willie Mae's house and restaurant, and many other volunteers have worked to assist repair of favorite neighborhood cafés and to help restaurant workers in need of finding new jobs. On the bright side, such fine new restaurants as Cochon and Longbranch opened in the months after Hurricane Katrina.

W. KENNETH HOLDITCH
New Orleans, Louisiana

R. W. Apple Jr., *New York Times* (31 May 2006); Pip Brennan, Jimmy Brennan, and Ted Brennan, *Breakfast at Brennan's and Dinner, Too* (1994); Marda Burton and Kenneth Holditch, *Galatoire's: Biography of a Bistro* (2004); Walter Cowan, Charles L. Dufour, and O. K. LeBlanc, *New Orleans: Yesterday, Today, and Tomorrow* (2001); John Egerton, *Southern Food: At Home, on the Road, in History* (1987); Lyle Saxon and Edward P. Dreyer, eds., *The WPA Guide to New Orleans* (1983); Kim Severson, *New York Times* (11 January 2006); William Makepeace Thackeray, *The Roundabout Papers* (1862).

Rice

As a tropical plant, rice had no position in the traditional cuisine of English settlers when they first came to the South. This situation continued for more than three centuries over most of the region. Two places were different, however: southern Louisiana and the Lowcountry of South Carolina and Georgia. Wheat, the familiar European cereal grain, did not thrive in these coastal plains. In the 1680s, therefore, when some seed rice came to Charleston by chance, people were receptive to a new way of farming and eating. The key to both processes was the presence of a large slave population from the Senegalese coast of West Africa. Rice culture was part of the heritage of that region. With the men's knowledge of canals and dikes, and the women's of seed selection, sowing, and processing, the new grain quickly established itself as a local staple. The distinguished food writer Raymond Sokolov has gone so far as to label the cuisine there "rizocentric," and many observers have noted the presence of a massive, silver rice spoon (about 15 inches long) on formal dinner tables.

In southern Louisiana, the second center of consumption, the history of the grain is unclear. African influences seem certain there as well, but perhaps

Aged woman near Crowley, La., using a
crude mortar and pestle to hull rice, 1938
(Russell Lee, photographer, Library of Congress
[LC-USF34-031664-D], Washington, D.C.)

through Caribbean intermediaries.
Rice is also a long-standing part of
Spanish culture. Traditional rice dishes
in Charleston include both red (with
tomato sauce) and green (with parsley, green peppers, and green onions)
rice, plus a large variety of pilafs (or
pilaus) where the grain serves as a bed
for native shellfish. Hoppin' John, the
simple blend of black-eyed peas and
rice now served every New Year's Day
throughout the South, also has its roots
in South Carolina. The list of rice dishes
in Cajun and Creole culture is similarly
large. It includes dirty rice (with chicken
gizzards and livers), jambalaya, red
beans and rice, and the New Orleans
breakfast confection called *calas*.

In 1956 each resident of Louisiana
and South Carolina ate an average of

36 and 26 pounds of rice, respectively.
These numbers were far above the national average of less than five pounds
per capita. In mainstream America,
including most of the South, people
lacked the assurance of cooking and
using rice found in the two older centers. They did not so much dislike the
food, according to surveys, but avoided
it simply because potatoes and other
starch sources were entrenched eating
habits. When pressed for details, non-
consumers said that rice was too much
trouble to prepare, starchy and fattening, tasteless, and Chinese. This set of
beliefs was the challenge faced by the
Rice Council, a nonprofit promotional
organization, when it was founded in
1959. Farmers in Arkansas, Louisiana,
Mississippi, and Texas had become
major producers of the crop by this time
and wanted to sell more of their output
domestically.

The council's initial advertising
campaigns stressed the versatility of rice
together with the ease of preparing its
so-called instant, or precooked, version. Then, in the late 1960s and 1970s
the council shifted to more aggressive
tactics. They first portrayed rice as chic
and nonfattening in comparison with
potatoes and followed this message by
photographs of sophisticated, youth-
ful people eating the food at exclusive
restaurants in Charleston and New
Orleans. Another campaign emphasized
rice as a health food—a good source of
protein, nonallergenic, easily digestible,
and low in both fat and sodium. These
varied efforts paid off, because national
rates for the grain's consumption rose to

eight pounds per capita by 1980 and to an amazing 26 pounds by 1998. All the success should not be credited to the Rice Council, however. Some studies have associated the eating of rice with an alternative, arcadian lifestyle that began to flourish in California and elsewhere in the 1970s. The grain certainly is common in the nouvelle cuisine that emerged at that time, with its stress on local foods and simple methods of preparation. Increases in rice consumption also are related to the greater presence of Asian and Hispanic populations in the country, to the concurrent popularity of ethnic restaurants, and to a heightened general concern with lowering cholesterol and eating healthier fare.

BARBARA G. SHORTRIDGE
University of Kansas

Judith A. Carney, *Black Rice: The African Origins of Rice Cultivation in the Americas* (2001); Henry C. Dethloff, *A History of the American Rice Industry, 1685–1985* (1988); John D. Folse, *The Evolution of Cajun and Creole Cuisine* (1989); Karen Hess, *The Carolina Rice Kitchen: The African Connection* (1992); David Littlefield, *Rice and Slaves: Ethnicity and the Slave Trade in Colonial South Carolina* (1981); James R. Shortridge and Barbara G. Shortridge, *Geographical Review* (October 1983); C. Wayne Smith and Robert H. Dilday, eds., *Rice: Origins, History, Technology, and Production* (2003); Raymond Sokolov, *Natural History* (February 1993).

Rice, Red

Sometimes called Savannah red rice, red rice is a pilau of long-grained rice simmered with tomatoes and seasoned broth until fluffy and dry. Originating in the rice-growing regions of the Georgia and South Carolina Lowcountry, it probably derives from the West African cookery introduced by slaves on the region's rice-growing plantations.

The names *red rice* and *Savannah red rice* appear to be modern. Annabella Hill (*Mrs. Hill's New Cook Book*, 1867) gives one of the earliest recorded recipes, calling it tomato pilau. It was also known as mulatto rice in Savannah (*The Savannah Cook Book*, Harriet Ross Colquitt, 1933) supposedly because its color resembles the skin tone of persons of mixed African, white, and Native American blood, although local historians claim that this was a confusion with a similar Geechee dish from Georgia's barrier islands.

Classic red rice is made by simmering long-grained rice with tomatoes and broth. The rice is sometimes sauteed briefly in fat to help ensure the dry, separate grains of a classic pilau. Some cooks bake the rice in a covered casserole. Some modern recipes do not follow the classic pilau technique: cooked or partially cooked rice is blended with tomato juice, bacon, and seasonings and baked in a covered casserole.

DAMON LEE FOWLER
Savannah, Georgia

John Egerton, *Southern Food: At Home, on the Road, in History* (1987); Karen Hess, *The Carolina Rice Kitchen: The African Connection* (1992); David Littlefield, *Rice and Slaves: Ethnicity and the Slave Trade in Colonial South Carolina* (1981); C. Wayne Smith and Robert H. Dilday, eds., *Rice: Origins, History, Technology, and Production* (2003).

Roux

Roux is a thickening agent traditionally made of equal portions of flour and fat (butter, oil, etc.) mixed and browned over a low fire. In Louisiana, roux production constitutes the first step in the preparation of several quintessential Cajun and Creole dishes, including gumbo, sauce piquante, and fricassée.

Pierre de Lune, a French royal chef, codified roux in the 14th century, and, by the 17th century, the thickening agent had become an integral part of classical French cuisine. French settlers brought the tradition to Louisiana. However, because wheat would not mature in lower Louisiana's semitropical climate, and because flour had to be imported at great expense, roux usage was reserved for special occasions. Like flour, butter was scarce and expensive in colonial Louisiana. As a consequence, colonial era cooks frequently substituted bear oil for butter. Although the documentary record sheds little light on the culinary fare enjoyed by colonial Louisianans in the New Orleans area, it appears that roux was utilized there in the production of gumbo and bisque by the early 19th century.

Roux usage gradually spread to the predominantly Acadian/Cajun settlements in rural southern Louisiana. Although predispersal Acadians produced large quantities of wheat in Nova Scotia, roux does not appear to have figured prominently in their culinary tradition—if at all. High freight charges levied by steamboats and flatboats made flour approximately twice as expensive in the Cajun parishes as in New Orleans. Cajun cooks consequently do not appear to have incorporated roux into their culinary repertoire until the late 19th or early 20th centuries, when improved transportation connections with New Orleans made flour more readily available and affordable.

Even after their adoption by Cajun and Creole cooks, roux-based foods have remained specialty dishes in the rural areas of French Louisiana. Roux production is quite labor intensive, requiring between 30 and 45 minutes to complete the browning process. Farm wives could not spare the time or the energy for roux production in their busy workweeks. Before the dawn of air-conditioning, cooks were obliged to stir the roux mixture continuously in sweltering kitchens. Hence, roux-based dishes were reserved for special occasions, particularly large family gatherings. Although much has changed in recent decades, Cajun and Creole cooks still have difficulty finding sufficient time in their busy schedules to prepare roux. Many south Louisianans consequently buy commercially prepared roux distributed by several local vendors. A variety of roux mixtures can be purchased at virtually every major French Louisiana supermarket.

This variety of commercial roux flavors reflects notable differences in subregional culinary traditions and individual tastes. Classical French cuisine, which emphasizes the use of butter, recognizes three roux types: white, blond, and brown. Cajun and Creole cooks substitute oil for butter, oil having a higher heat tolerance, resulting in potentially longer cooking times and darker roux. Darker roux provides a more robust flavor, more compatible with local tastes and ingredients.

RYAN A. BRASSEAUX

CARL A. BRASSEAUX

Lafayette, Louisiana

Mme. Bégué's Recipes of Old New Orleans Creole Cookery, (1900); Pip Brennan, Jimmy Brennan, and Ted Brennan, *Breakfast at Brennan's and Dinner, Too* (1994); Rima and Richard Collin, *The New Orleans Cookbook* (1987); Walter Cowan, Charles L. Dufour, and O. K. LeBlanc, *New Orleans: Yesterday, Today, and Tomorrow* (2001); John Egerton, *Southern Food: At Home, on the Road, in History* (1987); Peter S. Feibleman, *American Cooking: Creole and Acadian* (1971); Leon Galatoire, *Leon Galatoire's Cookbook* (1995); Lafcadio Hearn, *Lafcadio Hearn's Creole Cook Book* (reprint edition, 1990); *The Picayune Creole Cook Book* (1922).

Rum

In *The Westover Manuscripts: Containing the History of the Dividing Line Betwixt Virginia and North Carolina,* prominent Virginia planter and American colonial writer William Byrd (1674–1744) captures the conflicting feelings associated with rum since its inception in the New World. He claims that rum, "like gin in Great Britain, breaks the constitutions, vitiates the morals, and ruins the industry of most of the poor people of this country," meaning colonial Norfolk, Va. Yet Byrd goes on to say that "never was rum, that cordial of life, found more necessary than it was" when explorers slogged through the Dismal Swamp. "It did not only recruit the people's spirits, now almost jaded with fatigue, but it served to correct the badness of the water, and at the same time to resist the malignity of the air." Rum has been the notorious currency of the transatlantic slave trade, the demise of many American Indian tribes, a prize over which buccaneers and bootleggers alike battled, and a beverage that sparked wars and paved the road to Prohibition.

What exactly is rum? It can be made from molasses, cane syrup, or fresh cane juice that is fermented and distilled into an alcoholic liquor. It is traditionally aged in oak barrels for a period of time that varies depending on the type or style. Once known as "liquid gold," rum is the most lucrative by-product of the sugar industry.

Sugarcane cuttings arrived in the Americas on Christopher Columbus's second voyage in 1493. These initial transplants in Cuba and Hispaniola grew to be the dominant cash crop and central economic engine throughout the Caribbean "Sugar Islands" and parts of Central and South America, notably Brazil. The bulk of the actual sugar produced was exported to satisfy Europe's growing sweet tooth, and demand surged in the mid 1700s. Most of the West Indian molasses was exported to New England distilleries, where it was converted to rum.

Early American rum was not only an important trading medium domestically; it was also America's leading export well into the early 19th century. It was traded with American Indians for goods and land, ultimately facilitating the weakening of these indigenous cultures. In what came to be known as the infamous "triangle trade," ships would depart North American harbors loaded with barrels of rum to be sold in England and throughout Europe and exchanged for goods and human cargo from the west coast of Africa destined for the Americas. Sugar, molasses, and some island rum then became the main cargo leaving the Caribbean and South American ports headed back to North America, Europe, or Africa to repeat the cycle. It is estimated that more than half of the millions of captive Africans transported to the New World were sent to the West Indies to work the massive sugar plantations there. A constant stream of slaves was deemed necessary since death rates in the grueling and dangerous sugarcane fields were so high. While slave labor was used to produce nearly all of the agricultural commodities grown in the New World, it was primarily sugar and rum that fueled the transatlantic slave trade that endured for nearly four centuries.

Rum was the most popular distilled beverage during the colonial era, when alcohol consumption was rampant, often owing to a scarcity of clean water. Rum eventually became more popular than beer and hard cider, both of which were also consumed by men and women of all walks and ages in colonial America.

Rum fueled the growth of centralized, licensed taverns, which became the seats of social and political life in pre-Revolutionary America. Most of the colonial rum imbibed was produced in northern distilleries, but in many of the southern taverns, Caribbean rum, which came in through Charleston ports, was also prominent. Tavern goers drank rum straight, diluted it with water, and combined it in concoctions called *flip*, *sling*, *swizzle*, *hot toddy*, *rum punch*, and *grog*—a daily ration of which was served on British and American naval ships well into the 20th century.

Rum's nautical associations flow even further back, in fact. Barrels of rum were associated with pirates and other swashbucklers sailing the high seas throughout the 17th and 18th centuries. During periods of heavy maritime activity, more than a thousand ships carrying rum might be traversing the Atlantic at any time. "Rum-running" brought easy wealth for legitimate shipping companies and privateers, as well as those engaged in pure piracy.

In many ways, rum was the first American product that colonists, from North to South, coastal or inland, could call their own; in a sense it was a symbol of economic independence from England. This led to wars. As the British began to slap duties and taxes on molasses imported into American colonies from non-British territories (the Molasses Act of 1733 and the Sugar Act of 1764), colonial unrest ensued and culminated in the Revolutionary War as well as the subsequent War of 1812. The latter led to the demise of the early U.S. rum industry and gave rise to spirits made from locally grown grains like whiskey and bourbon. Nonetheless, rum was often the synonym for all alcohol throughout Prohibition (1919–33). State- and county-run "rum rooms" were designated to hold any type of alcohol seized by the government from bootleggers, and terminology like "demon rum" and "rum riots" were applied to all hard liquor and related unrest. Ironically, after World War II, rum—mixed with that most American of beverages, Coca-Cola—would become extremely popular after the Andrews Sisters recorded the hit song "Rum and Coca-Cola" (1944).

Today the vast majority of commercial rum is produced in the Caribbean. Nearly 80 percent of rum consumed in the United States is from Puerto Rico, the largest exporter and primary base for Bacardi, the world's biggest rum producer. There are many contemporary varieties and styles of rum. Rum is typically described as white (clear, colorless), light, silver, gold, dark, heavy, or black referring to its color or weight. Terms like *overproof* (151 proof or full strength), *premium distilled, aged* or *añejo* (Castillian for aged), *single mark, select, reserve, rare,* and *Demerara* are often used to describe rum's alcohol content, age, quality level, or geographic origin. Rum can be made as a white spirit, like vodka or gin, or as a brown spirit, like brandy or scotch; this versatility makes it a top-selling distilled spirit around the globe.

In the United States, outside of Hawaii, commercial sugarcane crops are grown exclusively in the South: Florida, Louisiana, and Texas, where the climates are hospitable to growing the semitropical reed. Mainland, southern artisanal rum makers include Prichard's Distillery in Kelso, Tenn., and Celebration Distillation, makers of Cane Rum in New Orleans, La.

Some well-loved modern rum drinks are the blue whale, daiquiri, mai tai, piña colada, rum punch, yellow bird, and zombie. Southern staples include the touristy "hurricane" out of New Orleans and a plethora of planter's punch recipes throughout the South, similar to plantation rum drinks from the West Indies.

Rum found its way from Caribbean sugar plantations into southern food culture, particularly Lowcountry cuisine, being added to main dishes and many fruit-based desserts. Bananas Foster, essentially sliced bananas sautéed in rum, is perhaps the most well-known fruit-based rum dessert, created in 1951 at Brennan's Restaurant in New Orleans. In some areas of the American South, as in other places in the African diaspora, rum extends beyond consumption and is also used as a sacramental offering in the voodoo religion.

TONYA HOPKINS
Brooklyn, New York

Julie Arkell, *Classic Rum* (1999); Hugh Barty-King and Anton Massel, *Rum Yesterday and Today* (1983); Charles A. Coulombe, *Rum: The Epic Story of the Drink that Conquered the World* (2004); John J. McCusker, *Rum and the American Revolution: The Rum Trade and the Balance of Payments of the Thirteen Continental Colonies* (1989); James E. McWilliams, *A Revolution in Eating: How the Quest for Food Shaped America* (2005); Susan Waggoner and Robert Markel, *Vintage Cocktails: Authentic Recipes and Illustrations from 1920–1960* (1999).

Sanders, Colonel Harland

(1890–1980) BUSINESSMAN.
To people all over the world the words "It's finger lickin' good" evoke the image of a quintessential southerner, the Kentucky colonel, personified by Harland David Sanders. Neither a native south-

erner nor an army colonel, Sanders built a chicken franchise empire that began in the back room of a filling station in Corbin, Ky., and grew to revenues totaling $3.5 billion by 1986, with 6,500 stores in 56 countries.

Harland David Sanders was born 9 September 1890 in Henryville, Ind., to Wilbert D. and Margaret Ann Sanders. Wilbert D. Sanders died when his son was young, and Sanders left home when he was only 12. He enlisted in the army at 16; then worked on the railroad; and after taking correspondence courses in law, began representing clients in court. What by some accounts was a promising legal career ended with a courtroom incident in which Sanders was charged with assault and battery by his own client.

Sanders began selling—first insurance, then Michelin tires. Realizing that he had a knack for business, Sanders in 1930 bought a Shell Oil service station in Corbin, Ky., on old U.S. Route 25, which went south to Atlanta and east to Asheville. At the foot of the eastern Kentucky mountains, Corbin lay in an area known locally as "Hell's Half Acre." Sanders soon moved his dining room table and six chairs into a storage room and began cooking and serving boardinghouse-style meals for truckers and travelers. He then expanded his operation from Sanders Cafe to Sanders Court, a motel with seven rooms, and began experimenting with pressure cookers and a fried chicken recipe given to him by a neighbor.

By 1949 Sanders had received from Governor Lawrence Wetherby his sec-

ond Kentucky colonel's commission, an honor typically bestowed for outstanding community service or as a political favor. Although Sanders himself said, "It don't mean a daggone thing," when he received the first commission from Governor Ruby Laffoon in 1935, he apparently took the second commission more seriously. He began signing his name "Colonel Harland Sanders," grew a moustache and a goatee, and allowed his nearly white hair to lengthen. Later he added the white suit and string tie to complete the Kentucky colonel image traditionally caricatured in popular films and literature: an aristocratic and chivalrous Dixie gentleman with a fondness for good horses and good bourbon (the Colonel, though, never touched a drop).

By 1950 the Colonel had settled on the cooking method and the 11 herbs and spices that would make his chicken world famous. In 1953 the first franchised Colonel Sanders' Kentucky Fried Chicken (KFC) was sold at the Dew Drop Inn, in Salt Lake City, Utah. To accommodate his daughter's distaste for dishwashing in her Florida restaurant, the Colonel came up with the notion of a "take-home" store. The prototype KFC franchise was erected in Jacksonville, Fla., and the fast-food industry was revolutionized.

By 1960 there were more than 200 franchises in the United States and Canada. In 1964 the Colonel sold KFC, Inc., to Kentucky businessman John Y. Brown Jr. and Nashville entrepreneur Jack Massey for $2 million. The Colonel was to continue in the services of the corporation as a goodwill ambassador. At times, he was more of an embarrassment than an asset, commenting publicly, for example, that under the new regime the gravy he had worked so hard to perfect "tasted like wallpaper paste."

In 1971 KFC Corporation merged with Heublein, Inc., in a $288 million deal. The tireless colonel, now in his 80s and in failing health, continued his promotional work for charities and KFC, and he attended the dedication of the Colonel Sanders Museum in Louisville in 1978. In 1980 he was hospitalized with pneumonia and died on 16 December. Colonel Harland D. Sanders, the man who personified an American dream and a southern myth, lay in state in both the Kentucky capitol and the corporate offices of KFC before interment in Louisville's Cave Hill Cemetery. Governor John Y. Brown Jr. eulogized the colonel, quoting from *Hamlet*: "He was a man. Take him for all and all. We shall not look upon his like again."

In 1982 R. J. Reynolds (now RJR Nabisco, Inc.) acquired KFC, and in July 1986, PepsiCo, Inc., agreed to buy the company for a book value of $850 million. There are more than 11,000 KFC restaurants now in more than 80 nations and territories. The restaurants are part of Yum! Brands, Inc., the world's largest restaurant system, which also includes such fast-food giants as Taco Bell and Pizza Hut. KFC annually serves more than a billion chicken dinners.

LISA N. HOWORTH
University of Mississippi

John Pearce, ed., *The Colonel: The Captivating Biography of the Dynamic Founder of a Fast-Food Empire* (1982); Harland D. Sanders, *Life As I Have Known It Has Been Finger Lickin' Good* (1974); Lawrence S. Thompson, *Georgia Review* (Spring 1953).

Sandwiches

The South has contributed to America's sandwich culture with a rich array of offerings that reflects key ethnic and social influences in the region. Of the many sandwiches popular in the South, some of the best known are pimento cheese, Kentucky's Hot Brown, and New Orleans's oyster loaf, po' boy, and muffuletta.

Pimento cheese sandwiches are served at events ranging from holiday celebrations and picnics to church gatherings and funerals. The origin of pimento cheese is unknown, but it's believed to have become popular coincident with the country store and the availability of hoop cheese. Pimientos, once a cash crop in the region, were plentiful and cheap. Frugal southerners combined the two ingredients and bound them together with mayonnaise. By the 1930s pimento cheese sandwiches had become popular, economical meals.

Kentucky is known for quality country hams, and one of the richest sandwiches in the South was born and bred there. The Hot Brown is a combination of toasted white bread, thin slices of turkey or chicken, ham, crisp bacon, and sliced tomato covered with cheddar cheese sauce and a sprinkling of grated Parmesan cheese that is broiled until hot and bubbly. Chef Fred K. Schmidt created the sandwich shortly after the 1923 opening of the Brown Hotel in Louisville. The hotel's nightly dinner dances drew more than 1,200 people, and at the end of the evening, famished guests headed to the dining room in search of something to eat. Having tired of the usual ham and eggs, patrons were delighted with the sandwich, and a new tradition was born. Today, the Brown Hotel still serves as the center of Louisville high society, and its namesake sandwich continues to sate the appetites of those accustomed to good eating.

New Orleans may well be the sandwich capital of the South. Two of its most famous sandwiches, the oyster loaf and the po' boy, are based on crusty loaves of French bread with a very light interior. The bread is produced in New Orleans's long-established bakeries founded by French immigrants and, later, French Creoles. The oyster loaf, filled with lightly breaded and deep-fried oysters, was created during the late 19th century when the locally available mollusk was plentiful and cheap. At the time, the oyster loaf was also known as *la mediatrice*, or mediator (or "peacemaker"), because husbands who had been carousing all night in the French Quarter would often bring one home in the hope of pacifying a jealous wife.

The po' boy sandwich is prepared with a variety of fillings, including ham, deep-fried seafood such as oysters or shrimp, Creole hot sausage, or roast beef with a dark, rich gravy called "debris." The codification of the po' boy is attributed to Benny and Clovis Martin, proprietors of Martin Brothers, a restaurant they established in New Orleans

in 1922. Former streetcar conductors, the Martins supported the 1929 streetcar strike by providing free sandwiches to their former colleagues, whom they termed "poor boys." This coincided with a new baking technique, introduced by New Orleans baker John Gendusa, that changed tapered French bread into equally proportioned 32-inch loaves, allowing them to be easily cut into three or four sandwiches. It's believed that one of today's most popular po' boys, economically filled with french fries and gravy, likely originated at the time of the strike.

The muffuletta represents an interesting ethnic influence on New Orleans' sandwich cuisine. Around the turn of the 20th century, immigrants from Italy began arriving in the city in significant numbers. Many were from Sicily, and they often found employment in the French Quarter's food industry. Legend has it that a Sicilian baker of Albanian descent first baked and sold the round loaves of bread, called *muffoletta*, which have been made since the 15th century in Piano degli Albanese, an Albanian colony near Palermo. Originally, the Sicilian workers would purchase and eat, separately from the bread, olive salad, cheeses, and meats. It wasn't long before Lupo Salvadore, who established Central Grocery in 1906, took note of what the workers were eating and began selling made-to-order sandwiches consisting of the same ingredients. It's believed the sandwich became known as the muffulletta simply because the grocer misspelled the name of the bread that he purchased from the baker.

Today, many of the South's signature

sandwiches have become so popular that they have spread beyond the region and appear on restaurant menus throughout the United States.

BECKY MERCURI
Rushford, New York

Brett Anderson, *Times-Picayune* (30 May 2003); John T. Edge, *A Gracious Plenty: Recipes and Recollections from the American South* (1999), *Southern Belly: The Ultimate Food Lover's Companion to the South* (2000); Becky Mercuri, *American Sandwich* (2004); *Sandwiches That You Will Like* (2002); Michael Mizell-Nelson, *Streetcar Stories*, VHS Video, Louisiana Endowment for the Humanities, New Orleans.

Saunders, Clarence

(1881–1953) CREATOR OF PIGGY WIGGLY SUPERMARKETS.

"His ears have been slashed. His toes cut off. His eyes cut out. His bones broken and face smashed. Over his mutilated form stand scores of mourners who tear at their hair and bite their fingernails while they yearn for the days when the demon of high prices ruled with an iron grip on the throats of consumers." With those words, written for a 1916 newspaper ad, Clarence Saunders of Memphis, Tenn., announced the birth of a bloodthirsty scion. His name was Piggly Wiggly. Economy was his virtue. Empowerment of the masses was his means. And if you believed the rhetoric Saunders spouted, his arrival foretold the demise of traditional grocers and the future of American retail.

Saunders's vision was simple. Rather than staff a grocery with clerks who retrieved goods from shelves and ferried purchases to the register, he supplied shoppers with baskets and opened shelf access to all. "You have a perfect right to take with your own hands the very thing that appeals to you," he told shoppers. "Open the meat box with your own hands. Open the bread box with your own hands and help yourself." Think of an inside-out assembly line, designed so that a company utilizes the free labor of its customers rather than the paid labor of its employees, and you have an inkling of how elemental, sound, and, yes, revolutionary the concept was.

Reduced labor costs allowed Saunders to undercut his competitor's prices. And he did not shy away from trumpeting low margins. But he also managed to convince patrons that Piggly Wiggly did not just smite the demon of high prices; Piggly Wiggly cared about the common shopper. "No store clerks gab and smirk while folks are standing around ten deep to get waited on," Saunders promised in an early newspaper ad. "Every lady will be her own clerk, so if she wants to talk to a can of tomatoes and kill her time, all right and well."

By way of his first Memphis store and the hundreds of Piggly Wiggly markets that followed, Saunders popularized the self-service grocery. And consumers soon embraced the Piggly Wiggly philosophy, an admixture of free will and low prices.

Emboldened—and enriched—by his success, Saunders began building a baronial estate with a bowling alley and a natatorium, flanked by two lakes and a private golf course. Saunders called it Cla-Le-Clare for his three children and promised that the million dollar mansion of pink marble would "stand for a thousand years." (It now serves as the centerpiece of Memphis's Pink Palace Museum complex.)

By the autumn of 1922, his empire included more than 1,200 Piggly Wiggly stores in 41 states and Canada. But his fall came as quickly as his rise. Soon after Saunders listed Piggly Wiggly with the New York Stock Exchange, traders executed a bear raid on the corporation, short-selling stock in what Saunders considered a de facto swindle. He fought back, pleading with the common man to join him in wresting control of Piggly Wiggly from these profiteers, to take a stand by way of taking stock in the South.

Saunders called the raid a second Yankee invasion, declaring the "battle has taken its firing line in front of the honor gates of Memphis. And the flag of Memphis must not be lowered." Boy Scout troops marched the streets of Memphis wearing badges that read, "We're One Hundred Percent for Clarence Saunders and Piggly Wiggly." Even competing merchants displayed signs that proclaimed, "A Share of Piggly Wiggly Stock in Every Home." But it was all for naught. In the spring of 1923 Saunders declared bankruptcy. He lost control of his company. He lost his home. And yet Saunders remained defiant. "They have the body of Piggly Wiggly," he said, upon being forced from the office of president. "But they cannot have the soul."

For years after, Saunders attempted many a comeback, including Keedoozle (as in *key-does-all*), an automated grocery that Saunders never managed

to perfect. From 1935 until his death in 1953, Saunders experimented with variations on a system that equipped shoppers with Bakelite-handled keys, which, upon insertion in the appropriate slot alongside a display of, say, canned peaches, registered the purchase through a vast web of solenoid relays and released a can stored in the bowels of the store. Although prototype stores opened every few years, beginning in 1937, each closed within months. And each time, Saunders pledged a rebound after working out a few bugs.

Keedoozle was just one of Saunders's unconventional—and unsuccessful—comeback attempts (which also included a professional football team and a cleaning solvent that effectively, yet unintentionally, shrank clothes). At the time of his death in 1953, Saunders was at work on Foodelectric. He pledged it would do everything Keedoozle could. And more.

JOHN T. EDGE
University of Mississippi

John T. Edge, *Oxford American* (Winter 2005); Mike Freeman, *Tennessee Historical Quarterly* (Spring 1992); James M. Mayo, *The American Grocery Store: The Business Evolution of an Architectural Space* (1993); Nitin Nohria and Bridget Gurtler, *Harvard Business Review* (24 May 2004).

Sazerac

Legend says that the Sazerac, a drink created in New Orleans during the mid-19th century, was the first cocktail in America identified by a brand of alcohol, although the claim has not been thoroughly documented. The origin of the word *Sazerac* is found in the French city of Limoges. The distillery known as Sazerac de Forge et Fils, which operated there, produced a brandy that was very popular in New Orleans during the 19th century. In 1859 John B. Schiller, the agent for the French distiller in New Orleans, opened the Sazerac Coffeehouse at 18 Exchange Alley in the French Quarter and began serving drinks made exclusively with the brandy, which had come to be known simply as Sazerac. As originally served at Schiller's establishment, the Sazerac cocktail also contained Peychaud bitters, a spicy herbal elixir produced about 1830 by the New Orleans pharmacist Antoine Amedée Peychaud. In 1870 Schiller's bookkeeper, Thomas Handy, acquired the coffeehouse, changing its name to Sazerac House. The new owner began substituting American rye whiskey for the original French brandy. At some point around 1870 another change in the Sazerac cocktail's formula occurred with the addition of a dash of absinthe, a wormwood-tinged liqueur produced in New Orleans until it became outlawed as a narcotic at the turn of the century. Credit for the absinthe innovation has gone to Léon Lamothe, then a bartender at Piña's restaurant on Burgundy Street in the French Quarter. The Sazerac's popularity extends to the present, although the recipe has undergone further revisions. Today the drink often contains Angostura brand bitters as well as Peychaud's, along with Herbsaint (a local anisette liqueur substituting for absinthe), rye or bourbon whiskey, and sugar water. The Sazerac also is the name of the bar and restaurant in New Orleans's Fairmont Hotel (opened in 1893 as the Grunewald and renamed the Roosevelt in 1923 and the Fairmont in 1970). Sazerac Co., a Kentucky distillery, now produces Herbsaint and Peychaud's bitters, as well as a rye whiskey carrying the brand name Sazerac.

GENE BOURG
New Orleans, Louisiana

Stanley Clisby Arthur, *Famous New Orleans Drinks and How to Mix 'Em* (1937); John F. Mariani, *The Dictionary of American Food and Drink* (1994).

Sorghum

Grain sorghum grows in a tassel of seeds on top of a stalk, and it ranks fourth in world grain production behind wheat, rice, and corn. In the South, however, interest in sorghum is focused not on the grain, but on the stalk. Sweet sorghum stalks are grown to make a sweetener known as sorghum syrup, sorghum molasses, or simply lassies. Today, in many parts of the South producers call their product "100% pure sweet sorghum syrup" because markets sell sorghum syrups that are mixtures of sorghum, corn syrup, flavorings, food coloring, and other additives.

Producing pure sorghum syrup begins with cutting sorghum stalks above the root, stripping the leaves, and loading the stalks on a wagon. At the sorghum mill, the stalks are pressed by heavy rollers to extract the green juice, which flows to an evaporator pan where heat is used to reduce it to a sweet syrup. The dark, thick, amber-colored syrup is then stored in jars and used to sweeten casseroles, sauces, breads, cakes, and candy. A traditional means of using the syrup is to heat it with a pinch of baking soda, causing heavy foaming. The bubbly syrup is then spread on buttered pancakes or biscuits, and on the palate, it sweetens the pastry as it adds a smoky, tangy flavor.

Prior to the second half of the 20th century, when sugar became more available, sorghum syrup was the primary southern sweetener, just as maple syrup was popular in the northern states. Even small farmers could produce sweet sorghum syrup, and with a half-acre plot yielding 50 to 100 gallons of the syrup, sorghum was a valuable cash crop.

As production of sorghum has fallen, the public has become confused about the product, using the terms *sorghum* and *molasses* interchangeably. Even in the traditional song "Liza Jane," recorded by Alan Lomax, the crops sugarcane and sorghum grass are confused:

> Goin' up the mountain
> To raise a patch of cane
> To make a barrel of sorghum
> To sweeten up Liza Jane.

The source of molasses is sugarcane, a perennial grass that cannot live through a frost. Sorghum, on the other hand, is an annual grass that grows in temperate as well as tropical climates. The more important distinction between sorghum and molasses, however, is that pure sorghum syrup is the primary product of sweet sorghum. Molasses is a by-product of white sugar production. In refining sugar, molasses is the residue left after the white sugar has been removed. Darker, stronger molasses contains more of the residue. Sorghum, however, does not come in degrees of thickness or flavor. Whereas the taste of cane syrup is one of straightforward sweetness, that of sorghum syrup offers a bit of a tang.

Sorghum is associated with the southern highlands, where most of the production of sorghum now occurs. Towns like Blairsville, Ga., Muddy Pond, Tenn., and West Liberty, Ky., boast annual sorghum festivals to celebrate the syrup and its place in southern culture.

MARK F. SOHN
Pikeville College

Alan Davidson, *The Oxford Companion to Food* (1999); National Sweet Sorghum Producers and Processors Association, *Sorghum Treasures* (1991); Fred W. Sauceman, *The Place Setting: Timeless Tastes of the Mountain South, from Bright Hope to Frog Level* (2006); Mark F. Sohn, *Appalachian Home Cooking: History, Culture, and Recipes* (2005).

Spoonbread

Spoonbread is a cornmeal-based dish that proved popular in 18th- and 19th-century America, particularly in the Tidewater South, and, to a lesser extent, in the Appalachian interior. It continues to have a considerable following today. Thomas Jefferson was very fond of the dish and served it to his guests at Monticello throughout his lifetime, offering it at morning, noon, and evening meals. It is still served in a few restaurants in the region, including the Boone Tavern in Berea, Ky., and is included in a number of southern cookbooks. John Egerton describes spoonbread as "the lightest, richest, most delicious of all corn bread dishes, a veritable corn bread soufflé."

So-named because it is eaten with a spoon, spoonbread is considered an excellent side dish to accompany many southern foods, including vegetables, chicken, ham and gravy, and various stews, plus hot fruit dishes and even salads. It has been often served in the South as a substitute for mashed potatoes.

The dish is said to have descended from *suppawn*, a Native American cornmeal milk pudding whose name derives from the Algonquin word *nasaump*—cornmeal "softened with water." This porridge-type dish was a favorite of colonists across the Northeast, including the Dutch in New York State, as well as settlers in the Seaboard South. Lila Pen repeated the legend that an earthenware crock of suppawn was left too long on the fire to cook. "By the time the forgetful housewife remembered it, it was no longer a porridge but had become crisp at the edges, although the center still remained creamy. It was eaten with butter and was called a masterpiece." Virginians, adding eggs and butter to provide a richer flavor, finessed the cooking of the delicacy to a fine art. A slightly different version was called Virginia Batter Bread.

JOSEPH DABNEY
Atlanta, Georgia

Joseph E. Dabney, *Smokehouse Ham, Spoon Bread, and Scuppernong Wine: The Folklore and Art of Southern Appalachian Cooking* (1998); Damon Lee Fowler, *Classical Southern Cooking: A Celebration of the Cuisine of the Old South* (1995); Sheila Hibben, *American Regional Cookery* (1946).

Squash

The word *squash* is of North American origin, deriving from Algonquian

Summer squash (Bill Tarpenning, photographer, United States Department of Agriculture)

askutasquash. In its original sense, the term applied only to the young, tender green fruit of several species of cucurbits, but primarily to young fruits of *Cucurbita pepo*. Today, botanists employ the term *squash* when referring to four cultivated species of cucurbits regardless of seasonality or size: *Cucurbita pepo, C. maxima, C. moschata,* and *C. mixta*. Of these four common species, the *pepos, mixtas,* and *moschatas* are most important for the South, since they are better adapted to a hot, humid climate. The *mixtas* and *moschatas* are not indigenous, and can be traced to Central America. They were introduced into the South early in the colonial period. In fact, the Seminole Pumpkin (*C. moschata*) of Florida is thought to date from early contact with the Spanish.

Unlike botanists, horticulturists generally divide squash into two broad types, the summer-fruiting varieties, which are indeed eaten young, and the fall-ripening varieties, which have hard shells ideal for over-winter storage. Large squash, regardless of species, are commonly referred to as pumpkins.

These horticultural designations are also found in culinary literature and in the historical garden literature. For example, William White's *Gardening for the South* (1856) recommended the striped cushaw (*C. mixta*) as a type of pumpkin, but also suggested that it would make a good substitute for any winter squash.

The cushaw was introduced from the Caribbean and is a variant form of another white-skinned "pumpkin" popularly known as the sweet potato pumpkin in many parts of the Upper South. Among the *pepos* recommended by White are both the summer crookneck and the yellow and white pattypans. These pattypan varieties are indigenous and are recorded as early as the 1580s. It is often referred to in cookery books as the "cymling" squash.

Southern manuscript cookery books do not often mention squash recipes, since Old South squash cookery was often orally transmitted and rather straightforward: stewed and served with butter, bacon drippings, or ham. The southern character of the dish did not hinge on the ingredients themselves so much as on the combination of squash with the other foods served. On the other hand, some published cookbooks were rather careful to include squash recipes. Mary Randolph's *Virginia House-wife* (1824) mentioned cymlings and winter squash, as well as sweet potato pumpkins, which she stuffed and baked—a very upper-class form of presentation. The range of squash recipes in cookery books nearly always included a pudding and a purée, and sometimes included a soup. Slices of squash were also tied up in soup bunches (bouquets of herbs and root vegetables) for making flavorful stocks.

Today, squash is employed in much more creative ways owing to the popularity of spicy Cajun-style cookery and to a quest for new kinds of cakes and breads using local ingredients. These imaginative new uses include inventions like hoppin' John's squashpuppies (hushpuppies made with squash) and Ronni Lundy's pumpkin grits pudding.

WILLIAM WOYS WEAVER
Drexel University

C. Paige Gutierrez, *Cajun Foodways* (1992); Ronni Lundy, *Butter Beans to Blackberries: Recipes from the Southern Garden* (1999); Martha McCulloch-Williams, *Dishes and Beverages of the Old South* (1913, 1988); Mary Randolph, *The Virginia House-wife* (1824); Anna Wells Rutledge, *The Carolina Housewife* (1847); John Martin Taylor, *Hoppin' John's Lowcountry Cooking* (1992); William Woys Weaver, *Heirloom Vegetable Gardening* (1996); William White, *Gardening for the South* (1856).

Stack Cake

The stack cake is distinct from other southern layer cakes in that rather than being a fancy festive cake, it grows out of an everyday tradition. In some areas the cake was called a washday cake because it was made the day before washday and served when the work schedule was heavy. During the latter half of the 20th century, however, stack cakes became a symbol of traditional Appalachian cooking, and they have earned a place as the centerpiece of Christmas or Thanksgiving dinner.

One hundred years ago, the cake was baked in the common cast-iron skillet,

Jenny Bonds's stack cake filled with apple butter, sold annually at the ramp supper (Lyntha Scott Eiler, photographer, Library of Congress, [CRF-LE-C083-17], Washington, D.C.)

and the recipe included six essential ingredients: dried apples, lard, sweet sorghum syrup, buttermilk, eggs, and flour. Except for flour, these ingredients were produced on the farm.

Given today's concern for health and the fact that the cake is made with from six to twelve layers, the cake's celebrity is well deserved. Stack cake recipes are light in both fat and calories. Recipes call for little shortening, and the "frosting," rather than being made of sugar or butter, is made of apples. In addition, the cake is convenient because it must stand for a day before serving so the apple filling will be absorbed by the layers and because it freezes perfectly.

Long before freezers became available, the cake was prepared in the fall or winter using apples, pears, peaches, or even berries. The most common filling is an apple filling, made with fresh or dried apples that are spiced and cooked until thick. Common apple stack cake spices include ground ginger, cinnamon, nutmeg, and cloves. Other stack cakes use cooked-down peach or pear butter, and a few use a blackberry filling. The filling is spread on the thin layers,

which are then stacked. The stack cake's many thin layers bring to mind Appalachian stack pies as well as the German-Austrian Dobosch or Dobos torte, a ten-layer sponge cake with a mocha filling and caramel glaze.

While the settler James Harrod may have brought the first stack cake to Kentucky when he founded Harrodsburg in 1774, the cake could not have been common until more than 100 years later when flour became readily available. In 1883 the White Lily Foods Company of Knoxville, Tenn., was established, and the firm was an early producer of flour. Not until that period did biscuits begin to replace cornbread and stack cakes come to be regularly made by southerners.

MARK F. SOHN
Pikeville College

Ronni Lundy, *Shuck Beans, Stack Cakes, and Honest Fried Chicken: The Heart and Soul of Southern Country Kitchens* (1991); Mark F. Sohn, *Appalachian Home Cooking: History, Culture, and Recipes* (2005), *Mountain Country Cooking: A Gathering of the Best Recipes from the Smokies to the Blue Ridge* (1996).

Sugar and Sugarcane

Before sugarcane made it to southern soil, the ancient grass had been grown for thousands of years in faraway Southeast Asia and India for its sweet juice and to make brown lumps of sticky sugar. Jesuit priests who in 1751 began their cultivation of sugarcane in what is now downtown New Orleans had no problem growing it, but turning its juice into sugar was expensive, unreliable, and unprofitable. In the 1790s,

Sugarcane farmers, Louisiana, 1938 (Russell Lee, photographer,
Library of Congress [LC-USF33-011831-M5], Washington, D.C.)

however, businessman Etienne de Bore and an expert sugar maker from Santo Domingo, Antoine Morin, granulated sugar and turned a profit. Their commercially successful venture on the site of present-day Audubon Park in New Orleans began what developed into an international sugar industry.

To make sugar, stalks of sugarcane are harvested and sent through rolling presses to extract the juice. The juice is then boiled into a thick syrup that is separated into sugar crystals and molasses. The sugar crystals are washed and filtered to make white, or refined, sugar. Originally, sugar was made in open cast-iron kettles, but innovations in the industry came rapidly and soon tremendous brick sugar mills housed sugar-making equipment that was used cooperatively by many plantations. One of the most significant advances in sugar

making came in 1834 when Norbert Rilleux, a free man of color, invented the triple-effect evaporator that is still used today.

As the sugar industry progressed and became one of the most lucrative businesses in the world, an entire economy and society based on sugar burgeoned as well. From the time de Bore began making money, the workforce needed to produce sugar increased dramatically each year. By the time the Civil War began, a staggering 300,000 slaves worked in the Louisiana sugar industry. The slave-based economy that powered the sugar industry created fabulous wealth, expansive plantations, and grand, columned houses that still line the waterways of south Louisiana. After the Civil War, the sugar industry crumbled without slave labor. But the demand for sugar remained high, and the cane fields were soon filled again with stalks of cane and thousands of men and women working as tenant farmers. As late as 1930, every stalk of sugarcane was harvested by hand. Soon thereafter, however, the advent of a mechanical harvester, along with a lack of labor during World War II, forced the sugar industry to mechanize quickly. By 1950 the entire commercial crop of sugarcane was machine harvested, and the incredible numbers of workers once needed to harvest the cane were without jobs.

As well as playing a large part in the southern economy, sugar is one of the most important ingredients of southern cooking. Along with the obvious foods—sweet tea, jams, jellies, cakes, pies, candy, ice cream, and all of the other desserts for which the South is famous—sugar is also included as an ingredient in ambrosia, coleslaw, and carbonated beverages, and it is used in curing meats. The by-products from sugar making are also put to good use. Molasses is used to make syrup and rum and is used as a food additive for animals and humans. Bagasse, or the crushed remains of cane after it passes through the rolling presses, is used for fiber, mulch, and fertilizer, and it was at one time burned for power to run the sugar mills.

In 1917, the Savannah Sugar Refining Corporation introduced the southern sugar brand, Dixie Crystals, produced in a large plant on the Savannah River built with the help of more than 400 workers brought from Louisiana's sugar industry. This sugar plant helped build Savannah's port activity and economy, transforming the city. In 1997, Imperial Sugar Company acquired Savannah Sugar Refining and has continued to sell Dixie Crystals as a distinctive southern sugar brand.

Today, sugar is an internationally traded commodity and a $.5 billion industry in Louisiana alone. Recently, Florida has passed Louisiana as the leader in production, but Texas, Louisiana, and Hawaii continue to produce substantial amounts of sugar, with South Carolina, Alabama, Mississippi, and Georgia producing far smaller amounts. The big business of sugar is also the subject of university study. Louisiana State University provides education, as well as research and development programs, for all aspects of the sugar industry. Appropriately, just across the street from the Audubon Research Institute on LSU's campus, one can see the original cast-iron kettle used by de Bore to granulate sugar and begin the sugar industry.

SCOTT R. SIMMONS
New Orleans, Louisiana

George C. Abbott, *Sugar* (1990); Hugh Barty-King and Anton Massel, *Rum Yesterday and Today* (1983); Sharon Tyler Herbst, *The New Food Lovers Companion*, 2nd edition (1995); Charley Richard, *Sugar Journal* (February 1995); J. Carlyle Sitterson, *Sugar Country* (1953); Robert Louis Stein, *The French Sugar Business in the Eighteenth Century* (1988); Wendy Woloson, *Refined Tastes: Sugar, Consumers, and Confectionary in Nineteenth-Century America* (2002).

Sweet Potatoes

The sweet potato (*Ipomoea batatas*), a member of the morning glory family, is rich in vitamins A, C, and E, folic acid, iron, copper, calcium, fiber, and beta-carotene, and low in fat. The sweet potato ranks seventh among the world's most-produced crops behind wheat, rice, corn, potato, yam, and cassava. Leading sweet potato producing states in this country include North Carolina, Louisiana, Mississippi, California, Alabama, Georgia, and New Jersey. White-fleshed sweet potatoes are common in Central and South America and have begun to appear in the parts of the United States where immigrants from these regions have congregated. Orange-fleshed sweet potatoes are more commonly cultivated and preferred here than in other countries.

Annual per capita consumption of sweet potatoes in the United States is usually only five pounds, primarily in pies or other dessert dishes. Lately other products such as yogurt, beverages, noodles, chips, fries, pancake mixes, and other flours are being made from sweet potatoes. Sweet potatoes have at least 124 medicinal and industrial uses. Researchers have shown that sweet potatoes contain bioactive components with antitumor, anti-HIV, anti–muscular dystrophy, antifungal, antibacterial, antihypertensive, and antidiabetic effects. George Washington Carver produced more than 118 different products from the sweet potato at Tuskegee Institute. The sweet potato is one of the crops selected for NASA's Advanced Life Support Program for potential long-duration lunar/Mars missions.

Freshly harvested sweet potatoes are high in moisture and, in the warm temperatures of the South, can be stored for only about a week at room temperature. Processing (such as pan frying, drying, freezing, or canning) increases the shelf life as well as increasing the palatability of sweet potatoes. New techniques such as vacuum drying of sweet potato slices and freeze drying are also being used. Some markets in Baltimore are beginning to offer sweet potato greens to consumers recently immigrated from West and Central Africa. White-fleshed sweet potato roots are used to produce starch and gasohol and made into pellets for animal rations. Orange-fleshed, high-moisture types of sweet potatoes, such as Beauregard, are erroneously called yams. True yams belong to the *Discorea* species, a tropical starchy tuberous root not commercially grown in the United States.

FATIMAH JACKSON
University of Maryland

ABDULLAH F. H. MUHAMMAD
Alcorn State University

LORRAINE NIBA
Virginia Tech University

Franklin W. Martin, Ruth M. Ruberte, and Jose L. Herrera, *The Sweet Potato Cookbook* (1989); Lyniece North Talmadge, *The Sweet Potato Cookbook* (1998); Jennifer A. Woolfe, *Sweet Potato: An Untapped Food Resource* (1992).

Tabasco

Tabasco Sauce, a brand of hot pepper sauce that is sold around the globe, is manufactured on Avery Island, near New Iberia, La. The tabasco pepper is short, a couple of inches of fiery red that grows upward from the leaf. It is the only one of its species, *Capsicum*

An intact vintage Tabasco bottle from the 1870–1906 period—and Tabasco today (McIlhenny Company Archives, Avery Island, La.)

frutescens, to be grown commercially in North America, although it is in common use in Latin America. The first seeds brought to Avery Island were possibly imported from the Tabasco region of Mexico. The pepper grows best in the bayou country of southern Louisiana, where it is generally known as a tabasco pepper.

According to one tradition, shortly after the Civil War an Avery in-law, Edmund McIlhenny, began growing the *Capsicum frutescens* and making the sauce on the island, which is a salt mound, about 2.5 miles in diameter, covered with a thin layer of rich soil over a huge dome of rock salt, where tabasco peppers grow well. Avery Island is 163 feet high and juts up out of Bayou Petite Anse, and the McIlhenny family was still living there and growing peppers in the year 2005, making over

700,000 bottles of the condiment each work day. When Edmund McIlhenny began it all, in the late 1860s, he first labeled his hot sauce Petite Anse Sauce, but shortly thereafter he changed its name to Tabasco Sauce. By the early 1870s a New York food wholesaler had begun selling Tabasco Sauce, and by the turn of the century, it occupied a niche of the national condiment market.

Among Edmund McIlhenny's descendants was Edward Avery McIlhenny, who assumed the presidency of the family company in 1898 and was a naturalist of considerable renown. He converted Avery Island into a natural wonderland. Its rich soil was favorable to the many species of trees and plants that he assembled from all over the world. Today it is home to a remarkable array of plant life, from a vast collection of bamboo to Indian rubber trees, and a wide variety of animals, from alligators to a roost of several thousand snowy egrets. Parts of Avery Island, and the Tabasco Sauce factory, are open to the public and were visited by about 100,000 people in 2004.

Tabasco peppers have always been harvested by hand. They break easily and come ripe at different times on the same bush, which makes mechanical harvesting difficult, if not impossible. The McIlhennys tried during the 1970s to develop a machine that could do better than human pickers, but with little success. Once the peppers are picked, they are crushed into a mash to which salt is added. The mash is stored in large, sealed white oak barrels and left to ferment for up to three years, then mixed with a little vinegar, strained, bottled, and sold. Its sharp bite and rich taste have made it almost as ubiquitous a North American product as Coca-Cola, and it turns up all around the world. In the early years of the 21st century Tabasco began to produce a number of new products, including sauces made with chipotle peppers and novelty products like candies spiced with original Tabasco sauce.

RICHARD SCHWEID
Barcelona, Spain

Shane K. Bernard, *Louisiana's Cultural Vistas* (Fall 2005); Paul McIlhenny with Barbara Hunter, *The Tabasco Cookbook: 125 Years of America's Favorite Pepper Sauce* (1993); McIlhenny Company Archives, Avery Island, La.; Richard Schweid, *Hot Peppers: The Story of Cajuns and Capsicum* (1987); www.tabasco.com.

Tasso

The word *tasso* is evidently a Cajun French corruption of the Spanish term *tasajo*, meaning smoked meat. In the Spanish context, *tasajo* usually refers to jerked beef, which is used as a flavoring agent in numerous dishes throughout Spain and Latin America. In French Louisiana, on the other hand, *tasso* specifies highly seasoned jerked and smoked pork. The transformation of the idiom and the food it represents is evidently the result of cross-cultural borrowing and assimilation in rural south Louisiana's unique melting pot. The origins of the Cajun practice are nevertheless uncertain. Various 18th-century Europeans reported the use of smoked meats by various Native American groups in the lower Mississippi Valley, including the reputedly cannibalistic Attakapas tribe, the indigenous population of south central Louisiana. This existing tradition appears—as the etymology of the food's name suggests—to have been reinforced by the culinary practices of Hispanic immigrants. In an attempt to Hispanicize the colony's French population in 1779, Louisiana's Spanish colonial government settled approximately 60 Malagueños along Bayou Teche at present-day New Iberia. These natives of Malaga, Spain, who subsequently moved to the shores of nearby Spanish Lake, were quickly absorbed into the region's much larger Cajun community. Although the Malagueños lost their language and identity in the assimilation process, a portion of the community's culinary tradition evidently lives on in the form of tasso.

The Cajun population engaged in ranching on the upper prairies west of Bayou Teche appears to have embraced the Spanish foodstuff most enthusiastically, perhaps because it provided a means of preserving beef during long cattle drives, which began at approximately the time of the Malagueño influx. Oral history fieldwork in the Cajun parishes suggests that the traditional usage of tasso was confined exclusively to those areas of the Cajun prairies that were most active in transporting cattle to 19th-century New Orleans markets. It is thus fitting that the term *tasso* first appears in the Louisiana documentary record in 1859 as the name of a prairie community near present-day Duson, in the heart of the early Cajun ranching country. In 1880 nationally famous local-color writer George Washington Cable, who collected notes on the Cajun community for a never-published addendum to the 1880 census report, recorded that "jerked beef (tassao)" and cornbread were the staples of the Cajun diet in the Carencro area, an early ranching center. Over the following century, Cajuns adapted well-established beef jerking techniques to the preservation of pork, which was more widely consumed among Cajun small farmers.

RYAN A. BRASSEAUX
CARL A. BRASSEAUX
Lafayette, Louisiana

Mme. Bégué's Recipes of Old New Orleans Creole Cookery (1900); Pip Brennan, Jimmy Brennan, and Ted Brennan, *Breakfast at Brennan's and Dinner, Too* (1994); Rima and Richard Collin, *New Orleans Cookbook* (1987); Walter Cowan, Charles L. Dufour, and O. K. LeBlanc, *New Orleans: Yesterday,*

Today, and Tomorrow (2001); John Egerton, *Southern Food: At Home, on the Road, in History* (1987); Peter S. Feibleman, *American Cooking: Creole and Acadian* (1971); Leon Galatoire, *Leon Galatoire's Cookbook* (1995); Lafcadio Hearn, *Lafcadio Hearn's Creole Cook Book* (1990); *The Picayune Creole Cook Book* (1922).

Tea Rooms

Contrary to the sweet-old-lady stereotype, southern-style tea rooms were often bastions of progressive women and precursors of modern fast-food trends. Refused use of meeting halls, southern women's rights leaders of 1880 met over tea in kitchens, fighting intemperance and lack of schooling for girls. Later, the first female graduates flocked to urban jobs during World War I. Unescorted they were banned from hotel dining rooms and from clubs. Industrious widows answered the need of young women with no place else to eat, calling their homes "tea rooms" and feeding them chicken pie, oyster bisque, and garden vegetable salads.

During Prohibition the tea room craze was at its height. Soups, casseroles, and toasted sandwiches were "fast food" for flappers and their beaus. Afternoon tea dances thrived in hotels from Memphis to Richmond, where "animal dancing" (the Turkey and Fox Trots) scandalized chaperones. Likewise, in Atlanta, the Apache was danced by Margaret Mitchell, *Gone with the Wind* author.

One enterprising tea room founder displayed her bobbed hair silhouette on a new Atlanta office building. Like other home economics/dietetics graduates, she studied the science of cooking, nutrition, and sanitation. Her light lunches and simple suppers replaced heavy sauces and fussy, five-course dinners favored by European trained chefs. Serving 2,000 patrons per day, "The Frances Virginia," as her tea room was called, was as busy as a modern McDonald's.

Tea rooms survived the Depression, showcasing tomato aspic or congealed fruit salad with almonds, made possible by the invention of Jell-O and by refrigerators replacing the icebox. Protestant diehards "revived" with delicate rum cream pies and prune whip with sherry custard sauce.

During World War II, hats flowered. "Tea room cafeterias" trilled with patriotic war brides and "old maid" aunts coming to the city to work, properly attired in gloves and girdles. Department stores advertised "Free Child Care," helping mothers to "lunch" in peace. Hubs of social and civic activity, they hosted fashion shows, bridal showers, rotary club meetings, employee interviews. Dealing with ration coupons, hot kitchens, and crowded dining rooms, hostesses promoted iced tea, thriftily sweetened while warm, and meatless vegetable luncheons that offered protein through milk or cheese sauce.

Wartime ended. Free nurseries ceased. Hometown tea rooms served Sunday dinner (at noon) with children's menus. Tea rooms now had furniture made just for juniors and highchairs for baby siblings. Gasoline was no longer rationed, and California iceberg lettuce arrived, plus deviled crab, and pink shrimp cocktails from the Florida coasts. Tea rooms catered to family

tradition, serving Thanksgiving turkey, cornbread dressing, and giblet gravy to relatives arriving by train, trolley, and taxi. They packaged tea room takeout turkey, turnip greens, and baked macaroni in cylindrical, cardboard containers for those who dined at home. Though the food was similar, the decor differed from that found in dark "grills" and smoky "restaurants," subtly suggesting "Men Only." Though segregated, tea rooms in black and white neighborhoods followed similar trends. Tea rooms began to decline in the 1950s. Owners and patrons aged. Chicken à la king could not compete with Elvis and pizza.

MILLIE COLEMAN
Atlanta, Georgia

Mildred Coleman, *The South's Legendary Frances Virginia Tea Room Cookbook* (1996); Pamela Goyan Kittler and Kathryn Sucher, *Food and Culture in America* (1989); Jan Whitaker, *Tea at the Blue Lantern Inn: A Social History of the Tea Room Craze in America* (2002).

Tomatoes

Many southerners have fond memories of going to the tobacco patch to harvest tobacco and to eat tomatoes growing in rows adjacent to the tobacco rows. The warm tomatoes, cut open with a pocketknife or simply pried open with the thumbs of both hands and liberally sprinkled with salt from a shaker carried in pants pockets, were (and are) a taste treat to be savored and remembered. Many also remember canning tomatoes, making tomato juice during brief times of surplus, and taking tomato sandwiches to school or to work, either on biscuits or loaf (white) bread smothered with mayonnaise.

Brought from South America, the tomato burst onto the southern landscape before traveling northward. Tomatoes came to America surrounded by a particular mythology that warned that they were a form of poisonous apple. In the early South, many gardeners and consumers remained suspicious of the tomato because of this legend. The tomato continued to entertain a controversial history in America, and even in the South, after such myths faded. S. D. Wilcox, editor of the *Florida Agriculturalist* reported that he ate his first tomatoes in 1836, as part of an experiment, in a pie without any seasoning or sweetening. He summed up his consequent dislike for the tomato: "[The tomato] is an arrogant humbug and deserves forthwith to be consigned to the tomb of all the Capulets. . . . [Anyone] who would have predicted that the tomato would ever become popular as an esculent or to be used in any utilitarian way except as gratification to the eye, would have been set down at once as daft or visionary."

Despite its early bad press, the tomato has long been a staple of southern family gardening and, in many southern states, commercial gardening as well. Prior to the development of commercial hybrids, most families saved their own tomato seeds or got them, by purchase or by trade, from neighbors. Such tomatoes are of many sizes, colors, shapes, and flavors. Among them are the well-known reds, of course, but also the Cherokee Purple, which came from the Cherokee Indi-

ans, and the German yellows (yellow with red stripes), which came from the Amish and Mennonites. Other older tomatoes include the multiple-origin oxhearts, with their heartlike shape (though no two are shaped quite the same); the Mortgage Lifter, which was developed through cross-breeding by a radiator repairman in West Virginia; and a host of varieties of ranging in color from white to black to those that remain green even when ripe. Many families also have their own variety of cherry tomato (tommy-toes), which may have been in the family for generations.

The South also has its own tomato breeding tradition most recently enhanced by the work of Randy Gardner of North Carolina State University. In his work at the Fletcher Experiment Station near Asheville, N.C., since 1976 Gardner has developed the "Mountain Series" of tomatoes widely sought after by commercial growers and by home gardeners as well. Through the use of traditional breeding techniques, Gardner has developed many varieties of disease-resistant tomatoes, most with excellent flavor. Originally from Hillsville, Va., Gardner experienced the problems of early and late blight as a farm youth and decided in graduate school to devote his career to trying to solve some of the most vexing problems facing both home gardeners and commercial growers. His varieties continue to be in high demand, and he is in demand as a speaker to commercial growers and home gardeners alike.

While hybrids have taken over much of the commercial trade in tomatoes,

Creole tomatoes for sale at market (Bill Tarpenning, photographer, United States Department of Agriculture)

the reemergence of farmers' markets, throughout the South and the rest of the nation as well, has given new prestige to (and generated new demand for) old-fashioned or heirloom varieties. Customers can buy freshly picked heirloom varieties and not have to worry about shelf life since the tomatoes will be eaten soon after purchase and certainly only a day or two after being picked. Farmers' markets have popularized shapes and colors of tomatoes unknown to many of today's consumers but common to their great-grandparents. Yellow tomatoes, with their high sugar content, and pink tomatoes, with their many blends of sugars and acids, are becoming increasingly popular, both with home gardeners and with market gardeners and their customers.

While tomatoes are increasingly popular in the United States and throughout most of the world, they have a special place in the lives of southerners, who grow many different types and who sometimes serve them three at meals a day during the summer—not to mention the tomato sandwiches enjoyed between meals. The tomato enjoys references across southern musical traditions, from blues artist Brownie Mc-Ghee's "Picking My Tomatoes" (1940) to southern folksinger Kate Campbell's "Jesus and Tomatoes" (2004), which tells the comic story of a woman who sees the likeness of Jesus in one of her homegrown garden tomatoes. Southern writers also recognize the important place of the tomato in southern culture. In her book *Truelove and Homegrown Tomatoes* (2003), author Julie Cannon constructs the seasonal life of a tomato patch as the central metaphor for joy and tragedy that mark the life of a family in Euharlee, Ga.

Along with the fresh tomato served

cold, southerners also claim two methods of preparing hot tomatoes: stewed tomatoes and fried tomatoes. Fried green tomatoes, a popular breakfast and lunch side dish, have distinctive southern origins. Through the work of Fannie Flagg's 1987 novel *Fried Green Tomatoes at the Whistle Stop Café* and the movie based on it, *Fried Green Tomatoes* (1994), this dish has become synonymous with southern culture and southern cooking. In the novel, the sharing of a plate of fried green tomatoes symbolically connects Evelyn Couch, a lonely middle-aged woman, with the childhood community, sisterhood, and secrets of her elderly friend, Ninny Threadgoode.

BILL BEST
Berea, Kentucky

FRANCES ABBOTT
University of Mississippi

Lee Bailey, *Tomatoes (1992)*; John Egerton, *Southern Food: At Home, on the Road, in History* (1987); Ronni Lundy, *Butter Beans to Blackberries: Recipes from the Southern Garden* (1999); Andrew F. Smith, *The Tomato in America: Early History, Culture, and Cookery* (1994).

Uncle Ben's

Uncle Ben's is one of the world's most successful brands of commercially prepared rice, thanks in large part to the marketing skills and dedication of the company's founder, Gordon Harwell. Harwell, a produce broker in Houston, saw an opportunity to fundamentally change the commercial rice market in the United States. Prior to the 1930s, short-grain rice was locally grown, milled, and sold. For the consumer,

such rice often varied in quality. Harwell believed that if he could market rice as a premium food rather than a commodity, he would be successful. Harwell bought rice grown in the Houston area and packaged it under the trade name Uncle Ben's, hoping that the African American symbol would "connote old fashioned goodness" to the customer. Unfortunately, the product still varied in quality, and Harwell needed a way to produce rice of a consistent appearance, quality, and taste.

The solution came in a new "conversion" process that was invented by Eric Huzenlaub, a chemist who emigrated from Germany to England in the 1930s. Under the conversion process, brown, long-grain rice is parboiled under steamed pressure to force water-soluble nutrients into the starchy endosperm and then dried and milled. After the process, the "converted rice" has more nutrients, less oil, and a harder texture than short-grain rice, and a white appearance that is similar to that of short-grain rice.

Harwell contacted Huzenlaub about licensing the conversion process, but Huzenlaub was not initially interested because he considered the United States too small as a rice market, especially compared to a country such as India. Eventually, Harwell persuaded Huzenlaub to grant him a license, and his converted-rice company was ready to launch. The United States military became the first large customer to try the product, then marketed as "Ehler's Converted Rice." The converted rice was easy to store, resistant to weevil infestation, and thus perfect to feed hungry soldiers in the South Pacific theater of World War II. By 1945, Ehler's Converted Rice was shipping 65 million pounds of its product to the military.

As World War II was coming to an end, Harwell understood that the military purchase orders were drying up and that he had to develop a consumer market for converted rice. He decided to focus the company's marketing efforts in the New York City area, believing that if they could make it there, they would make it everywhere. Harwell resurrected the "Uncle Ben's" brand he had used in the Houston area a decade before. The company advertised heavily in local media like the *New York Times*, and Harwell even hosted an all-rice-dish dinner for several New York food executives and restaurateurs. Harwell's focused sales campaign worked wonders, for soon "Uncle Ben's Converted Rice" became a household name in kitchens across the country.

Early advertisements for Uncle Ben's rice often emphasized the qualities of rice prepared in the "southern" or "South Carolina" method. In sharp contrast to the gummy mess that usually resulted when short-grain rice was cooked, converted rice, when cooked, still looked white, and it separated easily so that "every grain salutes you."

Although the company's website describes Uncle Ben as a legendary Texas rice farmer, there is not much information available about him. In some early press interviews, Harwell said that he wanted a persona who would connote the beginning of rice growing in the American South. He thought of the apocryphal blacks of the South Carolina

plantations who had so much to do with early rice growing. For the company logo, Harwell ultimately settled on a likeness of Frank C. Brown, an African American man who waited on, and impressed, him during a dinner in a Chicago restaurant.

We may never be able to separate myth from reality, but Uncle Ben's rice does hearken back to the forgotten days of African American achievement in rice growing and cookery. Throughout the slave trade, West African rice farmers were enslaved and targeted for sale to slaveowners in South Carolina, Georgia, and Louisiana who wanted to exploit their specialized knowledge and skills with rice. These enslaved Africans used rice to create some signature dishes of Lowcountry cuisine, like hoppin' John, pilau, and rice bread. Though the African American cook's reputation with rice was certainly forged in the South, it clearly made its way to the North. For example, *The Pentucket Housewife*, an 1888 cookbook published in Haverhill, Mass., featured a recipe, simply titled "A Black Man's Recipe to Dress Rice."

ADRIAN MILLER
Denver, Colorado

George Kent, *Washington Post* (16 January 1944); Marilyn Kern-Foxworth, *Aunt Jemima, Uncle Ben, and Rastus: Blacks in Advertising, Yesterday, Today, and Tomorrow* (1994); James J. Nagle, *New York Times* (24 May 1953).

Waffle House

When Bob Dole ran for president in 1996, he quipped that Bill Clinton was so shifty he had turned the White House into the Waffle House. With that pun, one of the most familiar sights of the southern roadscape fully arrived in the national consciousness. From its greasy beginnings as a short-order joint in Georgia, Waffle House has spread to more than 1,500 locations in 20-plus states. A smattering of the chain's yellow waffle iron signs appears in the Midwest and the Rocky Mountain states, but the great majority are in the Deep South, where the always-open restaurants have inspired something of a cult following among police officers, truck drivers, night owls, and overcaffeinated college students.

The first Waffle House opened on Labor Day 1955 in the Atlanta suburb of Avondale Estates. One of the founders, Joe Rogers Sr., had worked for a similar restaurant chain in Memphis, Toddle House, but quit because he could not get an ownership stake. Half a century later, Waffle House remains privately owned and based near Atlanta.

Unlike most franchise operations, Waffle Houses have a charmingly retro intimacy about them. The shoebox-shaped units are small, with a few hard plastic booths and counter stools facing an open kitchen where all the cooking is done in full view on toasters, irons, and a griddle top. The menu is basic: eggs, waffles, burgers, grits, hash browns. Waitresses seem to know all the regulars by name and call other customers "hon" or "darlin.'" Orders do not appear on a computer screen; servers stand at the end of a counter and bark them out in vintage diner slang.

To complete the truck stop atmosphere, every Waffle House has a juke-box stocked with corny, countrified tunes about eating at Waffle House. Among the titles are "Waffle Do Wop," "There Are Raisins in My Toast," and "844,739 Ways to Eat a Hamburger" (a Georgia Tech mathematics class actually calculated the permutations). Many customers know that some of the songs were recorded by Mary Rogers, the wife of the chief executive—another homey touch that no doubt enhances their feeling that when they eat at the Waffle House, they are among family.

JIM AUCHMUTEY
Atlanta Journal-Constitution

John T. Edge, *Southern Belly: The Ultimate Food Lover's Companion to the South* (2000); Bill Osinski, *Atlanta Journal-Constitution* (24 December 2004); Richard Pillsbury, *From Boarding House to Bistro: The American Restaurant Then and Now* (1990); Waffle House website: www.wafflehouse.com; Kristen Wyatt, "Still Dishing at Age 50," *Associated Press* (13 August 2005).

Walter, Eugene Ferdinand

(1921–1998) CULINARY ENTHUSIAST, WRITER.

A native of Mobile, Ala., Eugene Ferdinand Walter was a man of catholic tastes and insatiable intellectual curiosity. At various points in his career, he worked as a novelist, poet, essayist, artist, lyricist, actor, designer, translator, humorist, botanist, marionetteer, philosopher, and cookery writer. He was a founding contributor of the *Paris Review* and a contributor to a multitude of magazines and journals, including *Harper's, Botteghe Oscure*, and the *Transatlantic Review*. He published numerous chapbooks of poetry; collections of short stories, including *The Byzantine Riddle* (1985); and a prize-winning novel, *The Untidy Pilgrim* (1954).

Perhaps his most engaging work was in the broad field of culinary letters. His food writing was intelligent, worldly, and playful, worthy of comparison to the best of M. F. K. Fisher. Throughout his life, Walter espoused the virtues of good food and drink. Of Mobile natives he observed, "It's a toss-up whether they rank the pleasures of the table or the pleasures of the bed first, but it's a concrete certainty that talk follows close after."

Walter was a lifelong student of Mobile, a sort of unofficial curator of its quirky charms. In *The Untidy Pilgrim*, he introduced the world to his hometown. "Down in Mobile they're all crazy," he wrote, "because the Gulf Coast is the kingdom of monkeys, the land of clowns, ghosts and musicians, and Mobile is sweet lunacy's county seat."

Walter was not provincial. While on prolonged sojourn in Rome, during the 1950s and 1960s, he ate and drank with a group of friends that included Federico Fellini. He worked as a translator and actor in several Fellini films, including *8½* (1963), and wrote the lyrics for the song "What Is a Youth?" for Franco Zeffirelli's film of *Romeo and Juliet*. And yet, no matter where he might live, a love of southern food and frolic remained at the core of his being. "In Rome I live as I lived in Mobile," he wrote. "On my terrace garden I have five kinds of mint, five kinds of onions and chives, as well as four-o'clocks and sweet olive. I take a nap after the midday meal; there is always time for gossip and for writing letters."

Walter's dedication to the southern culinary arts brought him back home in 1969 to write *American Cooking: Southern Style*, among the best of the Time-Life Foods of the World series. In succeeding years, he wrote about culinary matters in *Gourmet* and numerous other publications. During his later years, Walter published two overlooked jewels: *Delectable Dishes from Termite Hall: Rare and Unusual Recipes* (1982) and *Hints and Pinches: A Concise Compendium of Herbs and Aromatics with Illustrative Recipes and Asides on Relishes, Chutneys, and Other Such Concerns* (1991).

The latter, suffused with Walter's fanciful pen-and-ink drawings of mango-eating monkeys, dancing cats, and crown-bedecked bulbs of garlic, is a funhouse encyclopedia of the culinary arts. (An illustration therein depicts a lady of aristocratic bearing, attired in a purple-and-gold-striped skirt, her hand resting on an oversized fork as if it were a scepter. The caption reads: "The Devil's dear Grandmother pondering what menu to serve when she invites Pat Robertson, Jerry Falwell and Jesse Helms to dine in Hell with Hitler and Mussolini.")

At turns erudite and irreverent, *Hints and Pinches* is not an easy book to encapsulate. It is a work of folklore: "Medieval magicians put celery seeds in their shoes," writes Walter, "believing this could make it possible for them to fly." It is a showcase for the author's prejudices: "Powdered cloves, like the dead dust sold as [ground, black] pepper, is as far from the flavor of a freshly ground clove as Helsinki is from Las Vegas." And it contains a surfeit of recipes, among them instructions for the proper preparation of persimmon jam, beet-tinted "Southern Belle" ice cream, chayote rellenos, nasturtium-infused vinegar, and baked bass flavored with yogurt, walnuts, and pomegranate seeds.

Eugene Walter died on 29 March 1998. He was interred at Mobile's historic Church Street Graveyard on 2 April after a spirited wake, during which, at Walter's instruction, celebrants feasted on "chicken salad sandwiches, port wine, and plenty of nuts." In the wake of his death, southerners have begun to rediscover Walter's culinary legacy by way of admirers like novelist Pat Conroy.

JOHN T. EDGE
University of Mississippi

Rebecca Barrett and Carolyn Haines, eds., *Moments with Eugene* (2000); Catherine Clarke, *Milking the Moon* (2001); Pat Conroy, *The Pat Conroy Cookbook* (2004).

Washington, George

(1732–1799) U.S. PRESIDENT, AGRICULTURALIST.

A third-generation Virginian who became a prominent military hero and statesman, George Washington brought hundreds of visitors to his home, Mount Vernon, each year and had the opportunity to extend hospitality to people ranging from neighbors on nearby plantations to a delegation from the Catawba nation and members of the noble houses of Europe. Some idea of the number of visitors welcomed to the estate can be found in Washington's diaries. For example, in the 16 years between their marriage and the Revolution, George and Martha Washington entertained at least 418 individuals at their home. Following the war, between 1784 and 1789, they accommodated at least 588 individuals at Mount Vernon. The figures remained high following Washington's retirement from the presidency. In 1798, for example, there were guests for dinner on 203 of the 310 days for which records exist. In terms of total numbers, in that year, the Washingtons had at least 656 guests for dinner. By the end of his life, the volume of traffic through his home sometimes led Washington, who once compared Mount Vernon to "a well-resorted tavern," to look back with longing to the days before he had become a household word. In a letter to a friend, he described a typical dinner, "at which I rarely miss seeing strange faces; come, as they say, out of respect to me. Pray, would not the word curiosity answer as well?" He went on wistfully, "and how different this, from having a few social friends at a cheerful board?"

Three to four meals were typically served each day at Mount Vernon. Because both George and Martha Washington rose before sunrise, breakfast was on the table at seven o'clock in the morning, about one to two hours earlier than on other Virginia plantations of the period. Despite the variety of meats, fish, breads, and beverages (tea, coffee, and chocolate) from which to choose, Washington invariably had hoecakes (cornmeal pancakes) "swimming in butter and honey," which he washed down with hot tea. The main meal of the day was the midafternoon dinner, served in three courses. The first course offered diners a large selection of meats and vegetables, while the second course included a like number of desserts and preserved fruits. Where Washington was partial to fish at this meal, his wife had a fondness for other types of seafood. The meal ended with a course of fresh fruits, nuts, and sweet wines, of which Washington is said to have particularly enjoyed walnuts and Madeira. Later in the day, about six or seven o'clock in the evening, the family had tea, a light meal consisting of bread, butter, perhaps some cold meat or cheese, cake, and the beverage that gave this repast its name. The Washingtons generally went to bed at about nine o'clock, so supper, another light meal served about that time in many households, was not usually offered, unless there were special guests with whom the general wanted to stay up to talk.

Washington once wrote to an old friend, "My manner of living is plain . . . a glass of wine and a bit of mutton are always ready, and such as will be content to partake of them are welcome, those who expect more will be disappointed." This was a bit of an understatement, for the tables at Mount Vernon were loaded with foodstuffs, both those grown and prepared on the plantation (beef, pork, mutton, dairy products, and a wide variety of fruits, nuts, and vegetables) and imported from around the world (spices, wines, cheeses, olives, nuts, tea,

coffee, sugar, molasses). As mistress of the plantation, Martha Washington oversaw the kitchen, the garden that supplied the table, the poultry yard, the dairy, and the smokehouse. She also discussed menus with the enslaved cooks on a daily basis. For inspiration in this task, she might have turned to either the manuscript cookbook she inherited from the family of her first husband, Daniel Parke Custis, or to her copy of the most popular English cookbook available in America at the time, *The Art of Cookery Made Plain and Easy*, by Hannah Glasse.

MARY V. THOMPSON
Mount Vernon Ladies' Association

W. W. Abbot, Dorothy Twohig, Philander D. Chase, et al., eds., *The Papers of George Washington, Colonial Series, Revolutionary War Series, Confederation Series, Presidential Series, and Retirement Series*, 46 vols. to date (1983–); George Washington Parke Custis, *Recollections and Private Memoirs of Washington, By His Adopted Son* (1860); Susan Gray Detweiler, *George Washington's Chinaware* (1982); Joseph C. Fields, ed., *"Worthy Partner": The Papers of Martha Washington* (1994); John C. Fitzpatrick, ed., *The Writings of George Washington from the Original Manuscript Sources, 1745–1799*, 39 vols. (1931–44); Karen Hess, ed., *Martha Washington's Booke of Cookery* (1981); Donald Jackson and Dorothy Twohig, eds., *The Diaries of George Washington*, 6 vols. (1976–79).

Watermelon

Watermelon is among the best examples of the mythic significance of food in southern culture. The eating of watermelon is one of the most symbolic rituals of southerners. To be sure, watermelon is not a unique possession of the American South. Watermelon seeds have been discovered in Egyptian tombs from thousands of years ago, and Mediterranean peoples have cultivated the plant for centuries. Northern Americans eat watermelon, although their climate enables them to raise only small-fruited and midget varieties.

An annual called *Citrullus lanatus*, southern watermelon is a member of the gourd family. It grows during the South's warm, humid summers, requiring a 120-day growing season. Southern watermelons are called "rampant-growing varieties," and they have regionally meaningful names such as the Dixie Queen, Dixielee, Stone Mountain, Charleston Gray, Alabama Giant, Florida Giant, Louisiana Queen, Carolina Cross, and Africa 8. Africans introduced watermelon to Europe and later North America, and Indians in Florida were cultivating it by the mid-17th century. Thomas Jefferson grew watermelons at Monticello, but they were found among the crops of yeoman farmers more often than those of planters. Garden patches that fed many an impoverished southerner in the postbellum South often included watermelons. They were a low-cost treat even during the Depression, and some southerners still call the watermelon a "Depression ham."

Watermelon has been especially associated in the United States with rural southern blacks. It became a prop identified with the stereotypical Sambo—the childlike, docile, laughing black boy was seen grinning and eating watermelon. This derogatory image was pervasive in popular literature and art, and watermelon-eating scenes later became stock features of films and newsreels. Watermelon has been, nonetheless, a cultural symbol used also in less negative ways as well by southerners and others. Folklore has long told of the proper ways to plant watermelon (by poking a hole in the ground and planting the seed by hand), and the ability to tell a ripe watermelon by thumping it was a legendary rural skill. Literature tells of the simple joys of eating watermelon. Tom Sawyer and Huck Finn (in Mark Twain's *Tom Sawyer, Detective: As Told by Huck Finn*) "snuck off" from Aunt Sally one night and "talked and smoked and stuffed watermelon as much as two hours."

The Skillet Lickers chose a traditional southern folk tune, "Watermelon on the Vine," for one of the earliest recordings of southern country music, and Tom T. Hall celebrated the melon in the more recent "Old Dogs, Children, and Watermelon Wine." The lyrics to the blues song "Watermelon Man" identified the succulent melon with sexual potency, and a 1970 Melvin Van Peebles film about the experiences of a white man who wakes up one morning with a black skin was also called *Watermelon Man*. The watermelon has been used as an advertising symbol, especially on roadsides to direct motorists to stands selling the delicacy. Miles Carpenter,

Watermelon vendors, Warren County, Miss., 1975 (William R. Ferris Collection, Southern Folklife Collection, Wilson Library, University of North Carolina at Chapel Hill)

of Waverly, Va., began carving wooden watermelon slices and painting them with enamel decades ago, and today he is recognized as an accomplished folk artist.

In the contemporary South the watermelon remains a part of the summer diet. Cookbooks have recipes not only for the traditional chilled melon, melon balls, pickled watermelon rind, and spiked melon, but also for watermelon and cassis ice, spiced watermelon pie, and watermelon muffins. But the importance of watermelon to southerners transcends its use as food. When popular periodicals discuss symbols of the region, they usually include watermelon (*Southern Magazine*, June 1987; *Texas Monthly*, January 1977). Summer recreation includes festivals, and watermelon is the central feature of festivals at Luling, Tex.; Hampton County, S.C.; Chiefland, Chipley, Lakeland, and Monticello, Fla.; Grand Bay, Ala.; Raleigh, N.C.; and Mize and Water Valley, Miss. The U.S. Watermelon Seed-Spitting Contest is held during the National Watermelon Association's annual convention in Moreven, Ga., the first week of March. Hope, Ark., may be the watermelon capital of the South. The town advertises itself with a logo that has a picture of a watermelon and the claim that Hope offers "a slice of the good life." Hope farmers regularly raise 100–150 pound watermelons. Another southern town, Cordele, Ga., claims the motto "The Watermelon Capital of the World" and is home to the Watermelon Capital Speedway. Every year, Cordele hosts the Watermelon Days Festival, which includes mass consumption of locally grown watermelons, arts and crafts, a parade, and seed-spitting competitions.

Southerners would likely still agree with a passage in Mark Twain's *Pudd'nhead Wilson*: "The true southern watermelon is a boon apart and not to be mentioned with commoner things. It is chief of this world's luxuries, king by the Grace of God over all the fruits of the earth. When one has tasted it, he knows what the angels eat. It was not a southern watermelon that Eve took; we know it because she repented."

CHARLES REAGAN WILSON
University of Mississippi

Ellen Ficklen, *Watermelon* (1984); Daniel Wallace, *The Watermelon King* (2003); William Woys Weaver, *Gourmet* (July 2004); John Edgar Wideman, *Damballah* (1998); David Scofield Wilson and Angus Kress Gillespie, eds., *Rooted in America: Foodlore of Popular Fruits and Vegetables* (1999).

Wilson, Justin

(1914–2001) CAJUN CHEF AND HUMORIST.

Born at Roseland, La., on 24 April 1914, Justin Wilson was the son of Harry D. Wilson, the Pelican State's commissioner of agriculture from 1916 to 1948, and Olivett Toadvin. One of six children, Wilson was reared in his native Tangipahoa Parish, part of the state's Anglo-American Bible Belt, before attending Louisiana State University at Baton Rouge. When Wilson left the university without a degree after "majoring in girls," he became an itinerant day laborer until two events changed his life. In 1935 he met Will Rogers, who inspired Wilson to pursue a career in public speaking. In addition, during the early 1930s, Wilson obtained a patronage job "policing the state's grain warehouse industry." His duties as a safety engineer occasionally took him into southwest Louisiana's predominately Cajun rice-producing region. During these travels, the engineer began to hone his skills as a comedic storyteller, basing his humorous tales on the Cajun community.

As he developed his stage persona, Wilson modeled his style on that of the state's leading contemporary storyteller/entertainer, Walter Coquille, whose *Mayor of Bayou Pom-Pom* radio show was perhaps the region's most popular Great Depression era program. New Orleanian Coquille masqueraded as Cajun Télésfore Boudreaux, mayor of the fictional Bayou Pom-Pom community.

Following Coquille's death in 1957, several emerging entertainers moved to fill the void, including Justin Wilson, who began making appearances on the regional convention and banquet circuit. Like Coquille's Boudreaux, Wilson's act combined elements of the same southern minstrel and storytelling traditions that produced Rod Brasfield, Minnie Pearl, and the popular *Hee Haw* comedy revue. The middle-class jokester poked fun at south Louisiana's Francophone working class by using fractured, Cajun-inflected English and malapropisms as bases for humorous stories. In the 1960s Wilson, who claimed to have learned to cook at the age of eight as a means of avoiding field work, launched another career as a cookbook writer. He released his first publication in 1965, a privately printed work simply entitled *Justin Wilson Cook Book*. In 1968 Wilson's career as a comedian and writer profited immensely from the burgeoning Cajun cultural renaissance, as he gained national and, later, international notoriety.

In the 1970s Wilson capitalized upon the mounting popular interest in the culture by launching a popular Cajun cooking show eventually syndicated on PBS. The show's success, in turn, contributed to the appeal of Wilson's comedy albums and cookbooks. The Library of Congress catalog lists eleven publications by Justin Wilson, all but two

"How y'all are?" Justin Wilson, a Louisiana legend (Courtesy Justin Wilson Holding Company)

of which are cookbooks. Four of these publications appeared during the initial surge of national interest in Cajun culture (1974–79), while three works appeared in each of the two ensuing decades. The Library of Congress catalog also indicates that Wilson released 12 comedy albums in the 1970s and 17 commercial recordings in the 1980s.

In the 1990s Wilson stopped releasing albums and devoted his attention to his syndicated cooking program. Fans of the cooking show, comedy albums, and cookbooks were charmed by the comedian's "quaint" language. On the other hand, some Cajuns, particularly academicians and cultural activists, took a very dim view of Wilson, regarding him as an offensive impersonator in the tradition of the 19th- and early 20th-century "ethnic comedians," who lampooned the nation's ethnic and racial minorities. Wilson countered his critics with the claim that he was part Cajun through his maternal line. That claim, however, is spurious. Olivett Toadvin was of French immigrant ancestry, not of Acadian/Cajun descent—a fact confirmed by a close family member in a recent interview. Nor was she French-speaking, according to the 1910 census of Louisiana.

It is thus ironic that Justin Wilson, the faux Cajun cultural icon, should reach the pinnacle of his success during the era of political correctness. Wilson, who spent his declining years in Summit, Miss., died on 5 September 2001 and was subsequently interred at St. William's Cemetery in Port Vincent, La. Wilson, who was married several times, was survived by three daughters.

CARL A. BRASSEAUX
RYAN A. BRASSEAUX
Lafayette, Louisiana

Justin Wilson, *Justin Wilson's Cajun Fables* (1982), *Justin Wilson's Cajun Humor* (1979), *Justin Wilson's Classic Louisiana Cookin'* (1993), *Justin Wilson Cook Book* (1973), *Justin Wilson's Easy Cooking: 150 Rib-Tickling Recipes for Good Eating* (1998), *The Justin Wilson Gourmet and Gourmand Cookbook* (1984), *Justin Wilson's Homegrown Louisiana Cookin'* (1990), *Justin Wilson Looking Back: A Cajun Cookbook* (1996), *Justin Wilson Number Two Cookbook: Cookin' Cajun* (1980), *Justin Wilson's Outdoor Cooking with Inside Help* (1986), *More Cajun Humor* (1984).

Wine

The South may be better known for bourbon and moonshine than for wine, but wine has always had a place in the social culture of the region—before 1776 and since. Imported wine was an accepted and popular social beverage among the elite of the colonial and antebellum South, particularly in port cities such as Baltimore, Richmond, Charleston, Savannah, Mobile, and New Orleans.

In many of the wealthier homes it was not uncommon to keep a decanter of port, sherry, or Madeira on the sideboard of the dining room or parlor. In the 1850s, wine clubs in Charleston and Savannah regularly hosted what were among the country's first wine tastings. Although moonshine and corn liquor were the beverages of choice for strong drink throughout the South, particularly in the rural highlands of the Appalachians and Ozarks, wine was also consumed, made from fruits and berries, wild or cultivated, and from herbs for medicinal and tonic uses.

America's culinary revolution in the last decades of the 20th century and the concomitant surge of interest in table wine (made solely from grapes) was a little slower coming to the South, but today it is firmly entrenched and still growing. Restaurants with top-flight wine lists of American and imported wines exist in all major cities of the South and even smaller cities and towns, be it Tampa, Fla., Raleigh, N.C., or Cleveland, Miss. Privately owned wine collections of international renown can be found in Nashville, Memphis, New Orleans, Houston, and Dallas, the environs of Washington, D.C., and Miami. Nashville's annual charity wine auction, l'Eté de Vin, is one of the largest and most lucrative in the United States.

The South is making history, however, with its own wine industry, which has flourished dramatically in the last 20 years. Southern wines—viognier and merlot from Virginia, cabernet and syrah from Texas, cabernet franc from Georgia, for instance—frequently garner awards in national wine competitions. Wines from Texas, Virginia, and North Carolina are available in several major metropolitan areas, including Los Angeles, New York, Washington, and Chicago; some are now exported to Europe, Scandinavia, and the Far East.

Surprising as it may seem, America's very first wines were likely made in the South. French Huguenots who had settled near what is now Jacksonville, Fla., in the 1560s produced wine from native grapes, probably the same wild varieties of muscadine spotted along the East Coast by Viking voyagers a thousand years ago. Some 500 years after the fabled Norse sightings, Sir Walter Raleigh made an early stab at making wine from the scuppernong grapes he found growing near the Carolina coast. His shipmasters noted the exotic scent of wild scuppernong (*Vitis rotundifolia*) along the shore: "The smell of sweetness filled the air as if they were in the midst of some delicate garden."

The Jamestown settlers of 1607 cultivated vineyards, though it is not known whether they actually made wine. Many of the early colonists imported European vine cuttings and encouraged wine growing, from Lord Delaware to Lord Baltimore to Governor James Oglethorpe in Georgia. None, however, was successful, just as Thomas Jefferson's efforts with European varieties failed—and for the same reasons. Jefferson believed that America, and

particularly Virginia, had great potential for wine growing; he viewed wine as a more temperate beverage, an antidote "for the bane of whiskey," whose abuses ultimately led to Prohibition. Jefferson's dream for producing classic wines such as those he tasted in Europe and imported for his own wine cellar never materialized, despite efforts at Monticello with varieties such as cabernet sauvignon, merlot, Sangiovese, and Riesling. The European vines (*Vitis vinifera*) succumbed to various assaults—January thaws followed by sudden freezes that killed the buds, mildew in the humidity of summer, or soil-borne pests that devoured the tender vine roots—problems finally solved only in the latter part of the 20th century. Jefferson would undoubtedly be pleased at Virginia's success with vinifera grapes today as the South's largest producer of vinifera wines.

Thomas Jefferson's passionate pursuit of wine growing at Monticello failed, but his interest in wine had significant impact on wine traditions in the young republic. During his five-year tenure in France as U.S. ambassador during the Washington administration, he acquainted himself with the best wines of that country, traveling extensively in the great vineyards of Burgundy, the Rhône Valley, and Bordeaux, as well as visiting wine regions in Italy and Germany. His personal records show numerous orders for shipments of fine wine to John Adams, Benjamin Franklin, James Madison, and George Washington, including one order of 40 cases of champagne for the president. Jefferson and Washington both prized good Madeira, maintained sizeable stocks of it, and were known to enjoy a glass of it almost daily.

Jefferson, recognizing the difficulty of adapting European vines to New World conditions, encouraged American grape breeders working with domestic grapes, including John Adlum of Maryland, who developed the Catawba grape; Samuel Maverick of South Carolina; and Dr. Daniel Norton of Virginia, who hybridized the Virginia seedling, or Norton grape, in the early 1800s. Later in the century, a Virginia red wine made from Norton took silver medals at the Paris Exposition of 1878. Today this same grape variety has produced several prize-winning wines from Virginia, Missouri, and Georgia.

By the 1870s several southern states had thriving wine industries, notably North Carolina and Virginia, but also Georgia, which, according to an 1880 Department of Agriculture report, was the sixth largest wine producer in the United States. In these states the native scuppernong and muscadine varieties produced huge quantities of wine shipped all over the country. Arkansas and Texas also produced quantities of wine from native grapes. It was, in fact, tough native rootstock grown in Texas and the Ozark highlands that saved the vineyards of Europe in the late 1880s when they were ravaged by a root pest, *Phylloxera*.

With temperance in full swing by the early 20th century, several southern states voted to go dry, and Prohibition virtually destroyed wine production throughout the United States. Even after repeal in 1933, however, Prohibition

maintained a stranglehold in the South, particularly in the Bible Belt, where some counties remain dry today. A significant breakthrough for winegrowers in all of the southern states came when they finally gained support from state legislatures for farm winery bills enabling them to produce and sell wine. Still, in one of those curiously southern quirks of religion and politics, there are a few counties that permit winery operation and the making of wine but prohibit sales of any alcoholic beverage.

The revolution in southern wines took its first leaps in the mid-1970s, when a handful of winegrowers in Virginia and Texas bucked scientific advice and planted the European wine varieties—*Vitis vinifera*—that supposedly could not grow east of the Rockies, and especially not in the South. These pioneers found it a struggle at first, trying to discover the keys to success in untried regions. Within a decade or so, however, improved viticultural techniques and better wine making began to pay off in wines of quality and style. The global success of California wine during the 1980s accelerated interest in and demand for good table wine in all parts of the United States. Momentum came also from America's gastronomic awakening, with its new awareness of regional specialties and homegrown food products.

As southern winegrowers began to understand the best spots for growing desirable grapes, as they gained experience in making stylish wines of better quality, they were able to capitalize on the flourishing interest in wine and attract local followings. By the mid-1990s wineries in several southern states were enjoying excellent success—and attracting attention nationwide.

The South's best wines come from a few states, notably Virginia, Texas, North Carolina, and Georgia, but quality wines increasingly pop up in Maryland, Arkansas, Tennessee, even Florida and Louisiana. Vineyard acreage is increasing in many areas, especially in the upland regions of the Upper South and in the mid-Atlantic states, where grape growing is considered a viable option to tobacco cultivation.

Many wineries still find it useful commercially to produce wines from French and American hybrids such as Seyval blanc, Vidal, Chambourcin, Catawba, and Cayuga, more prolific varieties that help with cash flow and ripen more reliably than *vinifera*. Improved quality and drinkability of these wines has gained greater acceptance, particularly important for regions where growing vinifera grapes is marginal or impossible, such as tropical and sub-tropical regions of the Deep South and Florida. Wineries in Florida, for in-stance, have benefited enormously from collaborative work with grape scientists at Florida State University developing new muscadine hybrids that produce sound dry and off-dry table wines.

Most wine consumers, in the South as elsewhere, prefer wines made from vinifera grapes, and southern wine-growers can now supply good char-donnay, merlot, cabernets, viognier, pinot grigio, syrah, and very appealing blended reds, though it is still necessary to sort out the well-made wines from the inferior. Most southern wineries are small, family-owned operations whose wines are available only locally. One popular way to discover them is the increasing number of wine festivals and tastings held throughout the South.

BARBARA ENSRUD
Durham, North Carolina

Leon Adams, *The Wines of America* (1990); Barbara Ensrud, *American Vineyards* (1988); James M. Gabler, *The Wines and Travels of Thomas Jefferson* (1995); John R. Hailman, *Jefferson on Wine* (2006); Thomas Jefferson, *The Garden and Farm Books* (1987).

Abbott, Frances, 27, 140, 143, 154, 155, 160, 210, 274
Albright, Alex, 172
Allen, Carol, 138
Auchmutey, Jim, 22, 244, 278

Barash, Bailey, 193
Best, Bill, 274
Bolsterli, Margaret Jones, 104
Bourg, Gene, 83, 212, 227, 238, 262
Bower, Anne L., 45
Brasseaux, Carl A., 32, 188, 195, 254, 272, 285
Brasseaux, Ryan A., 32, 188, 195, 254, 272, 285
Butler, Brooke, 170, 174

Cashion, Ann, 231
Chappell, Mary Margaret, 39
Chavis, Shaun, 125
Coleman, Millie, 273
Cowdery, Charles K., 127
Criswell, Stephen, 166, 185, 235

Dabney, Joseph, 264
Dean, Michael, 241

Edge, John T., 1, 77, 104, 261, 279
Egerton, John, 27, 141, 155, 175
Ensrud, Barbara, 287
Evans, Amy, 184

Ferris, Marcie Cohen, 47, 58, 67
Fisher, Brian, 196
Florio, Donna, 160, 207
Fowler, Damon Lee, 130, 154, 161, 182, 240, 253
Fussell, Fred C., 216

Gutierrez, C. Paige, 62, 177

Hanchett, Tom, 27
Harris, Jessica B., 15, 37, 122
Harwell, Richard B., 198
Hatchett, Louis, 182
Head, Thomas, 70
Hess, Karen, 189
Holditch, W. Kenneth, 249
Hopkins, Tonya, 255
Howorth, Lisa, N. 257

Jackson, Fatimah, 269
Jones, Loyal, 151

Kahn, E. J., Jr., 146
Kelly, Leslie, 112
Kolb, Carolyn, 177, 206

Lee, Matt, 245
Lee, Ted, 245
Lord, J. Dennis, 92
Luster, J. Michael, 203, 218, 221, 228

Makowski, Elizabeth M., 145, 186
McDearman, Karen M., 143
McGehee, Margaret T., 190
McMillen, Matt, 26
Mechling, Jay, 208
Mercuri, Becky, 259
Merrell, Mindy, 247
Miller, Adrian, 277
Miller, Mary Margaret, 158
Mosier, Angie, 79, 134, 222
Muhammad, Abdullah F. H., 269
Myers, Kendra, 226

Niba, Lorraine, 269
Norman, Corrie E., 95
Norris, Lucy, 219, 221

O'Kelley, Sarah, 193

Pilcher, Jeffrey M., 64
Pillsbury, Richard, 100, 162
Prewitt, Wiley C., Jr., 55, 147, 164, 213, 236
Purvis, Kathleen, 53, 110

Ragsdale, John G., 229
Rankin, Tom, 167, 199
Rowley, Matthew B., 200

Sauceman, Fred W., 18, 102, 119, 239
Schmidt, Aimée, 210
Schweid, Richard, 136, 219, 270
Shortridge, Barbara G., 50, 251
Simmons, Scott R., 129, 181, 234, 243, 267
Sohn, Mark F., 140, 168, 263, 266

Tartan, Beth, 41
Taylor, Joe Gray, 1, 73
Taylor, Saddler, 121, 131, 132, 179, 202
Thomas, James G., Jr., 109, 159
Thompson, Mary V., 281
Tipton-Martin, Toni, 104
Tucker, Susan, 190, 230
Tuten, Renna, 81, 159

Ward, George B., 115
Weaver, William Woys, 265
Wilson, Charles Reagan, 88, 122, 152, 204, 214, 282
Woodward, Stan, 179

Page numbers in boldface refer to articles.

Aaron, Hank, 192

Abbott, Shirley, 169

Abingdon, Va., 19

Acadians, 32–34, 158, 178, 195–96, 254

Adams, John, 288

Adlum, John, 289

Adventures in Good Eating (Hines), 183

African Americans, 11–12, **15–18**, 43, 47, 48–49, 51, 72, 77–79, 80, 102–3, 104–7, 110, 117, 121, 144, 184, 185, 225, 248, 278

Agee, James, 170

"Ain't the Gravy Good?," 169

Ajax Diner, 168

Alabama, 25, 43, 51, 52, 54, 67, 68, 94, 126, 131, 167, 176, 203, 229, 237, 238, 245, 269, 270

Alabama, University of, 44

Alabama First Lady's Cookbook, 43

Alaga Syrup, 124–25

Alciatore, Angelo (Antoine), 85, 250

Alciatore, Jules, 211, 212

Ale-8-1, 31

Alessio, Al, 248

Algonquians, 228, 229, 265

Allen & Son, 112

Allen Canning Company, 229

American Cooking: Southern Style (Walter), 280

American Indians. *See* Native Americans

American Southern Food Institute, 13

American Taste (Villas), 143

American Woman's Cook Book, The, 223

Anderson, Billy, 114

Anderson, Jay, 8

Anderson's Bar-B-Que, 114

Andrews Sisters, 257

Antique American Cookbooks, 44

Antoine (slave gardener), 218

Antoine's Restaurant, 85, 211, 212, 250

Apalachicola, Fla., 210

Appalachian foodways, **18–22**, 103, 169, 175, 230, 239, 240, 266

Applebee's, 101

Apple pie, 224

Apples, 21, 135, 224, 232, 267

Arawaks, 37

Arkansas, 28, 30, 52, 54, 94, 127, 169, 170, 229, 252, 289, 290

Arkansas, University of, 229

Armstrong, Ishmael, 191

Armstrong, Louis, 244

Arnaud's Restaurant, 85, 86, 211, 250

Arnold's Country Kitchen, 247

Art of Cookery Made Plain and Easy, The (Glasse), 41, 282

Asheville, N.C., 275

Athens, Tex., 126

Atlanta, Ga., 12, 29, 66, 78, 94, 101, 105, 146, 147, 182, 186, 191, 192, 215, **244–45**, 273–74, 279

Atlanta Constitution, 11, 106, 142, 171

Atlanta Journal, 42

Atlanta Journal-Constitution, 245

Atlanta Journal Sunday Magazine, 161

Attakapas, 272

Audubon, John, 149

Augusta, Ga., 226

Aunt Jemima, 13, **109–10**

Austin, Tex., 116

Avery Island, La., 46, 270, 271–72

Avondale Estates, Ga., 101

Awakening, The (Chopin), 72

Ayden, N.C., 112, 172, 174

Bachman, John, 149
Bagby, George, 8
Bagdad, Fla., 125
"Bake Me a Country Ham," 157
Ball Brothers Company, 233
Baltimore, Md., 154, 205, 270, 287
Banana pudding, 236
Barbados, 37
Barbecue, 8, 10, 12, **22–26**, 57, 61, 68, 82,
  91, 96, 100, 101, 150, 179, 180; Carolinas,
  110–12; Memphis and Tennessee, **112–
  15**; Texas, **115–18**
"Barbecue Bess," 82
Bar-B-Q Shop, 115
Bardstown, Ky., 128
Baro, Gene, 104–5
Barq, Edward Charles Edmond, 31
Barq's root beer, 31
Bartram, William, 216
Baton Rouge, La., 43, 88, 238
Bayougoula, 195
Beans, 3, 4, 18–19, 20, 21, 68, 106, **119–20**,
  151, 243
Beaufort, N.C., 204
Beaufort stew/Frogmore stew, **121–22**
Beef, **26–27**, 52, 80, 84, 115, 117, 163, 185
Begue, Elizabeth, 86
Begue, Hippolyte, 86
Belk, Sarah, 27
Bell Buckle, Tenn., 31, 199
Bell Buckle RC and MoonPie Festival, 199
Belmont, N.C., 167
Belzer, Arnold Mark, 69
Benét, Stephen Vincent, 151
Benne (sesame), 12, 103, **122**
Beranbaum, Rose Levy, 223
Berea, Ky., 264
Berendt, John, 77
Bessinger, Maurice, 78
Beverages, **27–32**
Beverley, Robert, 88–89, 116
Biedenharn, Joseph, 146
Big Daddy O's Patio, 234
Biguenet, Henry, 212
"Billie's Gumbo Blues," 179

Bill Neal's Southern Cooking, 13, 44, 140,
  205
Biloxi, Miss., 10, 31
Birmingham, Ala., 13, 44, 61, 78
Biscuits, 7, 79, 103, **122–25**, 168
Biscuits, Spoonbread, and Sweet Potato Pie
  (Neal), 205
Biscuitville, 124, 163
Bissinger, Karl, 194
Blackberry Farm, 239
Black Boy (Wright), 9
Black-eyed peas, 15, 16, 74, 103, 104, 120,
  122, **125–26**, 173, 252
Black Eyed Peas (hip-hop group), 120
Blacksburg, S.C., 204
Blair, Ezell, Jr., 77
Blairsville, Ga., 264
Blenheim, S.C., 31
Blenheim's Ginger Ale, 31
Bligh, Captain William, 38
Blount, Roy, Jr., 43, 82, 191
Blues music, 81–82
"Bobs of the Bayou Bank," 237
Bobwhite, 236–38
Bogan, Lucille, 82
Boggy Bayou Mullet Festival, 203–4
Bojangles, 95, 124, 163
Book of Southern Humor (Blount), 211
Boone Tavern, 264
Borden, Gail, 224
Botteghe Oscure, 279
Bourbon whiskey, 96, **127–29**, 198
Bowers, John, 229
Bowling Green, Ky., 183
Bowser, Pearl, 105
Bradham, Caleb, 29
Brasfield, Rod, 286
Breaux, Joseph A., 34
Breaux Bridge Crawfish Festival, 35, 159
Brennan, Dick, 87
Brennan, Ella, 87, **129–30**, 193
Brennan, Lally, 130
Brennan, Owen, 129
Brennan's Restaurant, 85, 87, 129, 250, 257
Breton Sound, La., 210

Brewer, Albert, 43
Brewer, Martha Farmer, 43
Bridges, Alston, 111
Bridges, Red, 111
Bridges Barbecue Lodge, 111
Brigsten, Frank, 213
"Bringing in the Sheaves," 81
Brookhaven, Miss., 204
Brooklyn, N.Y., 194
Broussard's, 85, 86
Brown, Frank C., 278
Brown, John Y., 258, 259
Brown, Marion Lea, **130–31**
Brown, Mel, 144
Brown, Milton, and His Musical Brownies, 82
Brownsville, Tenn., 113
Brunswick, Ga., 131
Brunswick County, Va., 131
Brunswick stew, 25, 56, 61, 92, 111, **131–32**, 179, 202, 230
Buckingham, Nash, 237
Buffalo (fish), 164
Buffett, Jimmy, 83, 179
Bullard, Mrs. W. L., 155
Bullock, Helen, 130
Burch Farms, 174
Burger King, 163
Burgoo, 25, 56, **132–33**, 179, 180, 202
Burlington, N.C., 130
Bush Brothers, 229
Byrd, William, II, 71, 88, 255
Byzantine Riddle, The (Walter), 280

Cable, George Washington, 273
Cadbury-Schwepps, 30
Cade, Robert, 29
Café des Réfugiés, 84, 249
Café Nicholson, 194
Cajun foodways, **32–36**, 43, 49, 56–57, 61, 63, 87, 158, 178, 188, 195–96, 230, 234, 252, 254, 266, 272–73, 285–87
Cakes, 42, **134–36**, 182
Calderón de la Barca, Fanny, 66
Caldwell, Joseph P., 173

California, 208, 210, 218, 253, 270
California Fruit Growers Exchange, 209
Callahan, Ed, 43
Callahan, Kevin, 205
Callus on My Soul (Gregory), 143
Camp, Charles, 9
Campbell, Christiana, 59
Campbell, Kate, 276
Campbell, William H., 167–68
Candler, Asa, 29, 146, 147
Cannon, Julie, 276
Canton, N.C., 22
Caramel cake, 135
Carême, Antonin, 83
Caribbean foodways, 23, **37–38**, 64–65, 210, 255–57
Carolina Housewife, The, 16, 122
Carolina Israelite, 77
Carolina Rice Kitchen, The (Hess), 9
Carpenter, Miles, 283–84
Carrboro, N.C., 205
Carter, Jimmy, 12, 176, 218, 237
Carteret County, N.C., 203, 204
Caruso, Enrico, 86
Carver, George Washington, 126, 217, 270
"Carve That 'Possum," 83
Casseroles, 55, 95, 253
Caste and Class in a Southern Town (Dollard), 145
Catawbas, 281
Catfish, 1, 8, 61, **136–38**, 167
Catledge, Turner, 175
Cazeneuve, Arnaud, 211
Centennial Buckeye Cook Book, 45
Center for the Study of Southern Culture, 13 (Oxford, Miss.)
Chapel Hill, N.C., 13, 49, 83, 112, 204, 205
Charbonneau, C. C., 165
Charleston, S.C., 12, 48, 68, 74, 75, 76, 77, 92, 135, 194, 205, 236, **245–46**, 251, 252, 256, 287
Charleston, W.Va., 19, 101, 191
Charleston Grill, 246
Charleston Receipts, 76
Charlotte, N.C., 30, 31, 66, 77, 111, 163, 199

Charlotte Observer, 173
Chase, Edgar (Dooky), II, 138
Chase, Leah Lange, 18, **138–40**
Chattanooga, Tenn., 31, 100, 163, 199
Chattanooga Bakery, 199, 200
Cheek, Joel O., 29
Cheerwine, 31
Chef Paul Prudhomme's Louisiana Kitchen, 179
Cherokees, 18, 19, 221, 239, 240, 275
Chess pie, **140–41**, 224
Chez Helene, 249
Chicago, Ill., 24, 66, 106, 109, 183
Chicken, 8, 39, 68, 80, 84, 92–93, 101, 104, 106, 178; fried, 3, 8, 12, 55, 70, 92, 99, **141–43**, 194, 258
Chick-fil-A, 245
Chiefland, Fla., 285
Chili, 65–66
Chili Pepper magazine, 115
Chiltoskey, Mary, 20
Chipley, Fla., 285
Chipman, N. P., 54
"Chitlin Cookin' Time in Cheatham County," 9, 144
Chitlin Strut and Other Madrigals, 143
Chitterlings, 2, 9, 89, **143–45**
Chopin, Kate, 72, 179
Chowchow, 18, 21, 75
"Church," 82
Church's Chicken, 95, 163
Cicala, Stephen, 49
Cincinnati, Ohio, 90, 218
Civil Rights Act of 1964, 78, 248
Civil rights movement, 17, 77, 139
Civil War, 6, 11, 17, **39–40**, 41, 54, 59–60, 132, 206, 232
Claiborne, Craig, 105, 145, 176
Clark, Guy, 169
Clayton, Ala., 135
Cleaver, Eldridge, 145
Cleveland, Miss., 287
Clinton, Bill, 278–79
Clinton, Catherine, 59
Clover (Sanders), 215

Clower, Jerry, 124, 157
Clutch, Ron, 157
Cobb, Ty, 215
Coca-Cola, 12, 29, 129, **146–47**, 198, 257
Coca-Cola cake, 31
Cochon, 251
Coconut cake, 136
"Coffee Grinding Blues," 82
Cold Mountain (Frazier), 60
Coleman, Mose, 207
"Collard Greens," 172
Collards. *See* Greens: collard
Colonel Sanders Museum, 259
Colonial Restaurant, 138
Colonnade, 245
Colorado, 234
Colquitt, Harriett Ross, 154, 253
Columbia, S.C., 78, 110
Columbian Exchange, 37
Columbus, Christopher, 141, 208, 220, 255
Columbus, Ga., 30, 42
Commander's Palace, 87, 129, 130, 193, 234, 235, 250
Compleat House-wife, The (Smith), 41
Confederate Receipt Book, 11, 39
Conroy, Pat, 281
Cook, Fanny A., 165
Cookbooks, **41–44**, 61, 63, 92, 98, 103, 105, 124, 130, 146, 182, 194, 232, 241, 266, 284; community, **45–46**
Cooke, Martha Neal, 124
Cooking with Soul (Hearon), 105
Coons and possums, **147–50**
Cooper's Old Time Pit Bar-B-Que, 118
Coquille, Walter, 285–86
Corbin, Ky., 142, 258
Cordele, Ga., 285
Corinth, Miss., 27
Corky's, 68, 115
Corn, 4, 6, 10, 16, 21, 33, 39, 51, 65, 76, 80, 84, 127, **151–52**, 196
Cornbread, 2, 3–4, 11, 18–19, 80–81, 99, 103, 104, 119, 123, 151, **152–54**, 171, 236
Cortez, Fla., 203
Cosmopolitan, 181

Country captain, **154–55**
Country ham, **155–58**
Country Ham (Clower), 157
Country music, 82
Covert, Mildred, 69
Cowpeas, 4–5
Cracker Barrel Old Country Store, 101, 249
Cracklings, 3, 152
Craig, Elijah, 96
Crass, James, 30
crawfish, 35, 36, 47, 49, 61, 63, **158–59**
Creole Feast (Lombard), 139
Creole foodways, 35, 47, 63, 74, 75, 76, 84, 88, 129, 130, 138–39, 158, 178, 181, 188, 212, 231, 235, 249, 250, 251, 252, 254, 260
Crews, Harry, 43
Crisco, 69, 223
Crook's Corner, 13, 49, 205
Cross Creek (Rawlings), 241–42
Cross Creek Cookery (Rawlings), 43, 186, 241–43
Cross Keys, 247
Cuba, 38, 66
Cuisine Créole, La (Hearn), 8, 181
Culinary Arts Institute, 223
"Culinary despotism," 12, 16
Cullman County, Ala., 94
Custis, Daniel Parke, 282
Cyrus, Billy Ray, 204

Daisy May's BBQ USA, 114
Dale, Thomas, 26
Dallas, Tex., 30, 287
Damon Lee Fowler's New Southern Kitchen, 160–61
Daniel, Jack Newton, 187
Daniels, Jonathan, 202
Darden, Norma Jean and Carole, 43
Davenport, Iowa, 218
Davenport, Rody, 100
Davidson's Country Store and Farm, 22
Davis, John, 198
Davis, R. T., 109
Davis, Varina, 40

Daytona Beach, Fla., 201
De Bore, Etienne, 268, 269
Decatur, Ga., 101, 195
Decoration Day, 54
Deep Run, N.C., 174
Deer, 56, 57. *See also* Venison
De la Valdéne, Guy, 237
Delectable Dishes from Termite Hall (Walter), 280
De Leon, Arnoldo, 65
Delta Wedding (Welty), 73
De Soto, Hernando, 88, 112
Deviled Egg Recipe Competition, 161
Deviled eggs, **160–61**
Dictionary of the Vulgar Tongue, 200
Dillon, Clarissa, 111
Diners, 100
Dishes and Beverages of the Old South (McCulloch-Williams), 223
Dixie beer, 29
Dixie Cook-Book and Practical Housekeeper, 45
Dixie Crystals, 269
Dixie Grape, 30
Dixon, Queenie, 124
Dog and Gun (Hooper), 237
Dole, Bob, 278–79
Dollard, John, 145
Dooky Chase Restaurant, 88, 138–40, 249, 251
Douglass, Frederick, 72
Dreamland, 24
Driftwood, Tex., 24
Dr Pepper, 30
Du Bois, W. E. B., 244
Dull, Henrietta Stanley, 42, 154, **161–62**
Dunn, N.C., 174
Dupree, Nathalie, 12, 44
Durham, N.C., 30
Dutch oven, 230
Dutrey, Louis, 86

Easton, Tex., 175
Eating, Drinking, and Visiting in the South (Taylor), 236

Economy Administration Cook Book, The (Rhodes), 42

Edge, John T., 44, 124, 161

Edgerton, Clyde, 53–54, 55

Edwards, Edwin, 210

Egerton, John, 13, 19, 27, 44, 103, 112, 124, 153, 154, 218, 236, 264

Eighteen Pounds of Unclean Chitlins and Other Greasy Blues Specialties, 144

"Eight Piece Box," 83

Eisenhower, Dwight D., 147

"Eleven Cent Cotton, Forty Cent Meat," 9

Elie, Lolis Eric, 114

Ellington, Duke, 169

Elliot, Sarah A., 42

Elliott, Charles, 237

Elliott, William, 56

Ellison, Ralph, 9, 144

Emancipation Proclamation, 17

Emeril Live, 193

Emeril's Delmonico, 193

Emory University, 147

English Huswife, The (Markham), 41

Esquire, 105

Essence of Emeril, The, 193

Ethnicity and food, **47–50**

Everett, Alberta, 69

Fabacher's, 86

Faison, N.C., 174

Farming, **50–52**, 93, 126, 151, 217

Fast food, 8, 23, 36, 81, 95, 101, 124, 142, **162–64**

Faucon, Xavier, 247

Faulkner, William, 9, 72, 120, 129, 174

Faust, Drew Gilpin, 59

Fayetteville, N.C., 30

Fearrington House, 194

Feast Made for Laughter, A (Claiborne), 146

Fellini, Federico, 280

Ferris, Marcie Cohen, 9

Filbert, S.C., 215

Finster, Howard, 200

Fish, rough, **164–66**

Fish camps, **166–67**

Fisher, Abby, 17, 43, 232

Fisher, M. F. K., 280

Flack, Captain, 117

Flagg, Fannie, 277

Floatplane Notebooks, The (Edgerton), 53

Flora-Bama Lounge, 203

Florida, 26, 28, 45, 52, 54, 62, 63, 64, 65, 88, 186, 197, 203, 208–10, 224, 237, 238, 241, 242, 257, 265, 269, 290

Florida, University of, 29, 197

Florida Agriculturalist, 275

Florida State University, 290

Flour, 7, 123, 223

Folks, 101

Fonseca, Denise, 207

Food History News, 111

Food Network, 193

Foodways, defined, 8

Foose, Martha, 141

Foreman, Clark, 78

Fossett, Edith, 189

Fowler, Damon Lee, 71, 214

Fox, William Price, 143

Franey, Pierre, 146

Franklin, Benjamin, 288

Frazier, Charles, 60

Freetown, Va., 13, 193

Fresh Air, 24

Freshwater Fishes in Mississippi (Cook), 165

Fried chicken. *See* Chicken: fried

"Fried Chicken," 143

"Fried Chicken and Gasoline," 83

Fried Green Tomatoes at the Whistle Stop Café (Flagg), 277

Frost, A. B., 109

Fruit butters, 21

Funeral food and cemetery cleaning, **53–55**

Gaines, Ernest, 179

Gainesville, Fla., 29

Gainesville, Ga., 94

Galatoire, Jean, 86

Galatoire's, 86, 250

Galveston Bay, Tex., 10

Game cookery, 1, 39, **55–57**, 92, 96, 131, 147–50, 236–38

Gar, 164–65

Garden Book (Jefferson), 122

Gardener's Latin (Neal), 205

Gardening for the South (White), 266

Gardner, Randy, 275

Garner, Bob, 111

Gaston, S.C., 174

Gaston County, N.C., 166, 167

Gastonia, N.C., 30, 111

Gatorade, 29

Gebhardt, William, 66

Gender and food, **58–62**, 72, 98

Gendusa, John, 260

Gendusa's Bakery, 228

Generall Historie of Virginia, The (Smith), 71

Genovese, Eugene D., 12, 16

Georgia, 23, 25, 31, 45, 52, 54, 68, 70, 73, 93, 94, 131, 132, 154, 155, 157, 173, 174, 182, 198, 213, 214, 215, 218, 230, 231, 237, 238, 241, 251, 253, 269, 270, 278, 279, 289

Georgia, University of, 208

Georgia Peaches, 215

Germantown Commissary, 112, 113, 114, 115

Giddings, Mrs. Jed, 42

Gift of Southern Cooking, The (Lewis and Peacock), 44, 194, 225

Glasgow, Ellen, 212

Glasse, Hannah, 41, 282

Glenn, Camille, 214

Glover, Thomas, 214

Gluck's, 86

Golden, Harry, 77

Goldsboro, N.C., 24

Gone with the Wind (Mitchell), 23, 72, 273

Gonzales, La., 188

Goodbody, Mary, 44

Good Hearts (Price), 157

Good Old Grits (Neal and Perry), 205

"Good Old Turnip Greens," 172

Goo Goo Clusters, **167–68**

Gordon, James, 56

Gourmet, 145, 280

Goya Foods, 66

Gracious Plenty, A (Edge), 44

Graham County, N.C., 240

Grand Bay, Ala., 285

Grand Ole Opry, 168

Gravy, 141, **168–70**. *See also* Redeye gravy

Great American Writers' Cookbook, 4

Great Depression, 11, 19, 93, 102, 173, 207, 233

Great Migration, 17

Green, Nancy, 109

Green, Paul, 174

Greene, Melissa Faye, 214

Greens, 16, 39, 104, 106, **170–72**, 228, 229; collard, 11, 74, 76, 171, 172, **172–74**; turnip, 172, **174–75**

Greensboro, N.C., 44, 77, 111, 192

Greenville, S.C., 191

Greenwood, Miss., 12

Gregory, Dick, 143

Griffin, Ga., 226

Grits, 4, 12, 43, 76, 123, 151, **175–77**

"Grunt Meat Blues," 82

Guizeta, Roberto, 147

Gulf Coast foodways, 10, **62–64**

Gumbo, 10, 16, 34, 47, 56, 63, 74, 84, 86, 92, 104, 139, **177–79**, 206, 235, 254

Gutierrez, C. Paige, 49, 196

Hale County, Ala., 170

Hall, Tom T., 283

Ham, 123. *See also* Country ham

Hamel, Paul, 20

Hamer, Gene, 205

Hampton County, S.C., 285

Handy, Thomas, 263

Hardee's, 124, 163

Harlan, Ky., 172

Harlem (New York City) 105

Harmon County, Okla., 126

Harper's Weekly, 181

Harris, Jessica B., 43

Harris, Julian, 171

Harris, Trudier, 72

Harrod, James, 267
Harrodsburg, Ky., 267
Hartman, Barney and Ally, 30
Harwell, Gordon, 277–78
Harwood, Jim, 43
Hash, South Carolina, **179–81**
Haskins, Creed, 131
Hatcher, Claud A., 30
Haverhill, Mass., 278
Hawaii, 208, 246, 269
Hawkins County, Tenn., 22
Hearn, Lafcadio, 8, **181–82**
Hearon, Ethel Brown, 105
Hee Haw, 286
Helena, Ark., 124
Hemings, James, 16, 189
Hemings, Peter, 189
Heritage Turnip Green Festival, 175
Hess, Karen, 9, 41, 235
Hetty Ray's Tea Room, 248
Highlands Bar and Grill, 13
Highlands, N.C., 30
Hill, Annabella P., 131, **182**, 235, 253
Hill, Sallie F., 154
Hillsville, Va., 275
Hines, Duncan, **182–83**
Hinrichs, K., 234
Hints and Pinches (Walter), 280–81
Hispanic American foodways, 49, **64–67**, 120
Historical Cookbook of the American Negro (Thurman), 43
History of the Dividing Line, The (Byrd), 71
Hobbs, Susan Moreton, 204, 205
Hog killing, 2–3, 11, 21, 89
Hogs, 52, 88–91, 100, 143, 155–56
Holly Farms, 94
Hominy, 4, 16, 39, 65, 151, 175–76
Hooker, John Lee, 54
Hooper, Johnson J., 237
Hope, Ark., 285
Hoppin' John's Lowcountry Cooking (Taylor), 43
Horne, Rose Marie, 98

Hospitality, 2, 23, 59, 71, 72, 99, 134, 247
Hot Brown, 259
Hot Springs, Ark., 24
Hot tamales, **184–85**
Housekeeping in Old Virginia, 140
Housekeeping in the Bluegrass, 45
Houston, Sam, 116
Houston, Tex., 101, 129, 205, 277, 287
Huddle House, 101
Hudson, A. P., 148
Hudson, Charles, 56
Hudson Foods, 94
Hunter, Kristin, 72
Hurricane Katrina, 88, 139, 250
Hurston, Zora Neale, 10, 28
Hushpuppies, 4, 25, 111, 153, **185–86**
Huzenlaub, Eric, 277

Iced tea, 28, 111
I'll Take My Stand, 72
Imperial Cabinet saloon, 238
Imperial Sugar Company, 269
"I'm Selling My Porkchops (But I'm Giving My Gravy Away)," 9
Incidents in the Life of a Slave Girl (Jacobs), 72
Indianola, Miss., 145
Inglenook Cook Book, The, 140
In Pursuit of Flavor (Lewis and Goodbody), 44, 107
Interstate Mullet Toss, 203
Intruder in the Dust (Faulkner), 9
Invisible Man (Ellison), 9, 144
Iowa, 90, 225
I Remember When (Layton), 41
Iroquois, 18
It's Grits, 176
"I Will Play for Gumbo," 83

Jack Daniel Distillery, **186–88**
Jack Daniel's Tennessee Whiskey, 128
Jackson, Andrew, 169, 176
Jackson, Ga., 24
Jackson Cookbook, 43

Jackson Symphony League, 43
Jacksonville, Fla., 258, 288
Jacobs, Harriet, 72
Jamaica, 38
Jambalaya, 63, 84, 92, **188**, 230, 252
"Jambalaya," 82, 159
Jamestown, Va., 175
Jaubert, Gus, 132
Jefferson, Martha, 189
Jefferson, Thomas, 16, 71, 122, 125–26, **189–90**, 206, 214, 218, 240, 264, 283, 288–89
"Jelly Whipping Blues," 82
Jerry's, 101
"Jesus and Tomatoes," 276
Jewell, J. D., 94
Jewish foodways, 48, 49, **67–70**, 75, 99
Jimmy Kelly's, 248
Johnson, James Weldon, 124
Johnson, Lyndon B., 23, 78, 116
Johnson, Robert, 184, 185
Johnson County (Tenn.) High School, 22
John Willingham's World Champion Bar-B-Q, 114
Jones, George, 82
Jones, Judith, 194
Jordan, Louis, and His Tympani Five, 82
Joyner, Charles, 121
Judd, Cledus T., 157
Julien, Honoré, 189
Justin Wilson Cook Book, 286

Kansas City, Mo., 25
Kansas Joe, 82
Kay, Terry, 124
Keen, Robert Earl, 82
Kelso, Tenn., 257
Kennedy, John Pendleton, 71
Kentucky, 3, 22, 25, 26, 28, 31, 45, 52, 90, 101, 124, 127, 128, 129, 132, 133, 155, 157, 162, 180, 198, 225, 258, 259, 263, 267
Kentucky Bourbon Festival, 128
Kentucky Fried Chicken, 12, 38, 95, 142, 162, 258, 259
Kentucky Housewife, The, 205

Kettenring, Elizabeth, 86
Kettle Restaurants, 101
Key lime pie, 224
Keystone Folklore Quarterly, 8
Key West, Fla., 197, 224
Killers of the Dream (Smith), 70
King, B. B., 123
King Biscuit Time, 124
King cakes, **190**
Kirkum, Henry, 211
Kleeman's, 247
Knife and Fork, 247
Knoxville, Tenn., 30, 267
Kolb's, 86
Körner, Polly Alice Masten, 41
Körner's Folly Cookbook, 41
K-Paul's Louisiana Kitchen, 87, 234, 235
Kreuz Market, 118
Krispy Kreme, **190–92**
Krystal, 100, 101, 163

Lady Baltimore (Wister), 135
Lafayette, Marquis de, 176
Laffoon, Ruby, 258
Lagasse, Emeril, 63, 87, 130, **193**, 249
La Grange, Ga., 182
Lakeland, Fla., 285
Lamothe, Léon, 263
Lane, Emma Rylander, 135
Las Vegas, Nev., 129
Latinos, 64
Latrobe, C. J., 198
Laurel, Miss., 45
Laurel Cook Book, The, 45
Laurens County, Ga., 161
Lawrence, Elizabeth, 205
Layton, Emma S., 41
"Lazy Bones," 168
Leaves of Green: The Collard Poems, 172
LeBeau, Joe, 191
Lee, Harper, 72, 197
Lee, Robert E., 39, 40, 135
Lemonade, 28
Le Moyne, Jean-Baptiste, 83

Leonard's, 113
Le Pavilion restaurant, 146
Leruth, Warren, 87
Leruth's, 87
Leslie, Eliza, 154
Lesson before Dying, A (Gaines), 179
Let Us Now Praise Famous Men (Agee), 170
Lewis, Aylene, 109
Lewis, Edna, 12, 18, 28, 44, 105, 107, 122, **193–95**, 225, 245
Lexington, N.C., 25, 110, 111
Lexington, Tenn., 114
Lexington (N.C.) Barbecue Festival, 111
"Life Is Just a Tire Swing," 83
Lincoln, Abraham, 39
Lineberger, Luther, 166
Lineberger's Fish Fry, 166
Literature, food in, 9, **70–73**
"Liza Jane," 264
Llano, Tex., 118
Locke, John, 74
Lockhart, Tex., 118
Logan, John, 54
Lomax, Alan, 264
Lombard, Rudy, 139
Long, Huey, 11, 171
Longbranch, 251
Longfellow, Henry Wadsworth, 54
Lonzo and Oscar, 31
Losing Battles (Welty), 73
Louisiana, 3, 6, 11, 32–35, 39, 46, 49, 51, 52, 54, 61, 63, 84, 87, 104, 120, 158, 159, 177–79, 181, 188, 190, 195–96, 198, 206, 207, 210, 212, 213, 218, 220, 230, 231, 233, 234, 251, 252, 254, 257, 268, 269, 270, 271, 272–73, 278, 285–87, 290
Louisiana State University, 269
Louisville, Ky., 259, 260
Louisville Courier-Journal, 169
Loveless Café, 248
Lovett, Lyle, 82
Lowcountry foodways, **73–77**, 122, 126, 180, 251, 253
Lowery, George H., Jr., 149

"Low Gravy," 169
Luling, Tex., 285
Lunch counters (civil rights era), 17, **77–79**, 248
Lundy, Ronni, 214
Lune, Pierre de, 254
Lynchburg, Tenn., 186–87
Lynn, Loretta, 223
Lytle, Andrew, 72

Mack, Lonnie, 82
Macon, Uncle Dave, 9
Madame Begue's, 86, 250
Maddox, Lester, 78
Madison, James, 288
Madison County, Ga., 182
Madisonville, La., 138
Magnolia's, 246
Mangus, Sister J. M., 140
Manhattan (New York City) 114, 145, 146
Manning, Eli, 168
Maque choux, **195–96**
Mardi Gras, 190, 244
Marion Brown's Pickles and Preserves, 130
Marion Brown's Southern Cook Book, 130
Markham, Gervase, 41
Marryatt, Frederick, 198
Martha White flour, 223
Martin, Benny and Clovis, 228, 260
Martin, Ti, 130
Martin Bros. Poor Boys, 228, 260
Mary B's Biscuits, 124–25
Maryland, 42, 90, 155, 186, 198, 221, 289, 290
Mary Mac's Tea Room, 245
Mary's Old-Fashioned Pit Barbecue, 115
Massey, Jack, 258
Matthews, Jimmy, 131, 132
Matzoh Ball Gumbo (Ferris), 9
Maurice's Piggy Park, 78
Maverick, Samuel, 289
Maxwell House coffee, 29
Maylie's, 250
Mayor of Bayou Pom-Pom, 285–86
McCain, Franklin, 77

McCall's, 105

McClard's, 24

McClung, Ollie, 78

McCrady's, 246

McCullers, Carson, 72, 120

McCulloch-Williams, Martha, 223

McDonald's, 36, 38

McGee Brothers, 82

McGhee, Brownie, 276

McGill, Ralph, 142

McIlhenny, Edmund, 271

McIlhenny, Edward Avery, 271

McNeil, Joseph, 77

McPhee, John, 208

McWhorter, Diane, 78

Meals, **79–81**

Medicinal uses, 171, 173, 175, 206, 220, 221, 229, 239

Melungeons, 239

Member of the Wedding, The (McCullers), 72, 120

Memorial Day (Decoration Day) (Schauffler), 54

Memphis, Tenn., 25, 68, 112–15, 137, 237, 261, 262, 273, 279, 287

Memphis Commerical Appeal, 112

Memphis Minnie, 9, 82, 124

Memphis Seven, 82

"Memphis Women and Fried Chicken," 9

Mercer, Johnny, 168

Merz, Valentine, 29

Mexico, 65

Miami, Fla., 66, 67, 163, 287

Michigan, 208

Mickler, Ernest Matthew, **196–97**

Mickler, Trisha, 197

Midland, Tex., 231

Midnight in the Garden of Good and Evil (Berendt), 77

Mikeska brothers, 118

"Milk 'Em in the Evening Blues," 82

Milton, Little, 176

Mint julep, **198**

Mississauga, Ontario, 192

Mississippi, 27, 31, 43, 52, 54, 56, 63, 83, 94, 105, 124, 137, 141, 148, 157, 176, 184–85, 213, 218, 252, 269, 270

Mississippi Delta, 24, 66, 137, 145, 184–85

Mississippi, University of, 13

Miss Kathleen's, 145

Miss Leslie's New Cookery Book, 154

Missouri, 54, 127, 289

Mitchell, Daniel, 174

Mitchell, Margaret, 23, 72, 198, 273

Mitchum, Robert, 201

Mize, Miss., 285

Mobile, Ala., 10, 17, 190, 231, 279, 287

Monk, Thelonius, 172, 174

Monk, Wayne, 111

Montana, 54

Montgomery, Ala., 125

Montgomery Biscuits, 124, 125

Montgomery County, Ky., 109

Monticello, Fla., 285

Monticello, Ga., 182

MoonPies, **199–200**

Moonshine and moonshining, 21, 82, **200–201**

Morehead City, N.C., 204

Moreven, Ga., 285

More White Trash Cooking (Mickler), 197

Morin, Antoine, 268

Morris, Willie, 43

Morrison, Toni, 72

Morton, Jelly Roll, 169

Moss, Kay, 111

Motlow, Lem, 187

Mountain City, Tenn., 22

Mountain Dew, 30

Mrs. Elliot's Housewife, 42

Mrs. Hill's New Cook Book, 182, 253

Mrs. Winner's, 163

Muddle, **202–3**

Muddy Pond, Tenn., 264

Mueller, Louis, 118

Muffuletta, 86, 260

Muir, Jim, 186

Mullet, **203–4**

Murphy Family Farms, 91

Murphy, Wendell, 52, 90–91

Music and food, 9, **81–83**

"Mustard Greens," 172

Mutton, 132

My Bondage and My Freedom (Douglass), 72

My Cousin Vinny, 176

Nappy Roots, 157

Nashville, Tenn., 29, 77, 115, 144, 167, 175, 191, **247–49**, 258, 287

Nathalie Dupree's New Southern Cooking, 12, 44

Nathalie Dupree's New Southern Memories, 44

Native Americans, 1, 18, 21, 41, 47, 56, 58, 62, 64, 91, 99, 104, 117, 151, 158, 170–71, 195, 202, 221, 255

Native Son (Wright), 106

Neal, Bill, 13, 44, 122, 123, 140, 153, 176, **204–5**, 236

Negro Chef Cookbook, The (Roberts), 189

New Bern, N.C., 29

New Deal, 51, 102, 233

New Iberia, La., 270

New Jersey, 66, 270

New Kentucky Home Cookbook, The, 98

New Mexico, 54

New Orleans, La., 8, 12, 16, 17, 27, 29, 34, 35, 61, 63, 68, 69, **83–88**, 129–30, 138, 139, 161, 163, 175, 177, 178, 179, 181–82, 186, 188, 190, 191, 193, 204, 211, 212, 218, 227, 228, 231, 234, 235, 236, 238, 239, 241, 243–44, 246, **249–51**, 252, 254, 257, 259, 260, 262–63, 267, 268, 273, 287

New York City, 161, 193, 235, 246

New Yorker, 197

New York Times, 105, 145–46, 175, 176, 205, 278

New York Times Cook Book, 146

Niceville, Fla., 204

Nicholson, John, 194

Nickerson, Jane, 145

Night in Acadie, A (Chopin), 179

Nola, 193

Norfolk, Va., 255

North Carolina, 21, 25, 30, 31, 49, 52, 53, 58, 67, 71, 90, 91, 94, 110–11, 114, 122, 124, 131, 132, 143, 155, 157, 163, 166–67, 173, 174, 176, 202–3, 205, 218, 226, 270, 288, 289, 290

North Carolina, University of, 25, 44

North Carolina Agricultural and Technical College, 77

North Carolina State University, 240, 275

North Texas State University, 44

Norton, Daniel, 289

Notes on the State of Virginia (Jefferson), 206

Nouvelle cuisine, 250, 253

Oak Grove, La., 229

Oakland, Calif., 197

O'Connor, Flannery, 174

O'Daniel, W. Lee "Pappy," 116

Oglethorpe, James, 288

O. Henry, 198

Ohio, 45

Oklahoma, 23, 26, 101

Okra, 11, 12, 15, 16, 34, 38, 68, 74, 80, 84, 103, 104, 122, 139, 177, 178, **206–7**, 222, 229

"Old Dogs, Children, and Watermelon Wine," 283

Old South Quartette, 212

Old Virginia Gentleman and Other Sketches, The (Bagby), 8

Ollie's Barbecue, 78

Oneonta, Ala., 199

Onions, Vidalia, **207–8**

Opelousas, La., 234

Orangeburg, S.C., 75

Oranges, **208–10**

"Oreo Cookie Blues," 82

Original Picayune Creole Cook Book, The, 178–79

Oscar Getz Museum of Whiskey History, 129

Our Best Recipes, 44

"Our Daily Bread," 241–43

Owensboro, Ky., 25, 133, 180

Oxford, Miss., 168
Oyster (Biguenet), 212
Oyster loaf, 259, 260
Oysters, 10, 62, 76, **210–12**
"Oysters and Wine at 2 a.m.," 212
Oysters Rockefeller, 211, **212–13**

Paddlefish, 165–66
Paducah, Ky., 191
Palm Valley, Fla., 197
Panfish, **213–14**
Paris Review, 279
Park, Roy, 183
Parker's, 112
Parkette Drive-In, 101
Patton, George S., 155
Payne, Guilford "Peach Tree," 215
Payne, Sonny, 124
Payne's, 115
Peaches, **214–15**
"Peach Tree Blues," 215
Peacock, Scott, 44, 122–23, 195, 225, 245
Peanuts, 1, 11, 12, 37, 52, 74, 76, **216–18**
Pearl, Minnie, 162, 286
Pecan pie, 225
Pecans, 11, 52, 61, 68, 120, **218–19**, 224, 225, 231
Pellagra, 6, 11, 65, 103, 151
Pelts, Don and Barry, 68
Pemberton, John S., 29, 146, 147
Pen, Lila, 265
Penn, Dan, 9
Penny, Hank, 143
Pensacola, Fla., 63, 231
Pensacola Bay, Fla., 10
Pentucket Housewife, The, 278
Peppers, hot, 74, 75, **219–21**
Pepper vinegar, **219**
Pepsi, 29–30
PepsiCo, Inc., 259
Percy, Walker, 129
Perdue Farms Inc., 94
Persimmons, **221**
Petersburg, Va., 130
Peychaud, Antoine Amedée, 263

Picayune's Creole Cook Book, The, 243
"Picking My Tomatoes," 276
Pickling, **221–22**
Pickrick Cafeteria, 78
Pie and Pastry Bible (Beranbaum), 223
Pierce, Billie and Dede, 179
Pies, 140–41, **222–25**
Pig & Whistle, 23
Piggly Wiggly, 261–62
Pike, Leonard, 208
Pimento cheese, **226–27**, 259
Pimiento, 226, 259
Pinch of Soul, A (Bowser), 105
Pineapple upside-down cake, 135
Pittsboro, N.C., 194
Pizza Hut, 36
Plains, Ga., 237
Plantations, 5, 51
Pleasant, Mammy, 17
Po' boy (poor boy), 87, **227–28**, 250, 251, 259, 260
PoFolks, 101
Poke sallet, **228–29**
Poke Sallet Festival (Harlan, Ky.), 172
Poke Salot Festival (Oak Grove, La.), 229
"Polk Salad Annie," 172, 229
Popeyes, 95, 163
Pork, 2–3, 6, 25, 26–27, 33, 39, 79, 80, 84, **88–91**, 102, 106, 110, 112, 115, 117, 119, 120, 143, 175, 178, 185, 223
Port Arthur, Tex., 63
Porter, Katherine Anne, 120
Port Vincent, La., 287
Port Wentworth, Ga., 174
Possums. *See* Coons and possums
Potlikker (pot liquor), 5, 11, 171, 173
Pots and skillets, **229–31**
Poultry, 3, 52, **92–95**
Pound cake, 134
Pralines, 18, 218, **231**
Preserves and jellies, **231–33**
Presley, Elvis, 26, 172, 226
Price, Reynolds, 157, 226
Proclamation of Blockade on Southern Ports, 39

Procter and Gamble, 183
Progressive Farmer's Southern Cookbook, 154
Prohibition, 12, 187, 200–201, 239, 256, 289
Prudhomme, Paul, 43, 63, 87, 130, 193, **234–35**, 249
Puddings, **235–36**
Pudd'nhead Wilson (Twain), 285
Puerto Rico, 257

Quail, **236–38**
Quaker Oats, 109, 110
Queen of the Turtle Derby and Other Southern Phenomena (Reed), 141

Raceland, La., 228
Ragan, Sam, 174
Raleigh, N.C., 111, 144, 287
Raleigh, Sir Walter, 288
Ramos, Henry C., 238–39
Ramos gin fizz, **238–39**, 249
Ramps, **239–40**
Randall, Joe, 43
Randle, Bill, 208
Randolph, Anne Cary, 240
Randolph, David Meade, 241
Randolph, Mary, 16, 41, 126, 141, 189, 206, 235, 236, **240–41**, 266
Randolph, Thomas Mann, 189, 241
"Ration Blues," 82
Rawlings, Marjorie Kinnan, 43, 186, **241–43**
RC Cola, 30, 199
RC Cola and MoonPie Festival, 31
Read, William A., 196
Recipes, 41–46, 75, 90, 98, 129, 134, 149, 242, 243, 284. *See also* Cookbooks
Red beans and rice, 120, **243–44**, 252
Redeye gravy, 19, 103, 123, 157, 169
Red Rooster's, 105
Red velvet cake, 136
Reed, Dale, 90
Reed, John Shelton, 25, 47, 90
Reed, Julia, 141

Reigel, George, 226
Religion and food, **95–100**
Remembering Bill Neal (Moreton Neal), 205
Rendezvous, 112, 115
Restaurant La Résidence, 205
Restaurants, 8, 12, 13, 73, 78, 80, 100–102, 162, 166–67, 183, 205; Atlanta, **244–45**; Charleston, **245–46**; Nashville, **247–49**; New Orleans, **249–51**
Revolutionary War, 232, 256
Reynolds, R. J., 259
Rhodes, S. R., 42
Rice, 10, 15, 16, 33, 52, 65, 68, 74, 76, 177, 178, 188, **251–53**, 277–78; red, **253**
Rice Council, 252–53
Richmond, David, 77
Richmond, Va., 30, 39, 40, 161, 241, 273, 287
Rilleux, Norbert, 268
River Road Recipes, 42
Roadside restaurants, **100–102**
Roanoke, Va., 140
Roberts, Leonard, 189
Robin, C. C., 196
Robinson, Anna, 109
Rockefeller, John D., 212
Rocky Mount, N.C., 174
Rodgers, Jimmie, 215
Rogers, Joe, Sr., 279
Rogers, Mary, 279
Rogers, Will, 285
Roosevelt, Franklin D., 102, 155
Rose Hill, N.C., 52
Roux, 11, 34, 84, 139, 169, 177, 178, **254–55**
Rudolph, Plumie Harrison, 191
Rudolph, Vernon Carver, 191, 192
Rum, 37, **255–57**
"Rum and Coca-Cola," 257
Rumford Complete Cookbook, The (Wallace), 42
Russell, W. H., 198
Rutledge, Sabe, 121
Rutledge, Sarah, 122
Rutt, Chris, 109

St. Augustine, Fla., 208
Saint Domingue (Haiti), 84
St. Joseph, Mo., 109
St. Louis, Mo., 30
St. Marks, Fla., 153
Salisbury, Md., 94
Salisbury, N.C., 31
Salley, S.C., 145
Sally Bell's Kitchen, 161
Salt Lake City, Utah, 258
Salt Lick, 24
Salvadore, Lupo, 260
San Antonio, Tex., 23, 66, 163
Sanders, Dori, 215
Sanders, Colonel Harland, 12, 142, 162, **257–59**
Sandwiches, 86–87, 227–28, **259–61**
San Francisco, Calif., 17, 232, 235
Satsuma Tea Room, 247, 248
Saturday Evening Post, 183
Saunders, Clarence, **261–62**
Sauveur, Bessie, 138
Savannah, Ga., 48, 69, 74, 76, 77, 92, 154–55, 168, 253, 269, 287
Savannah Cook Book, The (Colquitt), 154, 253
Sazerac, 249, **262–63**
Schauffler, Robert Haven, 54
Schiller, John B., 263
Schleicher County, Tex., 218
Schmidt, Fred K., 259
Scribner's, 181
Sea Islands, 16, 50, 121
Seafood, 10, 34, 35–36, 62–63, 84, 86, 177, 178, 195, 250
Seasoned in the South (Smith), 49–50
Seaton, Willie Mae, 251
Seeger, Guenter, 245
Sesame. *See* Benne
Seventeen, 105
7-Up, 30
Shange, Ntozake, 207
Sharecroppers, 6
Sheep, 132–33
Shelby, N.C., 110, 111

Shoenbaum, Alex, 101
Shoney's, 101, 248
Silver Sands, 247
Skillet Lickers, 169, 283
Skylight Inn, 112
Slaves, 6, 15–17, 38, 59, 74, 103, 110, 171, 189, 216, 220, 232, 256, 268
Slave trade, 15, 74, 125, 255–56, 278
Slugburger, 27
Smart-Grosvenor, Vertamae, 43
Smith, Bill, 49
Smith, Eliza, 41
Smith, John, 71, 176
Smith, Lillian, 70
Smith, Stephen A., 91
Smithfield Farms, 91
Smokestack Lightening (Elie), 114
Social class and food, **102–4**
Society for the Preservation and Revitalization of Southern Food, 13
Sokolov, Raymond, 251
Some Good Things to Eat, 135
"Song to Oysters," 211
Sonic, 101
Son's Place, 245
"Soppin' the Gravy," 169
Sorghum, 21–22, 40, 74, 79, **263–64**
Soul food, 12, **104–7**, 144, 172
Soul Food Cookbook (Harwood and Callahan), 43
Soul on Top o' Peachtree, 12, 105–6
Soul Power Cookbook, 105
Sound and the Fury, The (Faulkner), 72
South Pittsburg, Tenn., 230
South Carolina, 16, 18, 25, 28, 30, 31, 56, 73, 74, 75, 110–11, 121, 122, 131, 143, 166–67, 173, 174, 176, 179–81, 202–3, 215, 251, 252, 253, 269, 278, 289
Southern Cooking (Dull), 42, 154, 162
Southern Culture on the Skids, 83
Southern Food (Egerton), 13, 42, 236
Southern Foodways Alliance, 13, 88, 161, 194, 251
Southern Kitchen, 19
Southern Living, 43–44, 61, 141

Southern Magazine, 285

Southern Practical Cookery and Recipe Book (Hill), 235

Southern Progress Corporation, 61

Spano, Sarah, 42

Spartanburg, S.C., 98, 99

Spicer, Susan, 249

Spices, 16, 38, 75, 84, 122, 141, 178, 185, 225, 267

Spoonbread, 153, **264–65**

Spoonbread and Strawberry Wine (Darden), 43

Springdale, Ark., 94

Squash, 55, 76, 80, 84, **265–66**

Stack cake, 21, 135, 230, **266–67**

Stafford, Willie, 106

Stag, The (saloon), 238–39

Stamey, Warner, 111

Standard Candy Company, 167, 168

Steadman, John, 38

Stern, John Allen, 49

Stitt, Frank, 13, 176

Stowe, Harold, 167

Stowe's Fish Camp, 167

Strawberries, 19

"Stroke of Good Fortune, A," 174

Stuckey's, 218

Sturgeon, 165

Sudduth, Jimmy Lee, 229

Sugar and sugarcane, 37–38, 50, 52, 65, 97, 134, 232, 233, 255–56, 264, **267–69**

Sugg, Redding S., Jr., 153

Summit, Miss., 287

Sunburst Trout Farm, 22

Sun-Drop, 30, 31

Sunfish, 213–14

Sunflower, Miss., 145

Sunkist, 209

Swallow Barn (Kennedy), 71, 72

Sweet potatoes, 4, 5, 9, 12, 37, 39, 41, 43, 56, 68, 76, 84, 104, 106, 107, 225, 235, **269–70**

Sweet potato pie, 225

Sweet tea, 99, 106

Swett's, 247, 248

Swicegood, Jess, 111

Swindle, Michael, 204

Sylvan Park, 247

Tabasco, 46, 149, 220, **270–72**

Tampa, Fla., 63, 287

Tampa Red, 82

Tar Heels: A Portrait of North Carolina (Daniels), 202

Tarpon Springs, Fla., 63

Tasso, **272–73**

Taste of Country Cooking, The (Lewis), 13, 28, 44, 194

Taste of Heritage, A (Randall and Tipton-Martin), 43

Taylor, Joe Gray, 48, 102, 167, 236

Taylor, John Martin, 43, 161, 176, 214

Taylor, Tex., 118

Taylor, Walker, 112, 113, 114

Tea. *See* Iced tea; Sweet tea

Tea rooms, 248, **273–74**

Tennessee, 3, 21, 22, 26, 28, 30, 31, 90, 112–15, 127, 128, 129, 131, 140, 155, 167, 186, 187, 213, 225, 229, 239, 290

Texas, 3, 6, 23, 25, 26, 27, 46, 51, 52, 54, 62, 64, 65, 67, 115–18, 126, 208, 218, 221, 225, 231, 238, 252, 257, 269, 278, 288, 289, 290

"Texas Cookin'," 169

Texas Crawfish & Music Festival, 159

"Texas Hambone Blues," 82

Texas Monthly, 285

Tex-Mex, 65, 67, 116

Thackeray, William Makepeace, 249

Their Eyes Were Watching God (Hurston), 10, 28

Thelma's, 245

"Them Greasy Greens," 172

"They Made It Twice as Nice as Paradise and They Called It Dixieland," 81

"They're Red Hot," 184, 185

Through the Garden Gate (Lawrence/Neal), 205

Thunder Road, 201

Thurman, Sue Bailey, 43

Time, 105

Time-Life Foods of the World, 280

Tindall, George, 47
Tipton-Martin, Toni, 43
Titus, Mary, 72
To Dance with the White Dog (Kay), 124
To Kill a Mockingbird (Lee), 72, 197
Tomatoes, 20, 21, 41, 68, 74, 76, 80, 111, 178, 188, 222, 253, **274–77**
Tom's, 30
Tom Sawyer, Detective (Twain), 283
Toombs County, Ga., 207
Toussaint L'Ouverture, 84
Townes, Hap, 247
Transatlantic Review, 279
Travels in the United States (Davis), 198
Trigg County, Ky., 155
Trigg County Country Ham Festival, 155
Trillin, Calvin, 245
Trinidad, 38
Trout, Allan M., 169
Truelove and Homegrown Tomatoes (Cannon), 276
Tulane University, 44
Turci's Italian Garden, 86
"Turkey in the Straw," 81
Turner, Grant, 168
Turnips, 4. *See also* Greens: turnip
Tuscaloosa, Ala., 24
Tuskegee, Ala., 217
Tuskegee Institute, 126, 270
Twain, Mark, 283, 285
216 Club, 248
Tyson Foods, 94

Uncle Ben's, **277–78**
Uncle Henry's Oyster Roast and Seafood Restaurant, 211
Underwood, Charles, 109
United Daughters of the Confederacy, 45
U.S. Watermelon Seed-Spitting Contest, 285
Untidy Pilgrim, The (Walter), 280

Vanderbilt Agrarians, 72
Van Peebles, Melvin, 283
Varallo's, 247

Varsity, 245
Venison, 1, 57, 84
Vergos, Charlie, 112
Vergos, Nick, 112
Vibration Cooking (Smart-Grosvenor), 43
Vicksburg, Miss., 147, 233
Victor's, 86, 250
Vidalia, Ga., 207
Viking Range Corporation, 12, 61
Villa Teo, 205
Villas, Jim, 143
Virginia, 1, 25, 26, 28, 30, 31, 39, 41, 51, 52, 61, 71, 72, 73, 88, 90, 116, 125, 127, 128, 131, 132, 155, 189, 198, 206, 214, 239, 241, 255, 265, 281, 288–89, 290
Virginia (Glasgow), 212
Virginia House-wife, The (Randolph), 16, 41, 126, 141, 189, 206, 235, 236, 240, 241, 266
Vobe, Ann, 59
Vogue, 104
Vonderbank's, 86

Waco, Tex., 30
Waffle House, 101, 245, **278–79**
Wake County, N.C., 53
Wallace, Lily Haxworth, 42
Walland, Tenn., 239
Waller, Fats, 212
Wall Street Journal, 44
Walter, Eugene Ferdinand, **279–81**
Walton, Jack, 23
Warm Springs, Ga., 155
Washington, D.C., 287, 288
Washington, George, 23, 116, 125, 189, 218, **281–82**, 288–89
Washington, Martha, 281
Washington Post, 205
Water Valley, Miss., 285
Watermelon, 12, 122, **282–85**
Watermelon, Chicken, and Gritz, 157
Watermelon Days Festival, 285
Watermelon Man, 283
"Watermelon Man," 283
"Watermelon on the Vine," 283

Watershed, 245

Waverly, Va., 284

Welcome Table, The (Harris), 43

Wells, Dean Faulkner, 43

Welty, Eudora, 43, 73

Wendell Smith's, 247

West Carroll Parish, La., 229

Western Star (Benét), 151

West Liberty, Ky., 264

Westover Manuscripts, The, 255

West Virginia, 18, 54, 275

Wetherby, Lawrence, 258

What Mrs. Fisher Knows about Old Southern Cooking, 17, 43, 232

"What's the Matter with the Mill?," 82

"When It's Peach-Picking Time in Georgia," 215

Whiskey, 11, 28, 128, 187–88, 198, 200. *See also* Bourbon whiskey

White, Lucinda "Granny," 247

White, Tony Joe, 172, 229

White, William, 266

White, William Allen, 146

White Castle, 100

"White Lightning," 82

White Lily Foods Company, 61, 123, 223, 267

Whites, Lee Ann, 59

White Tower, 100

White Trash Cooking (Mickler), 196, 197

White Trash Cooking II (Mickler), 196, 197

Whitt, Doris, 13

Wilcox, Estelle Woods, 45

Wilcox, S. D., 275

Wilkesboro, N.C., 94

Williams, Ed, 112

Williams, Hank, Sr., 82, 159

Williams, Jonathan, 197

Williamsburg, Va., 41, 59

Williamsburg Art of Cookery (Bullock), 130, 134

Willie Mae's Scotch House, 88, 251

Willingham, John, 114

Wilmington, N.C., 211

Wilson, Justin, **285–87**

Wilson, N.C., 110, 112

Wilson's, 24

Winchester, Ky., 31

Wine, 189, **287–90**

Winston-Salem, N.C., 191, 192, 197

Wirtz, Billy C., 82

Wister, Owen, 135

Womenfolks (Abbott), 169

Wood, Memphis, 197

Woodruff, Ernest, 147

Woodruff, Robert Winship, 29, 146, 147

Woods, Marvin, 186

Woods, Sylvia, 18, 236

Woodward, Stan, 176

Woolcott, Anthony G., 197

Works Progress Administration, 233

World Championship MoonPie Eating Contest, 199

Wright, Richard, 9, 72, 103, 106

Wyatt-Brown, Bertram, 59

Yams, 38. *See also* Sweet potatoes

Yearling, The (Rawlings), 186

Yeoman farmers, 6, 89

"You're Not the Only Oyster in the Stew," 212

"Your Greens Give Me the Blues," 82

Zeffirelli, Franco, 280